ABBA: THE TRADITION OF ORTHODOXY IN THE WEST

Festschrift for Bishop Kallistos (Ware) of Diokleia

Abba

The Tradition of
Orthodoxy in the West

Festschrift for
Bishop Kallistos (Ware) of Diokleia

EDITORS

John Behr

Andrew Louth

Dimitri Conomos

ST VLADIMIR'S SEMINARY PRESS
CRESTWOOD, NEW YORK 10707
2003

The benefactors who made this publication possible
wish to dedicate it in thanksgiving for the ministry of
His Grace Bishop Kallistos Ware, and for their children,
Michael, David, King, Olivia, Karl, and Sophia.

❀ · ❀

Library of Congress Cataloging-in-Publication Data

Abba : the tradition of Orthodoxy in the West : festschrift for Bishop Kallistos (Ware) of Diokleia / editors, John Behr & Andrew Louth & Dimitri Conomos.
    p. cm.
  Includes bibliographical references.
    ISBN 0–88141–248–1
    1. Orthodox Eastern Church—History.   2. Orthodox Eastern Church—Doctrines.
3. Ware, Kallistos, 1934–   4. Ware, Kallistos, 1934– —Bibliography.   I. Ware, Kallistos,
1934–   II. Behr, John.   III. Louth, Andrew.   IV. Conomos, Dimitri E.

BX290 .A27 2003
281.9—dc21

2002037022

Contents

Part Two: Theological

Part Three: Spiritual

Foreword

Bartholomew

by the Grace of God Archbishop of Constantinople, New Rome, and Ecumenical Patriarch

T O THE MOST LEARNED SCHOLARS, beloved children of Our Humility in the Lord, who have diligently compiled this volume in honour of His Grace Bishop Kallistos of Diokleia: May the grace and peace of God be with you.

I applaud you for the agreeable initiative you have shown in producing this volume in honour of His Grace Bishop Kallistos, who is already highly celebrated for his scholarly achievements and service to the Church, and to promote a wider appreciation and recognition of his many-sided work.

It is, indeed, right for us to praise such an undertaking, for you honour thereby a scholar of worldwide reputation: a bishop whose contribution to theological enquiry, learning, and teaching follows the model of the holy fathers and teachers of the Church, whose lives, learning, speech and accomplishments in the Orthodox Church have been emulated by the hierarch to whom we now pay tribute. Rendering in this meritorious fashion "what is worthy to the worthy," you ascribe glory and blessing to the bountiful Giver of gifts, God Himself, who imparts the word of wisdom through the spoken utterances of those granted grace within His Church—those who in Christ-like humility care for the salvation of mankind and through their teaching and their theology make manifest in a profound way God's revelation in Christ and so enlighten the world.

To you who express appreciation to the shepherd and teacher and rightly extol his work, and to Bishop Kallistos himself, we happily confer our Patriarchal approval and the blessing of the Holy and Great Mother Church of Christ.

May the Lord our God abundantly bless both him and you and preserve you unharmed and in good health unto very many years, thereby to proclaim the Word of God and advance His sacred teachings, to the glory of His Holy Name and for the salvation of all the world.

On the 16th day of November 2002
†Archbishop of Constantinople, Bartholomew
Fervent Intercessor before God

Prologue

Gregorios
Archbishop of Thyateira and Great Britain

I FIRST MET BISHOP KALLISTOS almost forty years ago when, having recently arrived in London, I was ordained priest and appointed to the staff of the busy parish of All Saints in Camden Town. He had recently returned from Canada and was an intense, rather underweight young layman who was just about to establish a reputation for himself through his best-selling book, *The Orthodox Church*, and his scholarly *Eustratios Argenti: A Study of the Greek Church under Turkish Rule*. I was interested to learn that he had been received into the Orthodox Church some years earlier and that, in addition to his Double First in Classics from Oxford, he had also read Theology.

It was not surprising therefore that, on the election of Metropolitan Athenagoras of Elaea (who had been responsible for Canada) to the see of Thyateira and Great Britain in 1963, Timothy Ware (as he was then known) should contact him and, as a result, be offered a position as his lay assistant. As this, he experienced the growing pains of the diocese which had been reconstituted a year or so earlier; and he was called upon to share in the early difficulties with accommodation (or rather, the lack of it) and the consequent disorganization. This he did with a cheerful heart, which belied his rather severe appearance.

Recognizing his outstanding abilities, my predecessor of blessed memory urged him to accept ordination to the diaconate, ordaining him himself in the Cathedral of the Divine Wisdom in London's Bayswater, with foresight conferring on him the religious name of Kallistos in honour of St Kallistos Xanthopoulos (a late 13th and early 14th century Byzantine theological polymath), whose wide learning he was subsequently to imitate in so many respects. Indeed, it was I myself who gave him his *Symmartyria* or canonical letter of recommendation for ordination. Shortly afterwards, Archbishop

Athenagoras arranged for him to enter the monastery of which he himself was a monk, that of Patmos in the Dodecanese (Greece). Here, Deacon Kallistos was to encounter one of the leading figures of the twentieth-century monastic revivals, Archimandrite Amphilochios (Makris). Fittingly, it was Archbishop Athenagoras who, some time later, conferred the priesthood on him in the ascetic setting of the simple medieval church of All Saints belonging to the Monastery of St John the Baptist, which is situated a little outside the Essex village of Tolleshunt Knights (and that has subsequently become renowned on account of the outstanding personality of the late Archimandrite Sophrony).

His ordination to the priesthood coincided with his being appointed as Spalding Lecturer in Eastern Orthodox Studies in the Faculty of Theology at the University of Oxford in succession to the eminent Russian émigré theologian, Nicholas Zernov. His appointment to Oxford led to his being assigned to the parish of the Holy Trinity there under the jurisdiction of the Oecumenical Patriarchate. I remember him saying to me, shortly after his move there, that Oxford had now assured itself of a priest for the next fifty years! His years leading the parish have seen a phenomenal enrichment and growth of its membership, resulting in the need to build a church (which was done so in conjunction with the Russian diocese), and this building now needs to be significantly enlarged. In addition, there is now an assistant priest to help him with his pastoral work (and he is regularly assisted by clergy attracted to Oxford to study under his guidance).

From his position as Spalding Lecturer, he has had an immense influence on the progress of Orthodoxy in Great Britain, especially among those whose native language is English, through his teaching and writings (including the influential *The Orthodox Way*); and he has contributed significantly to the progress of Orthodoxy and the cultivation of good relations both with other Communions and Confessions in this country and with the Oxford collegiate bodies. In recognition of this and his own impressive theological learning, the Holy Synod of the Oecumenical Patriarchate of Constantinople in 1982 elected him as an assistant bishop within the Archdiocese of Thyateira and Great Britain, with the title of titular Bishop of Diokleia.

I began this Prologue by remarking on Bishop Kallistos' rather severe appearance as a young man. As he has matured both in age and in faith, his cheerful and optimistic heart has shone through to radiate the spirituality of one who has found his monastic "desert" among the "dreaming spires" of that most beautiful of seats of learning and at the door of whose "cell" (even though this may have been a university lecture-room) many have found their way to a balanced and authentic understanding of the teachings of our Lord and Savior, Jesus Christ, as they are uniquely to be found in Christian Orthodoxy. Now that he is retired after thirty-five years of university teaching, it is fitting that an academic tribute should be paid to him to mark his distinguished contribution to worldwide Orthodox Christianity by those who have either been associated with him or have been taught by him. That it should take the form of this *Festschrift* is to be commended.

London 1st September 2000

Biographical Sketch

Andrew Louth

TIMOTHY WARE was born in Bath, then in Somerset, on 11 September 1934; he was therefore, as his mother often remarked, a "Bath bun." His father was in the British Army, eventually rising to the rank of Brigadier; he had served in India, but returned to England shortly after Timothy's birth, and continued to serve in the army until after the Second World War. Timothy was the second child in the family, with an elder brother and two younger sisters. On his mother's side, he was related by marriage to the great philosopher and ancient historian, R.G. Collingwood, to whose college in Oxford Timothy himself (by then Archimandrite Kallistos) was eventually to belong as a Fellow. Collingwood, however, died before Timothy went up to Oxford, and by that time Collingwood's star had very much declined, most philosophers in Oxford in the period immediately after the Second World War having decidedly rejected his brand of idealism.

Timothy went to Westminster School, attached to the Abbey, in London. There he was initiated into what he has sometimes described, borrowing C.S. Lewis' phrase, as the education of "old Western man": that is, he had an elaborate education in Greek and Latin, learning not only to read these classical languages with great facility, but also to compose both prose and verse, as well as acquiring a first-hand acquaintance with the literature, history and philosophy that survives in these languages. It was an essentially literary education, with very little, if any, exposure to any of the sciences (save for some rigorous, but in twentieth-century terms elementary, mathematics). Already at school, the young Timothy displayed somewhat precocious philosophical interests. A story told by A.M. ("Donald") Allchin, who was several years senior to Timothy at Westminster and was to become one of his longest-standing friends, relates how, when Donald was supervising prep.[1] one

---

[1] "Prep.": that is, preparation, studies prescribed as preparation for the next day's classes, at boarding schools, like Westminster, done in the evening under the supervision of a prefect.

evening, Timothy's hand shot up and he requested that, having finished his prep., he might be given permission to read. "What are you reading?" asked the prefect. "Kant's *Critique of Pure Reason*," came the reply. Later, Bishop Kallistos himself would remark that his real philosophical love of his school-days was for the great English philosophers, Locke, Berkeley and Hume ("English" by language, for Berkeley was an Irishman and Hume a Scot), to whose clarity of expression and elegance of style he doubtless owes some debt. Among these, his favourite was, not surprisingly, Berkeley, whose deep sense of the primary reality of the world of spiritual beings derived in some measure from his knowledge of the Greek Fathers, especially Origen. It was not just philosophy that he took a delight in reading while at Westminster; novels and poetry also engrossed him. But there were other influences on the young Timothy, while he was at Westminster. One was the services of West-minster Abbey itself; the boys were required to attend Matins, and the young Timothy also delighted in the ceremonial splendour of the Sung Eucharist, especially that held annually in honour of St Edward the Confessor, the founder of the Abbey. These services made a lasting impression on him, one that continued when he went up to Oxford, where he frequented Sung Evensong, especially at New College. The great tradition of Anglican Church music, with male choristers—boys and men—conveyed a sense of what the Caroline divines of the seventeenth century called "the beauty of holi-ness" (Bishop Kallistos' love for Anglican Evensong has remained, with a connoisseur's appreciation for the clarity and line of the psalmody, rather than the brilliance of the anthem). Another, profounder, influence was extra-curricular. Not far from Westminster School was the Russian Church of St Philip's, in Buckingham Palace Road. There, just before he left Westminster School to go up to Oxford, Timothy by chance (though there is no chance in such matters) found himself in the church on Saturday afternoon during the Vigil Service. Bishop Kallistos has himself told of this occasion, in which he was caught up, from the noise and business of London, into "a world that was more real—I would almost say more *solid*" by the darkness, the stillness, the sense of overwhelming presence, a glimpse of the "beauty of holiness," not confected, but offered for participation.[2]

This classical education was completed by his studies at Magdalen Col-lege, Oxford, where he read Classical Moderations (i.e., classical literature)

[2]See Bishop Kallistos, "Strange yet Familiar: My Journey to the Orthodox Church," in *The Inner Kingdom*, vol. 1 of the Collected Works (Crestwood NY: St Vladimir's Seminary Press, 2000), 1–24. The account of his visit to St Philip's is on pp. 1–3, and the quotation on p. 3.

and *Literae Humaniores* (i.e., ancient history and philosophy, both classical and modern, with nothing much in between), known as "Mods" and "Greats," from 1952 to 1956, gaining first class honours. E.L. Woodward (later the first Professor of Modern History at Oxford) has remarked:

> The Oxford Greats School, on both its philosophical and its historical sides, adopts almost exactly the attitude of the late Roman pagans. It remains dominated by the peculiar circumstances of its Renaissance origin. All these circumstances have passed away, and the School is now, from the logical point of view, a meaningless anomaly. For in considering what may be called the problems of existence—so far as the School does seriously consider them—the Christian solution is tacitly set aside. It is not disproved: it never has the opportunity of stating its case; and this not for philosophical but largely for literary and "accidental" reasons.[3]

This residual paganism (perhaps more self-conscious in 1952 than in 1916 when Woodward wrote) made little impact on the undergraduate Timothy Ware, even though his tutors in Oxford—Geoffrey Warnock for philosophy and G.E.M. de Ste Croix for ancient history—were fine examples of this cast of mind, especially de Ste Croix. Despite this, de Ste Croix remained a friend, and urged his young pupil, when he turned to theology, to apply the same high standards of criticism to theology as he had done in classics, an injunction he certainly fulfilled. In 1954, Timothy offered himself for ordination in the Church of England, went to a selection board organized by what was then called CACTM (The Church's Advisory Council for Training for the Ministry), and was accepted for ordination. During his time at Magdalen, especially through Brother Peter of the Anglican Franciscan order, Society of St Francis, he came to know and experience much of the best of the Anglican tradition, with its combination of deep devotion, both personal and liturgical, a sense of mission, and an energetic concern for the needs of the poor and underprivileged. By the time he had finished Greats, his doubts over Anglicanism were beginning to grow, and he chose to stay on at Magdalen to read for the Honour School of Theology, rather than begin his theological studies at an Anglican Theological College. For during his time at Oxford his

---

[3]E.L. Woodward, *Christianity and Nationalism in the Later Roman Empire* (London: Longmans, Green and Co., 1916), 12–13 n.

interest in Orthodoxy had deepened and developed. He received little encouragement in his journey to Orthodoxy: far from it, he had been very much discouraged, both by his English friends (who warned him of "lifelong eccentricity"), and by the Orthodox bishop he had approached (Bishop James [Virvos] of Apamaea, of the Greek Cathedral of the Holy Wisdom in London). But Anglicanism itself he came to feel he could no longer embrace. What troubled him was the diversity of Anglican faith, leaving him with the oddness of affirming as an individual preference what he saw as something to be received as Tradition. Anglican involvement in the Church of South India, which troubled many fellow Anglicans, seemed to underscore such openness to ambiguity. The pull of Orthodoxy—its unambiguous embrace of Tradition, the continuing witness of its martyrs, its profound life of prayer, as well as the bonds of friendship being forged with such as Nicolas and Militza Zernov, and the influence of the theological insights of theologians like Vladimir Lossky, Fr Georges Florovsky and Fr John Romanides—became overwhelming. From Easter 1957, Timothy Ware ceased to receive communion within the Anglican Church, and on 14 April (1 April, Old Style), 1958, Friday in Bright Week, Bishop James received him into the Orthodox Church by chrismation. Despite his strong links with the Russian Orthodox Church (his spiritual father belonged to the Church in Exile), he was received into the Greek Orthodox Church of the Œcumenical Patriarchate (for reasons he explains in the article already referred to).

In the years following 1958, Timothy Ware first taught at a preparatory school and then spent a year in America as a scholar at Princeton University, wondering at this time if there might be more scope for his Orthodox vocation in the United States. Fortunately for us in England, he resisted this temptation. In 1960, he returned to Oxford, to do research under the supervision of the Anglican priest and expert on early monasticism, Fr Derwas Chitty, that led to the award of a doctorate (D.Phil.). During this period he travelled widely in the East, visiting the Monastery of the St John the Theologian on the island of Patmos, Mount Athos, and Jerusalem, where he spent six months in 1962–3.

His studies during these years were intense and diverse. In 1963 there appeared the first edition of *The Orthodox Church*, a Pelican Original (in later editions, from 1991 onwards, a Penguin book), that has continued in print ever since. Written by a young convert not yet thirty, and with less than five years' experience of being Orthodox, it is an astonishing book, remarkable for its careful scholarship and balanced objectivity. Nearly forty years later it remains far and away the best introduction in English (probably in any language: it has been translated into many) to the history and doctrine of the Orthodox Church.[4] (Thirty years later, for the 1993 edition, he extensively revised it, rewriting about a third of the text.) The next year, 1964, saw the publication of a rather different work, though equally scholarly and objective, *Eustratios Argenti: A Study of the Greek Church under Turkish Rule* (Clarendon Press, Oxford). This study, written at the request of the Argenti family, is a study of a period in the history of the Greek Orthodox Church, about which very little had been written when Timothy Ware was writing (Sir Steven Runciman's Birkbeck Lectures, on which the main part of his *The Great Church in Captivity* was based, were not given until 1966). Eustratios Argenti was a lay theologian, deeply involved in the polemical theology with the Latins, particularly the issue of the validity of Western baptism (and therefore any other sacraments). Timothy Ware's study is a model of clarity and careful judgment, even if a little dry, owing to the need to give a full account of the Argenti papers.

However, alongside this intensive study, both of the Orthodox Church in general and of Eustratios Argenti and his times in particular, Timothy was engaged in research for his doctorate, for which he successfully submitted his thesis in 1965. This was a study of the texts and the ascetic theology of St Mark the Monk (or "the Ascetic" or "the Hermit"), a writer of the fifth, or perhaps the sixth, century. It has, alas, never been published, though some of the material from the thesis has found its way into later scholarly articles. Even though the thesis, because unpublished, is less well known than the books he published in 1963 and 1964, it is the thesis of 1965 that foreshadows what was to be most characteristic of Timothy Ware's later academic endeavours. For it was ascetic theology (or "neptic" theology, the theology of watchfulness or waiting upon God), that he was to pursue for the rest of his academic career.

That career began in 1966, when he was appointed to succeed Nicolas Zernov as the Spalding Lecturer in Eastern Orthodox Studies, a post which he held until his retirement in 2001: remarkable evidence of monastic stability! These years—1965 and 1966—were crucial years for Timothy Ware for

---

[4]The original edition was published as one of a series, alongside others on Roman Catholicism (a remarkable book by Sebastian Bullough, OP), Anglicanism and Methodism (books remarkable in other ways), and indeed Mysticism and Buddhism. Timothy Ware's book is the only one on a Christian theme to stand the test of time (and the only one not to present its subject as an "-ism," or even an "-y"!).

other reasons. In 1965 he was ordained deacon, and given the name Kallistos by Archbishop Athenagoras of Thyateira and Great Britain, who ordained him. The following year, he was ordained priest and took monastic vows as a hieromonk ("priest-monk") of the Monastery of St John the Theologian on Patmos. He became Father Kallistos (later Archimandrite Kallistos). The name is a Greek superlative meaning "best" or "most beautiful"—not chosen by the ordinand, but conferred by his bishop—and was the name borne by an early second-century pope, whose compassion was pilloried as laxness, and by two fourteenth-century Patriarchs of Constantinople, both of them hesychasts, the later of whom, Kallistos II Xanthopoulos, was intended as his patron saint. It is affectionately abbreviated by his Oxford friends to "Super K." Although now a monk of Patmos, he made his home in Oxford, living with his parents, after his father's retirement, at 15 Staverton Road, in North Oxford. For over thirty years he lived at Staverton Road, looked after by his mother, Evereld, to whom he became very close. They spent a good deal of time together, especially after the death of his father, regularly spending their holidays together. Evereld was gradually drawn towards Orthodoxy, and eventually became Orthodox herself, being received by Archimandrite John Maitland Moir, a Scot of great simplicity and holiness, who became her spiritual father. Of her conversion to Orthodoxy, she would sometimes be heard to remark: "It has nothing to do with Timothy!"

From that base, Father Kallistos pursued what must seem like several full-time careers. He was a lecturer in the University of Oxford for thirty-five years; in 1970 he became Fellow and Tutor in Theology at Pembroke College, Oxford. As such, he lectured to undergraduates, principally in Greek Patristics, both dogmatic (for many years he gave a course of lectures on Christology from Ephesus to Chalcedon) and ascetic (notably a course of lectures on the theology of the human person in Greek theology), and also gave generously of his time through tutorials to undergraduates studying theology (mostly in Patristics, but also in later Byzantine theology: during his time in Oxford there was an optional paper in Byzantine Theology from St Symeon the New Theologian to St Gregory Palamas). He also supervised a growing number of research students in Greek and Byzantine theology (both dogmatic and neptic), several of them contributors to this volume. For much of his time in Oxford, one of his colleagues was the internationally renowned Syriac scholar, Sebastian Brock, Lecturer (and later Reader) in Syriac and Aramaic; together they set up the Eastern Christian Studies Seminar (and later, also, the M.Phil. in Eastern Christian Studies), which became an important focus for discussion and study of the Christian Orient, both Greek and Syriac, but also embracing Coptic and (especially after the appointment of Robert Thomson to the Gulbenkian chair in Armenian Studies) Armenian. Nor did he shrink from the burdens of academic administration, fulfilling the office of chairman of the Board of Studies in Theology at Oxford from 1992 to 1994.

Alongside this academic career, Father Kallistos also played a leading role in the development of the life of the Orthodox community in Oxford. In 1966 he founded the Greek Orthodox parish of the Holy Trinity in Oxford, which from 1973 shared a parish church with the Russian Orthodox parish of the Annunciation, built on the grounds of House of Sts Gregory and Macrina, an Orthodox and ecumenical centre, established by Nicolas Zernov. He remained the priest of the Greek parish until January 2002, when he was succeeded by his long-time assistant in the parish, Father Ian Graham. In addition to these heavy duties, Father Kallistos has taken on various roles outside Oxford. In 1982, he was consecrated titular bishop of Diokleia and appointed an Assistant Bishop in the Orthodox Archdiocese of Thyateira and Great Britain under the Œcumenical Patriarchate. He has also been involved for many years with SYNDESMOS, the international Orthodox youth federation.

But he is perhaps best known for his long engagement in the ecumenical movement. From 1973 to 1984 he was a delegate to the Anglican-Orthodox Joint Doctrinal Discussions, and from 1992–1996 was the Orthodox co-chairman of the Committee preparing for the proposed international Ortho-dox-Methodist dialogue. He has also for many years been one of the patrons of the Ecumenical Society of the Blessed Virgin Mary. But perhaps his engagement in the ecumenical movement has been most intense and long-lasting through his involvement in the Fellowship of St Alban and St Sergius, set up largely under the inspiration of Nicolas Zernov in 1928 to promote better understanding among Christians and particularly between the Anglican and Orthodox Churches. He and his one-time prefect, Donald Allchin, now an Anglican priest, for many years formed the permanent core of speakers at the annual summer conference, and he has long been one of the co-editors of the journal of the Fellowship, *Sobornost* (since 1979, incorporating *Eastern Churches Review*), where very many of his own lectures and articles first appeared. One should also add mention of Bishop Kallistos' long association with an even older association devoted to promoting understanding between Anglicans and Orthodox, the Anglican and Eastern Churches Association, and especially its pilgrimages, on which he has for many years been the Orthodox leader.

These three sides to Bishop Kallistos' life—the academic, the pastoral and the ecumenical—all find their coinherence in his life as a priest, a monk and a man of prayer. Although he has not made his home on the island of Patmos, he usually spends some time annually at the monastery; the importance to him of belonging to a monastic community of brothers can hardly be underestimated. (Another aspect of his engagement in monasticism is to be found in his association with the Friends of Mount Athos: see Graham Speake's contribution, below.) The monastic life is a life of prayer in which the truth and reality of God is acknowledged and rejoiced in. This sense of the wonderful, yet mysterious, *truth* of God informs the three aspects of Bishop Kallistos' vocation just mentioned. The academic is very obviously concerned with the patient discovery and exploration of truth; Bishop Kallistos' academic work combines rigorously scholarly methods with a delight in the truth discovered and an enthusiasm for passing such truth on. His pastoral concern follows from this desire to communicate the truths perceived by the saints; truth is not something to think about, it is the revelation of wonder and mystery, something that transforms the lives of those who come to know it. This truth is communicated through preaching, certainly—sermons are an important part of the celebration of the Divine Liturgy at Canterbury Road, coming immediately after the Gospel, not tucked away elsewhere—but also more tacitly in the very celebration of the mysteries. Coming to know the truth is something deeply personal: for Bishop Kallistos, pastoral concern is also expressed in his role, willingly embraced, as spiritual father to many in England and beyond. But if the Gospel is about the truth, then the fragmented state of those who call themselves Christians is not just unfortunate: it is a disgrace, something that we must work to remove. Here is the inspiration for Bishop Kallistos' tireless engagement in ecumenism, during a half-century in which the goal of ecumenism has seemed to recede almost daily.

The coinherence of these vocations—as academic, pastor, and ecumenical pioneer—in his fundamental vocation as hieromonk may help us to understand the way in which he has pursued each of these vocations. As a theologian, Bishop Kallistos might have performed for Byzantine and Orthodox theology the kind of role fulfilled by the Anglican (and Oxford) theologian, J.N.D. Kelly, in such works of lucid exposition as *Early Christian Doctrines*; his earliest book, *The Orthodox Church*, makes it plain that Bishop Kallistos was amply gifted in this respect. But his theological vocation took a different route. When Bishop Kallistos became Orthodox in 1958, Orthodoxy in the West was still in appearance very foreign: the Divine Liturgy was rarely, if ever, celebrated in English, and anyone who wanted to gain anything more than a superficial acquaintance with Orthodox theology and spirituality had really to start by learning Greek, or Russian and Slavonic, or all three (the situation was a little different in France, but then, as has been said in a different context, "they order this matter better in France"). If anything characterizes Bishop Kallistos' academic work as a whole, it is his determination to make available in English the riches of Orthodoxy. When Orthodoxy finally makes itself thoroughly at home in an English setting, it will owe an enormous debt to Bishop Kallistos' lifelong work. This task of making Orthodoxy available to the English may be considered under two headings: translation and exposition. There are two monuments to his engagement in the demanding task of translation. First, there is his part in the preparation of two of the service books of the Orthodox Church: *The Festal Menaion*, giving the services for those feasts of the Great Twelve Feasts of Our Lord and the Mother of God[5] contained in the several books of the *Menaion* (that is, excluding those found in the *Triodion* or the *Pentekostarion*), and *The Lenten Triodion*, which he prepared in collaboration with Mother Mary of the Orthodox Monastery of the Veil of the Mother of God in Bussy-en-Othe.[6] Secondly, there is his part in the translation (with one volume yet, and soon, to be published) of the great Athonite anthology of ascetic texts, prepared by Sts Nikodimos the Agiorite and Makarios, Bishop of Corinth, and published in Venice in 1782: the *Philokalia*.[7] All these translations were published in London by Faber and Faber, following a tradition established by G.E.H. Palmer, who had already persuaded Faber to publish two volumes of translations from St Theophan the Recluse's Russian translation of the *Philokalia*, as well

[5]Memorably described in an American *typikon* as "the Great Despotic and Theometoric Duodenary Feasts"!—a style of Orthodox translation Bishop Kallistos' translations have done much to render extinct (or at least worthy of extinction).

[6]*The Festal Menaion*, translated from the original Greek by Mother Mary and Archimandrite Kallistos Ware, with an introduction by Professor Georges Florovsky (London: Faber and Faber, 1969); *The Lenten Triodion*, translated from the original Greek by Mother Mary and Archimandrite Kallistos Ware (London: Faber and Faber, 1978). Both of these are still in print in paperback editions. In addition, there is a privately printed (xeroxed) supplement to *The Lenten Triodion*, published by the Monastery of the Veil of the Mother of God (1979), containing all the texts (mostly those for weekdays outside the first week and the Great and Holy Week) not included in the Faber volume for reasons of space.

[7]*The Philokalia, The Complete Text*, compiled by St Nikodimos of the Holy Mountain and St Makarios of Corinth, translated from the Greek and edited by G.E.H. Palmer, Philip Sherrard and Kallistos Ware, 4 volumes (out of 5), London: Faber and Faber, 1979–95. All now also available in paperback.

as a translation of St Theophan's version of St Nikodimos' paraphrase of two works, *Spiritual Combat* and *Path to Paradise*, by the sixteenth-century Theatine priest, Lorenzo Scupoli (a volume not universally appreciated in Orthodox circles: Fr Lev Gillet called it "spiritual piracy").[8] Faber's in-house editor for these early volumes from St Theophan was T.S. Eliot. Two further Orthodox volumes had appeared from Faber and Faber, in both of which Bishop Kallistos was involved: *The Art of Prayer*, compiled by Igumen Chariton of Valamo, to which anthology on the Jesus Prayer, drawn largely from St Theophan, Timothy Ware contributed an important introduction,[9] and *The Diary of a Russian Priest*, by Fr Alexander Elchaninov, the English text of which was prepared by Fr Kallistos from Helen Iwolsky's translation.[10]

It is evident from this list of publications that Bishop Kallistos' involvement from the beginning in the work of translation has gone beyond the actual engagement in the task of producing an accurate (and just as important, idiomatic) English translation. To make available some of the most-used Orthodox liturgical texts (for Lent and the Great Feasts are occasions of intense liturgical activity) and what is certainly the most influential anthology of Orthodox texts in modern times has been a major achievement. But beyond that lies the work of interpretation, the task of making these texts accessible within the West, both to the Orthodox themselves (especially the growing number of Western converts to Orthodoxy) and beyond. Bishop Kallistos was already engaged in this task in the works mentioned above: the *Festal Menaion* has a valuable introductory chapter on "The Orthodox Services and their Structure,"[11] which goes into the question of the meaning of the feasts, not just the structure of the services; the *Lenten Triodion* has a long preface by Archimandrite Kallistos on "The Meaning of the Great Fast,"[12] easily the most accessible introduction to the Orthodox practice of fasting, a practice now more or less abandoned by the Western Churches; his introduction to *The Art of Prayer* has been already mentioned; in the *Philokalia*,

---

[8] *Writings from the Philokalia on Prayer of the Heart, Early Fathers from the Philokalia, Unseen Warfare*, all translated from St Theophan's Russian by G.E.H. Palmer and E. Kadloubovsky (London: Faber and Faber, 1951, 1954, 1952).

[9] *The Art of Prayer: an Orthodox Anthology*, compiled by Igumen Chariton of Valamo, translated by E. Kadloubovsky and E.M. Palmer, edited with an introduction by Timothy Ware (London: Faber and Faber, 1966); the introduction is on pp. 9–38.

[10] Alexander Elchaninov, *The Diary of a Russian Priest*, translated by Helen Iswolsky, English edition prepared by Kallistos Timothy Ware, with an introduction by Tamara Elchaninov and a foreword by Dimitri Obolensky (London: Faber and Faber, 1967).

[11] *The Festal Menaion*, 38–97.

[12] *The Lenten Triodion*, 13–68.

there is an introduction in which the hand of Bishop Kallistos can be detected (though perhaps subordinate to that of Philip Sherrard),[13] and the prefaces to each of the authors that St Nikodimos provided have been replaced by brief scholarly prefaces by Bishop Kallistos. In addition to introductions to translations in which Bishop Kallistos himself had a hand, there are important introductions, sometimes almost like brief monographs, to translations by others, notably his introductions to Colm Luibheid and Norman Russell's translation of St John Climacus' *The Ladder of Divine Ascent*,[14] and to Sœur Claire-Agnès Zirnheld's French translation of Mark the Monk,[15] as well as his briefer foreword to the first volume of Ioan Ioniță and Robert Barrington's translation of Fr Dumitru Stăniloae's *Orthodox Theological Dogmatics*.[16]

But since 1964, there has been (so far) only one book: his immensely popular *The Orthodox Way*,[17] which complements *The Orthodox Church* with what might be described as a meditation on the doctrinal themes of Orthodoxy. But this has been supplemented by well over a hundred published lectures and articles (many more remain unpublished). This balance is significant: Bishop Kallistos has not set aside long periods of time alone in his study to produce the kind of published *œuvre* that would have gained him academic distinction; he has given himself unstintingly to those who want to know more about Orthodoxy. This has not excluded the scholarly community (witness to that is provided by several articles in major works of reference such as the *Theologische Realenzyklopädie* and the *Dictionnaire de Spiritualité*),[18] but he has given greater attention to other audiences, often quite small groups, of those who want to know more about Orthodoxy. For he is a great communicator, one who delights his audience as well as informs it. His lecturing style is quite distinctive, indeed inimitable, and might be said to give another dimension of meaning to the term "performative utterances," invented by Professor J.L. Austin, whose philosophy lectures Bishop Kallistos attended as

[13]*The Philokalia*, I, 11–18.

[14]John Climacus, *The Ladder of Divine Ascent*, translated by Colm Luibheid and Norman Russell (London: SPCK, 1982), 1–70.

[15]*Marc le Moine*, translated by Sœur Claire-Agnès Zirnheld, Spiritualité Orientale 41 (Abbaye de Bellefontained, 1985), ix-li.

[16]Dumitru Stăniloae, *The Experience of God* (Brookline MA: Holy Cross Orthodox Press, 1994), ix-xxvii.

[17]*The Orthodox Way*, Oxford: Mowbrays, 1979; now available from St Vladimir's Seminary Press in a revised edition (also translated into many languages).

[18]"Diadochus von Photice," "Gottesdienst: Orthodoxe Kirche" in *Theologische Realenzyklopädie* VIII (1981), 617-20, XIV (1985), 46–51; "Philocalie" in *Dictionnaire de Spiritualité* XII (1984), cols. 1336–52.

a student. But inform he does: something that will become apparent when his articles are rescued from periodicals, some not even readily available in libraries, and published in book form in the series of his collected works, now appearing under the imprint of St Vladimir's Seminary Press.[19] Bishop Kallistos' academic achievement was recognized by the Bolyai-Babeş University of Cluj-Napoca in Transylvanian Romania, when it honoured him with an honorary doctorate of theology in 1998. He has also received honorary doctorates from universities in Greece and America, and has recently been elected a member of the Russian Academy of Sciences, the first Orthodox bishop to be so honoured since 1917.

Bishop Kallistos has also given himself unstintingly in his supervision of research students, many of them Orthodox, including several, since the collapse of the Soviet Union, from Eastern Europe. All speak of his personal concern for them and their work, and his special ability to inspire them with a sense of the importance of the research they have been engaged upon. As one of his former students put it, "I have never left his office without the sense that my work is worthwhile and that it has just received new life; such is his great and special gift as a teacher." Many others, both colleagues and academics visiting Oxford, speak of having experienced such inspiration and encouragement. Some sense of the extent of this legacy to the Church may be gauged by mentioning that his former research students include one metropolitan, two bishops, many archimandrites, monks, nuns, professors, teachers and theologians (not only Orthodox).

This personal care for students and colleagues is difficult to separate from his pastoral care generally. Those who have had the privilege to be his spiritual children, or who have visited him to discuss theological matters, or even out of curiosity—in all these categories, non-Orthodox are to be counted as well as Orthodox—notice two things: first, that while they are with him, he seems to have time for nothing else than them and their concerns; but secondly, that when they arrive (generally at Staverton Road, now in Northmoor Road), after a warm welcome, they are asked to wait a few minutes while Bishop Kallistos lets some other visitor bring his business to a close, and after an hour or so, there is another ring on the doorbell, as the next visitor arrives.

---

[19]So far only vol. 1 (out of a projected eight, at the latest count!) has appeared: Bishop Kallistos Ware, *The Inner Kingdom* (Crestwood NY: St Vladimir's Seminary Press, 2000). Despite the title, this is not an English version (or even original) of the somewhat shorter collection published in France (and Greece) some years ago, entitled *Le royaume intérieur*, in the collection "Le sel de la terre" (Pully, Switzerland, 1993).

As already noted, for nearly thirty-five years, Bishop Kallistos has had pastoral charge of the Greek Orthodox parish in Oxford. This is an unusual parish, in that the parish church is shared by two congregations, one Greek Orthodox, one Russian Orthodox, each with its clergy and its parish council. The presence of both main Orthodox traditions in England is something Bishop Kallistos deeply values: his own spiritual roots are as much Russian as Greek, and his vision is of an Orthodox Church in England, neither Greek nor Russian, though deeply indebted to both (and to others: Serbs and Romanians, for instance), but English. But that vision is a long way from being achieved, and he must often have suffered from frustration at the lack of progress towards such a goal. One way of furthering that vision has been his establishment of the Fellowship of St John the Baptist in 1979, a group welcoming all Orthodox—Greek, Russian, Serb, Romanian, Bulgarian, as well as English converts, who often seem even more attached to the national character of the Church they have adopted than any émigré! With conferences and study days, a journal (*The Forerunner*), the publication of a calendar and a directory of Orthodox parishes and places of worship, the Fellowship has sought to foster a sense of Orthodoxy in Britain, transcending the national divisions, entrenched as they often seem to be in their separate (and not always cooperative) jurisdictions. Another aspect of this fostering a sense of British Orthodoxy can be seen in Bishop Kallistos' devotion to the Christian past of these islands—British, Celtic and Anglo-Saxon—when they were part of the undivided *oikoumene*. The saints of that time are well represented in the calendar published by the Fellowship and their memory thus preserved as Orthodox Saints, our Saints; Bishop Kallistos has further promoted devotion to them by his frequently leading pilgrimages to sites associated with these Saints.

Of his ecumenical work, the externals have been indicated above. From that it is evident that ecumenism means more to Bishop Kallistos than interchurch theological commissions: perhaps his most important contribution to ecumenism has been through his support for the Fellowship of St Alban and St Sergius, which has certainly reached beyond the world of the professional theologian and churchman. In these circles, Bishop Kallistos has witnessed to the truth of the Orthodox tradition, uncompromisingly, though not uncharitably. It may seem surprising that a convert from Anglicanism to Orthodoxy has played such an important role in promoting ecumenical relationships, not least between Anglicans and Orthodox. Much of the reason for this is that Bishop Kallistos' movement from Anglicanism to Orthodoxy had little that was negative about it; he continued to have a deep appreciation for what was valuable in Anglicanism, and saw his move as one towards a greater fullness of the truth. Those who under his guidance have followed his path into Orthodoxy can bear witness to Bishop Kallistos' concern that such a move should be made in a fundamentally positive spirit. It is characteristic of his approach that he has often observed that the encounter with Orthodoxy sometimes leads people to embrace Orthodoxy, but perhaps more frequently to return to their own traditions and discover there echoes of Orthodoxy that lend it greater depth and meaning. He is certainly prepared to find such echoes, especially in the writings of the poets—not simply among poets where this might seem obvious, like George Herbert, but even more in apparently less likely visionaries, such as William Blake.

If Bishop Kallistos' involvement in translation, focusing as it does on liturgical and ascetical texts, might be said to point to his monastic vocation, the bulk of his articles, based as they frequently are on lectures, talks and sermons, point to his vocation as a bishop, in which his love of teaching and communicating found its fulfilment. In the Orthodox Church, the different orders of ministers are ordained at different points in the Divine Liturgy, these points being determined by the role into which the candidate is entering. Deacons, therefore, are ordained at the end of the eucharistic prayer, so that they can help in the administering of Holy Communion. Priests are ordained at the Great Entrance, so that they can share with the bishop in the consecration of the divine gifts. Bishops, however, are consecrated before the Gospel, for their essential function is to proclaim the Gospel, to preach and teach; the bishop is pre-eminently a *didaskalos*. It is this teaching ministry that Bishop Kallistos clearly deeply loves, and in which he finds, perhaps, his greatest fulfilment.

This yearning to teach and communicate found its expression in the series of lectures he gave each autumn in the church in Canterbury Road in the late 1980s and early 1990s, organized by his friend and parishioner, Wendy Robinson. In these courses of five or six lectures, Bishop Kallistos would take a theme (for example "Heaven on Earth: the Orthodox experience of the Eucharist"), setting out clearly the Orthodox understanding of the matter and exploring its meaning and implications in various ways, drawing illustrations from art and literature, especially poetry, but also, as always, combining reflection on matters of great profundity with moments of delightful and at times hilarious humour. These lectures were very popular, attracting an audience of both Orthodox and non-Orthodox. Many of those who went found them a quite unforgettable experience.

This biographical sketch is incomplete: partly owing to the inadequacies of the author (a future biographer will find more to say about everything mentioned above, but also will need to explore the importance to Bishop Kallistos of his many friendships, not least those with Nicolas Zernov, Donald Allchin, Philip Sherrard, as well as Greek theologians such as Panayiotis Nellas, and also his involvement, grounded in his understanding of Orthodox asceticism, in the ecological movement), but mainly because its subject is still alive and well. He has retired from his academic career in Oxford, and from the immediate pastoral duties of the parish there. But his vocation, as bishop and monk, as teacher and spiritual father, remains. Perhaps in the next decade or so, if, God willing, he is spared to us, we may expect the fruits of his long acquaintance with, and experience of, the Orthodox tradition, its history, theology and spirituality: perhaps the long-promised history of the Greek Church during the *Tourkokratia*, a study on the Orthodox understanding of the Eucharistic sacrifice, and the gathering together, with further reflections, of *his* biographical sketches of several of those who have been most important for Orthodoxy in the West (Patriarch Athenagoras of Constantinople, Archbishop Athenagoras of Thyateira, Nicolas—and Militza—Zernov, Demetrios Koutroubis, Archbishop Basil of Brussels, Fr Lev Gillet, Fr Dumitru Stăniloae, Gerald Palmer, Philip Sherrard, not to mention those still alive). But above all, we look forward to many years of enjoying his gifts of mind, his wisdom, and his all-embracing charity. He is himself a remarkable example of "the human person," a subject on which he has lectured with a depth of insight that has inspired generations of students.

Χρόνια πολλά! Многая лета! Many years!

✿ A Friend of Mount Athos ✿

Graham Speake

I T IS WITH SOME DIFFIDENCE that I write on this topic. Mount Athos is such a special place for all Orthodox that it seems to me dangerous to speculate on the position that it may occupy in the hearts and minds of any of us who go there. I should not find it easy to define exactly what the Holy Mountain means to me. How can I presume to write about what it means to my spiritual father?

Interestingly, in May of 1994 Bishop Kallistos gave a talk to the Friends of Mount Athos entitled "Gerald Palmer, the *Philokalia*, and the Holy Mountain." Palmer (1904–84) had first visited Athos in 1948 and Bishop Kallistos described the circumstances of his encounter with Fr Nikon, a Russian hermit from Karoulia at the remote southernmost point of the peninsula, who happened to be making his annual visit to the monastery of St Panteleimonos at the time of Palmer's arrival. Fr Nikon was clearly a remarkable man. Highly intelligent, well educated, and extremely witty, he spoke fluent English and was a devoted reader of the *Illustrated London News* and the works of P. G. Wodehouse (of which he kept a complete set in his cell). At the same time he lived a strictly ascetic and solitary life in one of the most inhospitable parts of the Mountain where he devoted himself to the Jesus Prayer. The hermit invited Palmer to visit him at Karoulia where he introduced him to the Prayer and encouraged him to read the *Philokalia*. Inspired by Fr Nikon's example, Palmer was received into the Orthodox Church (but in London, not on Athos) and went on to produce two volumes of selected texts from the *Philokalia* which he translated from the Russian. It remained his hope one day to produce a complete translation of the entire corpus from the original Greek.

Bishop Kallistos, who had first visited Athos as an Orthodox layman in 1961, made four visits (the first in 1966, and three more in the 1970s) with Gerald Palmer, visits that were to bear fruit in their decision to collaborate with Philip Sherrard (1922–95) on an English translation of the complete text of the *Philokalia*. In his talk to the Friends he went on to reminisce about what he had learnt from walking with Palmer on Athos and looking at it through his eyes. He selected two things in particular that he owed to him:

> First, he greatly enhanced my sense of the Athonite environment, of the *physical reality* of the Holy Mountain. He made me aware—far more then I had been previously—of the Holy Mountain as in itself a sacrament of the divine presence. Athos is not only a mountain of holy monks, of holy monasteries, and holy icons. It is itself a *Holy Mountain*. The monks, the monasteries, and the icons are enfolded and contained within a wider framework, within an all-embracing context of sacred space. Walking with Gerald on the paths of Athos, I felt as he did that the very rocks and earth of the Mountain, with all its flowers, shrubs, and trees, possess an intrinsic sacredness. In Fr Nikon's words, which Gerald used to quote, "Here every stone breathes prayers. . . ." Gerald valued the monastic buildings, the icons, the human presence of the monks, the ever-renewed sequence of liturgical prayer. But all of this acquired its full meaning in his eyes because of the sacredness of the very Mountain itself.[1]

The second debt that Bishop Kallistos acknowledged to Palmer was something that many visitors to Athos in the past used to remark on but that is, at least superficially, harder to find there today.

> A second thing that Gerald taught me to feel and know more directly was the stillness of the Holy Mountain, its creative silence. By "stillness" (*hesychia*) I do not mean a total absence of sound, for of course there are always many sounds on the Mountain: of the wind and the sea, of the birds and the insects, of the *simantron*, the bells, and the chanting. But all these sounds stand out from an omnipresent background of silence—of a silence that is not an emptiness but a fullness, not an absence but a personal presence: "Be still, and know that I am God" (Psalm 46:10).[2]

Bishop Kallistos went on to quote Palmer's own description of the stillness of Athos in words that expressed just what the Holy Mountain had meant to him:

---

[1]Bishop Kallistos of Diokleia, "Gerald Palmer, the *Philokalia*, and the Holy Mountain," *Annual Report of the Friends of Mount Athos* (1994), 26–7.
[2]Ibid. 27–8.

It was midday on 6 August 1968. The motorboat from Daphni stopped at the harbour of Simonopetra. No one else landed, so after a friendly greeting from the monk on the jetty, I started climbing alone up the steep path as the motorboat went down the coast. After some twenty minutes or so, I reached the point where the path from the monastery of Grigoriou joins the track from the right. Here, at the junction, there is a small shrine with a Cross and stone seats under the shade of a roof; the open sides of the little building give wide views over the sea to the next peninsula. Having reverenced the Cross, I sat down in the shade and looked out across the sea, listening to the silence.

All was still.

Immediately I felt that now at last I was back on the Holy Mountain, and thanked God for once again giving me this immense privilege.

All was still.

This stillness, this silence, is everywhere, pervades all, is the very essence of the Holy Mountain. The distant sound of a motorboat serves only to punctuate the intensity of the quiet; the lizard's sudden rustling among the dry leaves, a frog plopping into a fountain, are loud and startling sounds, but merely emphasize the immense stillness. Often as one walks over the great stretches of wild country which form much of this sacred ground, following paths where every stone breathes prayers, it is impossible to hear a sound of any kind. Even in the monastery churches, where the silence is, as it were, made more profound by the darkness, by the beauty, and by the sacred quality of the place, it seems that the reading and chanting of priests and monks in the endless rhythm of their daily and nightly ritual is no more than a thin fringe of a limitless ocean of silence.

But this stillness, this silence, is far more than a mere absence of sound. It has a positive quality, a quality of fullness, of plenitude, of the eternal Peace which is there reflected in the Veil of the Mother of God, enshrouding and protecting her Holy Mountain, offering inner silence, peace of heart, to those who dwell there and to those who come with openness of heart to seek this blessing.

May many be blessed to guard here this peace or to bear it away as a lasting gift of grace.[3]

---

[3]Originally published anonymously in the periodical *Orthodox Life* (Jordanville, NY: Holy Trinity Russian Orthodox Monastery, Nov.-Dec. 1968), 33.

These then are some of the qualities of Mount Athos that Bishop Kallistos has identified as being of particular value to him. But can we go further and try to establish specific aspects of his life and work that have been influenced by the Holy Mountain? I think it is possible to detect from his writings three distinct areas in which Athos signifies—as a place of prayer, a place of inspiration, and a place of pilgrimage. There may of course be others; and it would be especially illuminating for his readers if he were one day to choose to write on this topic himself. In the meantime I hope that he will accept what follows as not being too wide of the mark.

A place of prayer

"Here every stone breathes prayers." This was a favourite saying of the Russian hermit, Fr Nikon of Karoulia, and, as we have already noticed, Bishop Kallistos is fond of quoting it too; and he adds: "This remains as true today as in the past."[4] Unlike other settlements in the so-called desert of Athos, Karoulia has not enjoyed much of the renewal that is now such a pronounced feature of most monasteries and sketes on the Mountain. It is stony ground. In fact there is precious little other than stones to be seen, which must make it specially fertile for prayer. This I think is perhaps the first debt that Bishop Kallistos would acknowledge to Athos: as a place of prayer. As he has written, "There is now, almost everywhere, a more attentive and recollected spirit of prayer, with a higher standard of chanting and reading, and a far greater emphasis on frequent communion."[5]

The notion of "breathing" prayers is striking, and reminds us of the words of St Gregory of Nazianzus who, writing in the fourth century, says: "Remember God more often that you breathe."[6] "Pray without ceasing" is the injunction of St Paul.[7] It is also the title of a paper by Bishop Kallistos which ends with these words:

> The Kingdom of heaven is within each of us. To pray is, quite simply, to enter into this inner Kingdom of our heart, and there to stand before God, conscious of His indwelling presence; to "pray without ceasing"

---

[4]*The Orthodox Church*, revised edn. (Harmondsworth, 1993), 132.
[5]"Athos after Ten Years: The Good News and the Bad," *Sobornost*, 15:1 (1993), 29.
[6]*Oration* 27.4 (*Theological Oration* 1.4).
[7]1 Thess. 5:17.

is to do this constantly. Although the full glory of this Kingdom is revealed to but few in this present age, we can all discover at any rate some part of its riches. The door is before us and the key is in our hands.[8]

The form of prayer with which Athos is most notably associated is that known as "noetic" prayer or prayer of the heart, as manifested especially in the Jesus Prayer. The traditions of hesychasm, which emphasize the value of prayer of the heart as a vehicle to induce a vision of divine and uncreated light, are very deeply rooted on the Holy Mountain, as indeed they are in Eastern Christianity as a whole, and can be traced back to the writings of St John Klimakos in the seventh century. The tradition was revived in Byzantium in the eleventh century by St Simeon the New Theologian, and again around 1300 by St Gregory of Sinai whose hesychast teaching was warmly received by the monks when he arrived on Athos. In the mid-fourteenth century, when the practices and claims of the hesychasts were challenged, they found a champion in the Athonite theologian St Gregory Palamas, later to be archbishop of Thessaloniki (1347–59). He had been tonsured at Vatopedi and had lived at the Lavra before becoming abbot of Esphigmenou, though he later abandoned that office to live as a hermit near Verria. The victory of the hesychasts, finally secured after no fewer than four church councils, had profound repercussions throughout the Orthodox world, as a result of which the Athonites acquired an unprecedented degree of influence and authority over the development of spirituality. By means of what Dimitri Obolensky has aptly termed this "Hesychast International," "the different parts of the Byzantine Commonwealth were, during the last hundred years of its existence, linked to each other and to its centre perhaps more closely than ever before."[9]

Nor did the influence of the hesychasts come to a halt in 1453. Far from it, as Bishop Kallistos has argued, it was the hesychasts—"those who emphasized the inner, spiritual values of the Greek Christian inheritance"—who provided the oppressed Greek Church with the strength to survive the long, dark centuries of Ottoman rule. And it was they who provided the inspiration for the compilation of the great anthology of spiritual texts known as the

---

[8] "Pray without Ceasing: The Ideal of Continual Prayer in Eastern Monasticism," *Eastern Churches Review*, 2:3 (1969), 253–61; reissued in *The Inner Kingdom* (New York, 2000), 75–87, here 86–7.

[9] D. Obolensky, *The Byzantine Commonwealth: Eastern Europe, 500–1453* (London, 1971), 390.

Philokalia, which was first published in Venice in 1782 and to which I shall return below.[10]

Furthermore, it is hesychasm that provides the spiritual basis of the monastic revival that is taking place on the Holy Mountain today. The injunction of Paul, echoed by Elder Joseph the Hesychast (d. 1959), one of the principal architects of the revival, to "pray without ceasing" is eagerly followed by the monks. At Philotheou, for example, where the monastic regime is particularly demanding, the monks regularly spend four hours a night (from 10 pm to 2 am) practising the Jesus Prayer in their cells, in addition to attending the morning office in church for the subsequent four hours. At Vatopedi the brotherhood frequently gathers in the kitchen after the evening meal for an hour to join together in a common task, usually the preparation of vegetables for the next day; but the only voice to be heard is that of the monk whose turn it is to recite the prayer which provides a spiritual as well as a physical rhythm to the mundane domestic activity. As Archimandrite Aimilianos, former abbot of Simonopetra, has written,

> Inner prayer is the attribute of the angels. It is the unceasing activity of the angelic hosts. It is the bread, the life, the language of these immaterial beings and their way of expressing their love of God. And the monks, who precisely live the angelic life in the flesh, affirm their love of God through the same unceasing prayer as that of the angels.[11]

In a particularly illuminating discussion of the Jesus Prayer entitled *The Power of the Name* Bishop Kallistos acknowledges his own debt to the hesychast tradition:

> To achieve silence: this is of all things the hardest and the most decisive in the art of prayer . . . The hesychast, the person who has achieved *hesychia*, inner stillness or silence, is *par excellence* the one who listens. He listens to the voice of prayer in his own heart, and he understands that this voice is not his own but that of Another speaking within him.[12]

[10]See his lecture, " 'Act out of Stillness': The Influence of Fourteenth-Century Hesychasm on Byzantine and Slav Civilization" (Toronto, 1995).

[11]Archimandrite Aimilianos, "Mount Athos: Sacred Vessel of the Prayer of Jesus," in Hieromonk Alexander (Golitzin) (ed.), *The Living Witness of the Holy Mountain: Contemporary Voices from Mount Athos* (South Canaan, PA, 1996), 182.

[12]Kallistos Ware, *The Power of the Name: The Jesus Prayer in Orthodox Spirituality* (London, 1989), 7.

A place of inspiration

If it was the hesychasts who provided the inspiration for the compilation of the *Philokalia* in the eighteenth century, it was Fr Nikon of Karoulia who provided the inspiration for its translation into English by Gerald Palmer, Philip Sherrard, and Kallistos Ware. This is made clear at the start of the first volume, which is "dedicated to the memory of Father Nikon (1875–1963) Hermit of St George's, Karoulia, on the Holy Mountain of Athos without whose inspiration this work would not have been undertaken."[13] As such, this translation, whose fifth and final volume is eagerly awaited, may be regarded as one of the most significant and tangible products of the twentieth-century revival on Athos.

The *Philokalia* is a collection of Greek texts, written between the fourth and the fifteenth centuries, by holy fathers of the Orthodox tradition. St Nikodimos, one of the compilers, describes it in his introduction as "a mystical school of inward prayer"; and though the texts range widely across what their authors call the art of arts and the science of sciences, a cohesive thread is provided by the recurrent references to the Jesus Prayer. In the words of its English translators,

> The *Philokalia* is an itinerary through the labyrinth of time, a silent way of love and gnosis through the deserts and emptinesses of life, especially of modern life, a vivifying and fadeless presence. It is an active force revealing a spiritual path and inducing man to follow it. It is a summons to him to overcome his ignorance, to uncover the knowledge that lies within, to rid himself of illusion, and to be receptive to the grace of the Holy Spirit who teaches all things and brings all things to remembrance.[14]

Though the texts were originally written by monks and for monks, it is clear that the compilation was intended from the start to be used just as much by laypeople living in the world. Several translations into Slavonic and Russian appeared in the course of the nineteenth century and exercised enormous influence on Russian culture and spirituality, as is demonstrated in the writ-

[13] G. E. H. Palmer, Philip Sherrard and Kallistos Ware (eds.), *The Philokalia. The Complete Text Compiled by St Nikodimos of the Holy Mountain and St Makarios of Corinth*, vol. 1 (London, 1979), 7.

[14] Ibid. 13–14.

ings of Dostoievsky. The *Philokalia* also features prominently in the anonymous Russian spiritual classic known as *The Way of a Pilgrim*.

> "Read this book," [the elder] said. "It is called *The Philokalia*, and it contains the full and detailed science of constant interior prayer, set forth by twenty-five holy Fathers. The book is marked by a lofty wisdom and is so profitable to use that it is considered the foremost and best manual of the contemplative spiritual life. As the revered Nicephorus said, 'It leads one to salvation without labour and sweat.' "
>
> "Is is then more sublime and holy than the Bible?" I asked.
>
> "No, it is not that. But it contains clear explanations of what the Bible holds in secret and which cannot be easily grasped by our short-sighted understanding. I will give you an illustration. The sun is the greatest, the most resplendent and the most wonderful of heavenly luminaries, but you cannot contemplate and examine it simply with unprotected eyes. You have to use a piece of artificial glass which is many millions of times smaller and darker than the sun. But through this little piece of glass you can examine the magnificent monarch of stars, delight in it, and endure its fiery rays. Holy Scripture also is a dazzling sun, and this book, *The Philokalia*, is the piece of glass which we use to enable us to contemplate the sun in its imperial splendour. Listen now, I am going to read you the sort of instruction it gives on unceasing interior prayer."[15]

In the twentieth century, translations of the *Philokalia* into modern Greek and western European languages were undertaken and attracted a wide readership. As Bishop Kallistos himself has written, "the *Philokalia* has acted as a spiritual 'time bomb,' for the true 'age of the *Philokalia*' has been not the late eighteenth but the late twentieth century."[16] In his 1994 talk to the Friends of Mount Athos he went further:

> The English *Philokalia*, as I can testify from the letters that I receive almost every week, has made a decisive impression, not only on Orthodox but on non-Orthodox, not only on Christians but on many persons of other faiths or of no faith at all. This immense and far-reaching

[15]*The Way of a Pilgrim*, translated by R.M. French (London, 1986), 9–10.
[16]*The Orthodox Church*, 100.

influence throughout the English-speaking world can be traced back to a single source: Gerald Palmer's visit to the Holy Mountain in May 1948 and his providential encounter with Fr Nikon.[17]

The *Philokalia* continues to be an inspiration to its many readers throughout the world. If Karoulia failed to yield a harvest of men comparable to that of some of the other sketes in the Athonite desert, its harvest of souls will be second to none as a result of the monumental achievement of this translation that was inspired by Fr Nikon.

A place of pilgrimage

In a paper entitled "The Spiritual Guide in Orthodox Christianity" Bishop Kallistos discusses the role of the spiritual father and his relationship with his spiritual children; and he also writes about what we are to do if we cannot find a spiritual guide. "We may turn, in the first place, to *books*," he says, ". . . above all the *Philokalia* . . ." He goes on:

> It is possible to learn also from visiting *places* where divine grace has been exceptionally manifest and where, in T. S. Eliot's phrase, "prayer has been valid." Before making a major decision, and in the absence of other guidance, many Orthodox Christians will go on pilgrimage to Jerusalem or Mount Athos, to some monastery or the shrine of a saint, where they will pray for illumination. This is the way in which I myself have reached certain of the more difficult decisions in my life.[18]

Here once again is an acknowledgement of the role that Athos has played in his life—as a place of pilgrimage. It is perhaps the role that the Mountain plays most conspicuously in the lives of all who go there, though many only become aware of this after they have completed their first pilgrimage. For Bishop Kallistos this was no doubt a key factor in his decision to support the formation of a society of Friends of Mount Athos, of which he has been Chairman since its foundation in 1990 (and now President since the death of Sir Steven Runciman in 2000).

---

[17] "Gerald Palmer, the *Philokalia*, and the Holy Mountain," 26.
[18] *The Inner Kingdom*, 147.

Sir Steven described the aims of this society in his Foreword to its first *Annual Report*:

This is not a society that aims at producing sensational results. Our role is described by our name. We know that the monasteries of the Holy Mountain form an autonomous religious republic whose members are proud to be living under the shadow of eternity, outside the modern materialistic world. But they cannot entirely separate themselves from the world; and we believe that they are grateful to have friends who are in it, and who will gladly give them such support and advice as they may need. We cannot offer direct financial aid, but I hope that we can, if asked, help with technical equipment and advice. We have no intention of meddling in politics, unless the integrity of the Holy Mountain is threatened. It is essentially as friends that we hope to operate, both as a society and individually; and I hope that we shall be joined by everyone who has a respect, a sympathy, and an admiration for that most beautiful of peninsulas and its holy way of life.[19]

Ten years on, the society has more than 600 members worldwide, it has acquired charitable status, and it has attracted royal patronage with both the Duke of Edinburgh and the Prince of Wales as active honorary members.

Bishop Kallistos has described the society as operating like a bridge between the Holy Mountain and the outside world, a bridge with two-way traffic on it. In one direction go the pilgrims to whom the society offers guidance and for whose benefit it arranges lectures, conferences, and publications; and in the other direction come the monks, sometimes seeking assistance with a specific problem, sometimes bearing spiritual gifts as they respond to an invitation to deliver an address. Traffic on the bridge continues to increase, in both directions. Bishop Kallistos's record of attendance speaks for itself: since the inauguration of the society in 1990 he has missed just one meeting of the Executive Committee and he has chaired every single AGM.

As I write towards the end of 2001, Bishop Kallistos is preparing to make his twelfth pilgrimage to the Holy Mountain, to celebrate the feast of the Nativity of Christ at the monastery of Simonopetra, whose feast day it will also be. It will have been nearly ten years since his last visit, in April 1992. What changes will he find?

---

[19]*Annual Report of the Friends of Mount Athos* (1991), 3.

When he reported on his 1992 visit, he wrote at length about the erosion of stillness, the damage done to the environment, and the persecution of minorities on the Mountain.[20] My impression as a more regular visitor is that there has been some improvement in all these respects. True, there are more visitors than ever, especially in the summer; and the numbers of roads and motor vehicles have continued to increase. But they seem less obtrusive than they did (or has one simply become accustomed to them?); the long-feared road connection with the mainland has never been built; and happily the desert remains a road-free zone. Meanwhile at the instigation of the Prince of Wales the Friends of Mount Athos has this year initiated a major new project for the restoration and preservation of what remains of the ancient network of footpaths and muletracks and their associated wayside shrines and fountains. Building work in the monasteries and elsewhere continues unabated; but it is mostly being done under careful professional supervision with close attention being paid to the choice of materials, the style of construction, and the preservation of harmony. Notable examples of recent refurbishment completed to a very high standard include the new library at Simonopetra, the new guesthouse at Vatopedi, and the new museum inside the Protaton Tower at Karyes, though the state of the frescos in the church of the Protaton is still a running sore. As for the minorities, no incidents of persecution have been reported in recent years and it would appear that they are mostly being left in peace. Numbers at all the non-Greek houses are rising, slowly but steadily; and the Romanians, for whom Bishop Kallistos made a special plea last time, are quietly flourishing not only at the sketes of Prodromou and Lakkou but also in some of the ruling monasteries where they often form the largest ethnic minority group. Far be it from me to anticipate his impressions; but I like to think that he will not be too disappointed by what he finds this time.

I should like to conclude by quoting the words with which Bishop Kallistos ended the report on his 1982 visit which seem to me, *mutatis mutandis*, every bit as valid today as they were when he wrote them:

> Friends of Athos, then, may look to the future with both hope and disquiet; hope, because of the undoubted strengthening of the monastic presence in the last fifteen years; disquiet, because of the increasing erosion of the Mountain's unique status as a sanctuary set apart. No

[20]"Athos after Ten Years: The Good News and the Bad," 29–35.

visible centre on earth, however precious, possesses ultimate value; the true wilderness, the only durable sanctuary, is within the heart. But at the same time visible symbols, areas in space that can serve as icons and sacraments, are an incalculable enrichment to the life of the Spirit. Each time I return to Athos, I feel this with an almost overwhelming physical intensity. When, after obtaining my permit at Karyes, I walk alone to the monastery where I am to spend the first night, with the silence growing more and more dense all around me, I thank God that I am once more privileged to return to this place where, as Fr Nikon used to say, "every stone breathes prayers." May our Saviour, at the intercessions of his All-Pure Mother, Patron of the Holy Mountain, long preserve this her heritage unimpaired, as a source of peace and stillness for all who dwell there or who come on pilgrimage.[21]

---

[21]"Wolves and Monks: Life on the Holy Mountain Today," *Sobornost*, 5:2 (1983), 68.

PART ONE

Historical

Theological Education in the Christian East: First to Sixth Centuries

Bishop Hilarion (Alfeyev) of Podolsk

I N A PAPER ENTITLED "Problems of Orthodox Theological Education in Russia,"[1] I called for a radical reform of the entire system of theological education existing in the Russian Church. The kind of reform that is needed, however, does not presuppose the invention of something fundamentally novel. On the contrary, we need to turn back to the ancient, long-forgotten legacy of theological education in the Christian East. In my view, the famous schools of the Christian East were vehicles of truly Orthodox theological education, and the present state of affairs in our system of theological education is largely a result of deviation from the principles underlying the activity of these schools. Perhaps, the substance of the reform that we need is to depart as far as possible from scholastic, medieval approaches to pedagogy and return to the truly Orthodox traditions of theological education.

In terms of their organisation, our present-day theological academies and seminaries are reproductions of medieval Latin theological schools. Many of the shortcomings that characterise theological institutions in Russia were inherited from their "foremother," the Kiev-Mogilyanskaya Academy, established in the 17th century after the model of the Jesuit schools of the period. Notwithstanding the three-and-a-half centuries that have passed since then as well as all the reforms that were carried out therein, the basic drawbacks of the medieval educational system have not yet been completely eliminated. This can only happen when the experience of a truly Orthodox theological school is implemented, that which existed in the Christian East long before Latin-style institutions following the Jesuit model began to spring up.

[1]Published in *Sourozh*, 71 (Oxford, 1998), 4–28.

In this article I would like to look at several theological schools that existed in the early Christian East. My objective here is not to present a comprehensive analysis of each variety of theological education from the early Christian centuries, but rather to draw the attention of the reader to some of the most vivid examples of theological schools active in the primitive Eastern Church. I would also like to ponder whether this legacy of early Christianity could be used today in forming and reforming Orthodox theological educational institutions.

I. Jesus Christ and His Disciples: The First "Theological School"

I shall begin with the apostolic community headed by Jesus Christ. This community was in fact the first Christian theological school. In it the pupils received divine revelation from the mouth of their Master, the incarnate Word of God himself. It was, above all, the assimilation of this experience that constituted the education of Christ's disciples. According to John the Theologian, the transmission of this experience to his disciples was, in the final analysis, the main purpose of the earthly service of the Word:

> And of his fullness have all we received, and grace for grace. For the law was given by Moses, but grace and truth came by Jesus Christ. No man hath seen God at any time; the only begotten Son, who is in the bosom of the Father, he has declared him. (Jn 1:16–18.)

Thus the incarnate Son of God "explained" (such is the exact meaning of the Greek verb ἐξηγήσατο, "expounded") his Father to the people and became God's first "exegete." During his earthly life, Jesus taught his disciples what it means to be "children of light."[2] This was the true goal to which the divine Master directed all of his efforts.

How did Jesus achieve this goal and what were the outward forms of his teaching? At the outset, it should be noted that Jesus himself enrolled his disciples, and he did this, so to say, without "entrance examinations" (see Mt 4:18–22). The disciples called Jesus their "Teacher" (διδάσκαλος) and "Lord" (κύριος), and Jesus took this as his due (Jn 13:13). He defined the task that his disciples had to fulfil, which was above all, the need to follow his example. Their feet having been washed at the mystical supper, Jesus told his disciples:

[2]Lk 16:8; Jn 12:36.

"If I then, your Lord and Master, have washed your feet; you also ought to wash one another's feet. For I have given you an example, that you should do as I have done to you" (Jn 13:14–15).

Aware also of the dignity due to a master, Jesus said: "The disciple is not above his master, nor the servant above his lord. It is enough for the disciple that he be as his master, and the servant as his lord" (Mt 10:24–5). At the same time, he emphasised that his disciples are not "servants" but friends who shared the master's knowledge of the divine mysteries: "Henceforth I call you not servants; for the servant knows not what his lord does: but I have called you friends; for all things that I have heard of my Father I have made known unto you" (Jn 15:15). Being a disciple is thus nothing other than a friendship with one's master, a close friendship wherein the master conceals nothing from his disciples. Jesus' attitude to his disciples differs from that to other people. He teaches the latter through parables without revealing to them everything that he might to his disciples. Certain things were concealed from ordinary people, while the disciples were made privy to the great and deep mysteries of the Kingdom of Heaven (see Mt 13:10–17).

Historically speaking, the community of Jesus' disciples was preceded by the prophetic schools of ancient Israel, the Essene communities, and gatherings similar to John the Baptist's circle of disciples. Outwardly, Christ's Twelve had much in common with them. This is indicated, in particular, by the words that the Evangelists use when speaking about Jesus as a teacher. Some points in the Gospel narrative have parallels in what we see in Talmudic literature, where disciples are especially directed to bear their teacher's shoes,[3] help their teacher overcome all kinds of difficulties, prepare the way for him,[4] make his paschal supper, bring him his ass, etc. All of these features can be seen in the community of Jesus Christ's disciples. What was foreign to it, however, was that complete, servile obedience which, in Talmudic tradition, had to be shown towards a rabbi. The disciples followed their Master everywhere, they accompanied him in his travels, listened to him as he taught the people and questioned him about the meaning of his parables. About all else, however, they ever remained his friends. The distance that, in Judaic tradition, separated a teacher from his disciples did not exist between Jesus Christ and the Twelve.

[3]John the Baptist's utterance (Mat 3:11) had a very specific meaning: John said that he was not worthy of being even a *disciple* of the Messiah.

[4]Cf. Mk 1:3 ("The voice of one crying in the wilderness, Prepare ye the way of the Lord, make his paths straight") and Mat 21:8 ("And a very great multitude spread their garments in the way; others cut down branches from the trees, and spread them in the way").

Although Jesus is referred to as "teacher" (διδάσκαλος) in the Gospels, he set himself over and above the other *didaskaloi* of his time. Thus he called Nicodemus, who came to him by night, "teacher of Israel" (διδάσκαλος τοῦ Ἰσραήλ, Jn 3:9–10). In the Hebraic understanding, the term "teacher of Israel" was used for a person who taught the way of God based on the Torah; sometimes such a person was called a "teacher of the truth." Jesus, however, when addressing his disciples said: "I am the way, the truth, and the life: no man cometh unto the Father, but by me." (Jn 14:6.) Not only does he teach the right way: He is himself the way that his disciples must follow.

Jesus Christ taught his disciples in order for them to hand down his teaching to future generations. After his resurrection, he charged them with a teaching mission: "Go ye therefore, and teach all nations . . . teaching them to observe all things whatsoever I have commanded you" (Mt 28:19–20). To carry out this mission, they required help from the Holy Spirit, who, according to the Master's promise, was to teach them all things (Jn 14:26). Once the Holy Spirit had descended on his disciples at Pentecost (Acts 2:1–4), they became apostles in the full sense of the word and embarked the path of teaching. Like Jesus himself, they began to teach in the temple, in synagogues and in private houses (see Acts 5:21, 5:42, 13:14, etc.).

The continuity of teaching handed down from generation to generation was an essential feature of every theological school. Jesus Christ as a Teacher was a successor of the Old Testament prophets and John the Baptist. Jesus' disciples, as well as the first generations of Christian teachers (*didaskaloi*), who are mentioned already in the Pauline epistles,[5] became the successors of Jesus. The task of these teachers was, in the first place, to teach catechumens and newly-baptised in the principles of the faith. Together with the presbyters and bishops, the teacher engaged in the evangelisation and catechisation of members of the young Christian communities.

A *didaskalos* taught the Church by unfolding the truths of the faith contained in the Tradition and in the Scriptures. Most if not all *didaskaloi* were learned theologians of the ancient Church, representatives of the theological discipline that serves the Church . . . Unlike pagan schools, they opened their schools where not only catechumens, but also the faithful wishing to learn more about the Word of God took instruction.[6]

[5]See Eph 4:11: "And he gave some, apostles; and some, prophets; and some, evangelists; and some, pastors and teachers (διδάσκαλοι)."

[6]N. Afanasiev, *Tserkov Dukha Svyatogo* [=The Church of the Holy Spirit] (Paris, 1971), 136.

It is on these schools, which aimed at preserving the tradition of Jesus Christ and his disciples, that the rest of this article will be focused.

II. Christian Theological Schools of the Hellenistic World

The preaching of Jesus Christ's disciples and their successors formed the foundation upon which all theological schools of the Christian East developed. As the Church expanded geographically, Christian teachers encountered cultural traditions different from those of Jesus' disciples. This was behind a complicated and sometimes painful process of the transformation of Christianity into a religion not conditioned by the implications of Jewish national tradition. The message about God incarnate, crucified and resurrected long remained "foolishness" to the Hellenistic world (cf. 1 Cor 1:23), which had to mature into its own Pentecost and find its own approach to the mystery of the Incarnation. The Hellenistic mind had evolved within a different cultural environment and called for an alternative pedagogical approach from the Christian *didaskaloi*. The experience of the apologists of the second and third centuries demonstrated how difficult it was to transmit the truths of revelation to classical society and to teach it how to live in Christ. This task, however, was successfully fulfilled by the catechetical schools of the ancient world, which will be the subject of our discussion.

About 100 to 150 years passed from the time of the apostolic preaching to the days when Christian schools, conditioned by their geographical location and succession of teachers, began to emerge. There is no reason to believe, however, that catechetical schools came into being all of a sudden. Catechism was an integral part of the spiritual and liturgical life of the Church. Thus, for example, judging by archaeological findings[7] and narrative information,[8] the Roman Christian community had an extensive body of catechumens, who were instructed by bishops, presbyters and *didaskaloi*. In the 2nd century, a Christian theological school supervised by Justin the Martyr was already active in Rome.

1. The Catechetical School of Alexandria, 2nd–3rd Centuries

The most lively and most interesting educational institution of the period was the Catechetical School of Alexandria. This school sustained its main

---

[7]For instance the wall drawings in the Roman catacombs dating from the late 1st and early 2nd centuries.

[8]Such as the First Epistle of Clement of Rome to the Corinthians.

practical objective, to instruct people in the faith and to prepare them for baptism. The instruction, in all likelihood, boiled down to an "introduction into Christianity" with emphasis on the reading of Holy Scripture. Particular attention was given to ascetic exercise and prayer alternating with theological studies. At the school, catechumens were gradually introduced into ecclesiastical life and teaching, and upon completion they were baptised, thus becoming fully-fledged members of the Church.

However, even as early as the 2nd century, under Pantaenus and Clement of Alexandria, the school began to be transformed from a purely catechetical institution into a kind of a "Christian university" offering instruction in a wide range of disciplines.[9] Clement's famous trilogy, his *magnum opus*, is nothing less than a "study programme" of Alexandria's Catechetical School. The basis of his *Protreptikos pros Hellenas* (Hortatory Discourse to the Greeks) was derived from lectures prepared for the school's "freshmen," that is, for those representatives of the Hellenistic tradition interested in Christianity and who were preparing for baptism. His *Paedagogos* (The Tutor) is a course in moral theology apparently intended for the newly baptised. As for his *Stromateis* (Miscellanies), they reflect the innermost Christian *gnosis* and were intended for those who aimed to grasp sublime divine knowledge. With such a flexible and academically elaborate programme, a teacher of the School of Alexandria was not merely an instructor in theology, but also a true *paidagogos*, "a man having the oversight of a child or youth," a preceptor giving personal spiritual guidance to his disciples in the faith and in ascetic practice. According to Clement, the comprehension of divine mysteries is inseparable from salvation; therefore Christian education is the implementation of God's will, a Christian act of faith.

From Clement's trilogy it is possible to form a clear picture of the course of subjects that he taught at the School of Alexandria. Initially, students were introduced to the sciences and arts (which constituted "worldly wisdom"), as well as to the entire repertory of the classical philosophical legacy. Next came the Holy Scriptures of the Old Testament, with special emphasis laid on establishing parallels between the Hellenistic and the Old Testament traditions. Finally were the Christian texts, in particular the Gospels and the Epistles of

[9]There is a hypothesis (founded on evidence provided by Theodore the Reader, a 5th-century historian: see Theodoros Anagnostes, *Kirchengeschichte* [Berlin, 1971], 160) according to which Athenagoras (2nd century) was one of the first heads of the School of Alexandria. If Athenagoras actually was the predecessor of Pantaenus and Clement as the head of the School of Alexandria, it was probably he and not they who played the main part in turning the school into a "Christian university."

Paul. Church Tradition, itself a field of study, was compared with the "traditions" of heretics. Clement gave particular attention to disproving Gnostic teachings and countering them with a truly Christian *gnosis*.

Why is it necessary to study the secular sciences and philosophy? Because, Clement answers, a person who is not learned will be able neither to distinguish between the truth and a lie, nor to guard properly the Christian faith against its enemies.[10] The so-called "preparatory" or "preliminary" sciences, which among other things, include music, geometry, grammar, and rhetoric, are, in Clement's opinion, necessary for ascending to a higher level, the study of philosophy.[11] The preparatory sciences are only needed to the extent that they are conducive to a more profound knowledge of the truth. A Christian, in Clement's view, must be a broadly educated person, but encyclopaedic learning is not an end in itself. Learning must be placed at the service of Christianity, which needs to be "guarded" against external assaults.[12]

Clement attached great importance to the study of philosophy and he believed that the Christian faith should not be opposed to it. He maintains that "philosophy does not drag us away from the faith," but rather, "by the use of an ampler circuit, obtains a common exercise demonstrative of the faith. Further, the juxtaposition of doctrines, by comparison, saves the truth, from which follows knowledge."[13] Clement says that "the way of truth is . . . one. But into it, as into a perennial river, streams flow from all sides."[14] One such stream is Greek philosophy, which is "a preparation, paving the way for him who is perfected in Christ."[15] Philosophy was given to the Greeks as a divine gift, as "the clear image of truth"[16]; it was to the Greeks the same schoolmaster to bring them to Christ (Gal 3:23–24) as the Mosaic law was to the Hebrews.[17] The very term "philosophy" was used by Clement in an extended sense: to him, philosophy was not Stoic, or the Platonic, or the Epicurean, or the Aristotelian teaching, but "whatever has been well said by each of those sects, which teach righteousness along with a science pervaded by piety."[18] "True philosophy," according to Clement, is the love of truth and a striving to know the true God. While among the Greeks philosophy not infre-

[10]*Stromateis* I.9.
[11]Ibid. I.5.
[12]Ibid. VI.10.
[13]Ibid. I.2.
[14]Ibid. I.5.
[15]Ibid. I.5.
[16]Ibid. I.2.
[17]Ibid. I.5.
[18]Ibid. I.7.

quently degenerates into sophistry, to Christians it always remains the way to acquire wisdom: "Those are called philosophers, among us, who love Wisdom, the Creator and Teacher of all things, that is, the knowledge of the Son of God; and among the Greeks, those who undertake arguments on virtue."[19]

In spite of all the respect Clement had for philosophy, he realised that studying it was, in its turn, a preparatory stage on the way towards comprehending real wisdom, Christian *gnosis*. For this reason, having given an overview of classical philosophical systems, Clement passed on to the Scriptures of the Old Testament. He told his disciples about its Greek translation[20] and about its author, identified with Moses.[21] This was followed by a detailed analysis of "parallels" between Moses and Plato. The aim of this analysis was to show that Plato had read Moses and borrowed considerably from the Old Testament.[22] The teaching of the Old Testament was also compared with the views of classical legislators, such as Minos, Lycurgus, and Solon.[23] At the subsequent stages of studying the Scriptures, Clement proceeded to refute Gnostic doctrines, continuing at the same time to compare classical conceptions with the Old Testament teachings.

Clement also offered students a course in the "exegesis" of the Holy Scriptures, in which he touched upon such key exegetical concepts as biblical anthropomorphism and the literal and allegorical interpretation of Scripture.[24] Questions of moral theology, which constituted the main part of the preparatory course (*Paidagogos*), were also touched upon at more advanced stages of study (moral exhortations are scattered all over the *Stromateis*). We cannot speak here about a systematic course in "dogmatics" as taught by Clement. There is no doubt, however, that at more advanced stages of studying, he introduced his disciples to the main "mysteries" of the Christian faith such as the eternal counsel and divine providence for the salvation of humanity,[25] the Lord's descent to Hades and his preaching to those of the heathen who had died outside of the faith,[26] and so forth. Clement also touched upon ecclesiological problems.[27] Questions of mystical theology are often reflected

[19]Ibid. VI.7.
[20]Chapter 22 of *Stromateis* I is devoted to this theme.
[21]See *Stromateis* I.23–24.
[22]Ibid. I.25.
[23]Ibid. I.26–28.
[24]See ibid. II.16 et al.
[25]Ibid. VII.2.
[26]Ibid. VI.6.
[27]See ibid. VII.17, where he speaks about the Church.

in Clement's work: he speaks about the vision of God to which Christians are called and about the deification of human nature.[28] Characteristically, however, the author of the *Stromateis* does not divide theology into "moral," "dogmatic," "mystical," and other compartments. Apparently, this is precisely what the "non-systematic" character of the *Stromateis*, which scholars have pointed to many times, means.

The fact that in Clement's works Christian theology is not sub-divided into various fields is determined, in my view, by the lack of such a division in the very course of study taught at the School of Alexandria. Clement certainly had a "system" of his own, which, as I have already mentioned, can be summarised as being a consecutive transition from a lower to a higher stage: from "preparatory sciences" to philosophy and from philosophy to theology. However, there is none of the fragmentation, so characteristic of today's theological schools, in the way Clement sets forth his material. "Christian science" was taught by Clement as a single whole, not divided into one or another "field." This is not, in my opinion, a shortcoming, but rather a meritorious method of instruction that was developed at the School of Alexandria. The students learnt Christian doctrine coherently, tracing the inseparable links between dogma, morality, asceticism, and mysticism.

2. *Origen and His Concept of the Theological School*

Let us now proceed to examine the pedagogical concepts of Origen, Clement's successor as head of the School of Alexandria, under whom the history of theological education in Alexandria reached its acme. Origen's role in the development of educational structures in the Christian Church cannot be exaggerated. He promoted and implemented a new method of teaching, genetically linked with the traditions begun by Clement, Pantaenus and their predecessors, yet at the same time sufficiently different from any kind of Christian pedagogy before his day.

An outstanding thinker, Origen was aware that Christian thought should encompass every field of human knowledge and that the deeper the spirit of Christianity penetrated every sphere of society's intellectual life, the louder Christ's message would be proclaimed in the pagan world. An ardent love of learning and education was combined in Origen with a profound spiritual life, asceticism, and broadmindedness. As a teacher, Origen gave priority to the interpretation of Scripture and to studying Christian dogmas. However,

[28]Ibid. VII.10.

before reading and examining the Bible, his students were offered a preparatory course, which included dialectics, physics, mathematics, astronomy, and geometry, followed by philosophy and theology. In this way, Origen followed in the wake of his predecessor heads of the School of Alexandria. Respect for classical learning had reigned supreme at that school since the days of Pantaenus and Clement, and Origen made every effort to keep this spirit alive. When Origen could no longer cope with the amount of teaching, owing to the increased number of students, he invited his disciple Heraclas, the future bishop of Alexandria, to assume the elementary instruction, leaving himself free for the advanced teaching of theology and the Holy Scriptures.

Compelled to leave Alexandria, Origen moved to Caesarea Palestine, where he founded a school after the model of the Catechetical School of Alexandria. The curriculum at Caesarea was approximately the same as in Alexandria. A unique piece of evidence has come down to us from that period. Gregory Thaumaturgus, who studied under Origen for five years, described in his *Oration and Panegyric Addressed to Origen* how his theological and spiritual moulding proceeded under the guidance of the great Alexandrian *didaskalos*. According to Gregory the Wonderworker, Origen included natural sciences, such as mathematics, geometry, astronomy, cosmology, and physiology into the curriculum.[29] He also gave particular attention to the study of classical philosophy and literature.[30] All the known systems of Greek philosophers were studied at Origen's school. Origen's lectures, however, were structured in such a way that they demonstrated the mutual contradiction of philosophic doctrines.[31] Introducing his students to the entire range of the classical philosophical legacy, Origen taught them how to orient themselves in it and to know the difference between right and wrong. Not only did Origen introduce certain classical or other teachings to his classes, but he also interpreted them in a Christian spirit and applied to them the criterion of conformity to the Christian message.[32]

An exceptionally great deal of attention was given at Origen's school to studying the books of the Holy Scriptures. Origen entrusted the teaching of other subjects to one or another of his disciples, but he left biblical exegesis for himself. Following Gregory, Origen may be described as an exegete whose penetrating spiritual eye missed none of the highly mysterious phrases in Holy

---

[29]Gregory Thaumaturgus *The Oration and Panegyric Addressed to Origen* VIII.
[30]Ibid. XIII–XV.
[31]Ibid. XIV.
[32]Ibid.

Scripture. Gregory also refers to Origen as a "hearer" of the divine Word, through whom the Word himself revealed the truth to the students. It was through Origen's interpretations that the students of the School of Caesarea learnt the meaning of the books of the Old and New Testaments.[33]

Particularly precious to us are the accounts of Origen's teaching method given by Gregory. The great *didaskalos*'s special concern was to cultivate in his students the ability to work directly with the sources. Origen was very much aware that his task was not to give his students a certain amount of knowledge but to teach them to answer by themselves the questions that arose in the process of learning one or another discipline. Like the earlier great teacher, Socrates, Origen did not give his students ready answers to their questions; rather, he persuaded each student "by his discourse, which acted like a bridle" in his mouth.[34]

Educating his students and acting as their guide, not only in scholarship, but also in the spiritual life, Origen, as can be seen, was relentless towards everything that prevented a young soul from knowing the fruits of truth. One should not think that Origen's students had exceptional abilities or that all of them were equally pious. Many students demanded of Origen greater teaching efforts, more patience and a more thoughtful approach. As we may assume, Gregory himself was one such "problem" student, with whom Origen was nonetheless able to cope:

Whenever he . . . detected anything in us not wholly fruitless and profitless and waste, he set about clearing the soil, and turning it up and irrigating it, and putting all things in movement, and brought his whole skill and care to bear on us, and wrought upon our mind.[35]

Between Origen and his disciples there was not that distance which quite often separates a teacher from his pupils. Despite his high position, Origen did not treat his students with indignity, neither did he humiliate them nor try to exact complete obedience from them at all costs. At Origen's school, the teacher and the students were united by ties of a strong and sincere friendship. Gregory testifies to this in the following manner:

... The stimulus of friendship was also brought to bear upon us—a stimulus, indeed, not easily withstood, but keen and most effective—the

[33]Ibid. XV.
[34]Ibid. VII.
[35]Ibid.

argument of a kind and affectionate disposition, which showed itself benignantly in his words when he spoke to us and associated with us.[36]

Again Gregory writes that Origen taught him the most important thing, the love of God. It was on this love, as on a strong foundation, that relations between the students and the teacher were built:

> And thus, like some spark lighting upon our inmost soul, love was kindled and burst into flame within us—a love at once to the holy Word, the most lovely object of all, who attracts all irresistibly toward himself by his unutterable beauty, and to this man, his friend and advocate.[37]

The panegyric written by Gregory Thaumaturgus may on first reading appear to be an idealised image of his teacher, were it not for the sincerity and auto-biographical quality that distinguish this work from many other similar writings. Gregory makes no mention of the negative aspects of school life which must have existed and which are virtually inevitable at any educational establishment. No materials have survived from second and third century catechetical schools similar to "The Statutes of the School of Nisibis" (discussed below) that would enable us to evaluate the major shortcomings and deficiencies of the educational system in these schools. What we do have, however, is a number of documentary records that tell us with indubitable veracity that these establishments were outstanding centres of spiritual culture where great *didaskaloi* (such as Clement and Origen) taught and where prominent students (such as Gregory Thaumaturgus) were educated. In the second and third century catechetical schools, learning was inseparable from piety as was theological education from spiritual upbringing. This is what constitutes their unquestionably great service to the Christian Church.

III. Theological Schools in the Syrian Orient

Let us now proceed to the next subject, the basic elements of theological education in the Syrian Orient. In spite of their differences in culture and historical circumstance, theological schools in the Syrian Orient developed in a

---

[36]Ibid.
[37]Ibid.

manner that was rather similar to that in which Christian theological educational institutions developed in the Hellenistic world. Those of the Syrian tradition, however, operated in a distinct manner, following their own intuition and their unique perceptions of theological education.

1. Syrian Christian Learning

Like the Hellenistic schools, the largest centres of Syrian Christian learning, the famous Schools of Edessa and Nisibis, grew out of small catechetical schools functioning in Christian parishes. According to Syrian sources, only boys studied at these parochial schools. One's education began with learning to read using the Psalter and reciting psalms by heart. Subsequent elementary education included learning the Old and New Testaments and becoming familiar with biblical exegesis. In addition, this programme of elementary education also required one to commit to memory the most important liturgical hymns and to acquire some experience in homiletics.

Our information about the early period of the School of Edessa is scanty and incomplete. We know that, after Nisibis was captured by the Persians in 363, many Christians abandoned the city to escape the cruel persecutions and settled at Edessa. Among them was Mar Aprem, better known to us as Ephraim the Syrian. At Edessa, he founded the theological "School of the Persians," so called because its first students and original masters were Persian Christian refugees in 363.

In Ephraim's lifetime and for several decades after his death, his interpretations of the Holy Scriptures were used at the School of Edessa as models of exegesis. In 420, however, Mar Qiiore, one of Ephraim's successors and rector of the school, decided to translate into Syriac the biblical commentaries of Theodore of Mopsuestia, which, unlike Ephraim's commentaries, covered practically all the books of the Bible. Once completed, the interpretations of Theodore of Mopsuestia replaced all others in the school's curriculum and Theodore himself began to be regarded as the main authority in theology and the principal exegete in the entire Eastern Syrian tradition: he was even called "the Blessed Interpreter." Theodore of Mopsuestia was a representative of the extreme Dyophysite school of Christological thought, which was subsequently identified with Nestorianism. After the condemnation of Nestorius by the Council of Ephesus in 433, the entire Eastern Syrian tradition was suspected of heresy. The debates between the Monophysite and Dyophysite factions directly affected the destiny of the School of Edessa. In 489, the school was declared a hotbed of the Nestorian heresy and closed by order of the Emperor Zeno.

Several years before the close of the School of Edessa, Mar Narsai, the head of the school, together with his disciples moved to Nisibis. By the end of the 5th century, the School of Nisibis became one of the major spiritual and theological centres of the Syrian Church. Mar Narsai was a remarkable person. He lived a long life that began in the fourth century and ended in the sixth (399—501) and his popularity in Nisibis was very wide. He was famous both as an ascetic and as an outstanding exegete. According to a chronicler of the day, people were most attracted by his following six qualities: the novelty of his thoughts, his ability to bear himself with dignity, his pleasant countenance, his understanding, his kind-heartedness, and his eloquence.[38] Under Narsai a highly interesting document, *The Statutes of the School of Nisibis*, which will be discussed below, was compiled.

Another famous rector of the School of Nisibis was Henana of Adiabene, who began his tenure in 572. Henana was a striking personality and an outstanding theologian. He made an attempt to replace the biblical commentaries of Theodore with his own. However, the authority of "the Blessed Interpreter" remained inviolable, and not only numerous theologians and monks, but also the bishops of the Syrian Church turned against him. Henana belonged to a school of Syrian theologians who sympathised with the Council of Chalcedon. It was for this reason that he wanted to destroy the legacy of Theodore of Mopsuestia, the "Father of Nestorianism." A struggle between Henana's adherents and opponents ensued at the School of Nisibis and it continued for quite a long time. But in spite of the late-sixth-century council prohibitions, Henana remained a respected authority even at the turn of the seventh century, when additional statutes of the School of Nisibis (discussed below) were made public: in them, Henana was described as "experienced in knowledge and glorious in humility."[39]

Let us now look at the teaching procedures at the School of Nisibis as well as its curriculum and structure. The course of study lasted three years and each academic year was divided into a summer and winter semester. Together with the Holy Scriptures, secular disciplines were also taught at the school.[40] Much attention was given to the teaching of rhetoric, whose teacher was called *mehageiana*. Philosophy was studied using primary sources: in particular, students read Aristotle, Porphyry, and Syrian authors. Instruction in

---

[38]The name of the chronicler is Barhadbeshabba (6th-7th centuries). See V. Pigulevskaya. *Kultura siriytsev v Sredniye veka* [=The Syrian Civilisation of the Middle Ages] (Moscow, 1979), 64.

[39]See V. Pigulevskaya, *Kultura siriytsev*, 70 and 102.

[40]See D. Miller, Epilogue to *The Ascetical Homilies of Saint Isaac the Syrian* (Boston Mass.: Holy Transfiguration Monastery, 1984), 489.

philosophic disciplines, one of the most important among which was logic, was given by the *baduqa*. *Sapera*, a "scribe," taught calligraphy. The *maqreiana* provided instruction in reading.

The key figure at the school was the *mepašqana*, the interpreter. His tasks included giving instruction in biblical exegesis. The *mepašqana* (exegete) did not only use the "standard" interpretations of Theodore of Mopsuestia, but also made use of interpretations by other Greek and Syrian authors. Besides, there also existed an oral tradition of interpretation that had been handed down from generation to generation. The *mepašqana* usually occupied also the office of rector (*rabban*), providing general spiritual guidance for the school. In matters of school administration the *mepašqana* relied on his chief administrative aid, the *rabbaita*. The latter was responsible for all school property, for its finances, for maintaining discipline, and for the upkeep of the library. The *rabbaita*, whose office was elective, had an aid, the *'aksenadakra*, who, in particular, took care of the school's hospital.

Although the rector and the *rabbaita* wielded unquestioned authority, the supreme authority at the school was exercised not by them but by the meeting of the community, in which both the teachers and the students (the latter having the deciding vote on account of their overwhelming majority[41]) always took part. At these meetings all major questions relating to the school's operation were discussed. The meeting elected the *rabbaita* and adopted decisions concerning the removal of one student or another from the school for misbehaviour. All of the community members, including the *rabban* and the *rabbaita* (who could not make important decisions without the sanction of the other community members), were accountable to the meeting.[42] This structure of the school ensured a high degree of mutual trust between the "faculty," on the one hand, and the students, on the other. To remove a student from the school by the private decision of a few school administrators was unthinkable. Naturally, one's attitude to the *rabbaita* was that of respect, for he was elected by the community, not appointed by a higher authority.

2. The Statutes of the School of Nisibis

To form an idea of how the School of Nisibis operated, it will be helpful to examine its aforementioned *Statutes*, which fortunately have come down to

---

[41]It should be noted that at different times the student body at the School of Nisibis numbered as many as 800 to 1,000.

[42]This information has been taken mostly from V. Pigulevskaya, *Kultura siriytsev*, 57–89.

us. Two sets of rules, the Canons of Narsai (496) and the Canons of Henana (590), still survive. The Statutes of the School of Nisibis are the first statutes of a Christian theological school known in history and, as such, they are of particular interest to us.

Unlike the aforementioned *Oration and Panegyric Addressed to Origen*, whose author, Gregory Thaumaturgus, emphasised positive aspects of his teacher's activities but said nothing about the negative features of the school's life, the Statutes of the School of Nisibis present, so to say, the other side of the ledger. In a lengthy introduction to the Statutes, we read how the need to adopt them was dictated by cases of waywardness at the school that transpired through the fault of certain "quarrelsome" and "envious" people.[43] The preface to the first part of the Statutes contains a warning to every violator of the school's regulations: he "should be anathematised from the fellowship of Christ, and from intercourse with the true believers."[44] In a school that views itself as a fellowship of Christ there should be no one who "should act with boldness and dare to destroy those [Statutes] which we have written, or to alter something in them to the contrary."[45]

The First Rule concerns the procedure for electing the *rabbaita*. He was elected on the recommendation of the *mepašqana*, doubling as the rector, by the general meeting of the school's teachers and students. The election was accompanied by contention and disputes. Parties, formed during the course of the election struggle, consisted of adherents who lobbied for one or the other candidate.[46]

According to the Second Rule, which also deals with the *rabbaita*, the latter was elected only for one year and the following rule defines how he was to manage the affairs of the school. In the first place, this rule provides for strict control over the *rabbaita's* financial activity. Moreover, it gives him the right, in consultation with the rector and the "outstanding brothers," to punish students for misbehaviour. Probably, this indicates corporal punishment, one of the most widespread and—one has to admit—the most effective of correctional measures in antiquity. The rule stipulates firmly that the *rabbaita* act

---

[43]Canons of Narsai, proem. (69–70). Here and below the two parts of the Statutes of the School of Nisibis (Canons of Narsai and Canons of Henana) are quoted (with some modifications) from: *The Statutes of the School of Nisibis*, edited, translated and furnished with a commentary by Arthur Vööbus.—Papers of the Estonian Theological Society in Exile 12 (Uppsala, 1961), 51–105.

[44]Ibid.

[45]Ibid.

[46]Canons of Narsai 1 (73–4).

following the counsel of the "brothers."[47] While a decision to punish an offender could be made by the school's administration (i.e., the *rabbaita* in council with the rector and the "outstanding brothers"), a decision to remove a student from the school had to be adopted by the general meeting.[48]

The Statutes of the School of Nisibis show that its students were addicted to the same vices that prevail in some modern educational establishments. Some students were not averse to drinking; others could become involved in fights with fellow students, steal their purses, etc. Those guilty of such offences would be expelled from the school. The penalty for pugilism, however, was less severe: the offender was to suffer public punishment.[49] Public punishment, however, was administered no more than three times. In case the offender failed to mend his ways, he was sent down.[50]

The students of the school were also forbidden to "go over to the country of the Romans,"[51] that is, Byzantium, without the *rabbaita's* sanction: the Roman Empire had for decades been a strategic enemy of the Persian Empire, and the students were obliged to be "politically correct." They were not allowed to "practise business or craft," except during the three months of summer vacation.[52] The penalty for theft from the library was expulsion from the school.[53] The severity of this punishment was determined by the fact that books, being exceedingly expensive, were among the school's most valuable assets. Even so, they were lent to the students.

Students (*'eskulaie*) were not allowed to be absent from classes in writing, reading and interpretation, nor to defect from the "recitation of the choirs"[54] (apparently common prayer). A student who accused a companion of a certain offence which he could not prove, himself received the punishment that corresponded to the alleged offence.[55] Students who had only recently registered in the school were forbidden to criticise the school's affairs; those guilty of this transgression were expelled.[56]

Noteworthy is the fact that punishment was administered not only to the school students, but also to the teachers. For example, a pecuniary penalty

[47]Ibid. 2 (74–5).
[48]Ibid. 3 (75).
[49]Ibid. 18 (82).
[50]Ibid. 19 (82–3).
[51]Ibid. 4 (75).
[52]Ibid. 5 (77–8).
[53]Ibid. 14 (81).
[54]Ibid. 8 (79).
[55]Ibid. 16 (82).
[56]Ibid. 13 (80–1).

was imposed on the *maqreiane*[57] and the *mehageiane*[58] for being absent from classes without permission.[59] By decision of the general meeting, even the *rabbaita* himself could incur a pecuniary penalty and be removed from the school. This happened if he violated the rules.[60]

The second part of the Statutes of the School of Nisibis, formulated a century after the adoption of the first, introduced a number of new and essential details to the school rules. In addition to his other duties, the *rabbaita* was now prescribed to "go around because of the needy brothers whether it is necessary to set bread before them, or whether it is necessary to aid them in the court."[61] The duties of the *ʿaksenadakra*[62] were also clearly defined: he had to take care for those students who are in the school's hospital, as well as exercise other administrative duties.[63]

The Canons of Henana, discussing the inappropriateness of drunkenness, refer to the vow taken by the student, forming the basis for their community:

> The brothers who are in the school, so long as they are in the school, shall not eat in the taverns and restaurants, they shall also not arrange picnics and drinking parties in the gardens and parks, but shall endure all in their cells as is becoming for the purpose and the manner of their *qeiama*.[64]

A student was forbidden to live in the town ("dwell with the Nisibeans, as long as the cells in the school are empty,"[65] or "leave under the pretext of righteousness the dwelling-place with the brothers and go out and build for himself a hut outside the town or by the side of the town")[66] or to miss the divine service.[67] At the time of harvest (called the "season of the workers") a

---

[57]"Lecturers," "teachers of reading": instructors in liturgical reading.

[58]Teachers helping to read syllables; perhaps, instructors in rhetoric.

[59]Canons of Narsai 20 (83–4).

[60]Ibid. 22 (85).

[61]Canons of Henana 3 (93–4).

[62]The curator of the hospital.

[63]Canons of Henana 1 (92–3).

[64]Ibid. 16 (99). *Qeiama* means "covenant" or "vow," and in this context refers to the vows of obedience to the school given by each student upon entry. *Benai qeiama* ("the sons of the covenant") was the most common designation for the semi-monastic ascetic order that prevailed in Syria before and during the 4th century.

[65]Ibid. 2 (93).

[66]Ibid. 4 (94).

[67]Ibid. 5 (94–5).

student could not "turn and deny the stipulation which he previously had made with his brothers regarding the work."[68] The students were not allowed to "live together with the physicians" ("in order that the books of the craft of the world should not be read with the books of holiness in one light")[69] or shelter captives under the pretext of righteousness or assist slaves to flee from their masters.[70] And, since the School of Nisibis was an enclosed community, open only to male students, measures were taken to ensure that the students should not overstep the mark in their contacts with women:

> No one of the brothers of the school is allowed to teach the women, *benat qeiama*[71], from the town or outside the town . . . Also no one shall have continuance of talk and prolonged conversation with women, in order that they may come to no offence and blasphemy through this cause. And when he is found that he acts otherwise, he shall be estranged from the community and go from the town.[72]

Finally, the Statutes paid attention to the students' outward appearance, stipulating that they should be neat in their dress and have closely cropped hair, so that they would be readily recognizable:

> Along with learning the brothers of the school shall be diligent also over the manner of the dress and hair: they shall not shave entirely, also they shall not grow curls like the seculars but they shall go about within the school and on the streets of the town in chaste tonsure and dignified dress that is far from luxury, so that through these both they shall be known to everybody . . .[73]

We can see that as early as the 5th and 6th centuries a Christian theological school needed to have detailed statutes in order to maintain order and strict discipline. This, however, was not "baculine" discipline based on compulsion. On the contrary, both teachers and students were called upon

---

[68]Ibid. 10.

[69]Ibid. 19 (100–101). Arabic version: "for the books of religion and the books of the world do not get on together" (101).

[70]Ibid. 21 (101).

[71]"The daughters of the covenant," i.e. members of the semi-monastic order referred to above (see note 64 above).

[72]Ibid. 18 (100).

[73]Ibid. 17 (99–100).

voluntarily and consciously to follow the school statutes and not to evade their observance using various excuses. The main concern of the drafters of the statutes was to preserve the school as a community of teachers and students united in a common goal and a common vision. Anyone who did not share this vision or who jeopardised the integrity of the school as an entity was expelled, something that occurred only by a decision of the general meeting and when the transgressions was particularly grave or repeatedly made.

Conclusion

We have looked at only a few examples of theological school typical of the early Christian East. To begin with the apostolic community was of interest to us because it was, above all, as the first "theological school," the only one of its kind founded by Jesus Christ himself. The Catechetical School of Alexandria provided us with evidence of a curriculum also known in Christian schools of the Hellenistic world. Later, Origen's understanding of theological education allowed us to draw inferences about the methods used by the great *didaskaloi* of the Christian East. An overview of Syrian Christian learning and, in particular, an examination of the Statutes of the School of Nisibis enabled us to see how the systems of discipline were enforced at theological schools in the early centuries of our era.

In conclusion, I would like to ponder on how the experience of early Christian schools can help us today in forming a new vision of the theological school. I would single out the following ten points that, in my opinion, deserve to be taken into consideration when developing a new model of theological school:

1. First and foremost, an early Christian theological school was a single community, a brotherhood of people united by a common goal and a common task (this equally applied to the disciples of Jesus, Origen's school and the School of Nisibis). What prevents us from reviving this spirit of fellowship and unity?

2. In an early Christian school, the relations between teachers and students were based on mutual trust. Both were united by ties of close friendship; there was no gulf between the "faculty" and the student body. A similar relationship could be revived today if the teaching staff could learn to respect and value the students. Teachers at theological schools should follow the example of Christ, who, while being "Master and Lord," washed his disciples' feet. In this way, atmosphere in our theological schools would change radically.

3. The key figure of a theological school in the Christian East was its rector, a pedagogue, a schoolmaster, a kind of a spiritual father to the students. As such, he determined the general procedural line of the school's work. The rector was not a school administrator, nor was he responsible for its finances or for maintaining school discipline: these were the responsibilities of others. The rector was a theologian, an expert in his field of knowledge (in particular, in biblical exegesis), and as such he enjoyed great prestige. What stops us from having this type of head as our model?

4. The supreme governing body at establishments such as the School of Nisibis was the general convocation of teachers and students. Should this tradition not be revived? Should we not give some thought to placing the key problems of academic life within the competence of a school general assembly?

5. Disciplinary questions, such as the expulsion of students from a school, should also be made the prerogative of the general assembly. Indeed, this would relieve theological schools from arbitrary actions by members of their administration. This would make it impossible for them to pass judgement on a student on the basis of a private decision which could have been influenced by their own personal likes and dislikes (under the existing system, there are not many theological school free from this).

6. The offices occupied by persons who are responsible for maintaining discipline in a school (inspectors, assistant inspectors, etc.) should be elected. Both teachers and students should be given voting privileges. This will substantially raise the level of students' trust in the administration.

7. In turning to the experience of the catechetical schools of the Hellenistic world (in particular, the School of Alexandria in the days of Clement), we could give some thought to making a gradual transition from today's fragmentation of theology into its numerous "disciplines"—dogmatic, moral, systematic and liturgical theology—to broader integration. Should we not, for example, link dogmatic and liturgical theology together and teach doctrine within the context of our liturgical life and experience? As a start we could at least develop a system of theological instruction in which various courses would be interrelated and complementary (under the existing system, these courses sometimes overlap one another and frequently are totally unrelated one to another).

8. The experience of the early Christian *didaskaloi* can teach us how to inculcate in students the habits of working independently (Origen, in particular, taught his disciples not only how to formulate questions but also how to

find answers to them unaided). Should we not consider an academic system that would replace rote learning by guidance in independent scholarship skills? Should we not reduce the number of lecture courses in order to make more time available for private research? Should we not formulate a new kind of lecture that would introduce students to the problems and the bibliography of a subject, leaving them free to do research on their own?

9. In the early Christian East, a substantial part of every curriculum was devoted to the philosophical disciplines. Do we now pay sufficient attention to such subjects as logic or dialectics? Do we study works by classical and modern philosophers? Are we concerned about cultivating in our students the skills of dialectical thinking? It is patently obvious that we should give further thought to ensuring a substantial improvement in the standards of teaching philosophy to our students.

10. Early Christian schools were not only theological centres, but also centres for the spiritual education of young adults. Theological schools formed a young Christian and laid in him the foundation for genuine attachment to the Church and for true Christian piety. Can we say that the graduates of our theological schools are more loyal to the Church and more spiritually mature when they leave school than they were when entering it? If not, should we not give serious thought to our shortcomings and try to amend them?

Many of the questions that have been raised in this paper may seem naive and many of the changes that have been proposed, impossible to achieve. Indeed, can you imagine an inspector in our theological schools being elected by the students rather than by higher authorities? And yet there was a time when such things were possible. In thinking about reforming our theological schools, we should not confine ourselves to changes in form. We should move further, radically changing the structure of the administration, the content of the study programmes and the entire approach to teaching itself. In my opinion, the experience of the theological schools in the early Christian East can be of substantial help to us in achieving these goals.

❀ The Changing Faces of ❀
St Ephrem as Read in the West

Sebastian Brock

O NLY TWO SYRIAC FATHERS were known and read in the medieval
West, St Ephrem and St Isaac "the Syrian." In both cases their works
had reached Latin by way of a Greek intermediary. In the case of Isaac, a substantial body of his works had been translated from Syriac into Greek in the
Palestinian Monastery of Mar Saba in the late eighth or early ninth century,
only a century or so after Isaac's death. From Greek, a selection of homilies
were put into Latin perhaps in the fourteenth century, and thence into a variety of Romance languages a century later—after which they received little
attention until the late twentieth century, when a spate of new translations
into European languages have been made.[1] The situation with Ephrem happens to be very different, and considerably more complicated. Latin translations (from Greek) of some works under his name are already attested in the
sixth century, and a small corpus of these were (to judge by the number of
manuscripts) widely read throughout the medieval period. This smaller corpus in Latin was considerably enlarged in the fifteenth century, and yet further in the late sixteenth. Only in the early eighteenth century, however, did
some of the Greek texts underlying the Latin receive publication (in Oxford),
while the original Syriac of Ephrem's main works (accompanied by a Latin
translation) had to wait until well into the eighteenth century before these
became available in Europe.

A further twofold complication in the case of Ephrem is that (a) in all
three languages many works under his name are not in fact by him, and (b)
only a small number of the texts in Greek and Latin have a known Syriac
counterpart; in the case of a few others a Syriac original may well have once

---

[1]Details of the translations of Isaac are given in my chapter on him in G. Conticello (ed.),
La théologie Byzantine (Turnhout, forthcoming), and "From Qatar to Tokyo, by way of Mar
Saba: the translations of Isaac of Beth Qatraye (Isaac the Syrian)," *Aram*, 11–12 (1999–2000),
475–84.

existed, but a large proportion of the remainder can only have originated in Greek (some of these are also transmitted in the manuscripts under other names, such as Makarios and John Chrysostom). Yet another difficulty lies in the fact that some of the Latin translations, in turn, have no known Greek counterparts, while others are closer to the Syriac originals than to the surviving Greek intermediaries. With such an array of problems, it is not surprising that the Latin and Greek texts under Ephrem's name have received very little attention from modern editors.[2] As a result, one still needs to consult early sixteenth-century editions for almost all the Latin texts, and the eighteenth-century ones for the Greek (though one of these has now been reprinted in Greece in a more convenient form).

Since differing texts under Ephrem's name have been read over the centuries in Europe the impression these have given of the character of their supposed author has altered, and so it is important to know upon which texts any particular portrait of Ephrem is based. This of course means that the veracity and appropriateness of any portayal of Ephrem, whether in words or in icons, will depend on whether the texts upon which it is based are authentically Ephrem's or not. As will emerge from the following rapid sketch, the texts available in Europe at any given time point to several rather different Ephrems, among whom the true Ephrem has only emerged within the last half-century or so.

Writing less than two decades after Ephrem's death, Jerome already knew of a Greek translation of one of his works (which cannot be identified with any surviving work under his name), and Sozomen, in the second quarter of the fifth century, states that works of Ephrem were translated into Greek during the author's lifetime and "are even now being made."[3] In Greek, as in Syriac, Ephrem soon suffered the consequences of popularity by having numerous works attributed to him which he had never written, and the impressive quantity of these can readily be ascertained by consulting the second volume of the *Clavis Patrum Graecorum* (CPG) where the entry on Ephrem Graecus runs to just over 100 pages, thus taking up more space than any Greek Father apart from St John Chrysostom.

---

[2]Valiant work, in making a start on sorting out the Greek tradition, was done by D. Hemmerdinger-Iliadou in a series of articles, the most important of which are to be found in the *Dictionnaire de Spiritualité*, IV (1960), 800–819, and in her posthumous "Ephrem: versions grecque, latine et slave. Addenda et corrigenda," *Epeteris Hetairias Buzantinon Spoudon*, 42 (1975/6), 320–73.

[3]Jerome *De viris illustribus* 115, dating from 392; Sozomen *Ecclesiastical History* III.16.

The first Latin translation

It so happens that the earliest Greek papyrus to have been studied in Europe[4] consists of some sixth-century fragments of the Greek work attributed to Ephrem on the Patriarch Joseph (CPG 3938). These had originally been preserved in the monastery of St Martin in Tours,[5] and it seems likely that the manuscript, fragments of which were later recycled in a binding, will have reached France at an early date; in this connection one recalls that towards the end of the sixth century Gregory of Tours made his translation of the Seven Sleepers of Ephesus, probably from Greek, with the help of a certain Syrian named Ioannes, and so it is not surprising that the earliest surviving Latin manuscript of a work under Ephrem's name also dates from the sixth century and also has a connection with the same town. The work in question is the very popular *Sermo asceticus*[6] and further testimony to the existence of an early Latin translation of this is provided by the quotations from it in Defensor of Ligugé's *Liber Scintillarum*,[7] dating from around 700.[8]

Another very early Latin manuscript, of the sixth or seventh century, contains a free rendering of the narrative poem on Jonah and the Repentance of Nineveh, whose Syriac text is almost certainly by Ephrem himself. The Greek intermediary was for a long time thought to have been lost, but it has now been published from a single known manuscript.[9]

[4]By B. de Montfaucon in his pioneering *Palaeographia Graeca* (1708).

[5]A detailed description of the fragments is given in K. Aland and H-U. Rosenbaum, *Repertorium der griechischen christlichen Papyri* II/1, *Kirchenväter-Papyri, Beschreibungen* (Patristische Texte und Studien 42; 1995), 171–96. A Latin translation of this work has been published from a ninth/tenth-century manuscript by L. Bailly, "Une traduction latine d'un sermon d'Ephrem dans le Clm 3516," *Sacris Erudiri*, 21 (1972/3), 71–80.

[6]Paris, BN Lat. 12634; the *Sermo asceticus* (CPG 3909; CPL 1143 vi) features in its collection of monastic rules. The Syriac sources for the Greek text are listed in the entry for CPG 3909. An early Greek uncial fragment has recently been identified as part of the underwriting in the famous Sinaiticus Syriacus (Sinai Syr. 30) Gospel manuscript: see S. Voicu, in *Scriptorium*, 38 (1984), 77–8.

[7]Defensor delightfully states that his aim in providing this collection of excerpts was "to spare readers the trouble of reading many volumes." (Since Ligugé was founded by Martin of Tours, this provides yet a further link between Latin manuscripts of Ephrem and that town).

[8]J. Kirchmeyer and D. Hemmerdinger-Iliadou, "S. Ephrem et le Liber Scintillarum," *Recherches de Science Religieuse*, 46 (1958), 545–50. Nine out of the fifteen quotations from Ephrem identified by the editor of the work (H.Rochais) are from the *Sermo asceticus*.

[9]The Latin text (CPL 1149, in Vatican, Palat. 210, the only known manuscript) was published by A. Mai, *Nova Patrum Bibliotheca* I (Rome, 1852), 193–204. The Syriac (= *Sermones* II.1) is edited by E. Beck, in the *Corpus Scriptorum Christianorum Orientalium*, 311–12 (1970); and the Greek (CPG 4082) by D. Hemmerdinger-Iliadou, in *Le Muséon*, 80 (1967), 52–74

By the ninth century a small corpus of eight Latin texts under Ephrem's name was circulating, six of which are normally found together.[10] Among these six are the *Sermo asceticus* (known under the title *de compunctione cordis*) and the *de paenitentia* (CPG 3915; CPL 1143 iii), whose great popularity in the Middle Ages is attested by the very large number of surviving manuscripts.[11] One further work, the *Life of Abraham and his niece Mary* (CPG 3937), was likewise to prove remarkably popular. This delightful narrative (whose authorship is left anonymous in the earliest manuscript of the Syriac original) must have been translated from Greek into Latin already in the sixth century, for the earliest surviving manuscript in Latin dates from the second half of the seventh century.[12] In the late tenth century the work caught the imagination of the enterprising Benedictine nun Hrotswitha of Gandersheim, who adapted it in what is often thought to be the best of her Terentian-style plays. Against the Life, she has the play open with a dialogue between Abraham and Ephrem:

ABRAHAM: Brother Ephrem, my dear comrade in the hermit life, may I speak to you now [about Mary, my niece], or shall I wait until you have finished your divine praises?

EPHREM: And what can you have to say to me that is not praise of him who said "Where two or three are gathered together in my name, I am with them"?[13]

(reprinted, with a Modern Greek translation, in Athens [no date] by the Kentron Meleton Hosiou Ephraim tou Surou). A table of the correspondence between the Greek and the Syriac can be found in my "Ephrem's Verse Homily on Jonah and the Repentance of Nineveh: Notes on the Textual Tradition," in A. Schoors and P.van Deun (eds), *Polyhistor: Miscellanea in honorem C. Laga* (Orientalia Lovaniensia Analecta 60; Leuven, 1994), 71–86 (esp. 82–5).

[10]See especially on these manuscripts D. Ganz, "Knowledge of Ephrem's writings in the Merovingian and Carolingian age," *Hugoye: Journal of Syriac Studies*, 2:1 (1999) [http://syr-com.cua.edu/Hugoye]. A pioneering work on the manuscripts of Ephrem in Latin is A. Siegmund's *Die Überlieferung der griechischen christlichen Literatur in der lateinischen Kirche bis zum zwölften Jahrhundert* (Munich, 1939) 67–71.

[11]T. S. Pattie, "Early printed editions of Ephraem Latinus and their relationship to the manuscripts," *Studia Patristica*, 20 (1989), 50–3, states that there are 128 for the former and about 90 for the latter. Both works were the source of prayers (e.g. Prayer 45 in the *Book of Cerne*): P. Sims-Williams, "Thoughts on Ephrem the Syrian in Anglo-Saxon England," in M. Lapidge and H. Gneuss (eds.), *Learning and Literature in Anglo-Saxon England*, (Cambridge, 1985), 205–26. T. H. Bestul, "Ephraim the Syrian and Old English poetry," *Anglia*, 99 (1981), 1–24, is perhaps rather too negative on the subject of the possible influence of the Latin Ephrem.

[12]Edited by A. Wilmart, "Les redactions latines de la Vie d'Abraham Ermite," *Revue Bénédictine*, 50 (1938), 222–45 (with another translation, also probably old).

[13]I use the translation by Christopher St John, *The Plays of Roswitha* (London, 1923), in

It would be nice to suppose that Theophano, the Emperor Otto II's Greek wife, met and chatted with Hrosthwitha on one of her visits to the Convent in Gandersheim.[14]

In the case of some of the early Latin translations of works under Ephrem's name there is evidence that the text developed over the course of the centuries, and it is even possible that the translations may at times have been revised on the basis of the Greek. One context where there does seem to have been direct contact with the Greek Ephrem is the School of Canterbury in the seventh century, and more particularly in the person of Archbishop Theodore of Tarsus, whose teaching has recently been shown to lie behind a collection of important biblical glosses, and who may also be the author of a work known as the *Laterculus Malalianus* (so named because it is in part a translation of a work by John Malalas): in each of these works Ephrem is cited as an authority, and the source for one of these references is a Greek work not known in Latin translation, while the other cannot be identified and is certainly not from the early Latin corpus.[15]

It has been said that in the medieval West "il n'était guère de monastère important dont la bibliothèque ne possédat son Liber Effrem."[16] This would consist of the standard corpus of the six works known under the Latin titles of *de poenitentia, de luctaminibus saeculi, de compunctione, de beatitudine animae, de resurrectione,* and *de die iudicii.*[17] At some date shortly before 1491 these were printed by Kilian Fischer (Piscator), and even today, as P. Petitmengin rather wistfully remarks, "l'édition la plus accessible [du texte latin] . . . est encore l'incunable publié à Fribourg par Kilian Fischer."[18]

---

preference to the very free rendering of K. M. Wilson, *Hrotsvit of Gandersheim. A Florilegium of her Works* (Cambridge 1998).

[14]Hrosthwitha's Abbess Gerberga II is said to have known Greek. For the influence of Ephrem on other medieval German writers see M.Schmidt, "Influence de saint Ephrem sur la littérature latine et allemande du début du moyen-âge," *Parole de l'Orient,* 4 (1973), 325–41.

[15]See B. Bischoff and M. Lapidge, *Biblical Commentaries from the Canterbury School of Theodore and Hadrian* (Cambridge, 1994), 402–3, with 514 (Lapidge also draws attention to the possibility that Theodore made a wider use of Syriac sources, whether or not by way of a Greek intermediary, cf. 233–40); and J. Stevenson, *The "Laterculus Malalianus" and the School of Archbishop Theodore* (Cambridge, 1995), 148–9; see also her "Ephraim the Syrian in Anglo-Saxon England," in *Hugoye,* 1:2 (1998) [see note 10].

[16]Thus D. Hemmerdinger-Iliadou, in *Dictionnaire de Spiritualité,* 4 (1960), 818.

[17]This is the sequence given by Vincent of Beauvais (d.1264) in his *Speculum historiale,* XIV.87 (he actually speaks of seven *opuscula* but lists only six—the *de compunctione* may have been treated as two books). The order in the manuscripts varies. See the Appendix for the corresponding Greek (and Syriac, where available) texts.

[18]In *Revue des Études Augustiniennes,* 17 (1971), 9. It is a pity that the opportunity of

Although a French translation of this was published in Paris in 1501, and the Latin text was reprinted at Basel in 1491, Cologne in 1547, and Dillingen in 1563, this particular Latin tradition subsequently fell from favour, being replaced by two much more extensive (and more recent) translations from Greek, one by Ambrosius Camaldulensis (Ambrogio Traversari), printed at the end of the fifteenth century, and the other by Gerard Vossius at the end of the sixteenth.

Two subsequent Latin translations

Whereas the contents of the early Latin translation correspond reasonably well with what Demokratia Hemmerdinger-Iliadou described as the pre-iconoclastic Greek collection, of Syro-Palestinian provenance, the fifteenth- and sixteenth-century ones evidently derive from a much larger Greek corpus: in the ninth century Photios already knew of a collection of 49 texts[19], and later Greek manuscripts often have even larger collections. It is thus not surprising that the two later Latin translations are much more extensive than the first.

The new early fifteenth-century Latin translation from Greek, made by the well-known translator of Greek patristic texts, Ambrogio Traversari (d. 1439), contained 19 pieces.[20] His work enjoyed a considerable popularity, to judge by the various reprints, and it was also the source used for various vernacular translations.[21] The translations include what is probably the earliest English version of any work under Ephrem's name; this was published in 1640 as an appendix to a translation of a work by Cardinal John Fisher (1469–1535; canonized in 1935).[22]

reprinting the text of this old edition was missed in Supplement IV (1966) to the *Patrologia Latina*, where a section is devoted to Ephrem Latinus (604–48).

[19]*Bibliotheca*, codex 196. Photios notes that, despite the *tapeinotēs* and *khudaiotēs* of the style (which he attributes to the translator), the *sōtēria* and *ōpheleia* of Ephrem's words was nevertheless apparent.

[20]The corresponding Greek texts in Assemani's edition are listed by D. Hemmerdinger-Iliadou, "Ephrem: versions grecque, latine et slave," 349 (see also the Appendix, below). She notes that no Greek manuscript known to her has the same order as the Latin translation.

[21]According to S. Mercati (*Bessarione* 1920, p.189) the first edition was 1481 (and not 1475, as is usually stated); this was followed by a number of further editions in the course of the next 25 years (I have used that of 1505, Cologne).

[22]Cardinal John Fisher, *A Treatise of Prayer and of the Fruits and Manner of Prayer, translated into English by R. A. B.* (Paris, 1640), 241–71. The translator nicely prefaces this with the following excuse: "Gentle Reader, by reason of these vacant pages, I thought good in respect this

A far more extensive collection of new Latin translations from Greek was made by Gerardus Vossius and printed in three volumes in Rome (1589, 1593, and 1598).[23] These contain over 120 texts. Among them is one that is particularly intriguing: in the third volume is a short piece entitled "Threni, id est, Lamentationes Virginis Mariae super passione Domini" (pp. 697–8), beginning "Stans iuxta crucem pura et immaculata virgo, salvatoremque in ea suspensum cernens, dirissimas plagas perpendens . . ." No source for this is known in the Ephrem Graecus corpus, but it now turns out that it corresponds exactly with an anonymous Greek Threnos.[24]

An intriguing feature of Vossius's edition is the portrait of Ephrem that prefaces the volumes. Ephrem, who is portrayed as a monk, stands holding a scroll with an inscription in Greek "Love and temperance (*enkrateia*) purify the soul." An accompanying note states that the portrait was derived from an icon "in the monastery of Sula, now inhabited by the Armenians." The Sulu Manastir in Constantinople, better known as the Monastery of the Theotokos Peribleptos, had indeed been transferred to Armenian hands over a century earlier to become the seat of the Armenian Patriarchate.[25] As it happened, the portrait was to prove influential, for it was taken over in the volumes of the great Roman edition of Ephrem's works (1732–1746); it might also be a candidate for the source, as yet unidentified, of the portrait of St Ephrem in the frieze with the heads of Sages in the Upper Reading Room of the Bodleian Library in Oxford, dating from 1618/19.[26] It likewise features in the recent Athens reprint of the Homily on Jonas.[27]

---

little Armour of S. Ephrem, doth something to conduce to the present Discourse to adde it as a postscript for thy further instruction" (the translator had dedicated his work to Lady Elizabeth Herbert of Powis Castle). "The Armour" corresponds to CPG 4020, and to Sermo 8 in Ambrogio's translation.

[23]The edition enjoyed at least two reprints (Cologne 1603 and 1616).

[24]Edited by M. I. Manousakis, in *Mélanges Octave et Melpo Merlier*, II (Athens, 1956), 49–60; I am most grateful to W. F. Bakker for this information and the reference (letter of 2 November, 1997). The Latin text was reprinted in the Assemani edition (III, 574–5).

[25]R. Janin, *La géographie ecclésiastique de l'empire byzantin*, I.3 [Constantinople;] *Les églises et les monastères* (Paris, 1969), 220 gives "1643," but this is incorrect: see the references given in my "A Medieval Armenian Pilgrim's Description of Constantinople," *Revue des Études Arméniennes*, NS 4 (1967), 98, notes 85–87.

[26]On the frieze see M. R. A. Bullard, "Talking Heads. The Bodleian frieze. Its inspiration, sources, designer and significance," *The Bodleian Library Record*, 14:6 (1994), 461–500; for Ephrem (no 188) see especially 493–4.

[27]See note 9, above.

The Greek text becomes available

Given the interest in making new Latin translations from Greek in the fifteenth, sixteenth and seventeenth century, it is astonishing that no humanist scholar should have edited any of the Greek texts themselves.[28] This task was left to the Oxford Anglo-Saxon scholar, Edward Thwaites (1667–1711). Like many scholars of his time, Thwaites could turn his hands to many things and in 1708 he was appointed Regius Professor of Greek. His edition of Greek works under Ephrem's name was published the following year, in 1709. The antiquarian Thomas Hearne, a former friend but with whom he was no longer on friendly terms, unkindly described the work as "a mean performance"; perhaps what he meant was that the presentation was hardly what would be called today "reader-friendly": there is no introduction, and not only the title page, but also the pagination, is in Greek (Thwaites modestly does not even put his name on the title page!). However, for the reader proficient in Greek it was a very valuable undertaking, and it is even provided with an index of incipits and of biblical references.

Much of Thwaites's work in fact lives on indirectly today, since it is the main source for what remains the standard source of reference to Ephraim Graecus, namely the first three volumes of the six-volume edition of Ephrem's works, edited by J. S. Assemani, *S. P. N. Ephraem Syri Opera Omnia* (Rome, 1732–46). In these volumes Assemani brings together a great deal of the Greek and Latin corpora, often deriving his material from earlier editions (and in particular, that of Thwaites for the first two volumes).[29] It is largely from these three volumes that the recent seven-volume Greek edition of Ephrem Graecus, edited by K. Phrantzolas, derives (Athens, 1988–98). Though a beginning was made on a critical edition of the Greek texts by S. G. Mercati at the beginning of the twentieth century, only a single fascicle ever appeared,[30] and the subsequent plans for an edition, by D. Hemmerdinger-Iliadou, who did so much to sort out the confused Greek tradition, were unfortunately never realised.[31]

---

[28]The only Greek texts of Ephraim printed in the seventeenth century seem to be some prayers, incorporated in a collection edited by M. Tzigala (Venice, 1681).

[29]The correspondences are given by D. Hemmerdinger-Iliadou, "Les manuscrits de l'Ephrem grec utilisés par Thwaites," *Scriptorium*, 13 (1959), 261–2.

[30]*S. Ephraem Syri Opera*. I.1, *Sermones in Abraham et Isaac, in Basilium magnum, in Eliam* (Rome, 1915).

[31]For her plans, see her "Vers une nouvelle édition de l'Ephrem grec," *Studia Patristica*, 3 (= *Texte und Untersuchungen*, 78, 1961), 72–80. The single edition by her that did appear was that of the important text on Jonah (see note 9); she died in 1976.

The arrival of the Syriac original texts

As late as the latter part of the seventeenth century it was possible for a great scholar such as Pierre Daniel Huet to suppose that, once Ephrem's works had been translated into Greek, their Syriac originals had got lost.[32] Huet must have overlooked Vossius's second volume, which includes a translation by Vossius that he had made "e Chaldaeo ac Syriaco," adding that he had done this on the basis of a literal translation he had asked the students of the Maronite College in Rome to make. In fact, already in the sixteenth century well-informed scholars like Andreas Masius were aware of the existence of Syriac works, no doubt thanks to information from his teacher of Syriac, the Syrian Orthodox priest Moses of Mardin, the man largely responsible for the magnificent first edition of the Syriac New Testament (Vienna, 1555). Moses would primarily have had in mind the vast number of hymns under Ephrem's name that feature in the Syrian Orthodox *Fenqitho*, or Festal Hymnary.

Vossius's Latin translation of a Syriac text of Ephrem probably has the distinction of being the first European translation from Syriac of a text attributed to Ephrem.[33] In the course of the seventeenth century a number of Syriac liturgical texts that included works under Ephrem's name were printed in Rome, mainly for Maronite use,[34] but these do not appear to have received any attention from those European scholars who had an interest in Syriac.

The men who altered the situation radically were Maronite scholars, for the most part from the Assemani family. Most prominent among them was Joseph Simon Assemani (1687–1768), editor of the Greek and Latin works in the great Roman edition of Ephrem, mentioned above. J. S. Assemani was a man of prodigious learning and had been sent to Rome to study at the tender age of eight. In 1715 (and again in 1717) he was sent by Pope Clement XI to Egypt, to buy ancient Syriac manuscripts from the library of the Syrian Monastery in the Wadi Natrun (between Alexandria and Cairo).[35] Thanks to a tenth-century abbot, Moses of Nisibis, this monastery had built up a

[32]Quoted by W. E. Tentzel in his *Dissertatio de Ephremo Syro* (Arnstadt, 1685), section 7.

[33]The Syriac text was subsequently published in Volume V (1740) of the Roman edition (336–8); it also features in several modern Syrian Orthodox anthologies.

[34]The Maronite Weekday Office (*Shehimto*) was first printed in Rome in 1624, and the Festal Hymnary *(Fenqitho)* in 1656. An edition of the Syrian Catholic Weekday Office (*Shehimo*), published in 1696, even mentions Ephrem in the title: *Breviarium Feriale Syriacum SS Ephraemi et Jacobi Syrorum iuxta ritum eiusdem nationis.*

[35]Already in 1707 Pope Clement had sent another member of the Assemani family, Elias, on a similar mission.

remarkable collection of very old Syriac manuscripts, but since the monastery had passed into Coptic Orthodox hands in 1636, these manuscripts were no longer of any direct interest to the monks. As a result of these visits the Vatican Library acquired its superb collection of Syriac manuscripts[36] (rivalled only by the British Museum—now British Library—which acquired an even better collection from the same source in the mid nineteenth century). Among the trophies brought back from Egypt were no less than three sixth-century manuscripts containing Ephrem's poems, all dated (519, 522, and 552). Luckily all three had escaped a dip in the Nile when a boat carrying a load of the manuscripts capsized in a sudden squall, and so were available to be used for the Syriac volumes (IV-VI) of the Roman edition of Ephrem's works. While the first three volumes, with the Greek and Latin works, contained little that was new, these final three volumes (1737, 1740, 1746) all contained hitherto unknown Syriac works by Ephrem, accompanied by a (remarkably free in places!) Latin translation.[37] Although the entire Roman edition is usually referred to as being the work of Assemani (that is, J. S. Assemani, the editor of the first three volumes), the editing for the three Syriac-Latin volumes was in fact largely done by Petrus Benedictus (Moubarak), though after his death the work was taken over by another Assemani (Stephanus Evodius).

The publication of these last three volumes made available for the first time in Europe, not only a large collection, in the original Syriac, of works attributed to Ephrem, but also of many that are certainly genuine and represent some of his finest poetry. It would be interesting to know something of its reception history, and in this connection it is tempting to suppose that John Wesley, who called Ephrem "the most awakening writer among all the ancients," might have been inspired by Ephrem for some of his hymns. However, when he read Ephrem aloud to Sophy Hopkey, with whom he had fallen in love in Georgia in 1736, this must have been from the Greek or Latin, since the first volume of the Syriac only came out the following year, and this volume happened to contain only prose works.[38]

---

[36]On the basis of these J. S. Assemani produced his massive (and still important) four-volume work on Syriac literature, *Bibliotheca Orientalis Clementino-Vaticana* (Rome, 1719–28).

[37]F. C. Burkitt, perhaps a little unkindly, described this edition as "one of the most confusing and misleading works ever published," *St Ephrem's Quotations from the Gospels* (Texts and Studies, VII.2; Cambridge, 1901), 4. On pp. 6–19 of this study Burkitt usefully identifies, where possible, the manuscript sources employed for the edition. The Latin text of all six volumes was subsequently reprinted in two volumes in Venice, 1755–6 (likewise in various volumes of A. B. Caillou's vast nineteenth-century *Collectio selecta SS. Ecclesiae Patrum*).

[38]On Wesley and Ephrem see G. Wakefield, "John Wesley and Ephraem Syrus," in *Hugoye,*

The Roman edition of the Syriac texts is not an easy one to use,[39] and so the vocalized edition of 19 poems taken from it by A. Hahn and F. L. Sieffert, in their *Chrestomathia Syriaca sive S. Ephraemi Carmina Selecta* (Leipzig, 1825), provided a considerably easier introduction to Ephrem's poetry, especially as the texts were now set out in verse form. Far more accessible to the ordinary reader, however, were the various translations that started appearing in the nineteenth century. The earliest to undertake the popularisation of Ephrem was Pius Zingerle, whose *Ausgewählte Schriften des hl. Ephräm von Syrien, aus dem Syrischen und Griechischen übersetzt* was first published in six volumes over the years 1831–1845, to be republished several times in different formats. Not surprisingly, Ephrem's writings appealed in England to the Oxford Movement, and an important product of this interest was J. B. Morris's *Select Works of Saint Ephrem the Syrian.*[40] Another person, but with no connection with the Oxford Movement, who translated selections from Ephrem's Syriac poems (including that on Jonah and the Repentance of Nineveh) was H. Burgess[41] (among the subscribers to the volume on the Repentance of Nineveh were Prince Albert and A. H. Layard). In some cases these early English translations have not yet been superseded. Some of Burgess's translations were versified for use as hymns by Horatius Bonar, while other hymn writers drew their material from the third volume of H. A. Daniel's *Thesaurus Hymnologicus* (Halle, 1841–6), which included material translated from Syriac (this was contributed by L. Splieth).[42]

Another person who deserves mention here is one of the more eccentric dilettante scholars of the nineteenth century, S. C. Malan (1814–1894). He

---

1:2 (1998) [note 10]. It is also possible that he might have read to her from the anonymous English translation (from Thwaites's edition) of the Sermo Compunctorius (CPG 3908): *A Serious Exhortation to Repentance and Sorrow for Sin and a Strict and Mortified Life*, printed by Wm. Bowyer (London, 1731); I am most grateful to Archimandrite Ephrem Lash for drawing my attention to this work.

[39]It is customary to refer to the Greek-Latin volumes as I-III, and the Syriac-Latin as IV-VI, even though they were not published in that sequence. CPG is the invaluable guide to Vols. I-III; for IV-VI, there are various ones, including my "A brief guide to the main editions and translations of the works of St Ephrem," *The Harp* [Kottayam], 3 (1990), 7–29, esp. 10–12.

[40]Oxford 1847. Morris's devotion to fasting earned him the nickname "Symeon Stylites"; the background is vividly described by G. Rowell, " 'Making the Church of England Poetical,' Ephraim and the Oxford Movement," in *Hugoye*, 2:1 (1999) [note 10].

[41]*The Repentance of Nineveh: a Metrical Homily on the Mission of Jonah by Ephrem Syrus* (London, 1853); and *Select Metrical Hymns and Homilies of Ephrem Syrus* (London, 1853).

[42]J. Julian, author of the excellent *A Dictionary of Hymnology* (1892; revised edition, London 1915), characterized the *Thesaurus* as "the work of a man who greatly loved his subject, but to whose mind the instinct of accuracy was in great measure wanting." On p.1113 Julian

was a man with an extraordinary facility for languages: besides knowing such tongues as Tibetan, Chinese and Japanese, he also had an interest in the various languages and literatures of the Christian Orient, including Syriac from which he translated several pieces.[43] Amongst his other remarkable linguistic feats was to preach in Georgian in Kutais Cathedral!

The nineteenth century saw the publication of a number of completely new texts by Ephrem, such as his *Commentary on the Diatessaron*, known at that time only from the Armenian translation.[44] Not surprisingly, the original edition of 1836, only in Armenian, did not draw much attention, and it was only when G. Moesinger published a Latin translation in 1876 that the work caused considerable excitement to the scholarly world. Further early Syriac manuscripts of Ephrem, deriving from the Syrian Monastery in Egypt, were acquired by the British Museum around the middle of the century. One of the first to make use of these was G. Bickell, in his edition of the important hymn cycle, the *Carmina Nisibena* (1866), while others were employed by T. J. Lamy in his four-volume *Sancti Ephraem Syri Hymni et Sermones* (Malines, 1882–1902); both editors also provided Latin translations, thus ensuring their much wider accessibility. A number of the texts in these two editions were translated into English in a useful volume in *Selections translated into English from the Hymns and Homilies of Ephraim the Syrian* (1898), in the Select Library of Nicene and Post-Nicene Fathers (II.13; Ephrem rather incongruously shares the volume with Gregory the Great). The work was edited by John Gwynn, a man who claimed to have learnt his Syriac on long train journeys between Donegal and Dublin.

A completely different side to Ephrem was revealed when C. W. Mitchell's patient decipherment of a palimpsest manuscript containing various prose refutations of heretics (notably Marcion, Bardaisan and Mani) was published in two volumes, the first in 1912, and the second, posthumously in 1921, having been completed and prepared for publication by F. C. Burkitt, Mitchell having been killed during the First World War. In this work one finds Ephrem referring to a number of Greek writers, such as Albinus.[45]

lists the various English metrical versions of Ephrem's poems used as hymns.

[43]*Repentance: Chiefly from the Syriac of St Ephraem, and other Eastern Sources* (London, 1866). There are also some included in his *Meditations for every Wednesday and Friday in Lent on a Prayer of St Ephraem* (London, 1859). (This well-known Greek prayer of St Ephrem has no known Syriac counterpart).

[44]About two thirds of it has now turned up in Syriac; there is a recent English translation by Carmel McCarthy (1993).

[45]Ephrem's surprising familiarity with Greek philosophy has recently been well brought out

As far as Ephrem's writings are concerned, by far the most important development of the twentieth century has been the re-edition (accompanied by German translations) of his poetry, on the basis of all the early manuscript evidence available; this was done single-handed by Dom Edmund Beck OSB, in a whole series of volumes in the Corpus Scriptorum Christianorum Orientalium over the years 1955–79. The publication of these excellent editions has led to a considerable revival of interest in his works (encouraged in the English-speaking world also by Robert Murray's many excerpts in his important *Symbols of Church and Kingdom. A Study in Early Syriac Tradition,* of 1975). As a result of this renewed interest, quite a large proportion of Ephrem's Syriac poetry is now at last available in English translations to the much wider audience that it deserves.[46]

*

It can be seen that St Ephrem has continued to enjoy a high standing in the western Christian tradition for at least a millennium and a half,[47] though on the basis of varying collections of texts. Has this made a difference to the picture of the man given to readers of these texts? Undoubtedly for readers in the medieval West Ephrem was essentially a monastic saint, and this is a perception which was subsequently actively encouraged when the Greek accounts of his life, in the fifth-century church historians, became known during the Renaissance, and when the sixth-century Syriac Life of Ephrem was published in the first volume of J. S. Assemani's *Bibliotheca Orientalis.* In recent years the study of the early Syriac ascetic tradition,[48] of which Ephrem

by U. Possekel, *Evidence of Greek Philosophical Concepts in the Writings of Ephrem the Syrian* (Leuven, 1999).

[46]The fullest collection is by K. McVey, *Ephrem the Syrian. Hymns* (New York, 1989), in the Classics of Western Spirituality series. A small selection is given in my *The Harp of the Spirit:18 poems by St Ephrem* (Studies supplementary to Sobornost; 2nd edition, London, 1983), while the small cycle of 15 poems on Paradise are translated in my *St Ephrem the Syrian. Hymns on Paradise* (Crestwood NY: St Vladimir's Seminary Press, 1990). Several further translations are announced for the new series Eastern Christian Texts in Translation (Washington/Leuven). An interesting small, and considerably earlier, collection of translations from Ephrem was published in India by Ann Anchor, *Ephrem the Syrian. An Eastern Contemplative* (Bangalore, 1939). (At the end is an announcement that she is the co-author, with a certain George Yesudas Martyn, of a planned volume entitled *Christian Spirituality and the Eastern Church,* in which the chapter on Ephrem is entitled "Hid Theology: The Way of the Spirit").

[47]At the beginning of the twentieth century this appreciation was formalized by Pope Benedict XV in his encyclical *Principi apostolorum,* of 5th October 1920, when he proclaimed St Ephrem a Doctor of the Church.

[48]A good guide to this is S. H. Griffith, "Asceticism in the Church of Syria," in V.L.Wimbush

was a part, has pointed to the anachronistic (and sometimes tendentious) character of these accounts.[49] Accordingly, it is now generally recognized that the most reliable portrait of the man is to be extrapolated from his own writings—and here it is essential to distinguish the genuine from the many works attributed to him. In the 1950s a lively controversy on this question was conducted between Dom Edmund Beck and another renowned Syriac scholar, Arthur Vööbus, who maintained that a number of texts, claiming to be by Ephrem and portraying him as a monk, were genuine. That Beck had the better judgement in this matter is now widely accepted. It thus emerges that already within a century or two of Ephrem's death two considerably different portraits of him had emerged: one was the historical Ephrem, the theologian-poet and deacon who was in all likelihood a representative of the distinctive form of Syrian proto-monasticism, living in the midst of the Christian community in Nisibis (until 363) and Edessa (from 363 until his death in 373), where (among other things) he established women's choirs and took an active role in famine relief, right at the end of his life; while the other was the monk, and sometimes hermit, who lived in isolation from the local Christian community, and who belonged to the wider monastic tradition with links with both Cappadocia and Egypt. The existence of these two Ephrems, "Ephrem Syrus" and "Ephrem Byzantinus" as they have been called by S. H. Griffith, can also be seen in the iconographic tradition, where the monastic Ephrem is, of course, the dominant one, and can be seen today (for example) on the cover of McVey's collection of translations (against the wishes of the translator!). A survival of another, presumably earlier, and certainly more reliable, tradition can be found in an icon in the Monastery of St Catherine, Sinai, of the Edessa Mandilion which must have been painted not long after the precious relic was transferred from Edessa to Constantinople in 944. In the lower right panel St Ephrem stands alongside St Basil (based on an unhistorical episode in the Life), dressed as a deacon.[50] It would be good if the modern iconographical tradition could revert to this image of the great saint.

and R.Valantasis (eds.), *Asceticism* (New York, 1995), 220–48. A brief orientation can also be found in my *The Luminous Eye: The Spiritual World Vision of St Ephrem* (2nd edition, Kalamazoo, 1992), chapter 8.

[49]Two important studies are by S. H. Griffith, "Images of Ephrem: the Syrian Holy Man and his Church," *Traditio*, 45 (1989/90), 7–33, and J. P. Amar, "Byzantine Ascetic Monachism and Greek Bias in the *Vita* Tradition of Ephrem the Syrian," *Orientalia Christiana Periodica*, 58 (1992), 123–56.

[50]Illustrated in K. A. Manafis, *Sinai. The Treasures of the Monastery of Saint Catherine* (Athens, 1990), 145.

Appendix

Contents of the early Latin corpus and of Ambrosius Camuldulensis's translation, with their correspondences in Greek and Syriac.

(a) The six Latin texts that by the ninth century formed a small corpus correspond as follows to Greek texts (for convenience, these are given in the sequence of CPG); where the titles in the Latin corpus differ these are given in brackets:

CPG 3909 *sermo asceticus (de compunctione cordis* I). The Greek corresponds in different places to different Syriac texts, none of which are certainly by Ephrem.

CPG 3915 *de paenitentia.* No Syriac text of this is known.

CPG 3920 *in secundum adventum Domini (de luctaminibus/de luctamine spirituali).* The opening of the Latin version has some of CPG 4002 *de virginitate,* and ends with the ending of CPG 3935(2). No Syriac text is known.

CPG 3925(2) *de beatitudine animae.* No Syriac text is known.

CPG 3940 *de iudicio et compunctione (de die iudicii).* No Syriac text is known.

CPG 3968 *catechesis ad monachos (de compuntione cordis* II). No Syriac text is known.

The other main texts available in an early Latin translation are:

CPG 3937 *vita Abrahamii et neptis eius Mariae.* Also known in Syriac, but dating from shortly after Ephrem's time.

CPG 3938 *in pulcherrimum Ioseph.* There seems to be no direct link with any of the various Syriac poems on Joseph (one of which is probably wrongly attributed to Ephrem).

CPG 4082 *in Ionam prophetam et de paenitentia Ninivitarum.* The Syriac original of this is almost certainly by Ephrem.

(b) The 19 texts translated by Ambrogio Traversari correspond to CPG as follows (Ambrogio's chapter numbers and titles are given; those marked with an asterisk are already found (at least in part) in the earlier Latin translations):

CPG 3909* = ch. 4, *de vita et exercitatione monastica*
CPG 3915* = ch. 9, *de conversione et paenitentia*
CPG 3916 = ch. 13, *de compunctione*
CPG 3919 = ch. 11, *de timore Dei*
CPG 3920* = ch. 10, *de secundo Domini adventu*
CPG 3921 = ch. 7, *ad monachos . . . de sanctis patribus*
CPG 3925 = ch. 1, *de paenitentia*
CPG 3928 = ch. 12, *de angustia qua premitur anima*

CPG 3933 = ch. 5, *quod non oportet ridere*
CPG 3938* = ch. 19, *de laudibus sancti Ioseph*
CPG 3940* = ch. 2, *de iudicio et resurrectione et charitate et compunctione*
CPG 3946 = ch. 16, *de antichristo*
CPG 4002(*) = ch. 17, *de virginitate*
CPG 4014 = ch. 3, *de iudicio et resurrectione*
CPG 4020 = ch. 8, *de armatura monachi*
CPG 4025 = ch. 14, *de passione Domini*[51]
CPG 4026 = ch. 18, *de laudibus martyrum*
CPG 4054 = ch. 15, *Ad eos qui filii naturam scrutari volunt*
CPG 4059 = ch. 6, *ad animam negligentem.*

Of these, corresponding Syriac texts have only been identified for CPG 3909, 3946 (requires verification), 4025 (attributed in Syriac to John Chrysostom), and 4054; details concerning these can be found in CPG.

A detailed bibliography of Ephrem's works in all languages is now available in K. den Biesen, *Bibliography of Ephrem the Syrian* (Giove in Umbria, 2002).

---

[51]English translation in E. Lash, "Sermon on the Saviour's Passion by Ephrem the Syrian," *Sobornost/Eastern Churches Review*, 22 (2000), 7–18.

The Greek Writings Attributed to Saint Ephrem the Syrian

Ephrem Lash

Introduction

SOME THIRTY YEARS AGO I sent Père François Graffin, principal editor of the *Patrologia Orientalis*, a postcard from Greece of a wall painting from the monastery of Varlaam in the Meteora depicting the Dormition of St Ephrem. On my return to Paris he remarked that he had had no idea that the Greeks gave St Ephrem "une telle importance." This icon, which is found in other monasteries, such as Iviron and Docheiariou on Mount Athos, shows in the foreground the dead saint lying on the bier surrounded by a crowd of monks, while the background shows a series of scenes depicting monastic life. Some of these paintings are very large, that at Docheiariou, for example, is four or five metres high and covers the whole north wall of the outer narthex of the catholicon. Pére Graffin had a point. I know of no other saint, apart from the Mother of God, whose death is treated on this scale and this fact alone demonstrates the importance of Ephrem the Syrian in Orthodox tradition.[1] Yet today he is seldom, if ever, mentioned in books and articles on Orthodox monasticism and Orthodox spirituality, except as the author of the "Prayer of Saint Ephrem the Syrian," used at all the offices on penitential days, notably on the weekdays of the Great Fast. This, however, is a prayer that reflects later coenobitic monasticism, of which Ephrem, who died in 373, would have known nothing, listing, as it does, a number of the endemic vices of monastic communities.

---

[1] There are, however, I have been informed a number of similar representations of the death of St Nicolas.

Lord and Master of my life, do not give me a spirit of sloth,
  idle curiosity, love of power and useless chatter.
Rather impart to me your servant a spirit of chastity,
  humility, endurance and love.
Yes, Lord and King, grant me to see my own faults and not
  to condemn my brother; for you are blessed to the ages
  of ages. Amen.

There is an interesting difference between the Greek and Slavonic texts.
Where the Greek has "idle curiosity," περιεργία, the Slavonic has "despon-
dency," уныніе, which in Greek would be that peculiarly monastic vice of
ἀκηδία. Whether this reflects a different Greek text behind the Slavonic, or
whether it is a reflection on national characters, I do not know. It is unlikely
to go back to a Syriac original, and Assemani, in his edition of the works of
Ephrem in Greek and Syriac, gives as his only source for the prayer contemporary Greek *Euchologia*.

The neglect of Ephrem is more surprising when we reflect on the fact that
the ascetic writings in Greek attributed to Ephrem the Syrian, who wrote
exclusively in Syriac and died in Edessa, the modern Urfa in southern Turkey,
are some of the basic texts of Orthodox monasticism. The *Triodion* prescribes
that they are to be read at Matins each weekday morning in Lent, after the
first two readings from the Psalter. On the Saturday before Lent, that of
Cheese Week, when we commemorate "All our venerable and God-bearing
Fathers who have shone in the ascetic life," the *Triodion* orders that Ephrem's
sermon on *The Fathers who have completed the course* be read in three sections. There are two sermons, of very different lengths, with this title, but
there is no way of knowing which of these is meant. The long sermon on
Joseph the All-virtuous is appointed for Matins on Holy Monday and that on
The Saviour's Passion for Matins of Good Friday. One of the Ambrosian
manuscripts listed by Assemani specifies that the *Sermon on the Second Coming and on Antichrist* is to be read on Carnival Sunday, that is, the Sunday of
the Last Judgement in the Byzantine rite. I do not know from when these
rubrics date, but it is not improbable that they originated in the Studite
monastery in the ninth century. Clearly the *Triodion* does not expect there to
be daily readings in Syriac in Greek or Russian monasteries, and so it must
be the Greek writings attributed to Ephrem to which the rubrics are referring.

From this I draw two conclusions. The first is that together with the *Lausiac History* of Palladios, prescribed to be read after the third reading of the

Psalter and the third Ode of the Canon, the *Ladder* of St John of Sinai and the *Instructions* of St Theodore the Studite, the writings of Ephrem should form part of the regular diet of non-biblical spiritual reading not only for monastics, but also for Orthodox Christians in general. In passing I note that of all these only the *Ladder* of St John of Sinai appears to be currently available in English.[2]

The second is that St Ephrem is considered in some sense to be, to put it no more strongly, a key model for the monastic life. The question, to which I have no proper answer, is "Why St Ephrem in particular?"

Sed Contra, as Thomas Aquinas might have said, he is almost never mentioned nowadays as a key influence in books and articles on Byzantine or Orthodox monasticism and spirituality. An exception is Olivier Clément's *The Roots of Christian Mysticism*.[3] The author deals exclusively, however, with the Syriac texts, merely noting in passing that Ephrem "has been translated, interpolated and imitated in Greek, Armenian, Coptic, Arabic and Ethiopic." He omits to mention Latin, Old Slavonic and Georgian, nor does he seem to be aware that the Syriac tradition was quite unknown to the Byzantine world.

What is certain is that Greek texts attributed to Ephrem were already circulating in his lifetime, or very soon after, and that they were very highly regarded by the Fathers, as they still are by those who hear them Lent by Lent in the monasteries and by those who encounter them, for example, in my English translations, which I am gradually putting onto my web page.[4] These texts are well worth studying in their own right regardless of whether or not they are by Mâr Afrêm himself.

This large corpus of Greek texts attributed to Ephrem the Syrian, which occupy three massive in-folio volumes in the Roman edition of Assemani, has also been greatly neglected by scholars, yet in the *Clavis Patrum Graecorum* the list of Ephrem's works comes second only to that of St John Chrysostom's and far exceeds those of St Basil the Great and the two Gregories. The only more or less complete editions are those published in the 18th century by Thwaites, in Oxford, in 1709, and by Assemani in Rome between 1732 and 1746, largely based on Thwaites, but much expanded. Joseph Simonius

[2]Since the writing of this piece, the English translation of the *Lausiac History* of Palladius has been reprinted.

[3](London, 1993), 328–330. The bibliography in this English edition is most inadequate and should be supplemented by that in *DEC*, 181.

[4]http://www.anastasis.org.uk/ephrem.htm

Assemani (1687–1768) was a Maronite from Tripoli in Syria who became Archbishop of Tyre and was Prefect of the Vatican library under the learned and enlightened Pope Benedict XIV. He should not be confused with his contemporary Joseph Aloysius Assemani (1710–1782), who edited the still valuable *Codex Liturgicus Ecclesiae Universae* in thirteen volumes between 1749 and 1746. Giovanni Mercati began a critical edition in 1915, but only one fascicle of the first volume ever appeared.[5] It contains the long poem on Abraham and Isaac together with those on Saint Basil and the Prophet Elias. In 1988 a corrected reprint, based on the two eighteenth century editions, together with a translation into Modern Greek, began to be published in Thessaloniki. This is now complete in seven volumes and the final volume contains a number of texts that are not in Thwaites or Assemani. This is extremely useful, though it is not a critical, but rather a practical, edition.[6] The most important work on Greek Ephrem in recent times is still that of the late Demokratia Hemmerdinger-Iliadou, which is summarised in her article in the *Dictionnaire de Spiritualité*, tome 4, published in 1960.

Early Testimonies

Of the early testimonies, the following are of importance.

St Jerome

St Jerome, c. 345–420, says that he had read "de Spiritu Sancto Graecum volumen," that someone had translated "de lingua Syriaca," "I recognised," he writes, "the acumen of a lofty intellect, even in translation." He also says that such was Ephrem's fame that in some churches his writings are recited—"recitantur"—after the readings from Scripture.

Sozomen

A little later, in the early 5th century, the historian Sozomen devotes to Ephrem a special chapter, to which there is nothing that corresponds in his model, Socrates. He is full of praise for his style and says that his works read as well in Greek as they do in Syriac, so that they surpass those of the most distinguished Greek writers, who works only lose in translation.

---

[5] *S. Ephraem Syri Opera* (Romae, 1915), Tomus Primus, Fasc. Primum. This is still obtainable from Herders in Rome at the original price.

[6] Κ. Γ. Φραντζολᾶς, Ὁσίου Ἐφραῒμ τοῦ Σύρου Ἔργα (Thessaloniki, 1988–1998). This edition has recently been incorporated into the TLG.

Severos of Antioch

A century later, Severos of Antioch has an extremely interesting passage about a *logos*, in Syriac *memra*,[7] which his Chalcedonian opponents claim to be by Ephrem, whom he calls "Teacher," *malphono*, in Greek *didaskalos*, entitled "On the Pearl." He says he has searched for it in Syriac, "for that was the language in which it was originally spoken. If indeed," he adds scornfully, "it ever was spoken," but has failed to find it. He has enquired in Edessa itself, but nowhere in the whole East was even the title known.[8] He also knows of numerous writings of St Ephrem that exist and circulate in Greek and which he could use to defend his position. This he will not do, he says, because one can prove anything by judicious selection of words and phrases.

St Ephrem of Antioch

However Severos's dismissal of the "In Margaritam" seems to have fallen on deaf ears, for later in the century we find one of his Chalcedonian successors, Ephrem of Antioch, using this precise text in defence of Chalcedonian orthodoxy.

St Photios the Great

St Photios the Great expresses his great admiration for Ephrem's doctrine, but he is distinctly less impressed than Sozomen by the Greek. Those who know Syriac, he writes, know how well Ephrem writes and so the inferior style of the Greek must be the responsibility of the translator. It is, he adds, amazing that such doctrine can be transmitted through such vulgarity of language. "It is not be wondered at if the vocabulary and style have nodded in the direction of popular and slipshod speech, because the fault lies not with the person who gave birth to the ideas, but with the one who translated them . . . The roughness of expression, then, is not remarkable. What is remarkable is that through such vulgarity of language so much that is salutary and profitable is offered to those who give it their attention."[9]

---

[7]Though he wrote in Greek, Severos's works, with the exception of a single homily, are preserved only in Syriac translation, the earliest of which date from the sixth century.

[8]This is extremely odd, since one of St Ephrem's best known works in Syriac are the five hymns on "The Pearl," which are included in the *Hymns on Faith*.

[9]*Bibliotheca*, ed. R. Henry, Photius. *Bibliothèque*, 8 vols. (Paris: Les Belles Lettres, 1959–1977).

Photios says that he has read a series of forty-nine discourses to the monks of Egypt. These texts are certainly not by Ephrem, but they are lively and full of practical advice on the monastic life. In our modern editions they number fifty and not all of them correspond to the ones Photios had in his library. For Photios the series starts with a piece in which the author laments his manner of life. This is very probably the text entitled *Elenchos kai Exomologesis* which is now an isolated piece. The forty-fifth discourse in Photios is a text explaining that the priest Eli was justly punished. This is also a separate piece in the modern editions. It is scarcely in place in the series and in the printed editions its place is taken by one on the text "It is better to marry than to burn." In Photios's edition the final discourse is one on the second coming and the call to repentance. It is difficult to identify which of the many texts on this subject this is. It may well be a *Logos Parainetikos* which includes a long section on the second coming.

Photios had also read the "One Hundred Chapters on Humility" and the "Sermon against indulging in laughter," both of which are in the printed editions. It may not be significant, but none of these texts is metrical.

The Enigma

There is, however, in connection with these Greek texts attributed to Ephrem a great enigma. Both Ephrem and Isaac were translated early into Greek, but whereas someone working on Greek Isaac can make use of the Syriac original to elucidate the meaning of the Greek, this is impossible with the Greek Ephrem, since, apart from one *memra* on Jonas and the Ninevites, there is virtually nothing in Greek Ephrem that corresponds to the genuine, or even the inauthentic, Syriac Ephrem. One result of this is that, since scholars have a tendency to be primarily interested in authentic texts, there has been little interest in the Greek texts for themselves.

Perhaps the greatest problem, which may partly be a result of this lack of interest, is the lack of available texts. To all intents and purposes we have still to rely on the eighteenth century editions of Thwaites and Assemani. The recent Greek edition contains the original Greek simply reprinted from Thwaites and Assemani, although the editor corrects obvious errors in the old editions and suggests a few emendations. However a number of his suggested corrections are simply wrong, as he disregards the metrical nature of many of the texts. Demokratia Hemmerdinger-Iliadou, published the *editio princeps* of the poem on "Jonas and the Ninevites" in 1967[10], but, since she did not know Syriac, she relied, for her comparisons with the Syriac original, on Burgess's English version of 1835. Moreover she declined to make any attempt at reproducing the metrical structure, which led her into a number of errors. A comparison of the two texts throws interesting light on the technique of the translator and this is well illustrated by the opening lines of the poem.

GREEK	SYRIAC
JONAS the Hebrew, * coming up from the sea,	Behold, Jonan preached in Nineveh,
preached in Ninevi * to the uncircumcised.	a Jew among the uncircumcised.
The prophet, having entered * the mighty city,	The vehement one entered the walled city
through his awesome message * he disturbed it,	and with terrifying words he terrified it.
a city, ruler of nations.[11] *At once ‹it› cowered in fear	The city of the nations mourned
through the preaching * of the son of Amathes,	by means of the Hebrew preacher.
and like the sea * it was shaken from every side	Like the sea it became troubled
through the message of the one * who had come up from the deep.	through Jonan, who came up from the sea.
	Tempests also rose up in it,
	like waves in the midst of the sea.
When he went down into the sea * he troubled it,	Jonan went down to the sea and troubled it;
and when he came up onto dry land * he at once raised a storm there.	he ascended to the dry land and terrified it.
The sea was shaken * by his flight,	The sea raged when he fled;
and the land was terrified * when he preached.	the dry land quaked when he preached.
The sea grew calm * by his prayer,	The sea became still by prayer;

[10]*Le Muséon*, LXXX (1967), 52–74

[11]There is a difficulty here. D. Hemerdinger-Iliadou has no punctuation after "nations" and prints the reading of the MS, which has "city ruler of nations" in the accusative. This leaves "cowered" without a subject. Phrantzoulas "corrects" this by putting a full stop after "disturbed" and making "city ruler of the nations" nominative. This is not necessary, if one simply starts a new sentence after "city ruler of the nations." The subject of "cowered" is quite easily "understood" from the context. This also has the merit of corresponding to the Syriac, though the verb there means rather "mourned".

and the land by God's * great
    compassion.[12]

the dry land also by repentance.

In the belly[13] of the great * whale
    he prayed;

He prayed in the great fish,

likewise the Ninevites * in the
    great city.

and the Ninevites in the great city.

Prayer delivered * Jonas from the
    whale,

Prayer delivered Jonan,

and supplication delivers * Nineve
    from the fall.

and supplication the Ninevites.

Jonas fled from the face of God *
    likewise the Ninevites from joy[14],

Jonan fled from God, and the
    Ninevites from purity.

and just judgement * shut them
    both up[15]

Justice imprisoned them,

like debtors, * and they brought to it

both of them, like debtors.

the two of them repentance, * that
    they might be redeemed

They offered him repentance,
    both of them, and were set free.

on both parts * of their own faults:

heaven's just[16] judgement * and
    repayment.

The Lord ordered * the whale in
    the sea

to keep Jonas safe * in the midst
    of the mainland.[17]

It[18] preserved Jonan in the sea,
    and the Ninevites in the midst
    of the dry land.

---

[12]D. has made a serious error here by adding the word ἐξέστη, with no warrant in the MS or in the Syriac. She gives no explanation for this and she is followed blindly by Phrantzoulas. In her introduction to the text she says she has not attempted to restore the poetic arrangement of the text into heptasyllables and octosyllables "devant l'arbitraire et les chevilles, qui sont inévitables en pareil cas." No more arbitrary, one might think, than adding words gratuitously to a text. Moreover, had she worked out the scansion, she would have realised that her addition destroys a perfectly clear series of heptasyllables, quite apart from making Ephrem say precisely the opposite of what he intended.

[13]Here D's proposed addition of κοιλίας may be accepted, because something is required to go with the article τῆς and it makes the scansion correct.

[14]Gk εὐφροσύνη. This is a little odd. The Syriac has "purity," "holiness," which makes better sense. A possible emendation might be σωφροσύνη.

[15]The Greek adds here ὡς ἐν φρουρᾷ, which violates the scansion and should be deleted. Interestingly the sixteenth century Latin version by Vossius of a lost Greek MS does not have the phrase.

[16]This adjective, οὐρανόδικος, is not attested in the lexica, though it should be in Lampe.

[17]This is very curious. I suspect a line referring to the Ninevites has fallen out, and the Syriac supports this idea.

[18]The subject in Syriac is "justice." It looks as though the translator has not understood this and supplied one. The alternative, that something has fallen out of the Syriac, is less likely.

For from himself * the prophet Jonas[19] learnt	By himself Jonan learned
that it is right * for those who repent to live.	that it is right that penitents should live.
Grace gave him * in himself an image.	Grace gave him, in himself, an example on behalf of sinners;
Jonas when he repented * came up out of the sea,	that as he was drawn out of the sea
so that thus he might bring up * the city that had drowned.	he should draw out the sunken walled city.
The city[20] was troubled, * just like the sea,	Nineveh, the lake, was troubled
through Jonas' voice, * when he had come from the deep.	by Jonan who sprang from the sea.
Jonas the just * opened his mouth	Jonan, the just, opened his mouth;
and Nineve, when it heard, * was at once disturbed.	Nineveh listened and mourned.
When the Jew preached * he made the city quail,[21]	A single Hebrew preacher made the whole city fear
distributing death * to his hearers.	His mouth spoke and delivered doom distributed death to his hearers.
The preacher stood up, * a physician among giants,	The feeble herald stood up in a city of mighty men
and from fear of him * they quailed like children.	
His voice broke * the hearts of kings,	His voice broke the heart of kings;
because he overturned * their city upon them.[22]	he overturned their city upon them.[23]
Cutting off with one word * all their hope,	By one word which cut off hope,
he made them drink a cup * full of anger and wrath.	he made them drink the cup of wrath.

Another indication of the importance of these texts is that, from late antiquity, they were translated into all the major Christian languages, including

---

[19]The Latin of Vossius adds "Jonas." The scansion requires this and the Syriac supports it.

[20]That there is nothing in the Greek corresponding to the word "lake" in the Syriac, may be without significance. But is worth noting that Syriac MS T has "city," rather than "lake."

[21]The Greek here seems to have omitted a verse, "His mouth spoke and delivered doom."

[22]This could also mean "he turned their city against them," as could the Syriac.

[23]This could also mean "he turned their city against them," as could the Greek.

Armenian, Latin,[24] Old Slavonic, Coptic, Georgian, Arabic and Ethiopic. In more recent times they have attracted the attention of people as diverse as Cardinal Ambrogio Traversari,[25] who published the Latin *editio princeps* in 1481 in a rare incunabulum containing nineteen texts of the Greek Ephrem, which went through a number of editions in the early sixteenth century and was translated into French, at the request of Cardinal Philippe de Luxembourg, and published in Paris in an even rarer incunabulum, undated, but in fact 1500,[26] and John Wesley, who had a particular fondness for Ephrem, and refers to him a number of times in his journals. In his *Fourth Savannah Journal*, on 12 October 1736 at Frederica in Georgia, he describes him as "The most awakening writer, I think, of all the ancients." Eleven years later, in Newcastle, he wrote in his journal on Ash Wednesday, 4 March 1747, "I spent some days in reading 'The Exhortations of Ephrem Syrus.' Surely never did any man, since David, give us such a picture of a broken and contrite heart." Wesley was almost certainly using the Oxford edition of 1709, since the Greek volumes of Assemani were only published in 1732, 1743 and 1746.[27] He cannot, despite what some of his biographers have written, have been using the Syriac texts, since these the first of these was only published in 1737; with the other two following in 1740 and 1743.[28] Wesley also seems to have known what is, I suspect, the earliest work of Ephrem to be translated into English, which was published by W. Bowyer in 1731.[29] It is a pamphlet of

[24]Edmund Bishop in a note on page 278 of Dom A. B. Kuypers edition of the *Book of Cerne* (Cambridge, 1902), writes, "In the early Middle Ages a collection of half a dozen ascetical tracts of St Ephrem had a wide circulation in the West; at what date the translation was made does not appear; the oldest manuscript that I have noticed containing any of these tracts is the S. Omer MS 33bis, assigned to the 8th century."

[25]1378–1439. A leading Florentine humanist cardinal and strong supporter of the papacy, who drew up, in Greek and Latin, the formula of reunion between the Greek and Latin churches at the council of Florence. His translation of nineteen sermons of Ephrem the Syrian is almost certainly the first of any of St Ephrem's works to be printed in any language. His work also exists in manuscripts in the Vatican library. The book was dedicated to the well-known Florentine humanist, Cosmo de Medici. A French translation of this work was published in Paris, at the request of Cardinal Philippe de Luxembourg, in 1500. Robert Watt writes of Ambrosius's version, "It is very excellent, and done by a person well versed in Greek literature" (*Bibliotheca Britannica*. Vol. 1, 26c. 1824).

[26]Cf. Brunet, *Manuel du Libraire*, t.2. Paris 1861.

[27]I do not know if eighteenth-century sea captains charged for excess baggage, but it is most unlikely that Wesley would have included Assemani's three massive in folio volumes in his luggage for a transatlantic voyage in the seventeen thirties.

[28]Thorvald Källstad is therefore quite wrong to suggest that Wesley might have read any of the texts which he lists on page 171 of his *John Wesley and the Bible* (Stockholm, 1974).

[29]Cf. John Nicols *Literary Anecdotes of the Eighteenth Century* (London, 1812), vol. 1,

some fifty pages in small quarto. Only seven copies are known to exist, three
of which are in the USA. Neither the British Library nor any Oxford library
possesses a copy; there is, however one in Liverpool University Library, which
I have been able to consult. The translator is anonymous, but was almost certainly the publisher, William Bowyer, who was a good Greek and Latin
scholar. The translation was made from Thwaites's Oxford edition of the
Greek, together with the Cologne edition of Gerard Vossius's 16th century
Latin translation. It is the sermon known as the *Sermo Compunctorius*, which
is to be found in the first volume of Assemani's edition on pages twenty-eight
to forty. Apart from this extremely rare edition, nothing of the Greek Ephrem
has been published in English, so far as I am aware, except for the *Prayer of
Saint Ephrem*, of which there are numerous versions. It is important to stress
that none of these earlier translators and readers had any knowledge of the
genuine, or even of the inauthentic, Syriac writings of Mâr Afrêm. Standard
works on Orthodox monasticism and spirituality make no mention of the
Greek corpus, though some mention the genuine Syriac texts, which in fact
had little or no influence on Western, including Byzantine, Christendom, until
the nineteenth century.[30] In English H. Burgess published two volumes of
translations from the Syriac in 1835 and ten years later J. B. Morris prepared
a further selection, with copious and useful annotation.[31] In 1898 John
Gwynn published a further collection as volume 13 of the Nicene and Post-
Nicene Fathers, which incorporated much of Morris's work.

This large corpus of Greek texts, which the *Oxford Dictionary of the
Christian Church* dismisses in a single clause,[32] is extremely heterogeneous
and much, if not most, of it is later than Mâr Afrêm himself. Many of the texts

---

47 2. The title is, "A Serious Exhortation to Repentance and Sorrow for Sin, and a strict and mortified Life; written about the Middle of the Fourth Century by St. Ephraim, the Cyrian [*sic*], Deacon of Edessa. Translated into English from the Greek and Latin compared."

[30] A modest attempt to start to redress the balance is the appearance of a brief article on
"Ephrem 'Greek' " in *DEC* (Oxford, 1999).

[31] This was published by Pusey in 1847, whose "Advertisement" might perhaps give the
impression that the translator had died: "The circumstances under which the present Work
appears, seem to require silence rather than explanation. It was commenced several years ago; it
was finished and in type before the English Church lost its translator." He concludes: "The circumstances of the present volume, render any thing approaching controversy, altogether
unseemly. It remains only to pray that, amid all these sorrows, the reverence and humble awe of
St. Ephrem may, by God's grace, deepen the same spirit in us which He has so mercifully reawak-
ened. DOMINE, MISERERE." Morris had become a Roman Catholic.

[32] "His works were translated into Armenian and Greek at a very early date, and via the latter into Latin and Slavonic; many of the works attributed to him in these languages, however,
are not genuine," *ODCC*, 3rd edition (1977), 551.

are clearly addressed to cenobitic monks and, since he died in 373 it is, to say the least, unlikely that he wrote to warn a fellow ascetic against the dangers of Nestorianism or quoted the definition of Chalcedon verbatim. On the other hand, as we have seen, these texts were known at least as early as the fifth century and they were certainly used by St Romanos in some of his kontakia.

Metrical Texts

A number of the Greek texts attributed to St Ephrem are written in verse, though this is not apparent in the various editions, which are all printed as prose, even though the original titles often note the fact that they are in verse. Some are written in octosyllabic lines, but the majority in heptasyllabic. The verse is strictly by count of syllables, no account being taken of either quantity, as in classical Greek, or of stress, as in the kontakia of Romanos and in general in all Byzantine liturgical hymnography. This is, so far as I am aware, unique in Greek, but is of course characteristically Syrian. Indeed the line of fourteen syllables, broken by a caesura, is known in Syriac as the "Metre of Mår Afrêm."

These metrical texts cover a number of different literary types.[33] One piece that stands somewhat apart is that *On those who scrutinise the nature of the Son*. This is of particular interest since it contains a number of echoes of the authentic hymns *On Faith*. Another that has a distinctly Syrian "feel" to it is the sermon *On the Passion of the Saviour*. This is also of particular interest since there exists in the British Library a Syriac manuscript which includes this piece, but attributed to St John Chrysostom. I am currently engaged on translating this and hope that a comparison of the two texts may shed some light on which is the original and which the translation.[34]

One of the most interesting texts in verse is the long poem on Abraham and Isaac, which was published in a full critical edition by Mercati in 1915. The text is closely related to the last part of a homily by Gregory of Nyssa *On the Divinity of the Son and the Spirit*. Since Mercati himself was of the opinion that the text was genuine Ephrem, he held that Gregory made use of Ephrem's sermon in composing his own work. Demokratia Hemmerdinger-

---

[33]I list a number of these in my paper, "Metrical Texts of Greek Ephrem," in *Studia Patristica*, xxxv (Leuven, 2001), 433–448. In this paper I also illustrate, by means of examples, how the metrical nature of these texts may be tentatively restored, even in the absence of proper critical editions.

[34]I published a translation of the Greek in *Sobornost* (2000).

Iliadou was inclined to agree. But if the sermon is not genuine Ephrem, then the relationship will be the other way round, and there are compelling reasons for thinking that the dependence does go the other way. The *terminus ante quem* for the sermon is the early sixth century, since the kontakion on Abraham by Romanos, who lived in the reign of Justinian, makes use of this text of the Greek Ephrem. The Greek text of the sermon is also to found among the *spuria* of John Chrysostom. The sermon contains a number of more less extended passages of a strongly christological nature, notably stanzas 10–19 and 96–109, and these have no equivalent in Gregory's text. Moreover in stanzas 20–27, the overtly christological ones, namely 21, 23 and 25–27 correspond to nothing in Gregory. This leads me to suggest that if the original sermon was a genuine work of Ephrem, it must have been reworked, with considerable theological additions, after its use by Gregory of Nyssa. But I believe that Gregory's text is the earlier and that the one attributed to Ephrem shows evident signs of padding, much of it, no doubt, *metri causa*.[35]

The most serious objection to the authenticity of at least some of the text are the references to the "Sabek plant." This is the reading of the LXX at Genesis 22:13 [ἐν φυτῷ σαβέκ], but not of the Syriac, which simply translates the Hebrew, "and behold, behind [him] was a ram, caught in a thicket by its horns." The Hebrew word *s^ebak* means something like "thicket," but the word itself is rare, only occurring here and at Is 9,17 and 10,34. It is unclear why the LXX should have transliterated the word rather than translated it. The Peshitta has, "a ram caught in a branch by its horns," while Ephrem in his authentic Syriac commentary on Genesis has "tree." The various texts of the Greek Ephrem that refer to the word *sabek* are, to put it no more strongly, unlikely to go back to a Syriac original. The meaning given to *sabek* is, by a mistaken etymology, derived from the Syriac *sh^ebaq*, that is "forgive." This meaning becomes a commonplace in the Fathers and in the Greek liturgical texts. The whole passage is worth quoting:

> Look too on the sheep * hanged by its two horns
> on the plant * that is called "Sabek."

> Look too on Christ, * the Lamb of God,
> hanged by his two hands * upon a Cross.

> The plant called Sabek * means "forgiveness,"
> for it saved from slaughter * the old man's child,

[35]The vivid and detailed description of iconographic depictions of the scene and its profound effect on the writer is found in both St Gregory and St Ephrem's texts.

It foreshadows the cross * that forgives the world
its sins * and grants it life.

The ram hanging * on the Sabek plant
mystically redeemed * Isaac alone,

While the Lamb of God * hanged on the cross
delivered the world * from Death and Hell.

It is perhaps worth noting that all three instances of the word "Sabek" occur
in a part of the text that has nothing corresponding to it in Gregory of Nyssa's
text.

Earlier in the poem, stanza 8 appears to have been padded out and stanza
9 to have been composed to introduce the long christological digression in the
next stanzas.[36]

> 8. *But the hope in God, * which flourished in them,*
>   was not only *unageing, * but also invincible.*

> 9. Therefore beyond hope * she *gave birth to Isaac,*
>   who bore in every way * the type of the Master.

In Gregory we have simply:

"*But the hope in God was unageing in them and flourishing.* In the
meantime *Isaac was born to them* so that the offspring might be manifested, not as a work of nature, but as a result of divine power."

It is far more likely that the sermon of the Greek Ephrem is a not unsuccessful pastiche of genuine Ephrem, which makes use of the sermon of Gregory
of Nyssa.[37]

Conclusion

Leaving aside the texts in the Greek corpus which are by other known
authors, how many suspects have we got, as Hercule Poirot or Miss Marples

---

[36]The words in italic are those that are also found in Gregory's text.

[37]On page 15 of Mercati's edition the author prints a number of stanzas in parallel with the
corresponding passages in Gregory's sermon. These seem to me to indicate quite clearly that the
metrical text of the Greek Ephrem is an adaptation of Gregory's prose one.

might ask? I will very tentatively distinguish three. The first, the author of the fifty *Exhortations to the Egyptian Monks*, is a down to earth cenobitic monk who writes largely to give practical advice to other monks, notably to beginners. He writes in prose vividly and colloquially, though he tends to indulge in lengthy parables which sometimes get out of hand and describe improbable situations tailored to the spiritual point he wishes to make. This is Photios's Ephrem: Here he is talking to novice monks:

5th Exhortation. To Novice Ascetics.

If someone comes to be a monk from an exalted station in life, let him guard himself from the demon of haughtiness, lest he fall into the spirit of pride and disobedience and harm himself. Beloved, it is no shame for you, if you are a subject in the Lord, nor if you work at what is good with your own hands; for the little distress and tribulation that you endure for the Lord becomes for you the cause of eternal life. And what more should I say? For like the person who changed a drachma into ten thousand talents of gold, so is every distress of the monastic life to the coming tribulation, which meets those who do ill. You then bring small things, and great ones are given you. Be vigilant then, beloved, like a good soldier. Do not neglect the gift which is in you, lest both things should come upon you: both to grieve human beings, that is your parents according to the flesh, and not to please God. But struggle, that those who see you may glorify God at your good way of life. For it is written, "Those who fear the Lord will see me and be glad." And again, "There is much peace for those who love your law, and there is no stumbling block for them." And so guard yourself from haughtiness, and the Lord will be your portion. To him be glory to the ages. Amen.

The second is also a monk, probably a cenobite, who has a deep sense of his own shortcomings and a intense awareness of the impending Judgement. This is John Wesley's Ephrem. Most of the fourth volume of the new Greek edition consists of texts on the Last Judgement and related themes. Many of these texts are metrical.

Here he is in the opening words of the discourse on "The Fathers who have completed the course":

My heart is in pain. * Have compassion for me, brethren.
Blessed servants, * come, listen to me.
My soul is grieved, * my nerves are in pain.

Where are tears, * where compunction,
that I may wash my body * with tears and groans?

Who will remove me * to an uninhabited place,
where there is no hubbub * which cuts off tears,
no confusion * which prevents weeping?

I raised my voice * and wept to God
with bitter tears, * and I said with groans,

"Heal me, Lord, * that I may be healed,
because my heart * is in grievous pain

and its groans * do not allow me to take
a moment's rest. * For I see, Master,
that like choice gold * you take your saints
from this vain world * to the repose of life.

Like a wise farmer * with understanding,
when he sees the fruits * have ripened well,
harvests them at once, * that they may not be spoiled
by any harmful damage, * so you, O Saviour,
gather in your elect * who have toiled in holiness.

But we the idle, * slack by choice,
have remained so * in our hardness,
and our fruit has always * remained unripe,

for we have not had * any firm intent to ripen well
by good works * and to be harvested in holiness
into the granary of life. * Our fruit
has no tears * to ripen it,
no compunction * to make it blossom
from the breeze of tears, * no humility
to shade it * from above
against the burning heat, * no non-possessiveness,
so that it is not weighed down * by enemies,

> no love of God, * the mighty root
> which bears fruit, * no non-anxiety
> for earthly things, * no vigil,
> no watchful mind, * alert in prayer."

The third is perhaps closer to Mår Afrêm himself in his use of Scripture, and his refusal to pry into the mystery of God. Here he is comparing the birth of Isaac to that of the Saviour:

> Therefore beyond hope * she gave birth to Isaac,
> who bore in every way * the type of the Master.

> It was not nature's work * that a dead womb conceived
> and breasts that were dry * gave Isaac milk.

> It was not nature's work * [for the Virgin Mary][38]
>   to conceive without a man and without corruption
> to give birth * to the Saviour of all things.

> He made Sara * a mother in old age;
> revealed Mary * a virgin after child-birth.

> An Angel in the tent * said to the patriarch,"
> At this time * Sara will have a son."

> An Angel in Nazareth * said to Mary,"
> Behold, you will bear a son, * O highly favoured."

> Sara laughed * seeing her barrenness,
> beholding her deadness, * disbelieving the word.

> "How, she said, will this be, * Abraham and I
> are both incapable * of having children?"

> Mary too was at loss, * seeing her virginity
> and keeping its seals * unbroken.

> "How will happen to me, * who do not know man?
> For this promise * is foreign to nature."

[38]There is one heptasyllable too many in this stanza. I bracket this one, since it is not grammatically essential, and the preceding stanza does not mention Sara by name. It has all the marks of a marginal gloss, or, since the phrase forms a heptasyllable, an unnecessary addition by a prosaically minded scribe.

But it was he, who beyond hope * gave Isaac to Sara,
who was born from the Virgin * according to the flesh.

All these writers implicitly acknowledge the greatness of the writer whose name they attach to their own work, and much of what they wrote has great value in its own right and merits not only scholarly study but prayerful meditation. I end this brief introduction to the Greek writings attributed to St Ephrem the Syrian, offered as a tribute of love and respect to one who has devoted much of his life not only to teaching the Orthodox monastic tradition, but to putting it into practice himself, with the opening of a set of Fifty-Five Beatitudes[39] by Ephrem the Greek, which might be used as a description of Mâr Afrêm himself, whose name they bear, and to which all Christians should aspire:

1. Blessed the one who has become wholly free in the Lord from all the earthly things of this vain life and loved God alone, the good and compassionate.

2. Blessed the one who has become a good ploughman of the virtues and raised a harvest of fruits of life in the Lord, like a ploughed field bearing wheat.

3. Blessed the one who has become a good husbandman of the virtues and planted a spiritual vine, plucked the grapes and filled his presses with fruits of life in the Lord.

4. Blessed the one who has made his fellow servants glad with spiritual gladness from the fruit of the virtues, which he planted by toiling to give back the fruit of life in the Lord.

5. Blessed the one who stands in the assembly and prays like an Angel from heaven, keeping his thoughts pure day by day, and has given no entrance to the Evil One to make his soul a prisoner, far from God his Saviour.

[39]Sir John Tavener tells me that he hopes to compose a musical setting of a number of these.

❧ Bishops and Charismatics in Early Christian Egypt ❧

Norman Russell

"THERE IS IN CHRISTIANITY," Bishop Kallistos has written, "no such thing as a spiritual *élite* exempt from the obligations of church membership. The solitary in the desert is as much a churchman as the artisan in the city. The ascetic and mystical path, while it is from one point of view 'the flight of the alone to the Alone,' is yet at the same time essentially social and communal."[1] This has not always been self-evident to the ascetics and mystics themselves. In early Egyptian monasticism the Platonist tradition of intellectualist mysticism (in Plotinian terms "the flight of the alone to the Alone"), mediated through the teaching of Origen and his fourth-century systematizer, Evagrius Ponticus, was regarded by many of the more educated ascetics as central to the correct understanding of the spiritual life.[2] The social and communal aspect, the monk's sense of solidarity with "the artisan in the city," was much less in evidence.[3] For most of the fourth and fifth centuries the activities of spiritual élites in the monastic settlements of Nitria and the Nile valley

[1] Kallistos Ware, *The Orthodox Way* (Crestwood, NY: St Vladimir's Seminary Press, 1979), 144.

[2] The papyrus evidence for the wide dissemination of Origen's spiritual writings is set out by C.H. Roberts, *Manuscript and Belief in Early Christian Egypt*, The Schweich Lectures, 1977, (London: Oxford University Press, 1979), 24–5. For an excellent account of the intellectual climate of early Egyptian monasticism see S. Rubenson, *The Letters of Saint Antony. Origenist Theology, Monastic Tradition and the Making of a Saint* (Bibliotheca Historico-ecclesiastica Lundensis 24) (Lund: Lund University Press, 1990), 89–125 [rev. edn.: Minneapolis: Fortress Press, 1995]. On Evagrius the classic work is A. Guillaumont, *Les 'Kephalaia Gnostica' d'Évagre le Pontique et l'histoire de l'origénisme chez les Grecs et chez les Syriens*, Patristica Sorbonensia, 5 (Paris: Les Éditions du Seuil, 1962). More recently, G. Bunge has challenged the view that Evagrius developed Origen's ideas in a heretical direction, but has not been entirely persuasive. See, for example, his "Origenismus–Gnostizismus: Zum geistesgeschichtlichen Standort des Evagrius Pontikos," *Vigiliae Christianae* 40 (1986), 24–54.

[3] The typical approach is illustrated by Ammonas (probably the Ammonas mentioned by Rufinus as one of Antony's disciples) in Letter XII: "You also know, my dear brethren, that ever

was a source of anxiety to the ecclesiastical establishment. The bishops of Alexandria, tentatively at first but then in an increasingly authoritarian way, sought to bring the monks into a closer relationship with the episcopal leadership. The welding together of monk and urban layman into a unified body with the same sense of the obligations of church membership was the result of a long and painful process.

During the episcopates of Athanasius, Timothy and Theophilus, the Egyptian church underwent a rapid expansion. What had previously been a relatively small community of confessors and students of *gnosis* came to be transformed by the early fifth century into an imperial church serving the broad mass of the people. This development had theological repercussions. An intellectualist idea of faith came to be replaced by one which was more "institutionalized," the emphasis shifting from knowing God through the contemplation of the timeless cosmic order to encountering him through his historical revelation in Jesus Christ.[4] The new emphasis was accompanied by a suspicion of intellectuals, a focussing more on the shared experience of the community. The first abbas, with their teaching on self-knowledge and spiritual ascent harked back to an earlier world. From the episcopal point of view it was important that the abbas' authority and prestige should be harnessed to the ecclesiastical needs of the new era and that whatever seemed incompatible with those needs should be eliminated.

The rise of monasticism in Egypt preceded the episcopate of Athanasius by more than fifty years. According to the relative chronology of the *Life of Antony*, Antony must have sold his possessions and embarked on the ascetic life in about 271, and even then he found an old man who had been a solitary

since the transgression came to pass, the soul cannot know God unless it withdraws itself from men and every distraction" (trans. D.J. Chitty, *The Letters of Ammonas* [Oxford: SLG Press, 1979], 16). Much rarer is the viewpoint expressed in the *Apophthegmata Patrum* under Antony 24: "It was revealed to Abba Antony in the desert that in the city there was someone like him, a doctor by profession, who gave to the needy from what was surplus to him and every day sang the *trisagion* with the angels." But this perhaps tells us more about rivalry among ascetics than solidarity with the ordinary faithful of the cities. A true sense of solidarity needed the development of Eucharistic teaching that we find in Theophilus and Cyril of Alexandria.

[4]On this transition see C. Kannengiesser, "The Spiritual Message of the Geat Fathers," in B. McGinn and J. Meyendorff (eds), *Christian Spirituality: Origins to the Twelfth Century* (London: Routledge & Kegan Paul, 1986), 63; D. Brakke, *Athanasius and Asceticism* (Baltimore and London: The Johns Hopkins University Press, 1998), 145–6, 268. Compare Antony, as reported by Evagrius: "My book is the nature of created things; and it is present for me, when I wish, to read the words of God" (*Praktikos* 92; quoted by Socrates *HE* 4.23) with Athanasius: "We have the divine Scriptures for salvation . . . . In these books alone the teaching of piety is proclaimed" (*Festal Letter* 39 [CE 367], trans. Brakke, *Athanasius*, 329).

since his youth to take as his spiritual father.[5] But it is only in the third decade of the fourth century that the monastic life acquired a political significance. Athanasius' election as bishop of Alexandria in 328 had been opposed by the powerful Melitian federation. Monastic support was important to him, partly to counter their influence. The strength of the Melitians lay in their claim to be an ascetic, morally superior manifestation of the church. Athanasius therefore had good reason to treat ascetic theory as part of dogma. The integration of the monastic life into the general life of the church became for him a key element of his search for doctrinal unity. This he sought to do in three ways: by appointing monks as bishops, by writing personal and encyclical letters of admonition or encouragement, and by publicising the monastic life to the church at large.

Athanasius' *Letter to Dracontius* gives us a valuable insight into the process by which monks were co-opted into the episcopate.[6] Dracontius had been head of a monastery. Having been been elected bishop of Hermopolis Parva, he had gone into hiding to escape what he saw as the destruction of his monastic vocation. Hermopolis, however, was a key nome capital in the "regio Alexandriae." The modern Damanhur, it was situated on the canal connecting lake Mareotis with the Canopic branch of the Nile. The monastic settlements of Nitria lay within its territory. Its bishop was therefore a vital link between Alexandria and the Nitrian ascetics. Athanasius deploys a formidable array of arguments to persuade Dracontius to return to his post. He must not be a stumbling block for the "little ones" (Mt 18:6) or put off pagans from becoming Christians. Nor should he bury his talent (Mt 25:27), or show contempt for church administration. He must imitate Paul and Old Testament figures who fulfilled their ministry, such as Moses, Jeremiah and Jonah, rather than the man in the Gospel who hesitated to follow Christ (Lk 9:61). After all, Dracontius is not the only monk to have been made a bishop—Athanasius mentions seven others, including Serapion of Thmuis and Paul of Latopolis. And in any case, as a bishop Dracontius can still live the ascetic life. By bringing monks into the episcopate, Athanasius "mitigated somewhat," as Brakke says, "the moral superiority granted to the monks."[7] He established a "principle of reciprocity" by which the monks had to serve the church as

---

[5] Athanasius *Life of Antony* 3.

[6] PG 25, 523–34; trans. L. W. Barnard, *The Monastic Letters of Saint Athanasius the Great* (Oxford: SLG Press 1994), 4–9. It should be noted that there were no metropolitans in Egypt apart from Libya and Cyrenaica. The bishops of the Delta and the Nile valley were all suffragans of Alexandria.

[7] Brakke, *Athanasius*, 110.

bishops if they wanted clergy for the monasteries. By the same token, the multiplication of monk-bishops tended to monasticise the episcopate.[8]

The rest of Athanasius' monastic correspondence fills out our picture of his relationship with the ascetic movement. In his *First Letter to Virgins*, writtten in 337–339, he discusses the respective merits of marriage and virginity.[9] Marriage belongs to human nature, but virginity transcends it. Purity of body, for example, enabled Elijah not only to overcome fire but even to be taken up in a fiery chariot. Virginity deifies its possessor, for its goal is "repose in the true light, Christ."[10] At the same time it is absurd "to despise what is lesser because it is not like what is greater than it."[11] Marriage and virginity are both laid down by divine precept. If you condemn marriage, you condemn virginity. This is the error of Hieracas, an encratite teacher of Origenist views who directed a community of ascetic men and women near Leontopolis in the Delta.[12]

A similar error is the subject of Athanasius' *Letter to Amoun*, written in the 350s.[13] Amoun, "the first of the monks to settle in Nitria,"[14] was the superior of a large group of solitaries. Some of the monks had apparently been taking an encratitic line on nocturnal emissions. These are not sinful, says Athanasius, when they are independent of the will. A middle course should be steered between libertarians who say that if our organs have been fashioned by the Creator, there is no sin in their genuine use, and rigorists who regard marriage as dishonourable. Marriage and virginity are two different ways to salvation, even if marriage is the more moderate and ordinary, and virginity the more angelic and perfect.

In two brief encyclical letters, written for a monastic readership during his third exile in 356–62, when he was hiding in the desert, Athanasius turned his attention to countering the influence of Arianism. His *First Letter to the Monks* was a covering letter accompanying a refutation of Arianism, probably the

---

[8]At the Council of Nicaea the monk Paphnutius, bishop of a city in the Thebaid, intervened to plead against the general imposition of celibacy on bishops (Socrates, *HE* I.11; Sozomen, *HE* I.23; Gelasius, *Hist. Conc. Nic.* II.32). But his was a minority voice.

[9]L. Th. Lefort, *S. Athanase: Letters festales et pastorales en copte*, CSCO 150, with Latin trans. 151, (Louvain, 1955), 73–99; trans. Brakke, *Athanasius*, 274–91.

[10]*First Letter to Virgins* 34; trans. Brakke, *Athanasius*, 285.

[11]*First Letter to Virgins* 24; trans. Brakke, *Athanasius*, 282.

[12]*First Letter to Virgins* 24–29; trans. Brakke, *Athanasius*, 282–83. Our chief informant for Hieracas, whose Origenism consisted in a belief in the preexistence of souls and the denial of a physical resurrection, is Epiphanius *Panarion* 67.

[13]PG 26, 1169–76; trans. Barnard, *Letters*, 1–3.

[14]*Historia Monachorum* 22.1.

History of the Arians.[15] It is striking how Athanasius adopts an approach guaranteed to appeal to the monks. Diffident in advancing his personal opinion and apophatic in his theological statements, he appears to be confiding his difficulties to them. In probing the divine law, he says, "the more I thought I understood it, the more I knew I failed to do so."[16] It is impossible to say what God is; it is only possible to say what he is not. For words are inadequate. The judgement of God in the matter is best seen in the manner of Arius's death, which elsewhere he describes in detail.[17] In the *Second Letter to the Monks* Athanasius is more specific about whom he is attacking: first, those who travel around the monasteries pretending to have come from him but actually spreading Arian propaganda, and, second, those who, while not professing Arian views, nevertheless worship with them. In the *History of the Arians* he reveals that the Arians have made an alliance with the Melitians.[18] It was therefore vitally important to draw firm boundaries round the orthodox community.

In his relations with the Pachomian federation Athanasius is more circumspect. He ignored the request of Serapion of Tentyra to ordain Pachomius against his will.[19] As a new bishop, he was probably still feeling his way carefully.[20] In any case he would certainly not have wished to alienate Pachomius. His supportive letters to Horsiesius in the difficult years after Pachomius's death suggest that he was prepared to allow a certain latitude to coenobitic communities, at least in the Nile valley, where he was most in need of support against the Melitians.[21]

His attitude to desert spirituality is summed up in his work as a monastic publicist. Recent studies have tended to confirm the Athanasian authorship of the *Life of Antony* and have demonstrated the dependence of some passages on Antony's *Letters.*[22] Athanasius takes Antony and uses his authority as a charismatic figure to underpin his programme—the demonstration of the

---

[15]PG 25, 691–93; trans. Barnard, *Letters*, 10–11. Athanasius also sent the *History of the Arians* to Serapion instructing him to return it after reading it.

[16]As Barnard comments, "an admission of fallibility unusual in Athanasius" (*Letters*, 10, n.1).

[17]Arius died in a public lavatory in Constantinople after Alexander, the bishop of the capital, had prayed to be spared having to communicate with him (*Letter to Serapion* 3).

[18]*Hist. Ar.* 78.

[19]*Vita Prima Pachomii* 30.

[20]On the issues involved see esp. Brakke, *Athanasius*, 113–20.

[21]PG 26, 977–80; trans. Barnard, *Letters*, 14–15.

[22]Rubenson, *Letters*, 126–44. See also the penetrating article of I. Perczel, "Mankind's Common Intellectual Substance: A Study in the *Letters* of Saint Antony and his *Life* by Saint Athanasius," in B. Nagy and M. Sebök (eds.), *The Man of Many Devices, Who Wandered Full Many Ways: Festschrift in Honor of János M. Bak* (Budapest: Central University Press, 1999), 197–213.

superiority of the ecclesiastical tradition over pagans and heretics.[23] The *Letters* reflect an Origenian spirituality centred on the primacy of the spiritual nature of the soul. Commenting on Wisdom 1:4, "He called all things out of nothingness into being," Antony says: "Such statements refer to our intellectual nature, which is hidden in this body of corruption, but which did not belong to it from the beginning, and is to be freed from it. . . . For this reason I tell you these things, refreshing you, and praying that, since we are all created of the same invisible substance, which has a beginning but no end, we may love one another with a single love."[24] In the *Life of Antony* Athanasius handles Antony's teaching very sympathetically. The chief idea concerns *to noeron*—not the intellectual element in the tripartite theory of the soul, but the soul's "intellectual state" or "intellectual nature."[25] Rational beings were created as a unique "intellectual substance," later broken up by the fall into individualized portions, each endowed with the "heavy body." Salvation therefore "consists in the return to this original intellectuality and in the recognition that this substance is what we really are."[26] Athanasius takes up the theme of "the spiritual substance of the soul" from Antony's *Letters*. "For virtue," he says, "consists of the soul preserving its intellectuality (*to noeron*) according to nature."[27]

After the brief episcopate of Timothy I (381–385), Athanasius was succeeded by Theophilus. Like Athanasius, Theophilus had many contacts with the Nitrian monks. The *Apophthegmata* retain the memory of a close association with them, in particular with Arsenius, whose name he is said to have had on his lips at the hour of his death.[28] The monks were of assistance to Theophilus not only as teachers of the spiritual life. He harnessed their iconoclastic energies to his campaigns against the temples. Once aroused, however, the monks could be dangerous allies. After his anti-anthropomorphite

[23]Rubenson: "The letters show that the purpose of the *Vita* was neither to 'humanize' a charismatic teacher nor to 'elevate' a simple monk, but to use the influence of Antony to depict the victory of Orthodoxy over pagans and heretics, the victory of the cross over the demons, of *gnosis* by faith over *gnosis* by education, of the 'man taught by God,' the *theodidaktos*, over the philosophers" (*Letters*, p. 187).

[24]Letter VI, trans. D. Chitty, *The Letters of Saint Antony the Great* (Oxford: SLG Press, 1975), 20–1.

[25]Perczel shows convincingly that Athanasius has derived his use of *to noeron* from Antony ("Intellectual Substance," 199–205).

[26]Perczel, "Intellectual Substance," 201.

[27]*Life of Antony* 20; trans. Perczel, "Intellectual Substance," 200.

[28]*Apophthegmata Patrum*, Arsenius 7, 8 and 28; Theophilus 5. Arsenius is not presented in the *Apophthegmata* as an intellectualist, in spite of his high culture.

pastoral letter of 399 they turned up in force in Alexandria threatening violence—successfully, according to Socrates and the Coptic monastic tradition
—to make him recant.[29] These sources portray Theophilus as dropping his
opposition to a literalist interpretation of the Scriptures out of deference to
the monks and embarking at once on his campaign against the Origenists.
Theophilus's own account is rather different. Writing from Constantinople in
403, he portrays himself as equally anxious to exclude both the crude ideas
of the "more rustic monks," the biblical literalists we might say, and the
sophisticated arguments of the allegorizing Origenists in favour of the subordination of the Son and the spiritualization of the resurrection.[30] He says
that in moving against the Origenists he was responding to reports of disturbances in the monasteries, which was probably true, but the timing of his anti-
Origenist campaign seeems to have been influenced by other, more political,
factors. Socrates draws attention to Theophilus's unseemly quarrel with
Isidore, his almoner and confidential envoy.[31] Accused of moral turpitude,
Isidore withdrew to the haven of his Nitrian cell and the company of his fel-
low-admirers of Origen. But Theophilus pursued him mercilessly, eventually
driving him out of Egypt altogether along with some 400 Nitrian monks.[32]

Can these varying accounts be reconciled? Certainly Isidore was more
than the mild saintly figure that pro-Origenist sources like to portray. When
Theophilus sent him to Jerusalem in 396 to broker a reconciliation between
its bishop, John, and a fiercely anti-Origenist and insubordinate Jerome, Isidore had compromised his mission by announcing in a private letter that fell
into Jerome's hands that his adversaries would be scattered on his arrival like
smoke in the breeze or wax before the fire.[33] This sabotaging of Theophilus's
efforts, however, did not prevent his bishop from putting him up in 398 as a
candidate against John Chrysostom for the throne of Constantinople. Yet two

[29]Socrates *HE* 6.7. The Coptic tradition is preserved in the story of the monk Aphou's visit
to Theophilus of Alexandria (published by E. Drioton, "La discussion d'un moine anthropomorphite Audien avec le patriarche Théophile d'Alexandrie en année 399," in *Revue de l'Orient Chrétien*, 2e série, 10 (=20) (1915–1917), 92–100, 113–128).

[30]M. Richard, "Nouveaux fragments de Théophile d'Alexandrie," in *Nachrichten der
Akademie der Wissenschaften in Göttingen. I. Philologisch-historische Klasse*, Jahrgang 1975,
Nr. 2 (Göttingen: Vandenhoeck & Ruprecht, 1975), n. 3, frgs 3–11, pp. 61–5.

[31]On Isidore's career see J.F. Dechow, *Dogma and Mysticism in Early Christianity. Epiphanius of Cyprus and the Legacy of Origen*, North American Patristic Society Monograph Series
13 (Macon GA: Mercer University Press, 1988), 161–4.

[32]See the account in E.A. Clark, *The Origenist Controversy. The Cultural Construction of
an Early Christian Debate* (Princeton, NJ: Princeton University Press, 1992), 44–50, 105–21.

[33]Jerome *Contra Johannem* 37.

years later Isidore was an object of hatred and fury, the "signifer hereticae factionis."[34] What had happened? Was it only then that Theophilus found out about Isidore's machinations? Perhaps. But once Isidore had withdrawn to Nitria, it would have been brought home to Theophilus that the intellectual leadership there was now hostile to him. In 398 Didymus had died, followed by Evagrius in 399. Each had been the centre of a devoted group. Rufinus describes Didymus as "a lamp shining with divine light" whose circle included monks such as the two Macarii, Isidore (of Scetis) and Pambo.[35] Evagrius, admired by Palladius as a "spirit-bearing" man endowed with the gifts of gnosis, wisdom and the discernment of spirits, was the great theoretician of the spiritual life.[36] With the deaths of these celebrated teachers, the leadership devolved on the four Tall Brothers: Eusebius, Euthymius, Ammonius, and Dioscorus, all of them close associates of Isidore of Alexandria.[37] Ammonius, who had cut off his left ear to avoid being made a bishop by Timothy, presided over a large community of ascetics. Dioscorus was bishop of Hermopolis Parva, appointed by Theophilus in the early 390s. Eusebius and Euthymius had been ordained to the priesthood by Theophilus and invited to Alexandria to assist in church administration, but had withdrawn to Nitria in disgust at the practices they had witnessed.[38] Theophilus could not afford to allow Nitria to become a centre of opposition to him. That is not to say that he wasn't motivated by genuine theological considerations. The statement attributed to him in the story of Aphou (the Coptic monk who went to remonstrate with him after his "anti-anthropomorphite" pastoral letter) that he had been intending to do something about the Origenists for some time, may well be true. From his own letters and homilies it is clear that his theological sympathies lay more with the literalists than the allegorizers. His study of Origen's writings had convinced him, he said, that Origen's views on the subordination of the Son, the embodied life of Adam and Eve as a punishment for pre-corporeal sin, the mortality of the resurrected body, and the cyclical nature of Christ's kingdom were fundamentally pagan. Theophilus had not fought his campaigns against the temples and their cult images only to blur the distinction between Christians and Hellenes.[39] His idea of the

---

[34]Theophilus *Synodal Letter* of CE 400 (=Jerome, *Ep.* 92.3.6).

[35]Rufinus *Apol.* 2.12. Jerome, too, was an admirer, mentioning Didymus in the same breath as Cicero, Plato and Aristotle (*Ep.* 50.2).

[36]*Hist. Laus.* 11.5 and 38.10.

[37]For prosopographical details see Dechow, *Dogma*, 164–9.

[38]Socrates *HE* 6.7.

[39]For a discussion of this aspect see my forthcoming article in *Origeniana Octava*,

church centred on the people gathered round their bishop and participating in the Eucharist, not on a circle of disciples sitting at the feet of a charismatic teacher showing them a higher way to heaven.

But if the boundaries between Christianity and paganism were so clear to Theophilus, how did he come to appoint Synesius bishop of Ptolemais in 410? Synesius, the neoplatonist philosopher and former student of Hypatia, had told Theophilus without any ambiguity that he could not renounce his belief in the preexistence of the soul or the eternity of the cosmos, nor could he accept the popular notion of the resurrection, and would only consent to ordination if he was permitted to be "one who philosophizes in private but mythologizes in public."[40] The situation in the Pentapolis, however, was very different from that of Nitria. Lying a considerable distance to the west of Alexandria, the Pentapolis was the only region within the archbishop's vast domain that had its own metropolitans. Unlike the numerous suffragans of Alexandria, the bishops of the Pentapolis needed to be men of sufficient standing to undertake onerous civic duties. Moreover, the area was troubled by Arianism and under constant threat from a warlike desert people, the Blemmyes. Synesius, who had represented the Pentapolis at Constantinople, did not disappoint Theophilus. He kept his philosophizing to himself and served his people well as their bishop, teaching them, judging their disputes, and organizing the defence of the city against the Blemmyes. But Nitria and Hermopolis Parva were another matter. The Tall Brothers and their followers may have been close to Synesius in some of their views, but they did not keep their philosophizing to themselves. Theophilus could not tolerate so close to Alexandria a circle of ascetics who seemed to hold the faith of ordinary Christians in contempt, especially when the local bishop through whom he would normally have communicated with them was one of their number.

Theophilus's measures seem to have been successful. It is many years before we hear again of problems in Egypt with Origenists. Of Cyril's correspondence only two documents deal directly with Egyptian monasticism, the *Letter to the Monks* of 429 clarifying the use of the term *theotokos*, and the *Letter to Calosirius* of uncertain date instructing the bishop of the Arsenoite nome to tighten up discipline among the monks of Mount Calamon. Both were

"Theophilus and Cyril of Alexandria on the Divine Image. A Consistent Episcopal Policy towards the Origenism of the Desert?"

[40]*Ep.* 105, PG 66, 1485C–1488B; cf. J. Bregman, *Synesius of Cyrene. Philosopher-Bishop*, The Transformation of the Classical Heritage, 2 (Berkeley, CA: University of California Press, 1982), 155.

written in response to reports by visitors to Alexandria of disturbances or "dangerous murmuring." Bishop Calosirius was obviously not as vigilant as Cyril would have wished. The catalogue of errors and abuses that he is to correct includes anthropomorphite ideas of God, the notion that the consecrated elements lose their efficacy if they are retained to the following day, the claim that devotion to prayer precludes manual labour, and intercommunion with Melitians.[41] The Melitians were to remain a problem for another century.[42] The rejection of work in favour of prayer, to which Cyril alludes, may indicate the presence of Messalians, or Euchites, in the monasteries of Mount Calamon. But Origenists are not mentioned. We hear of no reports reaching Alexandria in Cyril's time of disturbances in the monasteries involving them. Quite the contrary, the monks were among the fiercest champions of orthodoxy, putting pressure on the praefectus augustialis in his dispute with Cyril in the early days of his episcopate and then accompanying Cyril *en masse* to the Council of Ephesus in 431. In his commentaries, however, Cyril does take the trouble to refute the idea of the pre-existence of the soul and its punishment by embodied existence, a doctrine held by some (*tines*) that derives from the Greeks.[43] He also defends the reality of the resurrection, claiming that it is a body transformed by the glory of incorruptibility that we receive, not one that is attenuated and ethereal.[44] This suggests that Origenian ideas were current in Cyril's time, though not taught by any specific groups that Cyril could target.

It is often noted that no Greek source mentions Shenoute, even though according to the *Life* by his disciple Besa he had accompanied Cyril to the Council of Ephesus.[45] Shenoute, archimandrite of the White Monastery at

---

[41]L.R. Wickham (ed. and trans.), *Cyril of Alexandria: Select Letters* (Oxford: Clarendon Press, 1983), 214–20.

[42]At least so far as the central authority in Alexandria was concerned. Cf. the three contemporary bishops of Antinoopolis (Arian, Orthodox and Melitian) who seem to have got on amicably enough (Rubenson, *Letters*, p. 115).

[43]Cyril *In Rom.* 6, 6, Pusey III, p. 191.14–192.22. I owe this and the references in the following footnote to M.-O. Boulnois' forthcoming paper in *Origeniana Octava*, "La résurrection des corps selon Cyrille d'Alexandrie: une critique de la doctrine origénienne?"

[44]Cyril *In 1 Cor.* 15, 42, p. 312.3–14; *In Rom.* 8, 23, p. 217.27–218.3; *In Jo.* XII, 1, 1103b; *In Jo.* XII, 1, 1109a; cf. Origen *Com. Psalm.* 1, 5; *Strom.* apud Jerome, *Contra Johannem* 25–6, PL 23, 376C-377A.

[45]Shenoute was a prolific author, the first writer of original works in Coptic, but these do not seem to have circulated beyond his monastery. Although it is surprising that the Greeks ignored him, this does not imply any antagonism on their part. See further J. Timbie, "The State of Research on the Career of Shenoute of Atripe," in B. A. Pearson and J. E. Goehring (eds.), *The Roots of Egyptian Christianity*, Studies in Antiquity and Christianity (Philadelphia: Fortress Press, 1986), 258–70.

Atripe (modern Sohag) in Upper Egypt, was one of the great charismatic monks of the fifth century. In his building projects, his violent campaign against paganism, and his denunciation of heretics and oppressive landlords he stands as a monastic counterpart to Theophilus himself. With Shenoute the transformation from teacher of self-knowledge to standard-bearer of orthodoxy against pagans and heretics is complete. At some time between 444 and 451 Cyril's successor, Dioscorus, appealed to Shenoute to help him coordinate a purge of Origenism in the region of Panopolis (Shmin).[46] He sent him a memorandum for three bishops of the Thebaid on the need to enquire into the presence of heresy in their dioceses, together with a covering letter telling him about the relapse into Origenism of the priest Helias. Shenoute was to have the memorandum, which called for the "books and numerous treatises of the pest (*loimos*) named Origen and other heretics" to be weeded out of the monasteries of the area, to be translated into Coptic. Dioscorus clearly had the greatest confidence in Shenoute, trusting that he would see the matter through with zeal—and keep the local bishops up to the mark.

Shenoute's exhortation *Against the Origenists* may have been composed in response to the patriarchal initiative.[47] In this work, besides condemning recourse to magic and pagan shrines, the author takes issue with Origenist ideas on a number of matters, including their interpretation of the two seraphim of Isaiah 6:2 as representing the Son and the Holy Spirit, and their disapproval of prayer addressed to Jesus. With respect to the passage in Isaiah, Shenoute regards the Origenists' interpretation as equivalent to denying the *homoousion* of the Son and the Spirit and therefore as aligning them with the Arians. Denying the propriety of praying to the Son also implies an Arian position. In refuting it Shenoute presents a magnificent doxology of the holy name. The name of Jesus is to be on the lips of believers in their daily actions and in all the major events of their life. Heresy for Shenoute is not simply an intellectual matter. It is spiritual death, separating the believer from a living relationship with the Saviour.

[46]H. Thompson, "Dioscorus and Shenoute," *Bibliothèque de l'École des Hautes Études: Recueil d'Études Égyptologiques*, 234 (1922), 367–76. The letter is preserved in a 7th cent. Coptic manuscript.

[47]The exhortation was discovered and reconstructed by T. Orlandi. See T. Orlandi, "A Catechesis Against Apocryphal Texts by Shenoute and the Gnostic Texts of Nag Hammadi," *Harvard Theological Review*, 75 (1982), 85–95; idem, *Shenoute. Contra Origenistas. Testo con introduzione e traduzione*, Corpus dei Manuscritti Copti Letterari, (Rome, 1985). Cf. Dechow, *Dogma*, 230–40; Clark, *Controversy*, 151–8; A. Grillmeier with T. Hainthaler, *Christ in Christian Tradition*, vol. 2, part 4, *The Church of Alexandria with Nubia and Ethiopia after 451* (London: Mowbray, 1996), 180–208.

The Christianizing of Egypt called for the unifying of Egyptian Christianity under the bishop of Alexandria. Christianity was to be a faith for the masses, not just for an intellectual élite. During the fourth and fifth centuries the charismatic teachers of the desert became more and more closely identified with the episcopal programme. In tracing this transformation from searcher for *gnosis* to intransigent defender of orthodoxy, we have looked at three situations illustrating significant stages in the process: Athanasius adapting Antony's teaching; Theophilus purging the Nitriotes; and Dioscorus extending the campaign into Upper Egypt through Shenoute. At each stage charismatic monks served the church in an increasingly more direct fashion. But the monks could never be taken for granted. There is an eighth-century *Life* of St John the Little, which contains a telling story.[48] Theophilus is known to have built shrines and pilgrimage centres as part of his offensive against paganism. One of these was a church dedicated to Ananias, Azarias and Misael, the three holy youths cast into the fiery furnace (cf. Dan 3:13–33, LXX). Desiring to have their relics for the *martyrion*, Theophilus sent for Abba John, the superior of Scetis, for an angel had told him in a vision that only Abba John could procure them. On leaving Alexandria after his interview with Theophilus, John fell into an ecstasy, in which he travelled on a cloud to Babylon and spoke with the three youths. They told him that it was not possible for their relics to be translated. Nevertheless, "while the archbishop lives we will spiritually dwell in [the shrine] through signs and wonders."[49] The story closes with a piece of anti-Chalcedonian polemic: "And we will also remain with two of his successors after him, but after this, darkness will cover the whole earth. . . ."[50] Theophilus and his successors may have regulated the opinions of the monks in the first half of the century, but after the Council of Chalcedon spiritual authority, symbolized by John's direct access to the saints in his ecstasy, passed to the monasteries. In their long relationship with the bishops of Alexandria, the Coptic monks had the last word.[51]

❦ · ❦

---

[48]*Life of Saint John the Little* 75, trans. M. Mikhail and T. Vivian, *Coptic Church Review*, 18, nos. 1 and 2 (1997), 47–50.

[49]*John the Little* 49.

[50]*John the Little* 49.

[51]Vivian says that the anti-Chalcedonian polemic (not found in a fragment of the Sahidic version) may be interpolated. But the point still stands.

Music as Religious Propaganda: Venetian Polyphony and a Byzantine Response to the Council of Florence

Dimitri Conomos

AMONG THE 380 Byzantine manuscripts at the Library of the Dochei-ariou Monastery on the Holy Mountain of Athos there are preserved two very remarkable entries in an otherwise conventional anthology of Greek chants. What is so remarkable about these items is, first, that they are written in a polyphonic style (Byzantine music is *par excellence* monophonic plainchant); second, they are accompanied by an informative rubric indicating that the compositions are in the style of Latin chant; third, they were composed in the late fifteenth century by one Ioannes Plousiadenos, a Greek convert to Roman Catholicism resident in Venice in the aftermath of the Council of Florence; and, fourth, their purpose was, I believe, to introduce Western musical idioms into the Greek liturgy, this being part of a larger mission to enforce the so-called union of the Greek and Latin churches that had been ratified at the Council of Florence.

If these features alone do not demonstrate the uniqueness of these compositions, there is one further totally-unexpected aspect that singles them out: Neither their composer, Plousiadenos, nor the scribe of the Docheiariou manuscript, who copied them into his chant anthology around one hundred years after the pieces were written, could have imagined that these works would furnish music historians today with an involuntary record of a fifteenth-century Venetian musical practice that is rarely-encountered in Western musical manuscripts though is known to have existed.

These particulars, then, should explain the multi-thematic nature of the title of this essay. And we can begin our story by turning our attention first to some of the major protagonists—others will turn up later. First we have the propagator, Ioannes Plousiadenos (c. 1429–1500), second his mentor, Cardinal Bessarion (1402–1472) whose teachings constituted the single most important influence on Plousiadenos' religious outlook, and finally, the anonymous scribe of MS Docheiariou 315 who notated the Latin-influenced hymns in the late sixteenth century. Looming in the background is the Council of Ferrara-Florence (1438–1439) and its aborted union of the Greek and Roman churches. Looming also is the fall of Constantinople in 1453 and the subsequent flow of refugees, especially of refugee intellectuals, into the most Byzantine of Italian cities, Venice.

We should actually begin by looking at this background. Let us first consider the Union of Florence which, around fifty years after the Council sessions, provided the inspiration and the raison d'être for the writing of our alleged Latin-influenced polyphony.

After roughly three-and-a-half centuries of schism, preceded by a long period of estrangement, the churches of East and West, Latin and Greek, met in the Council of Florence in the years 1438 and 1439 to discuss unity.[1] Why they met at that time and in Italy was the result of many factors. On the Latin side there was a genuine desire to end the schism and, in an age of Latin councils (Pisa, Constance, Basle), a council seemed an apt means. The Latins also desired to extend the jurisdiction of the Papacy over all Christendom. On their side the Greeks had the same genuine Christian desire for Church union and had always insisted that only a council could achieve that. What made them accept the West as a venue of the council instead of holding out for Constantinople, was the fact that Constantinople, with a population of less than 50,000 inhabitants, was then nearly in its death throes since the Turks had conquered most of its ancient empire and, surrounding it on all sides, were only awaiting an opportunity to deliver the *coup de grâce*. The Byzantine Empire was in most urgent need of help to be able to defend itself. Hope for that lay only in the West. The one institution there that might channel effective aid was the papacy which had launched and directed so many crusades of European Christianity—not all of them particularly agreeable. It was clear, however, that the Byzantine emperor was willing to close his eyes to the plunder of the fourth crusade and to negotiate with the pope. The emperor was

---

[1]Bibliography on the Council is vast. Among the major publications in English are J. Gill, *The Council of Florence* (Cambridge, 1959); idem, *Personalities of the Council of Florence* (Oxford, 1964); J. M. Hussey, *The Orthodox Church in the Byzantine Empire* (Oxford, 1986), 267–86; G. Alberigo (ed.), *Christian Unity: The Council of Ferrara-Florence* (Louvain, 1991).

under the impression that the pope could speak for all Latins and raise immediate military help against the Ottomans. The best way of winning papal support would be the union of the churches. So the Greeks came first to Ferrara
in 1438 and then to Florence in 1439 to a joint council with the Latins to discuss unity. The change from Ferrara to Florence came about first, because of
the outbreak of a plague in Ferrara, and second, because Florence was willing to defray the costs of hosting an expensive council.

Indeed, it was not only the Greek Church that came but also the oriental
Church, for the Council of Florence was, to all appearances, the most ecumenical of all ecumenical councils. Emperor John VIII Palaeologus attended
and Joseph, Patriarch of Constantinople, also present in person, was accompanied by twenty Greek metropolitans, as well as bishops from Russia, Georgia and Moldowallachia. Moreover, five of the Greeks were procurators of
the oriental patriarchates, nominated by these patriarchates themselves.

A decree of union, finally signed on 6 July 1439, was the result, for agreement had been reached by the delegates on the main doctrinal points dividing the two churches—purgatory, papal primacy, the use of leavened or
unleavened Bread in the Eucharist and, more than anything else, the *filioque*—its legitimacy as an addition to the creed and its orthodoxy as a doctrine. Only Markos Eugenikos, Metropolitan of Ephesus who was later
canonised by the Orthodox Church, refused to sign. He represented the prevailing mentality of the Orthodox populations in the East. For the Union of
Florence, though celebrated throughout Western Europe (bells were rung in
all the churches of England) proved no more of a reality in the East than its
predecessor at Lyons. Emperor John VIII and his successor Constantine XI
both remained loyal to the Union; but they were powerless to enforce it on
their subjects and did not even dare to proclaim it publicly in Constantinople
until 1452. The Grand Duke Lucas Notaras had remarked: "I would rather
see the Moslem turban in the midst of the city than the Latin mitre."[2]

The bitter memory of the Latin occupation of a part of the Byzantine
Empire during the fourth crusade (1204–1261), even if ignored by John VIII,
had left a general distaste for and rejection of the politics and culture of "the
Franks" (as they were called) and the remarks of a fifteenth-century Russian
writer, attacking the Council of Florence, typify the prevailing negative
Orthodox attitude to Western Christianity. His main arguments against the
Latins are typically Russian. They have nothing to do with doctrine or theol-
ogy; they are about aesthetics:

[2]T. Ware, *The Orthodox Church*, 3rd edn (London, 1972), 81.

What have you seen of worth among the Latins? They do not even know how to venerate in the Church of God. They raise their voices as the fools, and their singing is a discordant wail. They have no idea of beauty or reverence in worship, for they strike trombones, blow horns, use organs, wave their hands, trample with their feet, and do many other irreverent and disorderly things which bring joy to the devil.[3]

We can only wonder in which Florentine church the writer had such an experience!

But it is true, of course, that the Muscovites had consistently opposed doctrinal agreement with the Latin Church, and the acceptance of the Florentine Union by the highest authorities of Byzantium came as a severe shock. This marked a turning point between Muscovy and Byzantium. Four-and-a-half centuries of unwavering loyalty to the Church of Constantinople had left them unprepared for this embarrassing betrayal.

However, although popular resistance prevented the union from materialising, there were among the Greek intellectuals, well into the sixteenth century, a small number of Latin sympathisers. One of them was the Metropolitan of Nicaea, Bessarion—a man of outstanding abilities and energy whose brilliant mind and powers of rhetoric were to be of singular importance not only in convincing all of the Orthodox delegation in Florence to accept Roman doctrines (that is, all but Markos of Ephesus), but also in shaping the career and activities of our composer, Ioannes Plousiadenos. Bessarion was the most prominent of the Byzantine émigrés who took up residence in Italy during the fifteenth century, and an appreciation of his qualities and influence will shed considerable light on the cultural and intellectual milieu in which Plousiadenos spent his formative years.

Bessarion has many claims to fame: He was a humanist, diplomat, philosopher, patriot, scholar, reformer of monasteries, theologian, Orthodox bishop turned Catholic cardinal, twice candidate for the papacy, and eventually Latin Patriarch of Constantinople. But he is best known as the apostle of union between the Latin and the Greek Churches. He was born in Trebizond in 1402 and educated in Constantinople. In 1423, at the age of 21, he took the monastic habit and developed a wide reputation as an orator. Eight years later, in 1431, he was ordained a priest after which we learn that he left the capital for the Peloponnese. There, at Mistra, he studied under George Gemistos

---

[3]Quoted in N. Zernov, *Moscow, The Third Rome* (London, 1937), 37.

Plethon (1431–36), the great exponent of Platonic philosophy, as a result of which Bessarion, too, became an ardent Platonist.[4] In 1436, he was called back to Constantinople to be the head of the Monastery of Saint Basil, and in the following year he was elected to the see of Nicaea. At the same time, three other monks with a reputation for learning were also consecrated bishops: Markos Eugenikos for Ephesus, Isidore for Kiev and Dionysios for Sardis. The election of all of these was not unconnected with the negotiations for a council of union between East and West, then reaching their climax, for, unlike the general level of learning of the oriental hierarchy (which left much to be desired), they were outstanding among the Greek clergy for their philosophical and theological ability.[5]

On this point it is well worth noting that in the early fifteenth century, the city of Constantinople was not only in a state of political decline but also intellectual decline. Shortly before the Council of Florence, the future Patriarch Gennadius Scholarius assessed the level of the capital's élite and was appalled. He found that only a few people (he says three or four) were devoting themselves to the pursuit of learning and that even these were concerned with appearances rather than substance. And when the Byzantines applied the Latin yardstick to themselves, they found their own culture wanting—confrontation with the West led some to recognise Latin cultural superiority.[6]

After 1439, when Bessarion had been created a cardinal by Pope Eugenius IV, he spoke bluntly to Emperor Constantine XII. The culture of the Byzantines, so high in the past, had sunk so low, he said, that they were considered ignorant by foreign powers. The wisdom and technological know-how of the Byzantines had disappeared, but it survived to a great extent among the Latins. In order to raise the level of culture, education and technology in

[4]See below ftn. 11.

[5]For further reading on Bessarion, see D. J. Geanakoplos, *Greek Scholars in Venice: Studies in the Dissemination of Greek Learning from Byzantium to Western Europe* (Cambridge, Mass., 1962); J. Gill, "Was Bessarion a Conciliarist or a Unionist before the Council of Florence?" in *Collectanes Byzantina* (Orientalia Christiana Analecta 204; Rome, 1977); idem, *The Council of Florence* (Cambridge, 1959); J. Harris, *Greek Emigrés in the West, 1400–1520* (Camberley, 1995); A. Keller, "A Byzantine Admirer of 'Western' Progress: Cardinal Bessarion," *Cambridge Historical Journal*, 11 (1953–55), 343–48; L. D. Reynolds and N. G. Wilson, *Scribes and Scholars: A Guide to the Transmission of Greek and Latin Literature*, 3rd edn (Oxford 1991); K. M. Setton, "The Byzantine Background to the Italian Renaissance," *Transactions and Proceedings of the American Philosophical Society*, 3 (1956), 1–76; J. W. Taylor, "Bessarion the Mediator," ibid. 55 (1924), 120–27; N. G. Wilson, *From Byzantium to Italy: Greek Studies in the Italian Renaissance* (London and Baltimore, 1992), esp. 57–67.

[6]I. Ševčenko, "The Decline of Byzantium seen through the Eyes of its Intellectuals," *Dumbarton Oaks Papers*, 15 (1961), 169–86, esp. 175–77.

the Peloponnese (under Venetian rule in the fifteenth century), Bessarion rec-
ommended that Constantine should invite Latin specialists there and send a
small group of Greek students to Italy. These half dozen students—he specifies three or four—should not be too young nor should they be too old, for
otherwise it would be too difficult for them to learn a foreign language. Their
programme of study should be technological: metallurgy, mechanics, arma-
ments, shipbuilding. The maintenance of what we would today call consumer
goods might be looked into also, but this was less important.[7] All of Bessarion's proposals must have sounded strange to some members of the Byzantine upper classes. When they were young, they had to memorise the elegant
periods of Aelius Aristides and Libanus in order to qualify for important positions—not a manual on shipbuilding.[8] Therefore Bessarion had to temper his
advice: he explained that *no loss of face was involved in learning from the
Latins*. First of all, the Byzantines would *only be receiving back what they
had given them in the past*.[9] Second, it was silly to be ashamed of acquiring
wisdom. If the Latins had been ashamed of receiving culture from the Byzantines long before, they would never have reached the cultural eminence they
were now enjoying.[10] As an interpreter of ideas between the Greek East and
the Latin West, Bessarion takes the prize. He was, as Lorenzo Valla describes
him, *Latinorum graecissimus, Graecorum latinissimus*.

"No loss of face in learning from the Latins . . . ," said Bessarion; "the
Byzantines would only be receiving back what they had given the Latins in
the past . . . Without the absorption of Byzantine culture the Latins would
never have reached their present cultural eminence." Statements such as these
made a deep impression on Greek refugee intellectuals like Ioannes Plousiadenos, a member of Bessarion's academy in Rome (a small group that gathered around the future cardinal). They stimulated Bessarion's compatriots
into a flurry of activity. Some offered more of Greek learning to the West
by producing accurate translations into Latin of unknown ancient Greek
authors,[11] others brought Western culture to the East—like Ioannes Plousiadenos with his new hymns in the Latin polyphonic tradition.

[7]Bessarion, *Letter to Constantine Palaeologus*, ed. S. Lambros; cited by Ševčenko, "Decline
of Byzantium," 177.

[8]Ševčenko, "Decline of Byzantinum," 177.

[9]In both instances the italics are mine.

[10]Ševčenko, "Decline of Byzantinum," 177.

[11]Bessarion himself translated into Latin Aristotle's *Metaphysics* (the standard Latin translation until well into the nineteenth century), Xenophon's *Memorabilia*, the metaphysical essay
of Theophrastus, and among other works he wrote a treatise "In Calumniatorem Platonis,"
directed against the Aristotelian views of George of Trebizond.

In 1453, when Constantinople fell to the Turks, Bessarion was in Bologna. Thereafter one of his chief preoccupations was to aid his fellow countrymen by fostering every prospect, however faint, of rousing Western princes to a crusade against the conquerors,[12] and by assisting unfortunate Greeks—some by providing ransoms to buy them or their families from captivity, others by receiving them in Italy and either giving them work to do or finding them a means of subsistence. This patriotic activity is also a feature which will soon be dramatically displayed in the life of Ioannes Plousiadenos.

Yet it was not only the military threat posed by the Turks that worried Bessarion, but the realisation that their capture of Constantinople might finally extinguish the inheritance of Greek Classical literature that had been preserved for so long under the Byzantine empire. According to his own account, after 1453 he embarked on a systematic rescue mission, collecting manuscripts of the Greek Classics to preserve them for posterity. His servants were sent as far afield as Constantinople and Trebizond to purchase Greek manuscripts, and a small army of scribes was employed to make copies of these works, both in Italy and in the Venetian colony of Crete.[13] The rich library that he acquired he bequeathed before he died to the Senate of Venice (which housed a public library for the preservation and dissemination of knowledge) where it became the foundation of the Marciana. He did this as a token of gratitude to the city of Venice for its constant goodwill towards him and his compatriots and in order to keep his collection of books together and make it more accessible to Greeks in Italy. He had between 800 and 900 manuscripts, some 600 of which were Greek. The Renaissance in Italy owed much to the Venetian link with Byzantium. Venice was a gateway to the East. It was also a gateway from the Greek East to the western world; and through this gateway much of the material flowed, in the form of manuscripts and scholars, for the revival of Greek learning in the West and for the Italian Renaissance.

At the council discussions in Florence, Bessarion began by demonstrating his distaste for western scholasticism and opposed the Latins vigorously, especially over the *filioque* issue. Gradually, however, he was shaken by their arguments and early in 1439 he ended up being convinced of the soundness of the Latin position. Eventually, not only did he believe that Greek and Latin

[12]In 1471 Bessarion published his *Oration to the Leaders of Italy Regarding the Imminent Perils*, in which he urged them to unite against the common enemy of all Christians.

[13]Bessarion himself contributed to the process both by copying manuscripts and by scouring Italian monastic libraries in search of long-forgotten codices. He is alleged to have scored a notable success in the Monastery of San Niccolò di Casole near Otranto, where he discovered the texts of works by Colluthus and Quintus Smyrnaeus.

theology were not incompatible but also that the West had much to offer the East in the way of culture and learning. Bessarion's *Dogmatic Discourse on the Union*, addressed to the Byzantine delegation, urged them to accept union with the Latin Church, the authority of the pope, and the Western creed with its controversial addition of the *filioque*, in the hope that military aid against the Turks would follow. When agreement was finally reached, Bessarion was accorded the honour of reading out the decree of union in Greek in the cathedral of Florence on 6 July 1439.

The year 1463 saw Bessarion in Venice as papal legate and in the same year he was made Latin Patriarch of Constantinople. When he died in 1472, neither of the two causes to which his main energies had been devoted succeeded. The union of the Churches was rendered largely ineffective by the resistance of the majority of the population in what remained of the Byzantine Empire, while the intimately related question of raising military support in western Europe to help defend Byzantium against the Turks, an uphill battle in any circumstance, faltered all the more as the Greeks' attitude became clearer.

In many ways the life of Ioannes Plousiadenos followed the same pattern as that of his patron.[14] He too was a scholar and master of many disciplines: hymnography, theology, calligraphy, music composition, singing and theory, diplomacy, and manuscript copying. Like Bessarion, he was a monk, priest, and finally Bishop of Methone who embraced Catholicism after reading and copying the acts of the Council of Florence. He was also a staunch patriot. The exact date of his birth is not known from any source but in one of his works he says that at the time of the Council of Florence he was still a child—not yet ten years of age. It is safe to assume that he was born around 1429. We do know that he was ordained as a priest in 1455, so the date 1429 for his birth seems quite reasonable. He was born in Crete and at first, like most Cretans, he was an anti-unionist. We know little of his activities as a youth but it seems clear that in Crete, which had been under Venetian control since

---

[14]Biographical information on Ioannes (Joseph) Plousiadenos may be found in numerous sources, including L. Petit, "Joseph de Méthone," *Dictionnaire de théologie catholique*, 8, ed. A. Vancant and E. Magenot (Paris, 1925), 1526–9; G. Hofmann, "Wie stand es mit der Frage der Kircheneinheit auf Kreta im XV. Jahrhundert?" *Orientalia Christiana Periodica*, 10 (1944), 106–11; N.Tomadakis, «Μιχαὴλ Καλοφρενᾶς Κρής, Μητροφάνης Β΄ καὶ ἡ πρὸς τὴν ἕνωσιν τῆς Φλωρεντίας ἀντίθεσις τῶν Κρητῶν», Ἐπετερὶς Ἑταιρεία Βυζαντινῶν Σπουδῶν, 21 (1951), 110–39, esp. 136–9; M. Candal, "La 'Apologia' del Plusiadeno a favor del Concilio de Florencia," *Orientalia Christiana Periodica*, 21 (1955), 36–57; M. Manoussakas, "Recherche sur la vie de Jean Plousiadénos (Joseph de Méthone) (1429?-1500)," *Revue des Études Byzantines*, 17 (1959), 28–51; S. G. Papadopoulos, Ἰωσήφ, Θρησκευτικὴ καὶ Ἠθικὴ Ἐγκυκλοπαίδεια, 7 (Athens, 1965), 117–119.

1204, he learned Latin and ancient Greek and had acquired a sound theological education, including lessons in chanting and notating Church music.

At that time in Crete there were centres of learning, particularly in monastic institutions, and there were also frequent contacts not only between the island and Venice but also Constantinople. In fact, even before 1453, the Capital's few intellectuals, realising that the Turkish onslaught was imminent, sought refuge in Venetian Crete. More, of course, followed after the fall. There, under an increasingly enlightened Venetian government, they could speak their own language, practise their own religion, and escape the blight of Turkish oppression.

It is quite likely that Plousiadenos spent several years of his youth in Constantinople and may even have been present at the final clash between the Byzantines and the Ottomans in 1453. After 1455, he became one of the twelve Byzantine priests who officially supported the decisions of Florence in the celebrated debates that followed the council meetings between the Greek anti- and pro-unionists. As a result, he and his companions were generally boycotted as religious and national traitors. In an encyclical dialogue he tried in vain to justify the group's position, and eventually they had to ask for financial aid from Venice and from the pope.

Plousiadenos must have known about Bessarion from his study of the acts of the council but their first meeting would have taken place between c.1466 and 1467 when Bessarion, now Latin Patriarch of Constantinople, selected Plousiadenos as "head of the churches" *(archon ton ekklesion)* in the orient and as *vice-protopapas*—a position that he held until 1481. He spent considerable time in Italy, chiefly in Venice with Bessarion and joined the latter's academy of Greek expatriate intellectuals.

A competent and diligent scribe, Plousiadenos was kept busy in Venice copying manuscripts of the acts of the Council of Florence to enlighten the Greeks, and some other works. Several of his autographs from this period survive today. They demonstrate a fine, accurate hand with much attention to detail and presentation. In 1492, he was elected to the see of Methone in the Peloponnese (also a Venetian colony and therefore a bastion of Greek Catholicism) and took the name "Joseph." In 1497, he visited Venice again and in 1498 we learn that he chanted the Gospel in Greek, and in the Greek manner, at the Papal Mass in Rome. He was about to visit his birthplace, Crete, in 1500, when he was informed of the impending Turkish attack on Methone. Like Bessarion, he was a true patriot; he hastened to the Peloponnese to provide whatever assistance he could, and, with Cross in hand, was killed there by the onrushing Turks.

Plousiadenos is best known for his constant support of the union of Florence, notably in his *Defensio synodi Florentinae*, a patristic defence of the five main elements in the decree of union, written after 1455 and often mistakenly printed under the name of Gennadius Scholarius.[15] He propagated his admiration for the Roman Church in the *Sermo apologeticus pro synodo Florentina*, the *Disceptatio de differentius inter Graecos et Latinos*, and in poetry, homilies and other minor works, most of which are published in the Patrologia Graeca.[16]

In 1995 I came across some unpublished compositions by Ioannes Plousiadenos when visiting Mount Athos. MS Koutloumousi 448, written in the early 17th century, has an interesting hymn to the Mother of God on folio 77r. It is made up of nine stanzas in lines of fifteen syllables. The initial letters of each stanza form the acrostic *BESSARION (BHCCAPIΩN)*, and an accompanying rubric reads: "By Ioannes Plousiadenos, the words and the music; I composed this for the Cardinal."[17] The hymn text and its music were therefore written between 1466 and 1472. Their presence in this manuscript shows that Plousiadenos' works were still being copied and sung in the seventeenth century.

There also exist by him two parahymnographical kanons.[18] The one, entitled "Kanon to Saint Thomas Aquinas," exalts the illustrious Western theologian. And the other, of special interest to our subject—the "Kanon for the Eighth Ecumenical Council which assembled in Florence"—is modelled on the musical, metrical and rhythmic patterns of one of the Sunday or Resurrection Kanons in Mode IV Plagal by the eighth-century hymnographer, Saint John Damascene. Neither of these works would have been welcomed in the Greek Churches of the East. The latter triumphantly celebrates the outcome of the Council of Florence where Orthodox acceptance of the *filioque* was allegedly secured (see below). Both kanons were designed for the Greek congregations in Venice, and like our polyphonic musical items, both belong to Plousiadenos' propaganda literature which was calculated to revive enthusiasm for a cause that was doomed almost from the outset:

---

[15]This is how it appears in Migne, PG 159:1109–1393.

[16]PG 159:1024–93 and 960–1024 respectively.

[17]Τοῦ Ἰωάννου τοῦ Πλουσιαδημοῦ τοῦτο ἐποίησα διὰ τὸν καρδινάλιον.

[18]A kanon is a hymnographic complex of eight canticles, based on the Old Testament canticles, which is sung during the Byzantine morning office.

Plousiadenos: Kanon for the Council of Florence

Canticle III: (Heirmos)

O Towers of piety, O defenders of the Churches. You shepherds and teachers of the universe. Today the theologians have piously proclaimed that the Holy Spirit clearly proceeds from both the Father and the Son.

Canticle V:

We loyally honour this venerable and holy Council devoutly assembled in Florence by the Holy Spirit Who has guided the irremediably-sundered Churches to unity.[19]

It is interesting that Plousiadenos borrows a familiar melody and poetic metre—those of St John Damascene—in order to propagate his views. In so doing he follows an ancient practice, one which is known at least as early as the fourth century in Syria where Saint Ephraim (c. 306–373) trained choirs of virgins and boys to sing his Orthodox hymns that were based on the metre and melodies of the heretical psalms of Bardaisan. Bardaisan popularised false doctrines through his greatly admired chants and by way of retribution Ephraim wrote substitute texts to match the heretic's melodies.[20] It is also reported that Saint John Chrysostom introduced processional chants in Constantinople in the fourth century, using the same technique, to counter the Arian innovation of popular marches and songs with erroneous teachings. This rather effortless replacement, known as *contrafactum* in music or *prosomoion* in liturgics, is no doubt older than the fourth century and continues throughout music history even to our own times. People enjoy a good, familiar tune—Plousiadenos knew that. And to ordinary folk, while the teachings in the text are of secondary bearing, through dint of repetition, the words and their meaning remain in the mind and germinate in the subconscious. Perhaps Plousiadenos knew that as well.

[19]The kanon to Saint Thomas Aquinas is published in R. Cantarello, "Canone graeco inedito di Giuseppe vescovo di Methoni (Giovanni Plousiadeno: sec. 15) in onore di San Tommaso d'Aquino," *Archivum Fratrum Praedicatorum*, 4 (1934), 145–85, see 151 ff. That for the Eighth Ecumenical Council (ed. Migne, PG 159:1095–1101) forms part of a discussion of this genre of Greek medieval literature in K. Mitsakis, "Byzantine and Modern Greek Parahymnography," *Studies in Eastern Chant*, 5, ed. D. Conomos (New York, 1990), 9–76.

[20]See the article, "Ephraem Syrus, St" in *The Oxford Dictionary of the Christian Church*, 3rd edn (Oxford, 1977), 551.

Let us return, once more, to Venice. It was a place that had attracted Greeks for many hundreds of years and, in fact, until the ninth century the patron saint of Venice was not Mark but the Greek Theodore. In the eleventh century, Byzantine workmen were summoned by the doge to embellish—perhaps to construct entirely, the Church of San Marco. Venetian-Byzantine contacts became more frequent in the late twelfth century as a result of the growth of the large Venetian colony in Constantinople, numbering some ten to twenty thousand. So close did relations between the two peoples become that intermarriage was common and the Venetians at home adopted Byzantine habits of dress, Greek titles, and ceremonies, and even introduced Greek words into the Venetian dialect. With the advance of the Ottomans in the East, many Greeks fled to Venice, including the intellectuals that had made a first stop in Venetian-held Crete. From Crete, Ioannes Plousiadenos' birthplace, it was an easy step to Venice, and it was not long before the solid nucleus of a Greek-speaking community had been established there. The Greek refugees who had lost their homeland found there a home away from home—some said "another Byzantium." The community there offered them a sense of security; newcomers automatically belonged to it by virtue of speech, race and religion. From 1456, Greek liturgies were being celebrated in Venetian churches and by the year 1470 the number of Greeks in Venice had risen to over four thousand. Thanks to Bessarion, who was the spiritual head of the colony from 1463, Venice displaced Florence as the leading centre of Hellenic studies in Europe.

As we have already learned, Bessarion was as much concerned to impart to his Latin co-religionists the intellectual and philosophical legacy of the ancient Greek world as he was to bring the contemporary sophistication, culture and education of the west to his compatriots. Ioannes Plousiadenos, one of his most faithful disciples, followed him in these endeavours. Not only did he copy out the ancient authors for the benefit of the west, but he also wrote out the acts of the Florentine Council, composed sermons, delivered orations and apologies, and was the author of a new hymnography that propagated the Latin doctrines which few were willing to accept. Now for the first time we observe Plousiadenos' involvement in musical composition to serve the same end. In an attempt to introduce a western sound into the Greek Churches, Plousiadenos conducted an unusual experiment. Using Byzantine musical notation, he wrote two communion chants in two simultaneous voice parts—an altogether unprecedented act in the East—and in a style only rarely seen in western manuscripts.

The first, a setting in Mode IV Plagal of Psalm 148:1 ("Praise the Lord from the heavens") is the communion verse for Sundays (see Example 1). It is preceded by the remark: "A double melody according to the chant of the Latins" (Διπλοῦν μέλος κατὰ τὴν τῶν ἑλατίνων [*sic*.] ψαλτικήν), and is written out in close score with both lines of notation—the upper voice in black ink and the lower in red—inscribed above the text. Perhaps one should not refer to these two voices as upper and lower in a strict sense, since the red neumes very frequently sail over the black. The second is a setting of John 14:9 with 6:56 ("He who has seen me has seen the Father and he who eats my flesh and drinks my blood dwells in me and I in him") the communion for Mid-Pentecost (Example 2).[21] Following a different format, the scribe has written out the music in two separate voice parts, as in Example 2a; the part for the lower voice in Mode IV Plagal is entitled "to keimenon" (τὸ κείμενον = "the text") and that for the upper voice in Mode IV authentic is given as "to tenōri" (τὸ τενώρει = "the tenor")—a curious reversal of normal nomenclature.[22] (For convenience this has been rewritten in close score as Example 2b.) Below this arrangement the scribe has noted: "This verse is chanted by two domestikoi[23] together; one sings the keimenon and the other the tenōri." (Ὁ αὐτὸς στίχος ψάλλεται ὑπὸ δύο δομεστίκων ὁμοῦ καὶ λέγει ὁ εἷς τὸ κείμενον καὶ ὁ ἄλλος τὸ τενώρει.) These words do not belong to Byzantine musical terminology; they are borrowed from the west. "Keimenon" may be a translation of "motetus," which in early western polyphony was the texted line above a slow-moving bass part. Here the context is unusual for such an explanation, but terms are known to change their meaning when transferred from culture to culture. "Tenōri" is also foreign and its application here as "tenor" is interesting. In early western polyphony, "tenor" refers to a *lower* line above which one or more voices are juxtaposed. Here our tenor is sometimes higher, sometimes lower, and sometimes in unison.

Now Plousiadenos may have been the earliest, but he was not the only Latinophile musician among the Greeks. A mid-sixteenth-century manuscript, now in the Athens National Library (no. 2401) preserves two more two-voiced Sunday communions on folios 328r and 216v, composed in a somewhat similar style of polyphony to the works of Plousiadenos by the

---

[21]MS Docheiariou 315, fols 66v-67r. These unusual items are noted in G. Stathis, *Τὰ χειρό-γραφα βυζαντινῆς μουσικῆς. Ἅγιον Ὄρος*, 1 (Athens, 1975), 352; Stathis also provides excellent colour facsimiles on pp.350–1. Plousiadenos' musical compositions are preserved in very many music anthologies, but these are the only known examples of polyphony by him.

[22]But see p. 132 and ftn. 28 below.

[23]That is, precentors.

EXAMPLE 1: Ioannes Plousiadenos, Psalm 148:1; Mount Athos,
Monastery of Docheiariou, MS 315, fol. 66ᵛ

Rubric: Διπλοῦν μέλος κατὰ τὴν τῶν ἐλατίνων [sic] ψαλτικήν
("A double melody according to the chant of the Latins").

EXAMPLE 2: Ioannes Plousiadenos, John 14:9, 6:56; Mount Athos, Monastery of Docheiariou, MS 315, fol. 67ʳ

Rubric: Ὁ αὐτὸς στίχος ψάλλεται ὑπο δομεστίκων [sic] ὁμοῦ· καὶ λέγει ὁ εἷς τὸ κείμενον καὶ ὁ ἄλλος τὸ τενώρει ("This verse is chanted by two domestikoi together; one sings the keimenon and the other the tenōri").

lampadarios, Manuel Gazes.[24] That is to say, both lines essentially describe the same melodic profile, except that the voices are separated by perfect intervals, at least for most of the time. The first piece (Example 3) carries the rubric: "This communion is sung [by] two [chanters]; one [follows] the black [neumes] in Mode IV [Authentic], and the other the red [neumes] in Mode IV Plagal." (τὸ τοιοῦτον κοινωνικὸν ψάλλοντο [sic.] δύο: ὁ εἷς τὰ μαῦρα εἰς ἦχον δ´: ὁ δὲ ἄλλος τὰ κόκκινα εἰς ἦχον πλ. δ´) The second (Example 4) bears the simple statement: "The red [neumes are] in the fourth plagal [mode]." (Τὸ κόκκινον εἰς τὸν πλάγιον τοῦ τετάρτου.)

Very little is known about this late-fifteenth/early-sixteenth century composer. Other manuscripts that transmit his purely Byzantine-style monophonic chants refer to him as a lampadarios, that is, leader of the left choir; but there is no mention of the city or church in which he sang. There are, however, two possible Western connections. First in MS 244 of the Leimonos Monastery on Lesbos, a sixteenth-century music anthology, there is preserved a doxology composed by Manuel Gazes which was commissioned, it says, by Leonardo, the overlord of Santa Mavra. Santa Mavra was the name given to the island of Lefkas in the late fifteenth century, and of the three overlords named Leonardo who ruled there, it must have been Leonardo II of the Tocco family who requested the work from Gazes. He was a patron of the arts, a friend of the last Byzantine emperor, and obviously attracted to eastern chant. The second possible connection with the West is evident in Gazes' two settings of the Greek Credo—one complete and one partial. The complete version is in a manuscript dated 1788, Θ 162 fol. 339v of the Great Lavra, Mount Athos; and the incomplete one is in the seventeenth-century music anthology MS sup. gr. 1171 fol. 51v in the Bibliothèque Nationale, Paris. It is interesting to note how this latter version omits the first section of the Creed and begins the musical notation at the critical article beginning: "And in the Holy Spirit . . ." It does not contain the *filioque*. While it is known that the Greeks occasionally sang the Creed before the ninth century, it is generally assumed that in medieval times, as today, it was simply recited by the whole congregation.[25] Gazes' settings in Mode IV and Mode I Plagal are without precedent in the East and it may be that they were composed under western

[24]Attention to Gazes' works was first paid by Michael Adamis, "An Example of Polyphony in Byzantine Music of the Late Middle Ages," *Report of the Eleventh International Musicological Society Congress, Copenhagen, 1971, 2,* ed H. Glahn, S. Sørenson and P. Ryom (Copenhagen, 1972), 737–47.

[25]For further details on the music of the Creed in the East, see K. Levy, "The Byzantine Sanctus and its Modal Tradition in East and West," *Annales Musicologiques,* 6 (1958–63), 40–2.

musical influence. Alternatively, having heard the Latins sing the Credo, he may have tried his hand at setting the Greek text. But neither the doxology nor the creed was set polyphonically: Gazes, following Plousiadenos' example, accorded this innovation solely to the psalmody of the communion antiphon. He also follows him in confining his polyphonic experiments to the fourth mode. As in the examples by Plousiadenos, Gazes here uses two signs and two inks—black for the upper voice and red for the lower—presumably to avoid confusion. Taken together, the four communion pieces constitute remarkable and unique evidence of attempts by musicians of the Greek East to compose in a western tradition.

There are a few questions that arise in connection with these four compositions. Which Latin tradition were they emulating? Were the melodies themselves of western origin? How do they compare in style with the known products of contemporary Italian sacred polyphony? How do they differ from Byzantine chant of the same period—or, to put it another way, from the two composers' other compositions in the conventional Greek style? Do they shed any new light on musical developments in either the West or the East?

A superficial glance at the examples reveals that we are dealing with a fairly uncomplicated species of polyphony—if this can be called polyphony at all—for the two lines are not contrapuntal but homophonic and homorhythmic. Except for a few isolated instances of contrary motion and the overlapping of parts, the two melodic lines in each piece travel along identical paths and are, for all practical purposes, the same. It is, therefore, erroneous to believe that one voice actually accompanies or is subordinate to the other. Each is a fully, self-contained melody, the two quite obviously written together, but operating within a rudimentary tonal logic. The mellifluous flow and melismatic treatment of the individual lines compare favourably with other ornate communion settings in the fourth mode that I have already examined;[26] they share many features with their common profile. This music belongs quite recognisably to the prevailing Byzantine kalophonic idiom that came into vogue at the beginning of the fourteenth century and is characterised by its embellishments and wide-ranging vocal lines. What I am suggesting here is that these are not cases of melodic borrowings from the West; as individual lines they have their place in the late Byzantine repertory. What is so completely unusual are the heard sounds resulting from chant that operates simultaneously at two sonic levels.

[26]D. Conomos, *The Late Byzantine and Slavonic Communion Cycle* (Dumbarton Oaks Oaks Studies, 21; Washington DC, 1985), esp. 82–170.

EXAMPLE 3: Manuel Gazēs, Psalm 148:1; Athens,
National Library of Greece, MS 2401, fol. 328ʳ

Rubric: Τὸ τοιοῦτον κοινωνικὸν ψάλλοντο [sic] δύο· ὁ εἷς τὰ μαῦρα εἰς ἦχον δ´·
ὁ δὲ ἄλλος τὰ κόκκινα εἰς ἦχον πλ. δ´ ("This communion is sung by two
chanters; one follows the black neumes in mode 4 authentic, and the other
the red neumes in mode 4 plagal").

EXAMPLE 4: Manuel Gazēs, Psalm 148:1; Athens,
National Library of Greece, MS 2401, fol. 216ᵛ

Rubric: Τὸ κόκκινον εἰς τὸν πλάγιον τοῦ τετάρτου
("The red neumes are in the fourth plagal mode").

Did these sounds resemble the kind of polyphony sung at the end of the fifteenth-century in Italy? In the late Italian quattrocento, we know that both monophonic plainsong and polyphony served the Mass and the Offices. Within polyphonic practice, two distinct repertories existed side by side. One was artistic, sophisticated and complex in its nature, typically committed to writing and informed by a spirit of experiment, exploration and change. The other was modest, simple and unassuming in its nature, passed along by example—essentially a performing tradition which only now and then is documented in writing. It is to the latter repertory, the simple, two-part, note-against-note type, that our Greek polyphonic pieces most readily relate. Where they differ is that the Greek examples are not based on pre-existing liturgical chant—a *cantus firmus*. Both voices are the creation of the composer.

According to the definition of the fifteenth-century western writer and theoretician, Prosdocimus of Beldemandis, this category of common polyphony was understood as *cantus planus binatum* (= "plainchant twice"), an expression that captures the inherent paradox and that may have served as the origin of the explanatory heading above Plousiadenos' Sunday communion: *diploun melos* (binatim cantus), "a *double melody* according to the chant of the Latins." Does this simple polyphony exist in western musical manuscripts? Can we make comparisons with these Greek experiments? According to Kenneth Levy, the testimony of this style in the West is meagre and it is destined to remain so for the very reason that improvisation and oral transmission sufficed. The simpler polyphony had very little cause to be preserved in manuscript, but when pieces of this kind make an appearance they are interesting both for what they say in themselves and for what they say about the hidden layers of improvised practice. Above all there is the fine line to be observed between what is written in books and what that written testimony says—or does not say—about the unwritten practice. In the end it will still prove difficult to glimpse the improvised practice, for each "improvised" example in manuscript is a contradiction, its testimony suspect because of the act that has put it on record.[27]

Both Plousiadenos and Gazes came to this tradition of polyphony as outsiders—it was not a part of their cultural, religious or artistic heritage. In fact, musicians in Byzantium were probably oblivious to the rise of polyphony in the West, particularly after the formal break between the two churches in the eleventh century. Our composers were obviously delighted by a sound that

---

[27]Kenneth Levy, "Italian Duecento Polyphony: Observations on an Umbrian Fragment," *Rivista Italiana di Musicologica*, 10 (1975), 11, ftn. 10.

was for them both new and engaging. Why did they compose these pieces? With Plousiadenos, in the light of his background and conversion, we can readily assume that his motivation stemmed from propaganda. Perhaps it was the same for Gazes; or perhaps he simply wanted to broaden his musical output. Can we rely on the authenticity of their witness to a western oral practice? I think we can, precisely because individuals who wish to propagate doctrine through the medium of an art form, having themselves been convinced of its veracity, and coming to the art as foreigners, would feel impelled to duplicate the tradition live and unadulterated rather than make creative departures from it. Ioannes Plousiadenos was a skilled musician and he must have imitated what he thought to be music worth imitating.

Evidence for this approach can be produced from a parallel episode in a much earlier period of sacred music's history. This time we see Latin musicians undertaking the translation of the heard sounds of Byzantine hymns into western neumes which would then be translated into the heard sounds of western performances. In the tenth and eleventh centuries we observe Latin renditions of Greek hymn texts that are accompanied by transcriptions of the Greek melodies into Latin notation. There are, for example, the western "Veterem hominem" antiphons for Epiphany (textual and musical translations of the Greek *Ton palaion anthropon*) and the Good Friday antiphon "O quando in cruce" (the Greek *Ote tō stavrō*). What they tell us with remarkable conviction is what western European listeners of the eighth to tenth centuries actually heard in the performance of Byzantine hymns. What the Latin musicians converted into their own melodic counterparts were musical settings that correspond closely to what our earliest Byzantine traditions for these hymns show.

Now the polyphonic communion chants are not melodic translations of Latin settings but they are melodies written *according to* or *in the style of* the Latins. Both Plousiadenos and Gazes composed their pieces in this fashion using as graphic tools the Byzantine neumatic and modal systems. In so doing they were confronted by serious notational problems, for the eastern neumes were never designed to render accurately two concurrent lines of music.

The preservation of these composers' pieces in eastern music manuscripts is certainly valuable for the history of western music since they constitute independent written testimony of a tradition of improvised practice and they bear out the persistence of simple polyphony about which so little is known precisely because in the West it was a performance, and not a written, tradition. Plousiadenos' settings may reflect the style of the sacred music that he had heard during his twenty-year stay in Venice before 1492, during which time he was made spiritual director of a small Greek community in that city. Our knowledge of Venetian music generally is very meagre, owing to the scantiness and vagueness of the relevant sources. For San Marco none exists. It was the private chapel of the doge and employed a large number of adult and young male singers, so it must have been the focal point of artistic, recorded music-making in Venice. It seems certain, however, that elsewhere in the city church music had progressed little beyond simple choral plainsong or a common, less artistic and unwritten polyphony.

Nevertheless, a few non-artistic pieces have come to light in western manuscripts which do permit one to make a few comparisons with our Greek imitations. They demonstrate that music of this kind was often only in two parts—sometimes in score or with one part coloured, sometimes with separate parts, invariably in a moderately melismatic note-against-note style. Both voices are written in the same range with frequent crossing of parts and some parallel motion in 5ths, 6ths and 7ths can be detected. In a couple of exceptional cases, both from the fifteenth century, the liturgical melody, the tenor, actually appears as the upper sounding voice.[28] All of this tallies well with our Byzantine examples. At all events, despite the paucity of the documentary evidence, I believe that the pieces of Plousiadenos and Gazes are a musical reflection, however imperfect, of fifteenth-century Italian, possibly Venetian, practice. At least the examples show what two Eastern musicians understood as church music "according to the . . . Latins," and they clearly suggest that the austere musical reforms of Pope Eugene IV were being put into practice in the second half of the fifteenth century.[29]

In matters of notation, these Byzantine polyphonic experiments assume broader and more significant interest. It should be emphasised here that normally in the East, communion psalmody is sung by a choir. Quite exceptionally, the rubrics for these four Latin-style chants are absolutely unambiguous: the melodies are exclusively designed for solo performance. The transcriptions

[28]Kurt von Fischer, "The Sacred Polyphony of the Italian Trecento," *Proceedings of the Royal Musical Association*, 100 (1973–4), 149–50, esp. exx. 2, 3.

[29]These reforms contributed decisively to the sharp decline of fashionable and progressive polyphonic invention in Italy after the Council of Ferrara-Florence. A new emphasis given to plainchant or, at best, polyphony strictly dependent upon it was accompanied by a condemnation of the artificiality of polyphonic practice, and it may well be that the Byzantine composers were observers of this renewal of enthusiasm for simplicity in sacred music. See N. Pirrotta, "Musical and Cultural Tendencies in Fifteenth-Century Italy," *Journal of the American Musicological Society*, 19 (1966), 135.

reveal that neither Plousiadenos' nor Gazes' compositions were recorded in an entirely satisfactory manner. It seems clear that the soloists must have relied heavily on free rhythm in order to perform the pieces intelligibly. It is reasonable to assume that the two chanters, probably singing from the same book and reading from score, would be sufficiently skilled to follow the scribes' intentions simply by observing the proximity of the neumes. And in this rather halting musical style, with its frequent long notes and short motivic runs, keeping together would not have constituted a difficulty.[30] At the heart of the matter is the problem of the unpitched, staffless, diastematic Byzantine neumatic system, totally unsuited for part writing and never intended for that purpose. Byzantine notation is quintessentially a notation for monophonic performance, and to impose on it an added musical dimension is to destroy its fundamental monodic capability. Little wonder, then, that exceptionally the pieces were given to soloists rather than to the choirs; little wonder, too, that they did not enjoy wide and lasting transmissions.

As a record of a western performance tradition, the Greek polyphonic communions are an involuntary record, for their copiers, the sixteenth and seventeenth century scribes of the manuscripts, did not consciously seek to transmit information on this point. Their intention, less exalted, was simply to transmit a novel Latin musical style, and it was no concern of theirs that, embedded in their transmissions were incidental allusions to an unwritten performance practice of the fifteenth century. Something of the same kind may be said for the composers, Ioannes Plousiadenos and Manuel Gazes. They, too, are involuntary witnesses. For in writing Latin-style liturgical chants, they sought only to enrich the liturgy and propagate western culture and western *musica sacra*. If they consciously alluded in their compositions to a performance practice of their day, this was for them a means and not an end. In a word, while our records belong to the end of the sixteenth and beginning of the seventeenth centuries, they record the testimony of two fifteenth-century witnesses, and if the records and the witnesses are equally ingenuous, they are by the same token equally and ideally trustworthy.

Apart from these isolated and independent examples, the experiment with Latin polyphony in the medieval East had run its course, and inevitably so. It was not until several decades later that the choral *ison* or drone singing was introduced into Greek Church music, marking a fundamental change from

---

[30]The extraordinary bravado finish of Example 4 must have occasioned some comment.

the centuries-old monophonic tradition.[31] But there was both a loss and a gain. For if the experiment failed, it has nevertheless provided the modern scholar with more information about the notational capabilities of the Byzantines than was ever available before. It has also allowed him the possibility of a glimpse into the obscure history of fifteenth-century Italian sacred polyphony.[32]

❀ · ❀

---

[31]The earliest notification of the custom appears to have been made in 1584 by the German traveller, Martin Crusius.

[32] Since this paper was written, it has come to my attention that Dr Alexander Lingas has continued research into late Byzantine polyphony in the context of larger Greco-Latin issues, particularly with regard to performance practice. See his forthcoming "Byzantine Chant and the Music of the Latin West after 1204," in A. Louth (ed.), *Byzantine Orthodoxies: Papers from the 36th Spring Symposium of Byzantine Studies* (Aldershot) and *Byzantine Polyphony: Edition and Commentary*, Music Archive Series (Harwood Academic Publishers).

Orthodoxy in Britain: Past, Present and Future

Metropolitan Makarios (Tillyrides) of Kenya and Irinoupolis

ALTHOUGH A CYPRIOT BY BIRTH, I have had many and close connections with the United Kingdom and have always admired the British people, their country and culture. I count the years I spent as a doctoral student at Oxford, supervised by Archimandrite (now, Bishop) Kallistos, as among the happiest of my life. As a theologian, a historian, and not least an Orthodox hierarch, I have always had a special interest in the glorious Christian heritage of the peoples of Great Britain and Ireland. It is a heritage which extends back almost to the dawn of Christendom.

For Orthodox Christians who find themselves in the West, there is both a sense of unfamiliarity and a desire to find some roots in the land of their earthly pilgrimage. This is true both of Orthodox of the diaspora—both Greek and Slav[1]—and also of those whose family roots are in the West, but in coming to embrace Orthodoxy have found this an experience of homecoming. The Christian landscape of the West, and of England in particular, is very different from in Orthodox countries: domes, onion-shaped or otherwise, are replaced by spires and towers. But if we go deep enough, or far enough back in history, we find ourselves—Eastern and Western Christians—on common ground. We find our common roots in the period, perhaps idealized, of the "undivided Church"; there we may find uncanny similarities of ascetic practice and devotional expression. One way of fostering this sense of discovering a common heritage is in restoring the practice of pilgrimage to the ancient Christian sites of Britain: something that Bishop Kallistos has

---

[1]Vladimir Lossky sought to discover his Orthodox Christian roots in the land of his adoption, something evident in the remarkable diary he wrote, as he tried to enlist in the French army as it fled before the German advance in 1940: see his *Sept Jours sur les routes de France, Juin 1940* (Paris: Éditions du Cerf, 1998)

promoted by regularly leading pilgrimages to Iona, or St Alban's, or Dorchester, and many places much less well known. Such pilgrimages have often
become ecumenical events, as Christians of East and West find their common
faith in praying at places sacred with the memory of those who did not know
the Christian divisions of the second Christian millennium.

The purpose of this contribution in honour of Bishop Kallistos is to recall
the Orthodox past of these islands, before the date of the Schism, to reflect
on present reality, and to look to the promise of the future.

The Past

Apart from the schisms of the Nestorians and Monophysites in the fifth and
sixth centuries, the "one holy, catholic and apostolic Church" of our Symbol
of Faith maintained its integrity until the Great Schism, conventionally dated
to 1054. Throughout the era of the "undivided Church," the British Isles
were singularly rich in saints. We Orthodox can claim them, both Celtic and
Saxon, as our own. Patrick of Ireland, David of Wales, Columba of Iona,
Aidan and Cuthbert of Lindisfarne, Piran of Cornwall, Augustine of Canterbury, Boniface of Germany and a host of others are as much Orthodox saints
as St Seraphim of Sarov and St Nektarios of Pentapolis. Incidentally, Augustine was neither Celtic nor Saxon, but Italian. It is time for British Orthodox
to enter into the richness of their heritage. There are encouraging signs that
they are doing so.

Christianity in the United Kingdom is ancient and deeply-rooted, although
its origins are obscure. There have been those who would like to believe that
our Lord himself, with his Mother, visited the land then known as Britannia.
Blake's well-known hymn, "Jerusalem," begins with a series of intriguing
questions:

> And did those feet in ancient time
> Walk upon England's mountains green?
> And was the Holy Lamb of God
> On England's pleasant pastures seen?
> And did the Countenance Divine
> Shine forth upon our clouded hills?
> And was Jerusalem builded here
> Among these dark Satanic mills?

This is all in the realm of fanciful conjecture. It must be admitted that there is no shred of evidence to support the theory that our Lord ever came to the Western Islands.

It has been suggested that Saints Peter and Paul also came to England and preached in London. The two great London churches, Westminster Abbey and St Paul's Cathedral are dedicated respectively to the two Apostles, according to some, in commemoration of their supposed visit. Here again, there is no evidence to support the supposition that Peter and Paul were ever in Britannia. There is a tradition that St Paul consecrated Aristoboulos "Bishop of Britain" (see below) which might later have led to the belief that he made his way to Britannia to give moral support to his disciples.

The Origins of British Christianity

There is much uncertainty concerning the identity of the first apostle to evangelize Britain. St Joseph of Arimathea is commonly reputed to have been first in the field. According to the legend, Joseph was part of a Christian mission to Gaul, led by Philip the Evangelist. Philip is said to have dispatched Joseph to Britain; and so the man of Arimathea (accompanied by "twelve apostles") came to Somerset and there, "with twisted twigs," built the first Christian church in Britain, which was later to develop into the abbey of Glastonbury. The legend adds that Joseph's staff was planted in the ground and took root, becoming a thorn, flowering twice a year. The historian William of Malmesbury (d. c. 1143) is our only source for this account of the British tradition of Joseph of Arimathea, and even William records it as "a tradition."

While the name "Glastonbury" is Saxon, the site of the town and its environs were once a Celtic settlement. In 1892, the remains were found of a Celtic lake-village built on an island in the middle of swamps. This has been dated by archaeologists to 300–200 B.C. The Britons called the area Ynys yr Afalon, the "island of Avalon," and it is replete with Arthurian connotations. While it can never be known whether Joseph of Arimathea was really in Avalon, this legend is strangely evocative: along with the legends of King Arthur, it represents an attempt to give vivid detail to the dim and shadowy legends in terms of which the British found their identity as Christians in these islands—the "matter of Britain." The legend about Joseph is not beyond plausibility. The Roman invasion of Britain was in A.D. 43, and by A.D. 80 the subjugation of the countries which later became England and Wales was complete. In other words, the early stages of the annexation of Britannia to the Roman Empire coincided with the very earliest phase of the Church. It was the *pax romana* which accounted in no small degree to the amazing rapidity with which the Christian faith was disseminated in every territory under Roman rule. It would have been perfectly feasible for Joseph of Arimathea to have been in Avalon before the end of the first century. In any event, English Christians have always regarded Glastonbury as the ancient cradle of their faith.

The name of St Aristoboulos is less well known, but the tradition concerning him is only slightly less strong than that of St Joseph of Arimathea. In Romans 16:1–15, the Apostle Paul sends his cordial greetings to a long list of Roman Christians, all of whom are evidently well known to him. In v.10 are the words "Greet those who are of the household of Aristoboulos." Aristoboulos is not mentioned elsewhere in the New Testament, a deficiency is made up for by tradition. According to the *Megas Synaxaristis*, which lists the names of our Lord's seventy disciples, one of them was Aristoboulos. He is also said to have been a brother of Barnabas, while their sister Maria was the wife of none other than Peter.

Aristoboulos is said to have accompanied Paul on some of his missionary journeys, and legend has Paul consecrate him "Bishop of Britain," where he came with a retinue of Greek followers. Here Aristoboulos built churches and ordained deacons and priests. His fate is uncertain. According to one account, he suffered persecution and eventually martyrdom at the hands of the barbaric Celts. Another account asserts that he died in peace. His feast day is October 31.

Another apostle who is said to have evangelized in Britain was St Simon the Zealot. As with Joseph of Arimathea and Aristoboulos, there is nothing more than late tradition to support this. Accounts of his martyrdom in Britain must be discounted, as it appears more probable that he suffered martyrdom in Persia.

According to Bede,[2] St Alban, the protomartyr of Britain, was put to death during the Great Persecution instigated by Diocletian (303–11); but the true date may well be a century earlier. That Verulamium was the site of his martyrdom is generally accepted; King Offa of Mercia built a church there c. 793, and the city of St Albans grew up around it, with a monastery soon being established. Of Alban himself apart from the circumstances of his martyrdom nothing is known. The only English pope (Nicholas Breakspear), Adrian IV (1154–59), thought so highly of Alban that he conferred on the abbot of St

---

[2]Bede *Historia Ecclesiastica* I. 7.

Alban's precedence over all other English abbots, a right that had formerly been the prerogative of the abbot of Glastonbury.

For British Christians, it is worthy of note that the first Christian Emperor, St Constantine the Great, was proclaimed "Augustus" in York (then Eboracum). Together with his father, Constantius I, Constantine had been campaigning against the Picts and Scots. When Constantius died on July 25, 306, the soldiers at once acclaimed Constantine as "Augustus" and successor to his father.

The Celtic Church

From time immemorial, the inhabitants of the British Isles had been Celtic in race and language, although, as a result of the Roman occupation, many Celts in the lowlands of England and Wales had, from the second century onward, embraced the language and culture of Roman society. Towards the end of the fourth century Roman military power had diminished, one consequence of which was the withdrawal of the Roman field army from Britain in 408. Groups of military men from the continent were probably initially invited to fill the vacuum thus created. The settlement in these islands of the Angles, Saxon and Jutes, three kindred people from what is now Denmark and neighbouring parts of Germany, marks the origin of the English nation (as opposed to the Scots, Welsh and Irish). The process, which took place in the course of the fifth century, resulted in the aggressive and pagan newcomers progressively dispossessing the native Britons. Those who resisted the overlordship of their one-time guests eventually receded or were driven into the mountains of Wales and the moorlands of Devon and Cornwall. There they came closer to those Celts who had resisted the Roman presence, and developed traditions independent of Rome, which differed in material respects from that of Roman Christendom, notably in the way the date for celebrating Easter was calculated.

Iona and Lindisfarne

The Celtic churches of Ireland and Scotland provided several of the brightest missionary luminaries of the early medieval Church. With these great men two tiny islands are associated: Iona and Lindisfarne. In 563, St Columba (an Irishman) founded a monastery on Iona, an island off the Inner Hebrides. This monastery quickly became a center for Celtic Christianity and the motherhouse of many monastic foundations. It was from Iona that Columba and his fellow missionaries went out to evangelize the Pictish tribes of Scotland and the Anglo-Saxons of northern England. Columba was famed for the holiness of his life and his many miracles. The last day of his life was Saturday, June 8, 597. When the bell sounded for the midnight office he was able to go unaided to the church. There, in prayer before the altar, he quietly reposed. The soil of Iona was regarded as being sanctified by the relics of Columba which were buried there, although they were removed to Ireland early in the ninth century. The sanctity of Iona has never departed, and it remains a holy island and a center of pilgrimage to the present day. It is the holiest earth of Scotland, as Glastonbury is of England.

In 635, St Aidan, a monk of Iona, founded a monastery on Lindisfarne, also known as Holy Island. This was done at the request of King Oswald of Northumbria. His people had been evangelized and professed Christianity but most of them had lapsed back into paganism. Aidan was consecrated and established his episcopal see on Lindisfarne. His mission was successful and the Northumbrians were restored to Christianity. Aidan reposed on August 31, 651.

Aidan's most distinguished successor as Bishop of Lindisfarne was St Cuthbert, who had been Prior of Melrose Abbey in Scotland. In 664 he was transferred to Lindisfarne as Prior where he devoted much of his time to evangelism on the mainland. Preferring an eremitical life, in 676 he became an anchorite on the tiny island of Farne, to the south of Lindisfarne. He remained in this quiet retreat for nine years. Persuaded to become a bishop, he was elected Bishop of Hexham, but exchanged sees with his former abbot Eata, and was consecrated bishop of Lindisfarne in 685. Early in 687, sensing that his end was near, he resigned his see and retired to his beloved island of Farne where he reposed on March 20. The ruins of a chapel can still be seen which are believed to mark the site of his cell. Besides his reputation for holiness, he is said to have worked many miracles.

The Mission of St Augustine

The Anglo-Saxons who occupied England and made it their own followed the rites of their Teutonic ancestors, which were idolatrous and polytheistic.

The inspiration for the evangelization of England came from Pope Gregory the Great. The story is well known of how Gregory, before he became pope, saw some youths for sale in the Roman slave market. Struck by their winsome appearance he asked their nationality and was told "Angles." "Non

Angli sed angeli" was his reply. When he became pope in 590, he did not forget them. Gregory had known Augustine, the prior of the monastery of St Andrew's he had founded on the Caelian Hill, for several years. Knowing he would be well suited for the mission, Gregory recruited him. Augustine now got together a team of forty monks and after saying farewell to the pope, they walked in procession through the Ostian Gate. From Ostia they sailed to the south of France. While in the south of France, for reasons which cannot be known, many of the young monks lost their nerve and wanted to abort the whole mission. Perplexed by this development, Augustine returned to Rome to take counsel with the pope. In a letter dated July 23, 596, the pope commanded the monks to obey Augustine as they would Christ. When Augustine rejoined the monks in France and showed them the pope's letter, they faced the task with renewed courage and resolve.

After spending Lent and Easter in France, they sailed for England, probably from Boulogne. Prior to the arrival of Augustine, Christianity already had a tiny toehold in Anglo-Saxon England. Although the King of England, Ethelbert, was a pagan, his Queen, Bertha, was a Christian. In Canterbury she had her own chapel, dedicated to St Martin of Tours, and a domestic chaplain, Bishop Liudhard. The chapel may have stood on the site of a chapel where Romano-Britons had worshipped before the coming of the Anglo-Saxons. The church of St Martin's, Canterbury, is reputed to be the oldest parish church in England. Most of the present building belongs to a period long after the sixth century, but some of the fabric may date back to the time of Ethelbert and Augustine.

Ethelbert's date of birth is unknown but he is believed to have become King of Kent about 560. In other words, by the time of Augustine's mission he had been king for 37 years. His kingdom encompassed a far greater area than the modern county of Kent. According to Bede, he was a Bretwalda or Overlord, who exercised suzerainty over the Anglo-Saxon rulers as far north as the Humber.

The arrival of Augustine at Ebbsfleet on the Isle of Thanet in April 597 was seminal. Because Augustine did not at that time know a word of English, while in northern France he had recruited some interpreters. Ethelbert initially received the missionaries with reserve. When a delegation of interpreters came to see him to tell him of the arrival of Augustine and his party, the King sent word that they were not to leave the Isle of Thanet. He then went to the Isle to meet them, traditionally under an oak tree. The king's reserve quickly melted. After hearing Augustine preach, he allowed the monks to go to his capital, Canterbury, provided accommodation and permitted them to evangelize. As Augustine and his fellow monks entered Canterbury they carried before them a processional cross and an icon of our Lord.

The conversion of the English to Christianity was completed between 597 and 686. Progress was rapid from the beginning, and during the last thirty years of this period paganism is said to have lingered only in remote areas. This may be doubted. There were various relapses back into paganism and some authorities believe that faith in the old gods was not finally extinguished until as late as the Norman Conquest. Perhaps it never completely perished. It is a bizarre sign of our own strange times that there are those in Germany, Scandinavia, England and elsewhere who are actively engaged in trying to resuscitate teutonic paganism.

At the outset, the conversion of the Kingdom of Kent was remarkably rapid. One of the first converts was King Ethelbert, who was baptized in his wife's chapel, probably on the vigil of Whitsun, Saturday, June 1, 597. It is to Ethelbert's credit that he never resorted to compulsion to spread Christianity.

Very soon after arriving in England, it became apparent to Augustine that he would need to be in episcopal orders if the work were to go forward. Later in 597 Augustine returned to France and was consecrated in Arles in either September or November. On his return, the great missionary had the joy of presiding over a mass baptism. Despite it being in the depth of winter, over 10,000 men and women of Kent were baptized in December. The mass baptism took place in the River Swale near the mouth of the Medway, the converts entering the water two at a time to be baptized. In 598 Augustine and his monks began the building of a monastery. In 601, Pope Gregory appointed Augustine Archbishop of Canterbury with metropolitan jurisdiction over all England, including York and the Celtic churches in Britain as well as all future bishops. Augustine's authority over York was not, however, inherited by his successors.

The Problem of Celtic Separatism

The first Archbishop of Canterbury wrestled with the separatism of the Celtic Christians. At the meeting known as the Conference of Augustine's Oak he tried in vain to persuade the Celtic Church to adopt the Roman observance of Easter. This, and Celtic separatism generally, was an issue which convulsed and tormented the English Church for generations. At the Synod of Whitby in 664, King Oswiu and the clergy of northern England declared their adherence to the Roman practice. It was not until 716 that the Celts finally submitted to the Roman observance, and it was only then achieved with shocking violence: Ethelfrith, King of Northumbria, massacred 1200 Celtic monks at Bangor who were adamant in their refusal to adopt the Roman usage.

Augustine was certainly the Apostle of Kent and he (and St Gregory the Great) is rightly regarded as the apostle of England, though he cannot be given credit for evangelizing the whole country. Wessex was converted by a freelance Frankish missionary named Birinus. Northumbria was converted to Christianity by Irish missionaries from Iona, notably Aidan; it also received a less successful mission from Paulinus, one of those who had joined Augustine's mission. King Penda of Mercia was staunchly pagan but immediately following his death in battle in 655, his people readily accepted the Gospel from Irish and Northumbrian missionaries. Essex owed its conversion to another Northumbrian evangelist, St Cedd.

It is to Augustine that the credit almost certainly belongs of being the founder of the first school in England. This institution still exists in Canterbury and is now known as the King's school. Its original purpose was to prepare boys for the priesthood. The evangelization of the Anglo-Saxons did not only make them Christians. It ushered in a Christian civilization which was to last for many hundred years.

King Ethelbert took an continuing interest in the spread of Christianity, which included making grants of money to found the see of Rochester in 604. By his promotion of Christianity, Ethelbert had played the same role in England as Constantine in Byzantium and Vladimir in Kiev. He is today honoured with Augustine as a saint of the Church. His feast day is February 25.

Of the forty monks who accompanied Augustine in 597, the names of only a few are known. Two of them also became Archbishops of Canterbury: Laurence who succeeded Augustine and Honorius who was fifth archbishop (627–653).

St Theodore of Tarsus and Canterbury

Although the orientation of the early English Church was towards Rome (which, we must remember, was not at that time in schism), it is an illustration of the oneness of the Church Catholic of that era that the seventh Archbishop of Canterbury was a Greek born in 602. His name was Theodore and his birthplace was the same as that of St Paul: Tarsus in Cilicia. St Theodore was one of the many Eastern monks who fled from the Middle East after either the Persian invasion (Tarsus was taken by the Persians in 613 or 614) or the Arab conquest of the 630s. He first made his way to Constantinople, but is later found among the many refugee monks in Rome, and may have participated, together with St Maximos the Confessor, in the Lateran Synod of 649, which condemned the heresies of monenergism and monothelitism. On the death of the sixth Archbishop of Canterbury, Theodore was invited by Pope Vitalian to fill the vacancy. After being consecrated in Rome, Theodore arrived in England in May 669. He was then no longer young. Indeed, by the standards of the seventh century he was, at 67, already in advanced old age; but this did not prevent his tenure as Archbishop from being one of continual and fruitful activity. He was also one of the most out-standing and innovative primates to occupy the throne of St Augustine. According to Bede, Theodore made a tour throughout the whole of England, correcting abuses and laying down the law concerning the canonical Easter. In 673, at Hertford, Theodore presided at the first synod of the English clergy. He presided over other synods in 679 and 684; at the former of these synods, at Hatfield, Theodore secured an affirmation of the authority of the first five Œcumenical Councils, as well as of the Lateran Synod of 649, and an asser-tion of the validity of the *filioque*. As Metropolitan, Theodore decided where bishops should have their episcopal seats and where their jurisdictions should extend. As a result of Theodore's labours, the formerly isolated bishoprics of Anglo-Saxon England were united and brought under submission to Canter-bury. It is believed that when Theodore first came to England he brought with him an entourage of Greek monks who played an important role in dissemi-nating classical and patristic learning throughout the English Church. The impact was profound and lasting.

Before the Anglo-Saxon invasions the country that became England was wholly Celtic. It was only natural that the Celts were bitterly resentful at hav-ing their country invaded by aliens who progressively dispossessed them and finally drove them into the wild mountains of Wales and the rugged moor-lands of the West Country. The bitterness of the Celts ran deep and was not healed by the conversion of the Anglo-Saxons. During the Anglo-Saxon pagan era, the Celts had to a great extent been cut off from Europe. For the Celts such distinctive features of their Christian practice as their method of dating Easter had acquired a cultural significance which they did not readily relinquish. Archbishop Theodore was neither Celt nor Anglo-Saxon but Greek and this neutrality perhaps enabled him to play a key role in helping to reconcile the Celts and the Anglo-Saxons. It is with good cause that Bede describes Theodore as "the first archbishop that all the English Church consented to obey."

One of the secular blessings of Theodore's archiepiscopate was national unity. Although the Anglo-Saxon invaders and conquerors of the fifth century were kindred peoples who spoke the same language, they arrayed themselves into many petty and often warring kingdoms, eventually reduced to seven. Theodore mediated between the warring monarchs and reconciled them. This laid the foundation of their eventual unification. In 829, England was united under King Egbert. By helping to foster this unity, Theodore had made an immense contribution to the secular well-being of the English nation.

Not least among the many achievements of Archbishop Theodore was the promotion of education and culture. After his death, the "Canterbury School," which he had founded, produced books of the highest artistic merit. They included the "Royal Gospels," described as "a large book with great purple pages in the Byzantine manner and an abundant use of gold," as well as a corpus of commentaries (recently discovered) on the Pentateuch and the Gospels. Theodore was also a founder of monasteries.

Very few British people today give a glance at Anglo-Saxon history and the name of St Theodore of Tarsus, seventh Archbishop of Canterbury, is almost unknown. In point of fact this great and good man is a towering figure of English ecclesiastical and secular history of the period. He had nobly served his adopted country which owes him an incalculable debt of gratitude. At the time of his death in 690, Theodore was 87 or 88 years old. His feast day is September 19.

The Evangelization of Germany

Christian England was to be the springboard for the conversion of pagan Germany. The Apostles of the Germanic lands were English saints, notably Willibrord of Northumbria (d. 738; feast day November 7), who evangelized the Netherlands, and Suidbert, who preached in the Netherlands. The greatest among these English missionary saints to pagan Europe, however, is St Boniface (680–754). A Devonshire man, born in Crediton, Boniface devoted his life to evangelizing Germany. After his consecration on November 30, 722, he applied himself with enormous vigor to the task of converting the people of his chosen mission field. In addition to his preaching and teaching he demolished idols, baptized thousands with his own hand and founded innumerable churches and monasteries. To help him in this work, Boniface recruited from England a team of outstanding missionary helpers, both monks and nuns. On June 5, 754, Boniface and a number of companions suffered martyrdom at the hands of a band of pagans.

The Northumbrian Renaissance

St Bede (c.672–735), or as he is generally known, the Venerable Bede, was a priest whose holiness of life deeply impressed his contemporaries. The Father of English History, it is to his masterly *The Ecclesiastical History of the English People* that we are indebted for our knowledge of the lives, works and miracles of so many of the English saints. Bede was an accomplished Greek scholar and the story is well known how, in the last hours of his life, he was dictating to an amanuensis his translation of St John's Gospel into English. This translation, unhappily, has not survived. St Bede's feast day is May 27.

It is from Bede that we derive our only knowledge of St Caedmon, the earliest English Christian poet. Caedmon's gift appears to have been supernatural rather than natural. Said to have been an illiterate herdsman, Caedmon one night had a vivid dream in which a stranger commanded him to recite a poetic account of "the beginning of created things," which he found himself able to do. He was taken to St Hilda who concluded that Caedmon had truly been blessed with a gift from heaven. The poet entered the monastery of Whitby and remained there for the rest of his life. From time to time the monks would expound to Caedmon various incidents or episodes from the Scriptures and Caedmon would render them into beautiful verse of the northern English dialect of his day. The topics of his poems include the Exodus, the Resurrection, the Ascension, the Second Coming and much else. Some of Caedmon's writings are extant. He reposed in the odour of sanctity c. 680, but there is uncertainty about the date of his death. His feast day is February 11.

One of the greatest women saints of the early Anglo-Saxon period was St Hilda of Whitby (614–680), who was related to the royal family of Northumbria. Born a pagan, she was converted and baptized at 13 by Paulinus. Her disposition from then on was strongly spiritual. Hilda did not enter the religious life until she was 33, devoting her earlier years to study and care for the poor. Hilda took the veil in 647. Ten years later she became the founder-abbess of the famous double monastery in Whitby. As a theologian she took part in the Synod of Whitby in 664, siding with her kinsman, King Oswiu of Northumbria in his decision to support the Roman dating for Easter, as opposed to the dating used by the Celts. Hilda was universally loved and revered and was the counselor and confidante of kings, bishops and humble peasants. Hilda reposed in 680, having suffered a painful illness for seven years. Her feast day is November 17.

A Royal Anglo-Saxon Martyr

On March 18, 978, Edward, King of the English, was treacherously assassinated at Corfe Castle in Dorset after a reign of less than three years. After his death, Edward was at once acclaimed by his people as a saint and martyr. The crime was probably inspired by his stepmother, Alfthrith, in a successful attempt to ensure the succession of her son, Ethelred ("the Unready"). Edward was the son by the first wife of King Edgar, "the Peaceful," who, with the great St Dunstan, had carried out an extensive reform of the monasteries where life and discipline had become lax. Edward continued these reforms and it is not impossible that unregenerate elements in the Church had conspired with those who assassinated him.

The British branch of the Russian Orthodox Church outside Russia (ROCOR) has a monastery in Brookwood, Surrey, dedicated to St Edward the Martyr. It is appropriate and a cause for joy to British Orthodox that the monastery is the custodian of the sacred relics of St Edward.

Alfred the Great

In the saga of English Christianity, King Alfred the Great (c. 848–900) is an outstanding figure. I am not concerned here with his brilliant achievements as a soldier and statesman. Alfred was a most devout Christian. In 853, when only five, he was sent to Rome where he was chrismated by Pope Leo IV. Two years later Alfred again went to Rome, this time with his father, King Ethelwulf. After the brief reigns and deaths of his three older brothers, Alfred became king in April 871. A generous financial supporter of the papacy, Alfred was in touch with the wider Church and corresponded with the Patriarch of Jerusalem, Elias III.

Although highly preoccupied, especially in the early part of his reign, in directing the defense of the nation against the repeated Viking incursions, Alfred found time to complete a number of learned writings, all with a high devotional content. An able Latinist, he also translated several spiritual works into Anglo-Saxon. The most important among these was a primer for the clergy by St Gregory the Great titled *Pastoral Care*. Alfred's translation of *The*

Consolation of Philosophy by Boethius achieved popularity in the Middle Ages as a rare example a philosophical manual in the vernacular. In this work occurs the sentence which might well stand as Alfred's epitaph: "My will was to live worthily as long as I lived, and after my life to leave to them that should come after, my memory in good works." The last of Alfred's works was an anthology, of which the first part was based mainly on the *Soliloquies* of St Augustine. This work ends with a sentence which yields a penetrating insight into the spiritual aspiration of the king who is so rightly ascribed "Alfred the Great": "Therefore he seems to me a very foolish man, and very wretched who will not increase his understanding while he is in the world, and ever wish and long to reach that endless life where all shall be made clear."

King Alfred the Great has not been canonized, but his devout wife has been so honoured. She was St Etheldwitha (d. 903, feast day July 20). She founded a convent in Winchester and entered it upon the death of her husband. Another saint in the ménage of Alfred the Great was the monk St Grimbald (d. 901) who was often consulted by the king.

Aelfric the Righteous Abbot

After Bede, perhaps the greatest author and theologian of Anglo-Saxon Church was Aelfric, called the "Grammarian." Aelfric was born about 955. He was educated in the Benedictine monastery in Winchester and soon gained a reputation as an outstanding scholar. He was for several years at the abbey of Cerne in Dorset. It was there that Aelfric began a series of homilies in Anglo-Saxon, compiled from the writings of the Latin Fathers. This could be regarded as a kind of early English precursor to the *Philokalia*. In a preface Aelfric deplored the fact that, except for the translations of King Alfred, Englishmen had none of the works of the Latin Fathers available to them in their own language. By his translations, Aelfric sought to remedy the deficiency. The first series comprises homilies for each Sunday and Feast Day of the Christian year. The second series covers Church history and doctrine. At the time of the Reformation, Protestants in England appealed to his authority as rejecting the doctrines of transubstantiation and the Immaculate Conception of the Mother of God. Although he may have been influenced in his Eucharistic theology by Ratramnus, his theology of the Holy Mysteries was fully Orthodox. In 1005 Aelfric became abbot of Eynsham in Oxfordshire where he reposed about 1020. In the latter years of his life he wrote textbooks and a guide to the systematic study of the Bible.

Our Lady of Walsingham

In 1061 came an event in which the Mother of God demonstrated her love of England and the English. In that year she manifested three visions to Richeldis de Faverches, the Lady of the Manor of Walsingham, a remote village in Norfolk. In these apparitions, Richeldis was told to build a replica of the holy house in Nazareth in which the Holy Virgin learnt from the Archangel that she was to become the Mother of our Lord. The shrine was built and throughout the Middle Ages it attracted a continuous stream of pilgrims. In his Catholic days, Henry VIII visited the shrine three times. After his break with Rome he had the shrine demolished together with every other monastery and pilgrim site in the land.

At the beginning of the twentieth century the shrine at Walsingham was restored by the Anglican Vicar of Walsingham, A. Hope Patten, and pilgrimages were revived. The Roman Catholics restored the Slipper Chapel as their shrine, and among the extensions to the shrine built in 1938 an Orthodox Chapel was included. Orthodox are now regularly among the thousands of pilgrims who go each year to Walsingham to venerate our Lady and to seek spiritual refreshment.

Schism and the Normans

Although no Byzantine sources seem aware of any significant rift between the Western and Eastern Churches in 1054, that date—the date of the exchange of anathemas between the papal legate, Cardinal Humbert, and the Œcumenical Patriarch, Michael Keroularios—has come to be regarded as the date of the Great schism. As a result, the British Isles is deemed to have passed into schism along with the rest of Latin Christendom. King Edward the Confessor (d. 1065) died 11 years too late to qualify as an Orthodox saint, although he was canonized by Pope Alexander III in 1161. For England, the conventional date of the schism almost coincides with the great caesura in English history known as the Norman Conquest. If there is a *dies nefastus* in English history it can be none other than September 28, 1066, when King Harold and his army were defeated at Hastings. The Norman victory resulted in immeasurable suffering to the native English and was to distort the history and culture of the nation for centuries to come. The fact that the Norman Conquest more or less coincided with the attempt by the papacy to refashion the Church along the lines of what has been called the Papal Monarchy (though the Normans themselves resisted such encroachment on their political power as fiercely as any continental monarch: witness to which is found in the exiles of the archbishops, Anselm and Edmund, and the martyrdom of Thomas Becket) means that for modern English Orthodox the period of the "undivided Church," where we are tempted to seek our roots, came to an end with the fall of the Anglo-Saxons.

The More Recent Past

Until about a century ago, Orthodoxy was almost completely unknown in the United Kingdom. Knowledge of the Faith was confined to a handful of theologians and those who had traveled in Orthodox countries. For the overwhelming majority of the British, Orthodoxy was as remote and as exotic as Shintoism.

Today, the situation is radically different. Throughout the United Kingdom the Orthodox presence maybe readily discerned. This is due largely to the Greek (including Cypriot) diaspora together with the influx of refugees from Russia and other Eastern European countries in the aftermath of the revolutionary rise of Communism. While there has been assimilation, the allegiance of the immigrants, of their children and grandchildren to the ancestral religion has been widely maintained. Moreover, the Orthodox of immigrant origin have been augmented by a continuous and growing stream of native British converts.

No one can gainsay that the diaspora—Greek and Slav—has been a blessing to the host countries. Britain has had its share of these quiet and industrious immigrants and it is first to the Greeks that the United Kingdom is indebted for the replanting of Orthodoxy on its soil. The first Greek Orthodox church of the modern era was opened in London in 1838, the year after Queen Victoria came to the throne. At first, the Greek influx was not particularly large, but it continued progressively. After Cyprus passed from Turkish rule to that of Britain in 1878, Cypriots also began to trickle in. The Turkish occupation of Cyprus has resulted in the arrival of yet more Greeks, which has been facilitated by the advent of the European Union. There are now believed to be about 300,000 people of Greek and Cypriot origin in the United Kingdom—in other words, a substantial ethnic minority.

A British Orthodox Pioneer

It is interesting to note that there was a pioneer English Orthodox priest during the nineteenth century. He was Father Stephen Hatherley. Father Stephen, who was born in 1827, was from a prosperous middle class home of staunchly Anglican faith. In 1853 he matriculated at New College, Oxford. The "Tractarian" movement had by that time spent its force but its lingering influence continued to make an impact on many earnest young students, of whom Hatherley was one. He corresponded with one of the leading figures of the movement, Dr Pusey. After graduating in 1856 Hatherley married and had a son.

Many of the "Tractarians" and those associated with them became Roman Catholics. Hatherley's spiritual quest led him to Orthodoxy and he was received into the Orthodox Church by Father Eugene Popov, the Chaplain of the Russian Embassy in London. In 1870 Hatherley visited Moscow and St Petersburg and the following year was in Constantinople where he was ordained a priest by the Œcumenical Patriarch. He returned to England and opened a church in Waterloo Road, Wolverhampton. Although his congregation was Greek, the reaction of the Anglican Establishment was one of marked hostility. An unpleasant controversy erupted involving the Turkish ambassador, and even the Prime Minister, Gladstone, was drawn in, with an accusation that Father Hatherley was seeking to "wound and estrange" the Church of England. Complaints were made to the Œcumenical Patriarch. Since he was anxious to remain on good terms with the Anglican hierarchy, the Patriarch became alarmed. He wrote to Father Hatherley to warn him that "proselytism" was not the Orthodox way.[3] As a result of the episode, Father Hatherley moved to Birmingham. The controversy soon died down and Father Hatherley later ministered to Greek parishes in Cardiff and Bristol, which are still active today. In addition to his labors as a priest, Father Hatherley was a composer and a literary apologist for Orthodoxy, and wrote one of the earliest books explaining the mysteries of Byzantine chant to the English. This valiant pioneer of modern British Orthodoxy reposed in Bournemouth on October 20, 1905.[4]

The Present

Facts and figures can have a certain interest, but the statistics of contemporary British Orthodoxy have to be given with the *caveat* that what is true

[3]The statement that Orthodoxy does not proselytize means that Orthodox missionaries do not use aggressive and intrusive methods like those of the Jehovah's Witnesses and other cults.
[4]A useful short biography titled *Stephen Hatherley: His Conversion to Orthodoxy* by A. Tillyrides is available, in Greek (Athens, 1989).

today may very probably be outdated tomorrow and also that the interpretation of statistics is fraught with peril. For many years British Christians have been lamenting the decline of churchgoing, a decline which has, for some denominations, become critical. A body named Christian Research has for several years carried out the "English Church Attendance Survey." This disclosed that the average Sunday attendance in 1998 for all the Christian churches was 3.7 million, which is 7.5% of the population and a drop of more than a fifth compared with 1989. Most "mainstream" churches suffered alarming falls in attendance over this 10-year period: Church of England, 23%; Roman Catholic, 22%; Methodist, 26%; United Reformed, 18%. As well as declining in numbers, the mainline churches have also lost much of their moral influence. Confronted with emptying churches and especially the loss of their young people, distraught denominational leaders are searching their souls. Many explain their losses in terms of deficiencies in their patterns of worship. To this downward trend, however, there are three exceptions. They are the churches attended by colored people, the Baptists, who recorded an increase of 2%, and the Orthodox who noted an astonishing 100% growth rate during the decade. The basis of virtually all British Orthodox communities is constituted by immigrants. Greeks, Russians, Ukrainians, Serbs, Bulgarians, Poles and Romanians have all contributed to the building up of the Orthodox Church in the United Kingdom; they have been joined by an increasing number of the British converts. The Orthodox community in the United Kingdom now numbers scores of thousands.

While there is much that is encouraging there can be no denying that there is a negative aspect to the situation: many young people who were baptized and chrismated have fallen away from the practice of Orthodoxy. Can such a person be legitimately classed as Orthodox? Canonically, yes; but for all practical purposes, no. As such I am hesitant to estimate the total number of Orthodox in the United Kingdom. In the paragraph above, I deliberately used the ambivalent phrase "scores of thousands." Roman Catholic statisticians and demographers regularly count the populations of whole large countries—for example, Spain, Italy and the countries of Latin America—as being Catholic when it is certain that a large majority of their citizens never practice the faith into which they were baptized. Such people have, *de facto*, seceded from the Church of their baptism and should not be classed as Roman Catholics at all. The same is true of the Orthodox. That interesting mine of information, *Operation World*,[5] gives the total of Orthodox "members" in

5(Carlisle: OM Publishing, 1993), 557.

the United Kingdom as 265,258 with a further 204,742 being "affiliated." The definition of "affiliated" is "the whole Christian community, inclusive membership, which includes children, non-member adherents, etc." These figures, totaling nearly half a million, cannot be taken seriously. According to an article in *Orthodox England*,[6] the number of *practicing* Orthodox Christians in the British Isles is between 50,000 and 100,000. These figures are realistic and it would be wise to regard the lower of the two as being more probable. While it is tragic that so many who would call themselves Orthodox seldom or never come to church, it nevertheless *is* a fact that the number of practicing British Orthodox is growing steadily. So also, is the number of clergy. The *Directory* of Orthodox parishes and clergy in the British Isles, published by the Orthodox Fellowship of Saint John the Baptist, lists all the active canonical clergy. This authority records that there are nine bishops resident in Britain (one of them English), 136 priests and 25 deacons. Of these clergy, about a third are of British ancestry. The *Directory* also lists the addresses of 85 Orthodox "places of worship" in England, six in Wales, 11 in Scotland, one in Northern Ireland and six in the Republic of Ireland. For many years, the strength of Orthodox clerical manpower has been growing, as has the number of "places of worship." There can be no doubt that both will continue to grow in the future.

While these figures are encouraging, there is the disturbing element of the multiplicity of jurisdictions. The allegiance of British Orthodox clergy and faithful is principally divided between the Patriarchs of Constantinople, Antioch and Moscow, though the Churches of Bulgaria, Serbia and Romania are also represented, as well as Russian Orthodox Church outside Russia. We can only hope and pray that before long this undesirable state of affairs will be rationalized.

Some ex-Anglicans have joined the Greek and Russian jurisdictions. However, the largest single group has joined the British Deanery of the Patriarchate of Antioch. The Deanery has 12 priests and one deacon, all ex-Anglicans. It has no resident bishop of its own and is at present dependent on an Antiochene bishop in Europe for episcopal ministrations, a situation which is clearly unsatisfactory.

[6](September, 1999), 5

The Future

In an article titled "The Orthodox Church in Great Britain," Sir Steven Runciman made these penetrating observations:

> The Orthodox Church has not yet abandoned itself to an orgy of modernism; and I hope that it never will. Reforms and adjustments may from time to time be necessary; for the Church is in the world. But it is concerned with eternity, and it respects the strength of tradition. I sometimes think that in a century's time the only great Christian Church to survive will be the Orthodox because it has not submerged itself in transient fashions. It is therefore of value to us in this country to have amongst us a Church which has not abandoned its traditions and its age-long standards and at the same time lives on and with God's grace will live on to fulfill the needs of its people.[7]

In an article also titled "The Orthodox Church in Great Britain," a theologian of the Church of Scotland, the Very Rev. Prof. T. F. Torrance, writes sympathetically on Orthodoxy from the perspective of a clergyman of the Reformed tradition. Professor Torrance states his firm belief that the theology most relevant to "our own modern scientific world," is that which goes back to Athanasius and Cyril of Alexandria, and to the first great Christian physicist, John Philoponos of Alexandria. Professor Torrance notes that one of the major achievements of the Protestant Reformation was the recovery of the evangelical doctrine of justification by grace. He then points out that this doctrine is "nowhere better expounded in all the history of theology than by the impeccably Orthodox Cyril of Alexandria." Torrance laments that so few of Cyril's theological writings are available in English and suggests that scholars of the Greek Orthodox Church in the United Kingdom could undertake the task of translation.[8] If undertaken and completed, there can be no doubt that this would confer an immense benefit upon the English-speaking Orthodox everywhere. It is significant that Professor Torrance affirms that "Orthodox theologians and Churchmen should be aware of the tendency of

---

[7] *Texts and Studies*, 2 (1983).

[8] A start has already been made by a priest of the Romanian jurisdiction, John McGuckin, in his book, *Cyril of Alexandria: the Christological Controversy* (Leiden: Brill, 1994), and by the Roman Catholic scholar, of Greek descent, Norman Russell, in his volume, *Cyril of Alexandria* (Early Church Fathers, London: Routledge, 2001).

non-Orthodox, for example Anglicans, to latch on to Orthodox spirituality without its deep-rooted theology and therefore only in a sort of sentimental way that is not very helpful to anyone."[9]

Orthodoxy in the Third Millennium

A new day is dawning, as Orthodoxy in the United Kingdom comes increasingly into its own. Those who have become sick at heart at the modernism and eccentricity which have overwhelmed British Christendom have for the first time a credible alternative to turn to. Moreover, far from being "exotic," Orthodoxy is, as I trust I have made clear, very much the "Faith of the Fathers" of all the indigenous people of the British Isles, whether of Celtic or Anglo-Saxon descent. Orthodox throughout the world are convinced that this third millennium of history will witness a vast new flowering of their faith. The United Kingdom will participate in this flowering; indeed, it is already doing so. It is visionary, but not absurdly so, to foresee that the Atlantic islands could be Orthodox once more.

[9]*Texts and Studies*, 2 (1983).

PART TWO

Theological

Faithfulness and Creativity

John Behr

ORTHODOX THEOLOGY was reborn in the twentieth century. The figures involved are too many to be recounted here, though their history deserves to be written. While antecedents can be discerned in the previous centuries, the real cradle of this renaissance was that group of Russian émigré theologians who eventually found themselves in Paris. It is perhaps not surprising, therefore, that this reawakening often developed in contradistinction to those things considered "Western." Paradoxically, however, this term was not really used to designate the geographical location in which they found themselves and where, ironically, many of the same concerns (for instance, the "return to the sources") were also evident, but rather as a designation for their own predecessors, whose "western captivity" they were finally shaking off.[1] Rather than the dry, scholastic exposition of formal dogmatic truths, characteristic Orthodoxy in the previous couple of centuries, this nascent theological consciousness expressed itself in a new style, with concerns held to be more immediate and spiritual, more "existential"—again echoing broader developments in the West. The dynamism of this theological reawakening was such that its influence extended beyond the limits of the Russian Diaspora,[2] though it was not welcomed by all; indeed, for some this phenomenon was itself evidence of a "western captivity."[3]

[1] A position developed most thoroughly by Fr. Georges Florovsky, on whom see K. Gavrilkin, "Church and Culture in the Thought of Father Georges Florovsky: The Role of Culture in the Making of Modern Theology" (M.Th. Thesis., St. Vladimir's Orthodox Theological Seminary, Crestwood, NY, 1998).

[2] Cf. C. Yannaras, "Theology in Present-Day Greece," *St Vladimir's Theological Quarterly*, 4 (1972), 195–214.

[3] For instance, N. Vasileiadis, in a letter published in *Eastern Churches Review*, 4.2 (1972), objects to Kallistos Ware's review of the French translation of P. N. Trembelas, *Dogmatic Theology*, which criticized the work for "the style of theology it represents," that is "*Western*," "*academic* and *scholastic* rather than liturgical and mystical." (*ECR* 3.4 [1971], 479–80, italics original), and points out that in the work of "the younger Greek theologians," to whom Ware refers, one finds "much Camus, a good deal of Heidegger, Jaspers and Kierkegaard, and not a

Given this relationship with their own past, it was inevitable that a favorite theme of Orthodox theologians in the twentieth century would be the interplay of faithfulness and creativity required by the particularly Orthodox understanding of tradition as *living tradition*.[4] For instance, in 1934 Fr Georges Florovsky spoke of tradition as being "not only *concord* with the past, but, in a certain sense, *freedom from the past*, as from some outward formal criterion. Tradition is not only a protective, conservative principle; it is, primarily, the principle of growth and regeneration."[5] At the end of the twentieth century, the same point is reaffirmed by Bishop Kallistos:

> True Orthodox fidelity to the past must always be a *creative* fidelity; for true Orthodoxy can never rest satisfied with a barren 'theology of repetition', which, parrot-like, repeats accepted formulae without striving to understand what lies behind them. . . . An Orthodox thinker must see Tradition *from within*, he must enter into its inner spirit, he must re-experience the meaning of Tradition in a manner that is exploratory, courageous and full of imaginative creativity.[6]

Examples of this sentiment could easily be multiplied. In part this reflects the dynamic mission of the Church herself, called to proclaim the Gospel to all nations, making them disciples and baptizing them in the name of the Father, Son and Holy Spirit (Matt 28:19). This revelation of God in Christ, as proclaimed in the Gospel, abides as the perennial subject of theological reflection, yet the permanency of the subject has not prevented the same truth being expressed in a variety of ways, a diversity to which Church history, both East

little Sartre, whereas only 'here and there' will you see St John Chrysostom, Basil the Great, Gregory the Theologian, etc.," a fault which Vasileiadis traces back to the Parisian émigré theologians, with their excessive preoccupation with the "mystical" side of theology (*ECR* 4.2 [1972], 179–181). For Kallistos' reply, see *ECR* 4.2 (1972), 181–2.

[4]A very important antecedent here is A. Khomiakov, whose work, *The Church is One* (1844/5) articulates many of the sentiments about tradition developed more extensively by twentieth-century theologians, and which is also clearly indebted to J. A. Möhler, *Die Einheit in der Kirche order das Prinzip des Katholizismus* (1825), a similarity noted by V. Lossky ("Tradition and traditions," in *In the Image and Likeness of God* [SVS, 1975], 142). Cf. S. Bolshakoff, *The Doctrine of the Unity of the Church in the Works of Khomyakov and Moehler* (London: SPCK, 1946).

[5]G. Florovsky, "The Catholicity of the Church" (1934), reprinted in idem, *Bible, Church, Tradition: An Eastern Orthodox View*, Collected Works of Georges Florovsky, vol. 1 (Vaduz: Büchervertriebsanstalt, 1987), 46–7.

[6]T. Ware (Bishop Kallistos of Diokleia), *The Orthodox Church*, rev. edn. (Harmondsworth: Penguin, 1997), 198.

and West, bears testimony. This belongs to the very imperative itself: the context in which the proclamation takes place continually changes, and consequently the proclamation and its explanation must respond ever anew. We will always need to "coin new words," as St Gregory the Theologian put it.

On a deeper level, the continuing nature of this challenge does not just derive from the changing situations and contexts in which we find ourselves. Rather the Church is continually *in via*, sojourning in this world but looking towards the heavens, in which lies our true citizenship and from where we await our Lord Jesus Christ, forgetting what lies behind and straining forward to what lies ahead, answering the upward call of God in Jesus Christ (Phil 2:20, 13–14). The Church, especially the reflection of those who belong to the Church, her theology, cannot and must not stand still. One might indeed apply the words of St Gregory of Nyssa concerning the spiritual life to the task of theology: that true perfection resides in never ceasing to grow towards what is better, never placing any limit or restriction on perfection or, in this case, never abandoning the attempt to give ever more adequate expression and witness to the truth.[7]

Tradition and Canon

This emphasis on the interplay between faithfulness and creativity unquestionably preserves an important truth. But it cannot be merely repeated; if it is to be truly appropriated, it requires that critical engagement of which it speaks. This is a much more challenging, and risky, task, yet one which cannot be avoided. It is precisely this creativity, imaginative yet rooted in what has been handed down, that is required today, as we enter the twenty-first century in a society (at least in the West, both geographically and culturally) which is finally abandoning any pretence at being Christian, but embraces an open pluralism in which any absolute claims are suspect and relativized, or integrated into a spirituality and religion of man's own creation.

However, unless we are sure about what exactly it is we must be faithful to, it will be difficult, if not impossible, also to be creative. Here, the distinction between "Tradition" and "traditions," frequently appealed to in the twentieth century, turns out to be less helpful than it might at first have seemed. Certainly not all things handed down possess the same importance,

---

[7]Cf. St. Gregory of Nyssa *On Perfection* (GNO 8.1, p.214.4–6).

and many things claiming to be part of the tradition of the Church might well be better designated as "customs," but an adequate criterion or canon for distinguishing these must still be given. To speak of "Tradition" as "the life of the Holy Spirit in the Church," is not sufficient. The issue becomes even more nebulous when, as is often done, Scripture is placed within tradition, as one, among many, of the outward forms or monuments of "Tradition." To argue for this on the grounds that the Church predates the writings of the New Testament, simply overlooks, in a Marcionite fashion, the existence of the Scriptures (the Law, the Psalms and the Prophets) in reference to which the Gospel was proclaimed from the beginning. Alternatively, to claim that as it was the Church that decided which books are to count as part of Scripture, the Bible is therefore the book of the Church and can only be understood properly within the Church and her tradition, still fails to address the issue of criterion or canon, for such is still required.[8] Such suggestions, framed largely in response to the problems posed by the polemics of the Reformation and Counter-Reformation, in which Scripture and tradition are opposed as two sources of authority, are not sufficient: a more creative solution is needed.

The recognition that the Gospel is proclaimed, from the beginning, "according to Scripture," forces us to look more closely at the way in which Scripture, tradition and canon fit together. It is revealing, for instance, that comparatively little attention was devoted, in antiquity, to the issue of which books were to count as Scripture and which not.[9] The "canon" was certainly discussed extensively, but this term did not (with a couple of possible exceptions) refer to a list of scriptural books, but to the "rule of faith" or the "rule

[8]A position anticipated by Khomiakov, adding the following extraordinary, but consequential, claim: "The collection of Old and New Testament books, which the Church acknowledges as hers are called by the name of Holy Scripture. But there are no limits to Scripture: for every writing which the Church acknowledges as hers is Holy Scripture. Such pre-eminently are the Creeds of the General Councils, and especially the Nicene-Constantinopolitan Creed. Wherefore, the writing of Holy Scripture has continued up to our day, and, if God pleases, yet more will be written." A. Khomiakov, *The Church is One*, trans. N. Zernov (London: Fellowship of St. Alban and St. Sergius, 1968), 24.

[9]See the meager sources collected by B. Metzger, *The Canon of the New Testament* (Oxford: Clarendon 1989), 209–38, 305–15. The only "conciliar" statements to which he can point are canons 59–60 of the Synod of Laodicea (c. A.D. 363) and canon 24 of the Synod of Carthage (A.D. 397), which summarized the now lost decision of the Synod of Hippo Regius (A.D. 393). He also notes that the Council of Trullo (692) recognized the decisions of the Synod of Laodicea and Fathers such as Athanasius and Amphilochius as authoritative, but "thereby sanction[ed] implicitly, so far as the list of Biblical books is concerned, quite incongruous and contradictory opinions." (*The Canon*, 216). The only conclusion to be drawn from this is that the listing of Biblical books was not an issue for those who met in Trullo!

of truth."[10] The concern was not to demarcate those books which then together constitute the sole source of revelation and authority in themselves. Scripture cannot, in fact, stand alone as a source of authority, for it is always the Scripture of a particular community and always needs interpretation—the inspiration of Scripture cannot be separated from the inspired use of Scripture within the Church. Yet it must also never be forgotten that the Gospel, upon which the Church is founded, itself refers back to the Scriptures, which are now used to understand and proclaim the death and resurrection of Christ. As such, it is also difficult to separate the tradition of the Church, the apostolic tradition, from this engagement with Scripture, to claim that Scripture is an expression of tradition, for the initial delivery (or "traditioning," cf. 1 Cor 15:3: παρέδωκα) is given with reference to Scripture.

Read in the light of what God has wrought in Christ, the Scriptures provided the terms and images, the context, within which the apostles made sense of what happened, and with which they explained it and preached it, so justifying the claim that Christ died and rose "according to the Scriptures" (1 Cor 15:3–4). It is important to note that here it is Christ who is being explained through the medium of Scripture, not Scripture itself that is being exegeted; the object is not to understand the "original meaning" of an ancient text, as in modern historical-critical scholarship, but to understand Christ, who, by being explained "according to the Scriptures," becomes the sole subject of Scripture—the Law, the Psalms and the Prophets.[11] This preaching, the

---

[10]R. Pfeiffer argues that the term "canon" was first used to designate "list" (the πίνακες drawn up by the Alexandrian literary critics) by David Ruhnken in 1768, and that "His coinage met with worldwide and lasting success, as the term was found to be so convenient; one has the impression that most people who use it believe that this usage is of Greek origin. But κανών was never used in this sense, nor would this have been possible. From its frequent use in ethics κανών always retained the meaning of rule or model" (*History of Classical Scholarship: From the Beginnings to the End of the Hellenistic Age* [Oxford: Clarendon, 1968], 207). Despite this recognition, Pfeiffer himself a few lines later describes the list of biblical books as its "canon," appealing to passages where κανών could equally be taken in the sense of "rule" (Origen *apud* Eusebius *HE* 6.25.3; Athanasius, *On the Decrees of Nicaea*, 18), cf. G. A. Robbins, "Eusebius' Lexicon of 'Canonicity,' " *St. Patr.* 25 (Leuven: Peeters, 1993), 134–41. The term "canon" does appear to refer to the listing of the accepted books in Amphilocius of Iconium, *Iambics for Seleucus* (cited in Metzger, *Canon*, 212–13). Most of the studies treating the canon of Scripture note that "canon" primarily meant "rule," yet presuppose that it should mean "list," and so devote most attention to cataloguing when, where and by whom, the various writings were accepted as Scripture. For a more considered discussion of the issues concerning canon and Scripture, see J. Barton, *Holy Writings, Sacred Text: The Canon in Early Christianity* (Louisville, KY: Westminster John Knox Press, 1997) and W. J. Abraham, *Canon and Criterion in Christian Theology* (Oxford: Clarendon Press, 1998).

[11]J. Barr makes a pertinent comment when he notes that "large elements in the text [of the Genesis story of Adam] cannot be made to support Paul's use of the story without distortion of

kerygma, provides what Hays describes as "the eschatological *apokalypsis* of the cross," a hermeneutical lens, through which Scripture can now be refracted with "a profound new symbolic coherence."[12] This coherence is epitomized, made flesh, in the canonical Gospels, where, in the descriptions of Christ and his activity, culminating in the Passion and always told from that perspective, there is constant allusion to scriptural imagery. In contrast, it is precisely this engagement with Scripture, read in the light of the *kerygma*, that is absent from noncanonical works such as the *Gospel of Thomas* or the Valentinian *Gospel of Truth*.[13] Thus, in the canonical Gospels, the very "beginning of the Gospel of Jesus Christ" in Mark is illustrated by the citation of a passage from Isaiah (Mk 1:1–3; Mal 3:1; Is 40:3). In Matthew, the same engagement with Scripture is found throughout, in terms of prophecy-fulfilment structuring the narrative. While in Luke it appears as the hermeneutic, the principle of interpretation, taught by the risen Christ, thereby enlightening his disciples: "Beginning with Moses and all the prophets, he interpreted to them in all the Scriptures the things concerning himself" (Lk 24:27, cf. Lk 24:44–49). This literary enlightening of the disciples is paralleled in John when Christ breathes on his disciples the Holy Spirit, the one he had promised, who would remind them of all things concerning Christ, leading them into all truth (cf. Jn 20:22; 14:26); Word and Spirit can never be separated, and both are at work in the task of interpretation. It is also in John where the relationship between the Scriptures and Christ is stated most emphatically, by Christ himself: "If you believed Moses, you would believe me, for he wrote of me" (Jn 5:46).

The first Father of the Church to treat explicitly the relationship between Scripture, canon and tradition, was St Irenaeus of Lyons. He lived in the second century, a period not unlike our own, an age of extreme diversity and

their meaning." This is simply because "Paul was not interpreting the story in and for itself; he was really *interpreting Christ* through the use of images from this story." (*The Garden of Eden and the Hope of Immortality* [Minneapolis: Fortress Press, 1993], 89). For the problems which arise when the synchronic character of Scripture, as the product of one author or as speaking of a single subject throughout, is replaced by a diachronic study of the text, attempting to reconstruct the "original meaning" of its various parts, see J. D. Levenson, "The Eighth Principle of Judaism and the Literary Simultaneity of Scripture," *Journal of Religion*, 68 (1988), 205–25.

[12] R. Hays, *Echoes of Scripture in the Letters of Paul* (New Haven and London: Yale University Press, 1989), 169.

[13] For Valentinus, see D. Dawson, *Allegorical Readers and Cultural Revision in Ancient Alexandria* (Berkeley: University of California Press, 1992). And, more generally, F. Young, *Biblical Exegesis and the Formation of Christian Culture* (Cambridge: Cambridge University Press, 1997), and J. Behr, *The Way to Nicaea* (New York: SVS, 2001), 17–48.

syncretism, abounding with figures claiming to have preserved the true, unadulterated Gospel or tradition. Unsurprisingly, he had to deal with exactly the same issues that concern us again today—the true identity of Christian faith, the canon of truth, and the dynamics of tradition. Like the modern writers considered earlier, the articulation of the canon, the rule of truth, which we see for the first time in the writings of Irenaeus, was not meant to curtail or prohibit creative, critical thinking. The canon functioned, rather, to make genuine theological reflection possible. This is a creative task, to be engaged in by each generation as they appropriate the apostolic deposit and proclaim it anew under the inspiration of the same Spirit, so preserving the youthfulness of the Church: as Irenaeus put it, the preaching of the prophets and apostles, preserved in the Church and received from the Church, is constantly renewed by the Spirit of God, "as if it were a precious deposit in an excellent vessel, so causing the vessel itself containing it [i.e. the Church] to be rejuvenated also."[14] That is, by preserving the preaching of the Church, the apostolic deposit, which the Spirit of God continually makes flourish, the Church herself is rejuvenated.

The coherence of Scripture, the scriptural texture of the apostolic preaching of the Gospel in its interpretative engagement with Scripture, is the basis for Irenaeus' appeal to canon and tradition, an appeal that utilizes important terms borrowed from Hellenistic epistemology and literary theory. After beginning his magnum opus, *Against the Heresies*, with a description of some of the Valentinian myths, Irenaeus criticizes their use of Scripture and discusses the role of canon and tradition. These people, he says, have a "hypothesis" (ὑπόθεσις) which does not derive from the Lord or the apostles, but is rather their own fabrication (πλάσμα), which they then explicate with words from the Scriptures, adapting the words of God to their own myths (μύθοις), in an attempt to endow it with persuasive plausibility. As such they "disregard the order (τάξις) and the connection (εἱρμός) of the Scriptures and, as much as in them lies, they disjoint the members of the truth." To illustrate their procedure, Irenaeus gives the striking analogy of someone taking a mosaic of a king, and rearranging the stones to make a picture of a dog or a fox, claiming that this is the original, true image (*AH* 1.8.1). After giving some examples of his opponents' exegesis, Irenaeus then gives a more literary example, describing how some people take diverse lines from the work of Homer and then rearrange them to produce homeric-sounding verses which tell a tale not found in Homer. While these centos can mislead those who have

---

[14]*Against the Heresies* (hereafter *AH*) 3.24.1.

only a passing knowledge of Homer, they will not deceive those who are well versed in his poetry, for they will be able to identify the lines and restore them to their proper context (*AH* 1.9.4).

The terms used here by Irenaeus, "fabrication" (πλάσμα) and "myth" (μῦθος), are terms which, in Hellenistic literary theory, describe stories that are, in the first case, not true but seem to be so, and in the latter case, manifestly untrue.[15] The Valentinians, according to Irenaeus, have based their exegesis of Scripture upon their own "hypothesis" (ὑπόθεσις), rather than that foretold by the prophets, taught by Christ and delivered ("traditioned") by the apostles. In Hellenistic times, the term "hypothesis" (ὑπόθεσις) had a variety of meanings, one of which, again in a literary context, was the plot or outline of a drama or epic (what Aristotle, in the *Poetics*, had termed the μῦθος).[16] It is what the poet posits as the outline for his subsequent creative work. It is not derived from reasoning, but presupposed, providing the raw material upon which the poet can exercise his talents. Although the Valentinian myths use the words and phrases from Scripture, they have adapted them to a different hypothesis, and so have created their own fabrication.

In the other arts, it is similarly the hypothesis, as that which is posited, the presupposition, which facilitates both action and inquiry, and ultimately knowledge itself. Hypotheses are, as Aristotle puts it, the starting points or first principles (ἀρχαί) of demonstrations.[17] The goal of health is the hypothesis for a doctor, who then deliberates on how it is to be attained, just as mathematicians hypothesize certain axioms and then proceed with their demonstrations.[18] Such hypotheses are tentative; if the goal proves to be unattainable or if the conclusions derived from the supposition turn out to be manifestly false, then the hypothesis in question must be rejected. The aim of philosophy, however, at least since Plato, has been to discover the ultimate, nonhypothetical first principles.[19] But even here, as Aristotle concedes, it is impossible to demand demonstrations of the first principles themselves; if they could be proved, they would be dependent upon something prior to them, and so one would be led into an infinite regress.[20] This means, as Clement of Alexandria points out, that the search for the first principles of

---

[15] Cf. Sextus Empiricus *Against the Grammarians* 12 (252–68). Cf. R. Meijering, *Literary and Rhetorical Theories in Greek Scholia* (Groningen: Egbert Forsten, 1987), 72–90.

[16] Cf. Meijering, *Literary and Rhetorical Theories*, 99–133.

[17] Aristotle *Metaphysics* 5.1.2 (1013a17).

[18] Cf. Aristotle *Eudemian Ethics* 1227b28–33; Meijering, 106.

[19] Cf. Aristotle *Republic* 6.20–1 (510–11).

[20] Aristotle *Metaphysics* 4.4.2 (1006a6–12).

demonstration ends up with indemonstrable faith.[21] For Christian faith, according to Clement, the Scripture, or more precisely the Lord who speaks in them, is the first principle of all knowledge.[22] The voice of the Lord, speaking throughout Scripture, is the first principle, the (nonhypothetical) hypothesis of all demonstrations from Scripture, by which Christians are led to the knowledge of the truth.

These first principles, grasped by faith, are not only the basis for subsequent demonstrations, but are also used to evaluate other claims to truth, acting thus as a "canon." Originally this term simply meant a straight line, a rule by which other lines could be judged: "by that which is straight, we discern both the straight and the crooked; for the carpenter's rule (ὁ κανών) is the test of both, but the crooked tests neither itself nor the straight."[23] Epicurus' *Canon* seems to have been the first work devoted to the need to establish "the criteria of truth,"[24] a need which, in the face of the Sceptical onslaught, made it almost obligatory in the Hellenistic period to begin any systematic presentation of philosophy with an account of "the criterion."[25] Without a canon or criterion, knowledge is not possible, for all inquiry will be drawn helplessly into an endless regression. It was generally held in Hellenistic philosophy that preconceptions (προλήψεις—generic notions synthesized out of repeated sense perceptions, later held to be innate) facilitate knowledge and act as criteria. But again Clement points out how even Epicurus accepted that this "preconception of the mind" is "faith," and that without it, neither inquiry nor judgement is possible.[26]

In the same manner in which Hellenistic philosophers argued against the infinite regression of the Sceptics by appealing to a canon or criterion of truth, Irenaeus, Tertullian and Clement of Alexandria countered the constantly mutating Gnostic mythology,[27] by an appeal to their own canon of truth.

[21]Clement *Stromateis* 8.3.6.7–7.2; cf. E. Osborn, "Arguments for Faith in Clement of Alexandria," *Vigiliae Christianae*, 48 (1994), 1–24, at 12–14.

[22] Cf. Clement *Stromateis* 7.16.95.4–6.

[23]Aristotle *On the Soul* 1.5 (411a5–7).

[24]Diogenes Laertius *Lives of Eminent Philsophers* 10.31.

[25]Cf. G. Striker, "Κριτήριον τῆς ἀληθείας," *Nachrichten der Akademie der Wissenschaften in Göttingen*, Phil.-hist. Kl. (1974), 2:47–110; M. Schofield, M. Burnyeat, and J. Barnes (eds.), *Doubt and Dogmatism: Studies in Hellenistic Epistemology* (Oxford: Oxford University Press, 1980); P. Huby and G. Neal (eds.), *The Criterion of Truth* (Liverpool: Liverpool University Press, 1989).

[26]Clement *Stromata* 2.5.16.3. Cf. S. R. C. Lilla, *Clement of Alexandria: A Study in Christian Platonism and Gnosticism* (Oxford: Oxford University Press, 1971), 120–31.

[27]According to Irenaeus, his opponents were obliged to devise something new every day. Cf. *AH* 1.18.1; 1.21.5.

Understood in this way, the appeal to a canon was not meant to curtail thought, but to ensure that it did not dissolve into endless regression or mythology.[28] Irenaeus' assertion that "we must keep the canon of faith unswervingly and perform the commandments of God" in faith, for such faith "is established upon things truly real" and enables us to have "a true comprehension of what is" echoes the concerns of many philosophers.[29] After criticising the Gnostics for their distortion of Scripture, as described above, Irenaeus continues:

> ... anyone who keeps unswervingly in himself the canon of truth (τὸν κανόνα τῆς ἀληθείας) received through baptism will recognise the names and sayings and parables from the Scriptures, but this blasphemous hypothesis of theirs he will not recognise. For if he recognises the jewels, he will not accept the fox for the image of the king. He will restore each one of the passages to its proper order and, having fit it into the body of the truth, he will lay bare their fabrication and show that it is without support (AH 1:9:4).

Irenaeus follows this by outlining the faith received from the apostles: "the faith in one God the Father Almighty, Creator of heaven and earth . . . ; and in one Jesus Christ, the Son of God, who was enfleshed for our salvation; and in the Holy Spirit, who through the prophets preached the economies" that is, the various aspects of Christ's parousia (AH 1.10.1). This description is clearly structured upon the same three central articles of belief found in the interrogatory baptismal creeds from the earliest times and going back to the baptismal command of Christ himself (Mat 28:19), though it is not given in the declarative form, as are the creeds used in baptism from the fourth century onwards.[30]

Thus the canon of truth does not simply give fixed, and abstract, statements of Christian doctrine, but expresses the correct hypothesis of Scripture

---

[28] Cf. E. Osborn, "The rule did not limit reason to make room for faith, but used faith to make room for reason. Without a credible first principle, reason was lost in an infinite regress." ("Reason and the Rule of Faith in the Second Century AD," in R. Williams (ed.), *The Making of Orthodoxy: Essays in Honour of Henry Chadwick* [Cambridge: Cambridge University Press, 1989], 40–61, at 57).

[29] *Demonstration of the Apostolic Preaching* (hereafter *Dem.*), 3.

[30] For the connection between the "canon of truth" and baptism, see also *Demonstration 7*; and for recent discussion on the connection between baptism, the rule of truth and the later creeds, see W. Kinzig and M. Vinzent, "Recent Research on the Origin of the Creed," *JTS* ns 50:2 (1999), 535–59.

itself, that by which one can see in Scripture the picture of a king, Christ, rather than a dog or fox. One must, for instance, hold that the God of the Law, the Psalms and the Prophets, is indeed the Father of Jesus Christ—the first article of any canon or creed—if one is not to end up with a falsified picture. As a canon it facilitates the demonstration of the incongruous and extraneous nature of the Gnostic hypotheses. By means of the same canon of truth the various passages, the "members of truth" (*AH* 1.8.1), can be returned to their rightful place within "the body of truth" (*Dem.* 1), Scripture, so that it again speaks of Christ, while exposing the Gnostic fabrications for what they are. The canon of truth is thus ultimately the presupposition that is the apostolic Christ himself, the one who is "according to the Scripture" and, in reverse, the subject of Scripture throughout, being spoken of by the Spirit through the prophets, so revealing the one God and Father. It is inextricably connected, for Irenaeus, with "the order and the connection of the Scriptures," for it presents the one Father who has made himself known through the one Son by the Holy Spirit speaking through the prophets, that is, through the Scriptures—the Law, the Psalms and the Prophets. It is striking that, in the fullest canon of truth outlined by Irenaeus in *AH* 1.10.1, all the economies of Christ recounted in the Gospels are presented under the article of the Holy Spirit, who preached these things through the prophets—Scripture when read according to the Spirit. In the later declaratory creeds, the economies described in the Gospel are presented under the second article, and so what it is that the Spirit "spoke through the prophets" is left unspecified. The canon of truth is the embodiment or crystallisation of the coherence of Scripture, read as speaking of the Christ who is revealed in the Gospel, the apostolic preaching of Christ "according to Scripture." Clement of Alexandria provides a concise definition of the canon when he states:

> The ecclesiastical canon is the concord and harmony of the law and the prophets in the covenant delivered at the coming of the Lord.[31]

The risen Lord reveals the symphony of the Scriptures, when he opens the books to show how they all speak of himself, the one presented by the apostles "according to Scripture." The pattern of this harmony is expressed in the canon of truth, enabling the demonstrations from Scripture to describe,

---

[31]Clement *Strom.* 6.15.125.3: κανὴν δὲ ἐκκλησιαστικὸς ἡ συνῳδία καὶ ἡ συμφωνία νόμου τε καὶ προφητῶν τῇ κατὰ τὴν τοῦ κυρίου παρουσίαν παραδιδομένῃ διαθήκῃ.

accurately, the portrait of a king, Christ.[32] The canon of truth thus provides the framework for the encounter with the Christ proclaimed by the apostles, an encounter which takes place through the engagement with the matrix of imagery provided by the Scriptures.

The key elements of the faith delivered by the apostles are crystallised in the canon of truth, which expresses the basic elements of the one Gospel, maintained and preached in the Church, in an ever-changing context. The continually changing context in which the same unchanging Gospel is preached makes it necessary that different aspects or facets of the same Gospel be drawn out to address contemporary challenges. However, whilst the context continually changes, the content of that tradition does not—it is the same Gospel. So, Irenaeus continues by emphasizing that though the Church is spread throughout the world, she nevertheless hands down the preaching and teaching harmoniously, for "the meaning of tradition (ἡ δύναμις τῆς παραδόσεως) is one and the same"; those who preside in the churches, however eloquent, cannot say anything else, and neither will a poor speaker subtract from the tradition, for the faith is one and the same (AH 1.10.2). However, as we have seen, the point of a canon is not to stymie inquiry and reflection, but to make it possible. So, although Irenaeus specifies that the content of the apostolic tradition remains one and the same, he nevertheless gives directions to those who desire to inquire more deeply into the revelation of God: theological inquiry is not to be carried out by changing the hypothesis itself (thinking up another God or another Christ), but by reflecting further on whatever was said in parables, bringing out the meaning of the obscure passages, by placing them in the clear light of the "hypothesis of truth" (AH 1.10.3).

Irenaeus further examines the relation between Scripture and tradition in the opening five chapters of his third book Against the Heresies, this time to counter the Gnostic claims to possess secret, oral traditions.[33] He begins by affirming categorically that the revelation of God is mediated through the apostles. It is not enough to see the "Jesus of history" to see God, nor to imagine God as a partner with whom one can dialogue directly, bypassing his own Word. Rather the locus of revelation, and the medium for our relationship with God, is precisely in the apostolic preaching of him, the Gospel which, as

---

[32]The need to remain true to a "pattern" is already felt by Paul, who urges Timothy to "follow the pattern of the sound words which you heard from me" (2 Tim 1:13); the "canon of truth" is the articulation of this "pattern."

[33]For a full analysis of these chapters, see Behr, The Way to Nicaea, 38–45.

we have seen, stands in an interpretative engagement with Scripture. The role of the apostles in delivering the Gospel is definitive. As Irenaeus puts it:

> We have learned from no others the plan of our salvation than from those through whom the Gospel has come down to us, which they did at one time proclaim in public, and at a later period, by the will of God, handed down (*tradiderunt*) to us in the Scriptures, to be the ground and pillar of our faith. . . . These have all declared to us that there is one God, Creator of heaven and earth, announced by the Law and Prophets; and one Christ the Son of God (*AH* 3.1.1–2).

So, for Irenaeus, both the true apostolic tradition maintained by the churches, and the apostolic writings themselves, derive from the same apostles, and have one and the same content, the Gospel, which is itself "according to the Scriptures." This allows Irenaeus to reject his opponents' appeal to a tradition which has been handed down in a secret oral tradition and without which, they claim, Scripture cannot be understood, for what the apostles taught in public is identical to what they wrote down; far from preserving an authentic tradition, Marcion and Valentinus have distorted the canon of truth and merely preached themselves (*AH* 3.2.1). Irenaeus, on the other hand, does appeal to tradition, and even imagines a scenario in which the apostles left nothing behind in writing, so that only the oral tradition exists, but in these cases the tradition he appeals to is again identical with what in fact is written down by the apostles (*AH* 3.2.2, 3.4). Irenaeus' appeal to tradition is thus fundamentally different to that of his opponents. While they appealed to tradition precisely for that which was not in Scripture, or for principles which would legitimise their interpretation of Scripture, Irenaeus, in his appeal to tradition, was not appealing to anything that was not also in Scripture. Thus Irenaeus can appeal to tradition to establish his case and at the same time maintain that Scripture cannot be understood except on the basis of Scripture itself, using its own hypothesis and canon.[34] Having established that the apostolic tradition does now exist in the Church, preserved through the successions of the presbyters who have preserved intact the true preaching, Irenaeus turns to "the demonstration from the Scriptures of the apostles who wrote the Gospel, in which they recorded the doctrine regarding God, pointing out that our Lord Jesus Christ is the truth, and that there is no lie in Him"

---

[34]Cf. *AH* 3.12.9: "the demonstrations [of things contained] in the Scriptures cannot be demonstrated except from the Scriptures themselves."

(*AH* 3.5.1). Scripture, as written, is fixed,[35] and though the tradition maintained by the succession of presbyters is similarly fixed in principle, in practice it is much less secure, and, in any case, it can never be, for Irenaeus, a point of reference apart from Scripture. The doctrine concerning God, and the truth that is Christ, is found in the exposition of the Scriptures as interpreted by the apostles, who alone proclaimed the Gospel, handing it down in both Scripture and tradition. In this way, the apostolic writings are recognized as belonging to Scripture, and are indeed used extensively as such, for the first time, by Irenaeus.[36]

In this way, Irenaeus established, in the chaos of the second century, amidst the numerous claims concerning the identity of the Christian faith, that there is indeed one Gospel, a Gospel which is of God, not of man (cf. Rom 1:1; Gal 1:11–12), just as there is one Lord Jesus Christ. The one Christ, the Son of God, proclaimed by the apostles in the one Gospel "according to the Scriptures," makes known (ἐξηγήσατο, "exegetes," Jn 1:18) the Father, just as the one God has made himself known through his one Son by the Holy Spirit who speaks about him through the prophets. Yet, this Gospel proclaims the Coming One (ὁ ἐρχόμενος), and so it is not finally fixed in a text, but is found in an interpretative engagement with Scripture, an engagement in which the student of the Word is also "interpreted" by the Word as he or she puts on the identity of Christ. This scriptural engagement cannot be avoided; even when John the Baptist was imprisoned and sent his disciples to ask Jesus "Are you he who is to come (ὁ ἐρχόμενος) or shall we look for another?" Jesus did not give a straightforward answer, but directed him to signs—the blind seeing, the lame walking—which can only be understood as "messianic" through the interpretation of them by Scripture (Matt 11:2–5). This hypothesis and canon calls for continual reflection, and the centuries that followed did so reflect and used all the means at their disposal. There are many monuments to this continual engagement with the Gospel proclaimed according to the Scriptures—writings of the Fathers and saints, schools of iconography and hagiography and so on—all of which have a certain authority to the extent that they point to the same vision of the King, the Gospel image of Christ. In the light of the canon of truth itself, other elements are also called "canons," such as the classical liturgical anaphoras, which epitomize the

---

[35]Though see B. Ehrman, *The Orthodox Corruption of Scripture: The Effect of Early Christological Controversies on the Text of the New Testament* (New York and Oxford: Oxford University Press, 1993).

[36]Cf. Y.-M. Blanchard, *Aux Sources du canon, le témoignage d'Irénée* (Paris: Cerf, 1993).

whole of Scripture, those saints whose lives and teachings embody the truth are "canons" of faith and piety, and similarly the decisions of the councils concerning the proper order for the Church and people of God in particular situations are "canons." The Word grows, as Acts puts it (Acts 6:7), in that as more and more people believe in it and reflect on it, there are ever new, more detailed and comprehensive explanations elaborated in defense of one and the same faith, the faith in what has been delivered from the beginning, the Gospel according to the Scriptures, the same Word of God—Jesus Christ, the same yesterday, today and for ever (Heb 13:8).

The Scriptural Christ – the Alpha and Omega

With Irenaeus, then, we have found a way of preserving the truth so dear to twentieth-century Orthodox theology, that the true tradition of the Church is preserved most faithfully in the creative response to Christ. Yet, as we have seen, the canon that makes this creativity possible expresses the hypothesis of Scripture, revealed in the apostolic proclamation of Christ "according to the Scriptures." Christian theology is centered upon Jesus Christ, the crucified and exalted Lord, understood and proclaimed "according to the Scriptures." This vitally important point, which might sound too obvious to mention, is too often obscured today. This is sadly true not only of theology, but of many other aspects of the life of the Church. It is too easy for the Church to become a vehicle for many other concerns and activities, which might themselves seem very religious and spiritual, pious and pastoral (such as Dostoyevsky's Grand Inquisitor, or the beasts described by St Ignaty Branchaninov, who worship the typikon rather than Christ); not to mention the ways in which the Church can be used for ends which are merely nationalistic or political, sectarian or escapist—anything rather than Christ and the Gospel, the truth which alone is able to set free (Gal 5:1; Jn 8:32). Such phenomena abound, but none of them are based in Jesus Christ as proclaimed in the Gospel, nor are they inspired and informed by the Spirit of God who leads us into the fullness of the truth revealed by Christ.

With regard to theology, a problem seems to arise, paradoxically, because of the abundance of riches. We are heirs to two millennia of theological reflection—from Fathers and Saints whose witness has been tested by sweat and blood. Although the Orthodox have not taken the lead in matters such as preparing good editions and translations of the texts, we have, over the past century, come to appreciate increasingly this heritage (the "return to the sources"—again, largely following Western trends) and we have become conscious of the value of this inheritance: the rebirth of Orthodox theology in the twentieth century, mentioned earlier, took the form of a "patristic revival" and resulted in a "neopatristic synthesis."

However, it is easy for our very familiarity with the reflections of the Fathers and the results of the various dogmatic controversies and conciliar resolutions to blind us to the focal point of those reflections and debates: Jesus Christ, the crucified and exalted Lord. Looking back on twentieth-century theology, it can sometimes seem as if theological reflection in this period *began* with the results of the dogmatic debates, rather than the questions that they were seeking to answer.[37] It is noticeable, for instance, that there is very little serious engagement with Scripture, or the pre-Nicene period, by Orthodox theologians in the twentieth century. The tendency is to begin with Nicaea, and then look for anticipations of Nicene theology in the earlier periods. But, it is methodologically faulty to begin with the results of the controversies or with these results already synthesized into dogmatic systems by later generations. Doing this, we start with what we think we already know and look back to the Fathers simply to find confirmation—and then we will find that they all taught the same thing, which turns out to be what we already knew![38] Not only is there no serious engagement with the writings of the Fathers when approached in this manner, but the risk of misconstruing what they were saying is great: if the questions being debated are not understood, it will be difficult, if not impossible, to understand the answers. We all certainly stand in tradition, and so have a context for looking back at history, but we must also make sure that we allow our understanding of tradition to be challenged by history, rather than reduce everything to our own presuppositions.

Trinitarian theology is a good example of this problematic. Nicene Trinitarian theology is too often reduced to shorthand formulae such as the "three hypostases" of the "consubstantial Trinity." The reflection that lies behind

[37]For a fuller analysis of this problem, see J. Behr, "The Paschal Foundation of Christian Theology," *St. Vladimir's Orthodox Theological Quarterly*, 45.2 (2001), 115–36.

[38]A similar point was already noted by N. Berdyaev: "I have also noticed that, while the newly-converted advocates of Orthodoxy were studying and propagating the Church Fathers with great enthusiasm, they often ascribed to them views and beliefs which it is not possible to find in them, or tended to read between the lines where no 'between' could possibly be detected." *Dream and Reality*, trans. K. Lampert (London: Bles, 1950), 178. I thank N. Behr for drawing my attention to this passage.

these phrases is immense, but to begin with the results tends to detached the formulae from the debates that forged them and so devoid them of the content they encapsulate. Begun from such a starting point, Trinitarian theology concerns itself with reflecting on how there can be three eternally distinct persons, without the plurality destroying the unity or the unity undermining the reality of the distinctions. Such theology concerns itself with the metaphysics of three divine persons, and projects a history, or better a mythology, describing how, after interacting in various other ways, one of these persons eventually became man (though why it is the second person is never really explained).[39] Theological attention is now focused on the heavenly existence of three divine persons, and their relationship, as persons in communion, is taken as the constitutive element for our own existence in the image of God.

But this does not really do justice to the Fathers who articulated the teaching of Nicaea. The formulae "three hypostases, one ousia" in fact occurs very rarely in their writings.[40] Moreover, the great Fathers of the fourth century urge great caution in using numbers at all: "When the Lord taught us the doctrine of the Father, Son and Holy Spirit, he did not make arithmetic a part of this gift! . . . He did not say one, two and three."[41] This point is echoed by Vladimir Lossky: "In speaking of three hypostases, we are already making an improper abstraction," he notes, for there is no common definition of the three hypostases, no common concept of "hypostasis" (by which we would be able to count three, and then elaborate a metaphysics of personhood and communion), for anything common belongs to the one essence—by definition.[42]

More importantly, in this style of theology, Christ is actually marginalized. Not only is theological attention no longer focused on the given revelation of God in Christ, but that revelation is now retold in a different manner: the Word of God is no longer the locus of God's self-expression (for from the time of Augustine it is held that any of the three appeared in the Old Testament theophanies), and the Incarnate Word, Jesus Christ, is not so much "the exact imprint of the very being" of the Father (Heb 1:3), but is rather the

[39]Cf. K. Rahner, "The Theology of the Incarnation," in idem, *More Recent Writings*, Theological Investigations, vol. 4 (Baltimore: Helicon Press, 1966), 105–20. According to Peter Lombard, though it is still a common presupposition, that while it was the Son who became man, as Jesus Christ, it was nevertheless possible, and still is, for the Father and the Spirit also to be incarnate (cf. *Libri IV Sententiarum* 3.1.2).

[40]Cf. J. T. Lienhard, "*Ousia* and *Hypostasis*: The Cappadocian Settlement and the Theology of 'One *Hypostasis*,'" in S. T. Davies, D. Kendall, and G. O'Collins eds., *The Trinity* (Oxford: OUP, 1999), 99–121, esp. 99–103.

[41]St Basil the Great *On the Holy Spirit* 44.

[42]V. Lossky, *In the Image and Likeness of God*, 113.

incarnation of a divine person which could have been otherwise if so desired. Rather than concerning itself about the heavenly existence of three divine persons, the point of Nicene Trinitarian theology is to confirm that what we see in Christ, as proclaimed by the Gospel, is indeed truly is what it is to be God, that he is divine with the same divinity as his Father, a recognition only possible in the Spirit, who alone enables us to recognize Christ as Lord, the bearer of the Divine Name (cf. 1 Cor 12:3; Phil 2:8–9). Similarly, it is not, according to the New Testament and the Fathers, the communal existence of a trinitarian God that is the paradigm for our existence in the image of God, as persons in communion, vertically with God and horizontally with each other; rather it is Christ alone who is the image of the invisible God (Col 1:15), in whose pattern Adam was already moulded (Rom 5:14), and to whose image we are conformed (Rom 8:29) when we are crucified with him (Gal 2:20 etc.).

One could make the same point about all the dogmatic controversies, and their resulting formulae—that they are ultimately reflections about Christ, who opens the books of Scripture (Lk 24), making known the Father (Jn 1:18), from whom, in Christ, we receive the Spirit. The dogmatic formulae of the Church are not abstract, detachable statements which we can use to construct a metaphysical system responding to our existential or philosophical concerns. Of course, theological reflection became ever more abstract, but the point of such ongoing reflection is not to describe ultimate structures of "reality," to elaborate a fundamental ontology, whether of "Being" or "communion" (or both), which then tends to function as if it constitutes the content of the revelation itself. We must be very careful not to substitute the explanation for that which it seeks to explain. The aim of such theological reflection was and is to articulate as precisely as possible, in the face of perceived aberrations, the canon of truth, so as to preserve the undistorted image of the Christ presented in the Scriptures.

As we have seen, the Christ with whom we are concerned is the Scriptural Christ: the Christ who appears in Gospels as the crucified and exalted Lord, understood and presented through the medium of the Scriptures—the Law, the Psalms and the Prophets. It is *this* Christ who is the subject of our faith, not the Christ of historical reconstruction, individual mystical experience or metaphysical explanations. The Scriptures thus form the basic context or matrix within which all theology develops. Tradition, as we have seen, is not a supplementary source alongside Scripture, nor does Scripture exist within Tradition, for from the beginning the Gospel, which calls the Church into being, is proclaimed through the medium of Scripture. For the early Church, "tradition" is, as Florovsky put it, "Scripture rightly understood."[43] This is equally evident in our liturgical tradition, where Christ is praised and worshipped, giving glory through him to the Father in the Spirit, in hymns whose imagery and poetry are drawn directly from the treasury of Scripture. This Scriptural context seems to be diminished today, not only in the increasingly secularised world, but, more tragically, within the Church and even in the discipline of theology.[44] General familiarity with the basic narratives of Scripture, the books that informed and formed the imagination and thought-world of previous centuries, is being lost at an accelerating rate. It may be that more people today claim themselves to be Christians, but the Christ that they turn to is more likely to be "my personal saviour who helps me find happiness and true selfhood" or "the Christ of an abstracted theology whose incarnation effects my deification if I can only connect myself with the divine energies," rather than the Scriptural Christ, in whose light we can know both ourselves as we truly are, sinners living in death, and also the greatness of God, whose strength is made perfect in weakness (2 Cor 12:9). If we are to take seriously the creativity and faithfulness so extolled in the twentieth century, we must focus on Jesus Christ, the crucified and exalted Lord, as understood and proclaimed in Scripture. We need to return, as St Polycarp already in the early second century urged his readers, to "the Word delivered in the beginning."[45]

[43]G. Florovsky, "The Function of Tradition in the Early Church," *GOTR* 9.2 (1963), 182; repr. in idem, *Bible, Church, Tradition* (Vaduz, Büchervertriebsanstalt, 1987), 75.

[44]For some profound reflections on the problems that this raises, see G. Lindbeck, "Barth and Textuality," *Theology Today*, 43 (1986), 361–76.

[45]Polycarp *To the Philippians* 7.2.

On God and Evil

Thomas Hopko

BISHOP KALLISTOS is fond of quoting John Henry Newman's description of the theological enterprise as "saying and unsaying to a positive effect."[1] This description is nowhere more fitting than in discourse about God's relation to evil according to the Christian canon of faith centered in the crucified Christ. May my words on this subject be an apt illustration of Cardinal Newman's insight and a contribution worthy of Bishop Kallistos' extraordinary achievements.

My understanding of God's relation to evil according to Christian teaching is given in twenty-seven sentences.

1. **God is good and in God is no evil at all.** This foundational affirmation plays on the saying of the first letter of John that "God is light and in him is no darkness at all" (1 Jn 1:5). Orthodox theology, following canonical Christian scripture, rejects any teaching which posits two metaphysical absolutes, one light and good, and the other dark and evil. Christian orthodoxy rejects all forms of metaphysical dualism. God alone is absolute. God alone is good. God is only good. There is no "dark side" of God, no "tragedy" in the Godhead, no "fall" of God in any form.

2. **"Divine darkness" has nothing to do with evil.** When Christian mystics speak of "divine darkness" they are not referring to evil in God. They are rather saying that what God is is so glorious and splendid that it may be spoken of paradoxically as "luminous darkness." God's dazzling darkness is, in this sense, the blinding light of God's resplendent reality. The use of the term "darkness" in this poetic way affirms the canonical scriptural teaching that "God dwells in unapproachable light" and that "in him is no darkness at all"

[1]E.g. See Bishop Kallistos' address on *Theological Education in Scripture and the Fathers* at the International Conference of Orthodox Theological Schools sponsored by SYNDESMOS in Halki, August, 1994.

(1 Tim 6:16, 1 Jn 1:5). It affirms as well that what God is cannot be comprehended by creatures.[2]

3. God is beyond good and evil. Speaking in another way, it can be said that there is a sense in which God is beyond good and evil, and so, too, beyond light and darkness, and being and nothingness. This is so because God is beyond all created realities and categories. There is nothing in creation comparable to God. God is completely different. He is, as the saying goes, wholly other (*totaliter aliter*). God abides in a realm of reality uniquely his own before which creatures can only wonder and worship, and submit and surrender.

4. There is a sense in which God is not good. The positive (*kataphatic*) way of speaking about God affirms things of God and denies these same things, strictly speaking, to creatures. In this sense we say that God is good and in him is no evil at all, and that creatures cannot really be said to be good. The Bible generally speaks this way (see Mk 10:18). The negative (*apophatic*) way of speaking of God affirms things about creatures and denies them, strictly speaking, to God. In this sense we say that since we call creatures good, God can be said to be "not good" because what God is in God's divine (or supra-divine, or supra-non-divine) reality is wholly beyond anything that words and images used for creatures can accurately convey. We may then go on to say that God is even not "not good" because the negation presupposes an assertion which, in this way of speaking (which is often that of church fathers and mystics), is also not completely accurate or precise.[3]

5. God can never be said to be evil. Whether we use biblical ways of speaking of God, or patristic ways; whether our words are scholastic or poetic, mystical or intellectual; whether we make affirmations or negations, or even negations of negations, one thing is for certain according to Orthodox Christian teaching: we can never say that God is evil. God can be said to be good. God can be said to be "not good" in comparison to created good. God can also be said to be "beyond good and evil," as these categories apply, strictly speaking, solely to creatures. But God can never be said to be evil.

6. God creates everything good. To continue our saying and unsaying, hopefully to a positive effect, we can now say that God creates everything good

---

[2]See Dionysios the Areopagite *Mystical Theology* 1. Vladimir Lossky, *The Mystical Theology of the Eastern Church* (Crestwood, NY: St Vladimir's Seminary Press, 1976), 2.

[3]See John of Damascus *The Orthodox Faith* 1.12.

and that the goodness of what God creates reflects, imitates and participates in the goodness of God. All that creatures are and have is from God. We are even constrained to say that all that creatures are and have somehow exists in God in a divine (or supra-divine, or supra-non-divine) manner beyond human comprehension and imagination. Creatures are not autonomous or independent. They have nothing their own, and are nothing in themselves. They belong to God and are what they are only to the measure that they reflect God and abide in communion with him. Human goodness, therefore, whether people acknowledge it or not, as well as the goodness of the natural world, are always from God as created expressions, reflections and imitations of God's incomprehensible and boundless goodness in which creatures participate.

7. **Evil has no substantial existence.** Evil is a perversion of goodness. It is a parasite. It has no being of its own. Evil is always a misuse and abuse of something positive and good. Evil, therefore, cannot be considered as simply an "absence of being," or an "absence of goodness," something somehow "non-existent." Evil exists as a presence and a power, albeit a negative presence and a destructive power. Thus there is no such thing as "evil as such" or "evil in itself." Evil is always rooted and grounded in something good made by God. As such, evil is a distortion and corruption of the good (which is also necessarily the true and the beautiful) which is never completely lacking in the evildoer in whom the evil is found and through whom the evil is enacted. Seen and spoken of in this way, it must be said that Satan and the demons are originally and essentially good, as are all evildoers.

8. **Evil comes from creatures.** Evil originates in creatures. It does not come from God. It is not the will of God. Creatures bring evil into God's good creation by misusing and abusing the good things given by God, beginning with their own being and life. Sicknesses and diseases, and even natural disasters and the ravages of beasts, are, according to Christian scriptures and saints, somehow the fault of creatures who have broken their relationship with God. If human beings were perfectly good, Christian tradition contends, and if they remained in perfect communion with God, acting freely by God's Good Spirit and not enslaved by evil spirits, the elements and the animals would be in their control and would thereby be deprived of their destructive and death-dealing powers. This cosmic peace is exactly what is expected in God's coming kingdom under the lordship of Christ at the end of the ages. It is already witnessed in Jesus' earthly life, according to the scriptures, as well as in the lives of saints.

9. **Evil's origin is creaturely choice.** It is often said that the origin of evil lies in choice, and that sin is the making of bad choices. This is true when properly explained, but it seems more consistent with Christian scripture and tradition to hold that the origin of evil is found in the presumption that creatures have choices at all. The point here is simple. If God exists, what choices can creatures possibly have? Their only real choice is to love and trust God, and to do God's will. This seems to be what the Genesis stories are written to tell us. It is also what Jesus, the second and final Adam, witnesses when he says that he has no words, no works and no will of his own, but that all that he says, does and wills is in obedience to God his Father. It is impossible to imagine that Christ would presume to *choose* anything, or even think that he had a choice. Even more impossible is it to imagine that Jesus would hold that his freedom and dignity derive from the many choices available to him in his alleged autonomy![4] Jesus obeys God his Father with absolute love and devotion. He says "yes" to the Father's will in every circumstance, even when he asks his "Abba," to whom all things are possible, to remove the cup of suffering which he must drink at the hands of evildoers. In this understanding, the cause of every evil lies in the lie that creatures have choices. In this way of looking at things, the making of choices demonstrates an egregious failure on the part of creatures to abide in communion with God. It demonstrates a disobedience and rebellion that inexorably lead to destruction and death.

10. **God wills that there be evil.** Although God did not create evil, God clearly wills, according to Christian scripture and tradition, that evil and wickedness exist. The fathers, interpreting scripture, make this subtle point by saying that though God does not will evil *metaphysically,* God certainly does will evil *providentially.*[5] This is proven by God's creating those whom he knew would be evil. God does this, the scriptures testify and the saints explain, because God in his love creates all that can be created, both good and evil. He does this so that creatures who come to see themselves in the light of God's goodness, and recognize themselves as being both creatures and sinners, can repent of their evils by being tried, purified and glorified for unending life in communion with God through what they suffer. It is therefore inevitable that there

---

[4]St. Maximos the Confessor was mutilated for insisting that Christ, having divine and human natures, wills, energies and operations, had no "gnomic will," which is to say that he never made choices based on deliberations since he possessed perfect freedom in his perfect union with God the Father (a condition which is also theoretically possible to "mere human beings" by faith and grace.) The Sixth Ecumenical Council confirmed this doctrine.

[5]See John of Damascus *The Orthodox Faith* 2.22–30.

be evil. God wills the existence of evil as a creaturely perversion of good in his decision to create. And he uses evil, in all its horror and ugliness, for the ultimate glory of his creatures. In a word, God either has a world with evil, or God has no world at all.

11. **God hates and loves evildoers.** Reflecting on God's relationship to evil-doers provides a perfect example of the need for "saying and unsaying to a positive effect." Christian scriptures and saints insist on God's hatred for evil-doers. Yet the Christian good news, fulfilling the law and the prophets, pro-claims God's love for sinners. In creating a world with evil, and ultimately destroying evil by Christ's crucifixion at the hands of evildoers, God demon-strates his ultimate love for the wicked. If God loved only those who love him, he would, according to Jesus, be no better than a sinner himself. But it is per-fectly proven in Christ that God loves his enemies. He blesses those who curse him. He speaks to those who do not speak to him. He gives to those from whom he has no hope to receive back again. He is kind to the ungrateful and the selfish (see Lk 6:32–36). God's very wrath for the wicked is an expression of his love, for God cares enough to be angry over evildoers whom he ulti-mately forgives and redeems in his son Jesus. Thus we must say, paradoxi-cally, that God hates those whom he loves when he sees them sinning, and loves the sinners whom he hates when he does all that he can to save them.

12. **God cannot create only those who are good.** Some people ask why God does not create only good people in a good world. At least three answers seem possible to this question. The first is that there are no completely good peo-ple (including those who put the question), or, at best, very few who are right-eous by faith and grace but who nevertheless are still subject to innocent human failings and weaknesses.[6] The second is that all who are saved for everlasting life with God are saved through sin and repentance. The third is that all human beings, to become truly like God and totally deified, must, without exception, confront and endure evil without being overcome by it. Good people must prove their goodness by their love for God through love for their neighbors, including the most egregious doers of evil. They must come by God's grace to imitate God's love and to overcome evil by good which inevitably requires the enduring of evils, suffering and death.

---

[6]See St. Silouan's comments on the sinlessness of Christ's mother Mary in Archimandrite Sophrony's *St. Silouan the Athonite* (Crestwood, NY: St Vladimir's Seminary Press), 392.

13. **Human beings have been evil from the beginning.** According to Judeo-Christian scripture evil exists from the very beginning of human life. There is no history of sinless humanity on earth. The attempt to be godlike without God through the experience of evil is a primordial action of human beings. It is inspired by a serpentine "wisdom" described in scripture as "earthly, psychic and demonic" which is rooted in "bitter jealousy" and "selfish ambition" (Jas 3:14–16). It is the wicked suppression of the truth which leads to every manner of evil through the refusal to give glory and gratitude to God whose divinity and power can be clearly seen in the things that exist (Rom 1:18–32). It is a defiant act of rebellion which results in the murder, carnality, presumption, arrogance and pride described in the biblical stories from the disobedience of Adam and Eve to the destruction of Sodom and Gomorrah at the time of Abraham who received God's promise of salvation for all the families of the earth through his seed who is the Christ (Gen 1:1–19, Gal 3:16).

14. **Human beings are born into a corrupted world.** Human beings from the beginning are conceived in sinful conditions and born into a sinful world, if indeed they are permitted to survive in their mothers' wombs after being conceived (Ps 51:5).[7] The children of Adam and Eve are formed in the distorted image and likeness of their parents (see Gen 5:3). Ancestral, generational and corporate sins draw people into all sorts of wickedness from before their birth. The kind and degree of perversion in human beings depends on heredity and environment, on nature and nurture. The more parents are perverted in mind, soul and body, the more perverted are their children. No one and nothing in this world are untouched by evils and unscathed by sins. The world lies in wickedness, and everyone and everything in it are involved in evil to a greater or lesser degree.[8]

15. **Human beings are a complex of good and evil.** The Bible knows no real atheists. It knows *fools,* who say that there is no God; *apostates* who turn their back on God and rebel against him; *idolaters* who make gods in their own images and worship them in place of the only true God; *hypocrites* who pretend outwardly to be godly and good, but inwardly are evil and wicked; and *blasphemers,* like the demons, who in their rebellious madness hate God

---

[7]Orthodox tradition generally interprets Psalm 51 as saying that the blessed act of procreation occurs in a condition corrupted by evil and condemned to death. It does not understand, as is sometimes claimed, that the procreative act is in itself sinful.

[8]See T. Hopko, *Sin: Primordial, Generational, Personal.* Audio Casettes (Crestwood, NY: St Vladimir's Seminary Press, 1999).

and refuse to submit to his righteousness. Some evildoers know what they do and knowingly draw others into their madness. Some have been deceived and deluded and act wickedly without really knowing what they do. All, especially at this late point in human history, including those who call on the name of the Lord, are a complex mixture of good and evil, of knowledge and delusion. All are in desperate need of God's word and God's grace in order to be healed and saved.

16. **Good acts done without love profit nothing.** Objectively good acts, like working for justice, aiding the sick and helping the poor, including good acts done in God's name, profit a person nothing if they are done without love (see 1 Cor 13). Such good deeds can be done from arrogance, pride, vanity, anger, contempt for others and for many other ungodly and vicious reasons. Thus we understand Christ's terrible words: "Not everyone who says to me 'Lord, Lord,' shall enter the kingdom of heaven, but he who does the will of my Father who is in heaven. On that day (of judgment) many will say to me, 'Lord, Lord, did we not prophesy in your name, and cast out demons in your name, and do many mighty works in your name?' And then I will declare to them, 'I never knew you; depart from me, your evildoers' " (Mt 7:21–23). The Father's will is that we love.[9]

17. **The worst possible evils are those done in God's name.** No evil is greater and more heinous than that done in the name of God, especially the God of Jesus. Such evils may be done knowingly, with the rankest hypocrisy. Or they may be done by those who have been deluded and deceived by the wickedness of others, having fallen into the hands of false prophets and teachers. Or they may be done through the inspiration of demons appearing as angels of light. Whatever the case or the cause of such evils, it is clearly possible for people to call light darkness and darkness light, good actions evil and evil actions good (Isa 5:20–21). It is possible even for people to kill and to think that they are offering service to God (Jn 16:2, Mt 23–24).

[9]Reasons are found in classical Christian teaching about why God allows unloving people to prophecy, perform miracles and do good deeds in God's name only to be condemned at the end as "evildoers." Among them are that God does what he wills and it is not for us to question; that God defends his name by working through the wicked; that God uses evildoers for the benefit of the faithful, the poor and the needy; and that God provides all things to his people, even prophecies and miracles, so that those who are ultimately lost for lack of love will be without excuse or accusation against God, having been given everything possible for repentance and salvation.

18. **God is the Lord of good and evil.** It is sometimes said that God is Lord of good, but not evil, of light but not darkness. In this view, evil is independent of God and outside his control. A version of this view is that the Lord permits evil to exist outside his control, although he could in fact control it, because he respects the freedom of his creatures. Such an understanding, it seems to me, is contrary to Christian scripture and tradition. The teaching is rather that God creates a world in which evil exists through creaturely rebellion, and that when evil emerges through the wickedness of creatures, God can literally do nothing about it except use it for good according to his providential purposes, and take it upon himself to destroy it from within through the crucifixion of his Son. The Orthodox doctrine, therefore, seems to be that the God of gods and the Lord of lords rules over good and evil by ordering a world and accomplishing a providential plan which includes the existence and employment of evil for divinely designed purposes and ends. As the biblical songs declare, it is God who kills and makes alive, who brings to sheol and raises up, who wounds and heals, who makes poor and rich, who brings low and exalts.[10] The greatly stricken Job, whom God himself offered to Satan, responds to his wife's counsel that he "curse God and die" with the stark question: "Shall we receive good at the hand of God, and shall we not receive evil?" (Job 2:9–10) The biblical answer is obvious.[11]

19. **God uses evil for good.** The biblical story, which Christians see recapitulated in the gospel of Christ, is the story of God using evil for his ultimate victory over evil by good. In Hebrew the word for salvation and the word for victory is the same word. *Savior* and *victor* are synonyms in the Bible. God uses evil to chasten, cleanse and instruct his People. He brings evils upon the proud and glorious of the earth in order to bring them to their senses that they might repent of their evils and return to God.[12] He sends diseases, afflictions, terror, invasions, plagues and disasters in order to instruct and chasten his people that they may ultimately be saved.[13] In the person of Christ, God

---

[10]E.g. Deut 32:39–42, 1 Sam 2:6–7.

[11]Job argues with God for forty chapters only to "repent in dust and ashes" when he sees the Lord with his eye (Job 42:1–6). What did Job see? Perhaps it was the messianic mystery.

[12]At Lenten Matins in the Orthodox Church the faithful sing a solemn "Alleluia" interspersed with lines from Isaiah's canticle which include the verse: "Bring more evils upon them, O Lord, bring more evils upon the glorious ones of the earth" (Isa 26:15 LXX). It is a common teaching in Orthodox spiritual literature that evils are God's sole means for converting and saving sinners.

[13]The Lord *sends* the tribes of the north and Nebuchadnezzar, the king of Babylon whom

destroys human wickedness by reconciling all people to himself by the folly and scandal of the cross. Christ takes upon himself all the evils of the world and overcomes them. He does this by becoming their innocent victim through his broken body and spilled blood in the curse of crucifixion. Jesus' execution is the most magnificent and compelling example of God's use of evil for good.

20. **God chastens evildoers for salvation.** The biblical story tells of God's violence towards evildoers, especially those called to be his people, until he establishes his reign in the universe. God's chastening acts of evil toward creatures are seen in scripture in the light of God's ultimate act of forgiveness and redemption in Christ. This is the clear proclamation of the prophets whose warnings and woes and bitter lamentations of God's sending of evils are always crowned by the word of God's mercy and restoration for all who repent. This is finally God's gospel in Jesus who takes upon himself the sins of the world and expiates them all in his crucified flesh. Seen in this light, it can be said that God both punishes the wicked, and does not punish them. Again we are constrained to "say and unsay to a positive effect." The Lord chastens in order to bring to repentance and ultimately to save. He does not punish in the sense that he inflicts pain upon the wicked as a punitive payment for their evil deeds. If we can speak of such a punitive payment at all, we must immediately announce the good news that Isaiah's prophecy of the Lord's Suffering Servant is fulfilled in Jesus who brings God's redemption to the world through his innocent death at the hands of the wicked. Christ was wounded for our transgressions and bruised for our iniquities when he made himself an offering for sin. God placed upon him the chastisement that made us whole so that by his wounds we might be healed (Isa 53:4–6).

21. **Victims of evil are closest to God.** Those who suffer at the hands of evildoers are closest to God. And those closest to God inevitably suffer from evil. This hard teaching is witnessed in scripture and testified to by the saints. The repentant persecutor Paul boasted of his manifold sufferings as proof of his being an apostle sent by God to proclaim and explain the gospel of the crucified Christ, the only gospel of God that there is in this world. The same apostle testified that God sent "an angel of Satan" to harass him in order to prove

he calls "my servant," against Judah and Jerusalem in order to "utterly destroy them and make them a horror, a hissing and an everlasting reproach" (Jer 25:8–9). The apostle Paul says that God *sends* "a strong delusion" upon those who "refused to love the truth" in order to "make them believe what is false, so that they all may be condemned who did not believe the truth but had pleasure in unrighteousness" (2 Thess 2:10–11).

that God's "grace is sufficient" and that his "power is made perfect in weakness." Paul's "thorn in the flesh" was also given, he said, that he might learn to be "content with weaknesses, insults, hardships, persecutions and calamities" for the sake of being glorified with Christ (2 Cor 12:7–10). Innocent sufferers and those who give their life for God and their neighbor are believed by Christians to be certainly saved. These include first of all those who suffer innocently from the "sins of the world," such as those providentially called to endure severe disabilities and diseases. They also include those who suffer from others, like the victims of all kinds of abuse, especially in childhood. They also include those who suffer and die defending and saving the lives of others, and those who die in love for the name of God who is Love. God glorifies these people by their endurance of evil. He never allows them to be tried beyond their strength (however outrageously untrue this may seem), as he uses them to "complete what is lacking in the afflictions of Christ" for the sake of those who are to be saved through his pains and theirs (See 1 Cor 10:13, Col 1:24).[14]

22. **Christ pays the debt to redeem evildoers.** The apostle Paul teaches that God made his sinless Son to be sin so that sinners might be made the righteousness of God (2 Cor 5:21). He says that Christ became a curse by hanging on the tree of the cross so that evildoers might be redeemed by his perfect self-sacrifice (Gal 3:13–14). The teaching of Paul, that "the living God [in Jesus] is the Savior of all human beings, especially of those who believe" (1 Tim 4:10), is confirmed in writings attributed to Jesus' beloved disciple John who says that Jesus is "the expiation for our sins, and not for ours only but also for the sins of the whole world" (1 Jn 2:2). The debt that Christ pays for all in his death on the cross is in one sense the punishment that is due to sinners, the inevitable "wages of sin" which is suffering and death (Rom 6:23). But it is more than that. It is also the offering of glory and gratitude to God through the payment of the debt of love to God and neighbor which creatures owe as their fulfillment of God's law (Rom 12:8). In this sense Jesus shows himself to be truly the last, real and perfect Adam, the unique "son of God" who accomplishes in his death what the first transgressing Adam, who was "the type of him who was to come," failed to accomplish in his life. For the

---

[14]Human beings do not "co-redeem" the world with God. God alone is the world's redeemer in Christ. What is "lacking" in Christ's affliction is the believer's imitation of it and participation in it which is necessary for their redemption and that of others. It must also be affirmed that Christ suffers in and with all the afflicted, especially those who suffer for, in and with him in love. See, e.g., 2 Tim 2:10–13.

first Adam brought all manner of evils into the world that lead to death. And the last Adam by his death brought to the world the fullness of goodness and everlasting life (Rom 5:12–21, 1 Cor 15:45–50).

23. Human beings must accept God's redemption in Christ. In Jesus Christ the whole world is saved. All sinners are forgiven. All evildoers are reconciled to God. This is God's gospel in Jesus. To become effective for creatures this good news must be received and believed. It must be loved and lived. It is not automatically enacted. It cannot be enforced against the will of creatures. It must be freely acknowledged and joyfully accepted. The final chance for this to happen is at the *parousia* of Christ at the end of the age. When Christ appears in glory, all flesh will have the final chance to repent of their sins and to glorify God through Jesus. This does not necessarily mean that all will in fact be saved, though, with Bishop Kallistos and eminent others, we may hold that hope, and pray for it fervently, though we dare not preach it.[15] It seems rather to mean, according to scripture, that salvation is freely given to all. For those who accept it, life will finally be paradise completely free from evil. For those who resist it, the very mercy, love and forgiveness of God will be a punishment and torment added to their own self-punishment and the torment afflicted upon them by their fellow creatures who also oppose God's loving victory in Jesus.

24. Evil will be separated from good at the end. Christian scriptures teach that in God's coming kingdom evil will be separated from good. The very word judgment (*krisis*) means separation. Evildoers who persist in evil will no longer be able to harm those who repent of their evils and accept God's mercy. They will be tormented by God's presence, by their own madness, by other evildoers and by evil spirits who cling to darkness in their blasphemy of God's Holy Spirit. The persistence of evil will not spoil the joy of the repentant because nothing more can be done for those who are established in evil. All that can be done for them has been done by Christ on the cross. If the sinners' refusal to repent would cause suffering to the saved, the victory would

[15]See Bishop Kallistos Ware, "Dare We Hope for the Salvation of All?" in idem, *The Inner Kingdom* (Crestwood, NY: St Vladimir's Seminary Press, 2000), 193–215. See also Kenneth Carveley, "From Glory to Glory: The Renewal of All Things in Christ: Maximus the Confessor and John Wesley," and Peter C. Bouteneff, "All Creation in United Thanksgiving: Gregory of Nyssa and the Wesleys on Salvation," in S T Kimbrough, Jr (ed.) *Orthodox and Wesleyan Spirituality*, (Crestwood, NY: St Vladimir's Seminary Press, 2002).

be theirs. It would be exactly what they, in their perversion, desire: to make the righteous miserable forever. Their containment, however, even without conversion, will be a joy to those made righteous by faith whose delight will be due not to any supposed punishment of the evildoers, since, as a matter of fact, no punishment is inflicted. Their rejoicing will rather be because the evil actions of the wicked can no longer harm the innocent. If the wicked should at some point repent and surrender to God's love, the joy of the just would be all the greater. But there seems to be no clear evidence in the scriptures that this is likely to happen, though faith and love still constrains us to hope and pray that it may.

25. Evil is revealed to be everlasting. Christian scripture seems clearly to teach that evil for some creatures will go on without end. This does not mean that God will inflict ceaseless punishment upon the wicked. It means rather, according to the overwhelming majority of Christian teachers through the centuries, that evildoers who refuse to repent of their evil-doing will be the more greatly enslaved to evil as they stubbornly refuse to surrender to God's loving presence. Among the most terrifying mysteries of evil seems to be that God's mercy makes confirmed evildoers even more vicious and violent. The prophet Isaiah quotes the Lord himself in this regard when he declares that "if favor is shown to the wicked, he does not learn righteousness; in the land of uprightness he deals perversely and does not see the majesty of the Lord" (Isa 2:10). The new testament scriptures seem to demonstrate this truth beyond doubt. The greater the love of Jesus and his apostles for their enemies, and the more brilliant their light, the more convincing their words, and the more charitable their deeds, the greater the violence of the opposition against them. In John's gospel Jesus makes this point most strongly when he says that "this is the judgment, that the light has come into the world, and human beings loved darkness rather than light, because their deeds were evil. For every one who does evil hates the light, and does not come to the light, lest his deeds be exposed. But he who does what is true comes to the light, that it may be clearly seen that his deeds have been wrought in God." (Jn 3:19–21) Is love of darkness not what the Lord warns about in the gospels when he says that "every sin and blasphemy will be forgiven men, but the blasphemy against the Spirit will not be forgiven . . . either in this age or in the age to come" (Mt 12:31–32). Those who sin in this grievous way, Jesus declares, are "guilty of an eternal sin" (Mk 3:28–30).

26. **God's judgment of evil is his mercy on all.** God shows mercy on whomever he wills, and he wills to show mercy on all. This is the biblical teaching. It is God's gospel in Jesus. It is God's judgment on the world. Writings attributed to the apostle Paul tell us that we are to "have hope on the living God, who is the Savior of all people, especially those who believe" (1 Tim 4:10). Christ's beloved disciple John tells us that he is writing to us that we may not sin, but that "if anyone does sin, we have an advocate (*parakletos*) with the Father, Jesus Christ the righteous; and he is the expiation for our sins, and not for ours only, but also for the sins of the whole world" (1 Jn 2:2). Universal salvation is given in Christ. The return of all things to God (*apokatastsis tōn pantōn*) is realized in Jesus seated in glory at the Father's right hand, made the head over all things through what he suffered at the hands of evildoers (Eph 1:20–23). This is the judgment of creation: God's universal and unconditional act of mercy in Christ for which every creature under heaven will one day have to answer and account.

27. **God will be all and in all through Christ.** At the coming of Christ, when the Lord submits everything with himself to God the Father who subjects all things to him, God will be "all and in all," or (as some English translations of scripture would have it) "everything to everyone" (1 Cor 15:28, cf. also Col 3:11). Paul puts this teaching another way when he writes that "at the name of Jesus every knee should bow, in heaven and on earth and under the earth, and every tongue confess that Jesus Christ is Lord to the glory of God the Father" (Phil 2:10–11). Such sayings lead some people to think that everyone and everything will be saved when all creatures will be compelled to worship God and his Son through whom God will be "all and in all." There is, however, no logical or theological necessity in drawing such a conclusion. As my dogmatics professor, Serge Verhovskoy, would put it: God will be all and in all, but not all will like it; every knee will bow before God and his Christ, but not all will enjoy it. The scriptural teaching seems to be that the same presence of God that brings refreshment to the faithful brings torment to the wicked.[16] This seems to be Paul's teaching when he says that unrepentant

[16]Compare Acts 3:19 where God's "times for refreshing" for the righteous come "from the presence (or face) of the Lord [*apo prosopou tou kyriou*]" with 1 Thess 1:9 where God's "punishment of eternal destruction" for the unrighteous comes also "from the presence (or face) of the Lord [*apo prosopou tou kyriou*]." The word "exclusion" found in the RSV rendering of the Thessalonian text is not in the original Greek. The apostolic texts are clearly inspired by OT prophetic writings which ascribe both the Lord's mercy and judgment, with his comfort for the just and his judgment on the wicked, to the Lord's same terrible appearing.

evildoers will pay the penalty of "eternal destruction from the presence (or face) of the Lord and from the glory of his might" (2 Thess 1:9), and that Lord Jesus will "destroy [the lawless] by the appearance (*epiphania*) of his coming *(parousia)*" (2 Thess 2:8).

We sum up our "saying and unsaying" about God and evil by once more insisting that God is not evil and does not create evil. Evil comes from creatures and inevitably exists as the perversion of good in a human world. God uses evils for positive providential purposes. God orders and orchestrates evil for his ultimate glory and that of his servants. The ways of the Lord, who sends evils upon whom he wills so that they might repent before his terrible justice and majestic mercy, are beyond creaturely comprehension and questioning (Isa 55:8–9). When believers in the Christian God witness earthquake, flood, fire, war, invasion by enemies and evils of every kind, they believe that they are being visited by God for their chastening, repentance and everlasting salvation. They surrender in love and obedience to God who sends these evils upon them for their instruction and purification, and overcomes them in Christ for their salvation and glorification. They do this by affirming the Lord's victory on the cross and his coming in glory by co-suffering with him in love through the crosses which he provides for their glory. The refusal of God's victory in Christ, with the refusal to suffer in love with the Lord for good, results in a misery and torment which may well last forever.

The biblical psalms proclaim in the most perfect way what Christians believe to be the truth about God and evil in this present age. They declare God's sovereign dominion over good and evil, and his steadfast love for those who come to adore his majesty and accept his mercy. For Christians, the psalms are the words of Christ.[17] They "say and unsay" to every possible positive effect everything that human beings can possibly "say and unsay" in the face of evil, before the face of God, until the Lord's coming.

---

[17]See Patrick Henry Reardon, *Christ in the Psalms* (Ben Lomond, CA: 2000); Dietrich Bonhoeffer, *Psalms: The Prayer Book of the Bible* (Minneapolis: Augsburg Fortress Press, 1970).

Mary: The Flower and Fruit of Worship: The Mother of God in the Orthodox Tradition

Wendy Robinson

E CAN ONLY APPROACH the Mother of God with more silence than words. The words we find are only what can be held in cupped hands, out of the great sea of meanings which flows all around her. She is, in the west as well as in the east, the star of that sea, the guide for lost and weary travellers. For many women in our age, for a variety of cogent and sometimes tragic reasons, her star has not been visible through the lowering clouds of controversy, anger and painful searching about the place and meaning of women and men together in the Church. Some of us who have entered the Orthodox Church in adult life have come to experience her presence slowly, yet surely. Some of us have been helped by Bishop Kalllistos' devotion to the Mother of God expressed in celebration of the mysteries, when she is so constantly evoked, or in talks on pilgrimages to Walsingham or to the Ecumenical Society of the Blessed Virgin Mary.

I remember Nicolas and Militza Zernov talking to me of the importance of the Mother of God in worship and iconography. "As goes Mary, so goes the church," they would say. The future of the Church is intimately linked with the living life and prayer of the Mother of God in our midst. She is in our midst in worship, always pointing beyond herself to Christ. How important is that gesture of transcendence, which Christ, too, makes in his earthly life to the Father, and to the coming of the Spirit; which the Father makes to the beloved Son; which the Spirit makes in our hearts as we pray: the beyond that is yet in the midst. The Mother of God is in the midst with open heart, revealing in the icon of Tenderness (so commonly found now in the West, too) a tender love being met by a tender love, or her presence in the heart of suffering at the foot of the Cross, or in the heart waiting on God at Pentecost in the upper room. In such wise the Mother of God leads us to the place of the heart, the deep centre of our theandric personhood. As she, like her Son, "ever lives to make intercession for us" in that "place of the heart," herself a living symbol of hesychia, or inner stillness, in what other place would we choose to stand if we were living our life at its deepest and fullest?

In one of his poems the western Catholic poet, Gerard Manley Hopkins compares the Mother of God to the air we breathe.[1] The Mother of God is the air we breathe in worship, the atmosphere of the church at its deepest and fullest. In Orthodox worship there are particular moments when a palpable attention and devotion are noticeable among the worshippers. One such moment is always in the making of the sign of the Cross and the looks directed to the icon of the Mother of God when she is addressed in the litanies. "Commemorating our all-holy, pure, most blessed and glorious Lady, Mother of God and ever-virgin Mary with all the saints, let us entrust ourselves and one another and our whole life to Christ our God"—even as she entrusted herself. In the Orthodox tradition it is often said that Mary, Theotokos, does not belong to the outer world of declared dogma but to the secret inner life of the Church, to be discovered there. She is present as the flower and fruit of worship, ripened in tradition.

So where dogma is experienced in its seeds, in its roots, in worship and in prayer, Mary, as flower and fruit, is revealed. The stories we hear about her in worship surround and protect the truth of the incarnation of the Son, the second Person of the Trinity. Many of the stories come out of the *Protevangelium of James*. In historical terms we cannot set out to prove events from them. But they are "telling tales," effective and affective, revelatory stories rooted in faith and belief. As we repeat them year by year in the great cycle of feasts and fasts, they become a creative matrix of story and image, of mystery and silence, that nourish and "hold" the truths of faith which maintain us.

The deepest level of the human soul is where *poesis* happens—a creative energy which throws up for us dreams and images and is symbol-making and story-telling. ("The symbol touches the depth long before it reaches the surface";[2] long before it engenders thought and rationality.) What from the point of view of rationality we call rhetoric, or figures of speech, refers to the deepest activities of the human soul when we learn to read it, to know its

[1]*Poems of Gerard Manley Hopkins* (Oxford: Oxford University Press, 1950 [1930]), 99.
[2]Gaston Bachelard, *The Poetics of Space* (Boston: Beaca, 1940), 131.

transformations and to use it creatively, "under the Protection." That deep place of making gives rise to thought but it is wise for thought to keep its tap root in the creative matrix, where truths are invocatory, celebratory, proclamatory, rather than set out as rational propositions. That is why when inquirers want Orthodox people to say something about ourselves we have to say: "Come and worship with us." You can't just learn the truth in talk or discussion or reading. You have to meet it in worship, in the making, in touch with the creative matrix. In that meeting and making of worship you will find us always commemorating the one who is "more honourable than the cherubim and incomparably more glorious than the seraphim, our all-holy, pure, most blessed and glorious Mother of God and ever-virgin Mary . . ." There is always a certain silence around the mysteries, an awe in the worshipping experience of God's love and truth and presence. And so it is for the Mother of God, too. There is a certain silence around her mysteries. Yet this numinous, awe-inspiring and luminous, light-giving silence has always been endlessly inspirational. One moment we have teaching on the apophatic need to move beyond images, to honour silence and venerate the mysteries. The next moment we have images pouring forth as if from a breathtaking treasure-house. There is even a risk of satiety for those of us not born and bred in this tradition. The Akathist hymn to the Mother of God (used particularly on Fridays in Lent) with its flow of images drawn from cosmos and biblical culture, weaves a glorious robe of attributions around the Mother of God, "Unwedded Bride; Bride without bridegroom":

> Hail, beam of the spiritual Sun;
> Hail, ray of the moon that never wanes;
> Hail, lightning flash that shines upon our souls;
> Hail, thunder . . . Hail, dawn . . . Hail, spring . . .
>   water . . . cup . . .
> Hail, Height hard to climb even for thoughts of men,
> Hail, Depth hard to scan, even for the eyes of angels.
> Hail, Bride without bridegroom.
> (Akathist Hymn to the Most Holy Mother of God, Ikos One)[3]

Again, the Lamentations in the services of Holy Week are expressive and full of deep emotion, almost causing through their reiterative rhythms a

---

[3] *Akathistos Hymn to the Most Holy Mother of God*, trans. Kallistos Ware (Ecumenical Society of the Blessed Virgin Mary, 1987), 18.

physical withdrawal into reticence, endurance and silence around the mystery of the Passion:

> When she beheld her Son and Lord hanging on the cross, the pure Virgin was torn by grief and weeping bitterly with the other women, and she cried out: "Woe is me! I see thee, dearest and beloved Child, hanging on the cross and my heart is wounded bitterly . . . How am I deprived of Him who is my hope, my gladness, of my Son and God. Woe is me, my heart is filled with anguish . . ." (Holy Friday, Small Compline, canticle one).[4]

Indeed, rhythm and repetition in liturgical forms seem to carry a deep experience of feminine discourse that we otherwise meet in the rituals, rhythms and repetitions around the birth and nurture of small babies and children, as well as in expressions of grief and mourning around death. Learning to live in this creative matrix we discover slowly over time what it means to be Orthodox—to find the rhythms of its tides and waves, how it ebbs and flows around us, carrying us. We don't need to sustain it except by our cooperation in it, but it sustains us.

In that matrix in worship we meet the Mother of God as the pivotal point through which we turn, bringing the cosmos with us, through our personhood, towards God, offering ourselves through her. As we say at Christmas:

> What shall we offer thee, O Christ, who for our sakes has appeared on earth as man? Every creature made by thee offers thee thanks. The angels offer thee a hymn; the heavens, a star; the Magi, gifts; the shepherds, their wonder; the earth, a cave; the wilderness, a manger; and we offer thee a Virgin Mother. (Vespers of the Nativity of Christ)[5]

She is our great offering through whom we offer ourselves to God. At times we have to struggle with the pains, fears, doubts and glories of our individual journey and struggle to follow St Paul's injunction: "Therefore I urge you, in view of God's mercy to offer your bodies as living sacrifices holy and pleasing to God—this is your spiritual act of worship" (Rom 12:1, NIV). But in our shared worship we can offer ourselves in and through and with the

---

[4]*The Lenten Triodion*, trans. Mother Maria and Archimandrite Kallistos Ware (London: Faber and Faber, 1978), 617.

[5]*The Festal Menaion*, trans. Mother Mary and Archimandrite Kallistos Ware (London: Faber and Faber, 1984), 254.

Mother of God; an act of simple joy even in the midst of suffering, in gratitude for the incarnation. At those moments we are deeply aware of the one who is called most truly the "Joy of all Creation."

It is always impossible to present an even remotely adequate account of the experience of the rite, which is only discovered through participation in it, sharing in the mysterious, corporate, sacramental and symbolic "language" of ritual which is not reducible to the language of the conscious individual self.[6] We can only say, "Come and see."

What I do know is that it has been a transformative experience for me as woman, as psychotherapist and as a human person, caught up in the theandric vision of what it means to be truly human: "My life is hid with Christ in God," as St Paul says (Col 3:3). Yet I remain terribly conscious of the struggles both within myself and within those who share their lives with me. Many people have been alienated from the Mother of God because of what the history of religious culture has made of Mary in terms of the history of women. The Mother of God is a tender, protective presence and companion to the suffering, the poor and the afflicted. I do not think she minds if we bring her our problems and our searchings about who she is and what she means for us. Some of the struggles may seem alien to those born into the Orthodox tradition and who have always "known" the presence of the Mother of God. Some of the conflicts as people express them can seem distasteful, so that any discussion of "woman" in some Orthodox circles will be dismissed as secularised feminism. Mercifully, there are people like Bishop Kallistos and Elisabeth Behr-Sigel who encourage us to remain open to the pressing questions about our understanding of sexuality and gender within the understanding of the Church, priesthood and other related and sometimes burning issues.

Marina Warner, in her fascinating book about the Marian tradition in the West, *Alone of All Her Sex*, points even in the title to something of what the problems for women have been about. The title is taken from a translation of Caelius Sedulius:

> She . . . had no peer
> Either in our first mother or in all women
> Who were to come. But alone of all her sex
> She pleased the Lord.[7]

[6]Roger Grainger, *The Language of the Rite* (London: Darton, Longman and Todd, 1975), 7ff.
[7]Marina Warner, *Alone of All Her Sex: The Myth and the Cult of the Virgin Mary* (Picador, 1990 [1985]).

"Alone of all her sex . . ." encapsulates the danger, as women see it, that sometimes the Mother of God is celebrated as so special, so different, that we lose
a sense of her solidarity with us and that is an appalling loss. She ceases to be
that representative "Everywoman" who is also "Everyman," through whom
we offer ourselves to Christ as she did. The application of Mariology has led,
tragically, to certain kinds of encultured trouble. It has seemed at times to promote a particular image of woman which has certain beauties and may provide an idealised image of how men would sometimes like women to be, but
assuredly does not carry the total reality of women's lives and their way to
God. For what it has sometimes done in family life or in schools (particularly
some convent schools) is to bring about a rather narrow band of piety, of
what was acceptable behaviour for a woman. It was conveyed that she should
be quiet, preferably silent, humble, pure and good, in a domestic interior,
devoted and submissive, knowing her place. Girls brought up in that strict
tradition will sometimes talk about how much they gained from it (plenty of
convent-raised girls have been spirited lasses!) but also about the difficulties
that were engendered in it. They feel that they learned an ambiguity about the
body (their embodied reality as women) with a sense of shame that took a lot
of overcoming. They felt bad and ignorant about their sexuality. They could
not talk about menstruation without much shame. They found it was difficult, even if they had "saved themselves" for marriage, to cope with desire
and sexuality within marriage. They felt they were acceptable if they were
kind and nice and clean and good. But alas! They also sometimes found that
they wanted to be clever, well-educated, to take part in the public world, to
argue for the sake of truth, to be angry in the cause of justice, to be stroppy
and sexy and searching; in fact women who did not know their place in terms
of traditional piety. So the problems leave us in the midst of things, always in
the womb of things, always on the road, travelling and searching women—
and we have to be able to bring all that reality to the Mother of God.

There is an extreme danger that across the centuries the Mother of God
has been presented as less human in some ways than her Son, somehow not
being tempted, more remote from our fallen humanity, and less a woman of
desire who has to find the long road to compassionate and mutual selfless
love. Theologically, that represents a supreme irony. She who became known
as "Theotokos" in order to protect the truth of incarnation can become in
religious culture dangerously dehumanised, *dis*carnate. That is one temptation, but there is another. If we place in Mary certain characteristics of compassion, mercy, of nearness, of tenderness—and leave other things to Christ,

such as stern judge, Pantocrator—it leads to a devastating split in how we experience the divine. There are a number of amusing stories which illustrate this dangerous tendency. For instance, Christ came to St Peter at the gates one day and said: "How is it that there are so many people around in heaven? I can't believe they were all meant to be here." St Peter answers, "Well, I do my best. I say no, but the Mother of God is round at the back door letting them in." It is a story that touches matters that are recognisable and arguable between men and women, and how characteristics on the human plane can get unhelpfully split between the sexes too. It also touches the nervy place in all of us about the Last Judgement.

Discussions about sexuality and gender have often tended to be acrimonious. At times women have expressed much anger towards men and their apparent hold on power and domination: sometimes more apparent than real. It helped me recently, when I was looking through a book of paintings of Mary in all their richness and variety, to realise that they were all of them painted by men. I realised again that there is something about this image of woman, Virgin and Mother, that speaks particularly to a reality in man's soul. Perhaps the image expresses the tender, virginal side of man, and the longing for the mother, which as women we do well to treasure and cherish and respect, even if at times we are having to talk with them firmly about our earthy and varied humanity as women. I experience the insistent hand of the Spirit on our current preoccupations, as if God is wanting to restore a fuller Christian anthropology—and is having to find a new way to reach us as encultured images and ideas have become too ingrained and stereotyped. No transformative change happens without unrest, conflict and risk, but sometimes the living God requires it of us.

So, then, if we turn to the great images of the Mother of God as Virgin Mother, how can we learn to understand them? To quote a simple and telling poem by San Juan de la Cruz, in translation:

> The Virgin comes walking
> The Word in her womb:
> Could you not give her
> Place in your room?[8]

What is the meaning of the Virgin? We can ask questions that end in reductive biology and a dismissal of the whole story. But if we ask instead a

[8]From *Centred Love: The Poems of St. John of the Cross*, trans Marjorie Flower, O.C. (Carmelite Nuns, NSW, 1983).

"Who?" question, it can lead us to the hypothesis of the person. She who is
Virgin: what does that mean for us? We know that biblical and patristic stories of Mary's virginity safeguard the incarnation. "Virgin" carries with it a
spiritual meaning, which is that of a total givenness to God. "She learnt what
she was FOR," as a student once said. We speak of her three-fold virginity—
the one who was given to God, in innocence, in experience and ever. The
"ever-ness" informs all the rest: a total givenness to God. Here we sense that
virginity is not a state, and is certainly not a possession, but is rather an eschatological reality. It is a reality that calls to us from the fulness of time, from
the pleroma, from the way things will be because that is how they truly are
ontologically. This reality is not just a perfectionist ideal, which floats above
us and haunts us and taunts us for not being able to measure up to it, but a
reality, a deep truth in which we have to learn to participate. It has its place
in origins, in innocence, in the beginning—in body and biology. It moves
through experience, through fallenness and our struggles to find our true personhood and transformation in Christ. It exercises an eschatological pull on
our lives, full of future promise. How can we make real that total givenness
to God? Virginity in that sense is something into which we must grow. It lies
ahead of us in our becoming ever more real in givenness. It is linked with our
restoration in Christ, our transformation in the Spirit, our divinisation. It
makes of our lives a theandric reality. It comes through our working together
with the energies of God. It is an ascetic path which can include all our bro-
kenness, all the consequences of the Fall. We can discover again and again
that the touch of God restores virginity, our capacity for total givenness to
God—when we come in tears, in sorrow, with a desire for *metanoia*. Thomas
Merton describes that kind of virginity:

> At the centre of our being is a point of nothingness ("le point vierge")
> which is untouched by sin and by illusion, a point of pure truth, a point
> which belongs entirely to God, which is never at our disposal, from
> which God disposes of our lives, which is inaccessible to the fantasies
> of our own minds or the brutalities of our own will. This little point
> of nothingness in us and of absolute poverty is the pure glory of God
> in us. It is his Name written in us.[9]

Sometimes I find the approach to that reality can come through the phrase
"spiritual integrity." I can use that phrase with people who are sexually active

[9]Thomas Merton, *Conjectures of a Guilty Bystander* (Burns and Oates, 1965), 142.

or celibate, and particularly with those who suffer, believers or not. Our fallen state can lead to the most appalling abuse—spiritual, emotional, sexual—of other human beings. There are always the *anawim* (the poor of the biblical tradition) whose integrity of body, soul and spirit has been invaded overwhelmingly, who have been battered by the accidents of birth or nurture and who feel totally broken, abject (i.e. thrown away) and lacking in any sense of their own integrity. It sometimes takes a long and loving journey with a compassionate other before they can find a sense of that "virgin point" within, expressed in Psalm 139:

> For you created my inmost being. You knit me together in my mother's womb. My frame was not hidden from you when I was made in the secret place, when I was woven together in the depths of the earth. Your eyes saw my unformed body (Ps 139:13,15,16).

There is an integrity, a virginity, which can be restored in Christ, through encounter, through baptism, through sacraments, through feasts and fasts, through supreme spiritual effort, *podvig,* through tears, through failure, through love—through God's grace enabling all our efforts, forgiving all our abject failures. Virginity in that sense represents a potent integrity. And so we offer ourselves through the one who stands in our midst as Virgin—and with her and through her prayers we find that we too are capable of God. With her we can offer God our finite freedom and entrust it to his eternal freedom, in order that we can find the true freedom that comes from doing God's will.

There is in us as human beings a potent receptivity; a receptivity for which the word passivity is not accurate, though it has often been used for feminine receptivity. We have to find ways in which our will learns to work together with the will of God, as Mary did at the Annunciation. It requires of us a receptivity to the Presence of God and what he asks of us. It may have to come via the earthy sanity of doubt: "How shall this be, since I know not a man?" I sometimes find when I am talking with women who are very much against men, perhaps because of an abusive history, that we have to become aware that there is a way in which as women we have to find our sexual receptivity which is equal in its potency to the phallic power of penetration of the male. That receptivity belongs to the capacity to receive God. The Other may seem strange to us, almost overwhelming, but we have to find our receptivity so that we can meet with the other and be totally available: to be able to put ourselves at the disposal of the other. Our egotism, our self-obsession, our self-protectiveness goes deep. We have to find the place of choice: our sovereign freedom to say "Yes" to God. That choice is his gift to us with all its terrors. The eventual "Yes" may carry the creative "No" of the ascetic path, or the questioning of our doubts. In order for Christ to be born again and again in the human spirit, not yesterday, not tomorrow but *now*, we have to find our way to receptivity and choice so that we can say our "Let it be so." The whole of our faith hung on that response at the Annunciation. More than we may ever know may hang on our response, too. That is why we offer ourselves through the Mother of God who discovered the place of ultimate choice. We need to find a listening, receptive obedience to God.

T. S. Eliot in *Four Quartets* points out that there is not only the one annunciation, but a "lifetime of annunciations." We meet each one and have to make something of what has come, however strange and alien it may seem at first—painful decision by painful decision sometimes. In the end, the annunciation we have to take on is death: how to give birth to the fact of one's own death? As Eliot said, "The bone's prayer to Death its God. Only the hardly, barely prayable/Prayer of the one Annunciation."[10] Sometimes, life's refusals of what we most desire (a partner, a child, an ambition . . .) has also to be accepted and taken in, so that we can find the otherness of the will of God for us.

Yet annunciations can bring rejoicings, too. We hear in the Gospel how Mary went to her cousin Elizabeth in the hill country. Elizabeth said: "As soon as the sound of your greeting reached my ears the baby in my womb leapt for joy" (Lk 1:44). Out of that meeting of the two women comes the great song of the Magnificat, held between them. It celebrates surely the Unexpected Joy (another of the liturgical and iconic titles of the Mother of God). "From now on all generations will call me blessed. The Mighty One has done great things for me and holy is his Name." It is a strange song, too: that great song of reversals. "He has scattered the proud in their innermost thoughts. He has brought down the mighty but has lifted up the humble" (Lk 1:51). No pious passivity is noticeable there. I respond to the way Mary is inspiringly active and courageous. She is like David's wife, Abigail, who saddled up her ass and set out into the wilderness, or the Shunamite woman who did the same. The Mother of God could, too, as it were, saddle up her donkey and set out for the hill country, or Bethlehem, or Egypt, or Jerusalem—risking the journey into the wilderness of God, dependent on the mysterious divine guidance as the meaning of what was happening to her unfolded. She too was a travelling woman, who can travel with searching women today.

[10]T. S. Eliot, *Collected Poems 1909–1962* (London: Faber and Faber, 1964), 208.

So, discovering the Virgin in experience can be joyful and celebratory as well as a massive risk, an offering that can be sacrifice—a total offering of self to the givenness of God. Virginity can be fecund, fruitful. It carries within it the fruitful womb. So Mary is not only Virgin, but Virgin Mother.

The Bible has many stories in it of children of promise who were born to barren women, way beyond the restraints of biology. The child of promise may be an actual child or may be the birth of the new in many forms. Even in periods of terrible spiritual sterility and barrenness, the Word of God still comes asking to be born in us. "Sing, O barren woman, you who have never borne a child, burst into song, shout for joy, you who were never in labour, because more are the children of the desolate woman than of her who has a husband" (Isa 54:1). The true meaning of the Gospel is full of these songs of reversal, of mind-splitting and heart-warming paradoxes and oxymorons, whose meanings only unfold through participation in life, and the life of faith.

There are spiritual meanings to the biological fact of womb. Phyllis Trible, in her book *God and the Rhetoric of Sexuality*,[11] links the Hebrew word for womb with the one meaning tender, loving compassion. Certainly in a life of faith we need to find the spiritual meanings that the womb engenders—and of which women may be the guardians but not the possessors of experience that belongs to the truly human. The spiritual womb can help us to bear, to carry, to gestate, to suffer things in order to wait for the right time for something to come to birth; equally to be able also to bear with the miscarriages, the abortions, the stillbirths that happen in all the situations which life in its raw, its fallen state, has to endure. How are we to become in the Church "mothers-and fathers-in-Israel" for each other, in the company of the Mother of God and her great, varied and even morally questionable ancestresses? How can we learn spiritually to nurture, feed, train, give each other enough but not too much, without smothering each other with parasitic love which does not allow enough relational space for the other to become who they are? Sometimes the pains and sufferings involved will take us into having to learn from God what is told to us in Isaiah 45:3: "I will give you the treasures of darkness, riches stored in secret places . . ." Dark times may be where the Lord most is:

> . . . without darkness
> Nothing comes to birth,
> As without light,
> Nothing flowers.[12]

[11]P. Trible (London: SCM, 1978).
[12]May Sarton, *Collected Poems, 1930–1993* (W.W. Norton and Co,, 1993), 326.

In the Mother of God, we have the one who could make something of the dark times. She was the one who learnt to take the hard sayings and "treasure them in her heart," able to do that which tests us all—how to endure not just our own suffering but the suffering of the Beloved. Mary found a way that kept her nailed to the foot of the Cross, when that was what was happening.

Times of testing can make us feel very alone. The only icons in which Mary appears to be alone she is not truly so. For in reality the Mother of God Orans (the praying Mary) is joined with us and with her Son in his ever living to make intercession for us. Other than with her, as representing our offering to God in total self-givenness, so that he might come again and again and be incarnate in the human heart, where could we wish to be? To be with her as representing the ongoing life of the Church to worship and to pray for the sins and darkness of the world, which God loves—how could we settle for doing otherwise? Other than with her, essentially there is no other place where we as women and men in the Church can stand. She shows us the courageous and even daunting journey that has to be made. The "feminine matrix" that her feasts give in liturgical form in the Orthodox tradition is a deeply satisfying resource for women in the Orthodox Church as it is for men. There may have to be transformations in the cultural application of some of the images, but the Presence of the Mother of God transcends them all with her "Protecting Veil" that encompasses us all.

To sum up, I quote from Saint Silouan: his vision of the Mother of God.[13] I first heard this passage read in an illuminating talk given by Bishop Kallistos:

We cannot fathom the depth of the love of the Mother of God, but this, we know: the fuller the love, the fuller the knowledge of God. The more ardent the love, the more fervent the prayer. The more perfect the love, the holier the life. The greater the love, the greater the sorrow. Never by a single fault did the Mother of God sin, nor did she ever lose grace, yet vast were her sorrows. When she stood by the Cross her grief was as boundless as the ocean and her soul knew pain inconquerably deeper than Adam's suffering when he was driven from Paradise, for the reason that the measure of her love was beyond compare, greater than the love with which Adam loved when he was in Paradise. We cannot discern to the full the love of the Mother of God.

---

[13]"On the Mother of God," in Archimandrite Sophrony (Sakharov), *Saint Silouan the Athonite* (Tolleshunt Knights, Essex: Stavropegic Monastery of St John the Baptist, 1991).

And so we cannot comprehend all her grief. Her love was complete. She stands in our midst as the one who calls us to give ourselves totally to God.

Human Uniqueness and Human Unity[1]

Nonna Verna Harrison

T HE QUESTION OF HUMAN IDENTITY is a pressing concern in contemporary culture as well as in our personal reflections. We ask ourselves, "Who am I? How is who I am related to who other people are?" Then there are further questions. What is it about myself that constitutes the core of my identity, and what aspects of my being, activity and experience are more peripheral? Which aspects are transient and which are permanent? In what ways am I the same as other people and in what ways am I different, and is the center of my identity located in my likeness to others or in my distinctiveness? Such questions have probably been at issue in all human cultures. In the Orthodox Christian tradition, much has been said about these issues, both by the ancient fathers and by more contemporary theologians. This paper will consider how the uniqueness of the human person is related to the unity of humankind.

At the risk of gross oversimplification, one can recognize disparate "eastern" and "western" experiences of human identity. The "eastern" experience begins with a fundamental unity with others that is presupposed and provides a firm foundation for community life and the distinctive roles different people fulfill within it. Hence *sobornost*, mutual interrelatedness, is a given, and one's identity is constituted by one's embeddedness in a web of relationships with others. The limitation of this model is that any personal distinctiveness or uniqueness that goes beyond tribal or cultural solidarity and prescribed social location can become submerged in group identity. The modern "western" experience begins with an awareness of one's personal uniqueness and

[1]This paper was presented to a meeting of the Oxford branch of the Fellowship of St Alban and St Sergius in February 1999. A lively discussion followed, graced with many insightful comments by Bishop Kallistos of Diokleia, who was chairing the meeting. Some of his suggestions have been incorporated into the final version.

the ability to create one's own identity and build a nexus of freely chosen relationships with others appropriate to one's unique character. There is great potential for positive creativity in this model and authentic mutual love and self-giving grounded in freedom, but there are also grave risks. One may perceive oneself as an isolated, self-enclosed individual, unable to create an identity acceptable enough to other people to enable any connectedness with them at all. Then one's identity appears to oneself to be insubstantial and without foundation.

Surely each of these models of human identity is incomplete without the other. Either collectivism or individualism left to itself becomes oppressive and ultimately inhuman. Human identity is often incomplete, flawed, defaced or truncated in our sinful world. In its present fallen condition, human identity is not fully realized but is often broken and fragmented. There are often divisions and conflicts within and among human persons where, in God's creative intention, harmony can and should unite the different parts. Yet we can still discern the outlines of a genuine wholeness. Initially we can identify at least four aspects of likeness and difference, all of which are included in authentic human identity.

(1) The first aspect is a *personal uniqueness* ultimately comprising a depth of mystery, the human image of divine incomprehensibility. This uniqueness cannot be reduced to an identifiable list of talents, weaknesses, character traits and life experiences. It is rather a greater reality that lies within, beneath and beyond such characteristics. People perceive this unique personal presence in those they love. It is also manifest in the great achievements of art, science and, above all, spiritual endeavor. Contemporary Orthodox theologians have brilliantly analyzed this dimension of personhood.

(2) Each person is endowed with a distinctive set of talents, weaknesses, character traits and life experiences. Some of these characteristics are uniquely individual. Others are shared by groups of people. Some of the group characteristics are shared activities or interests like law, medicine, fly fishing or embroidery. Some are the broad categories that many regard as central to human identity, such as culture, ethnicity, gender and class. These broad categories often unite people with some of their fellows while dividing them from others, which can become dangerous and destructive. So as St Paul (Col 3:11, Gal 3:28) and many of the Greek fathers have observed, it is a mistake to regard these characteristics as the core of human identity. This is because they simultaneously produce partial unity and division in humankind. They can be employed to suppress the personal uniqueness expressive

of freedom and the universal unity expressive of love, both of which are more central to our identity than they are.

Yet all these *individual and group characteristics*, which are aspects of human nature, are important to the actualization and manifestation of personal identity. When used rightly, they serve as the indispensable artistic media through which the person expresses his or her unique presence and offers himself or herself to others as a gift.

(3) Besides individual and group characteristics, there are important ways in which all human beings are *alike*, in body and soul, in that they are human. These include the many common features of the human nature and its attributes and energies. The fact of unique personhood present in each, with its attendant freedom of choice and capacity for self-fashioning and self-determination, is also universally human. The common human nature and its universal characteristics have been downplayed by many contemporary Orthodox theologians, but their central place in human identity is emphasized by the Greek fathers, the ascetic tradition and some contemporary theologians who are deeply rooted in these sources. They emphasize that the right use of universally human faculties, activities and experiences comprises the heart of the way of life that leads to salvation. This is a point whose importance cannot be overemphasized. I will return to it below.

(4) Finally, there is humankind's *unity*, which occurs on several distinct but interrelated levels. There is an ontological unity of human nature as such, since God has created humankind as one. This unity of nature is the milieu within which the incarnate Christ present in the particular humanity he assumed enters into communion with other humans, thereby imparting to them his divine life. We become aware of this unity and affirm it in practice in two seemingly opposite but mutually supportive ways, one arising from our common nature and the other from our unique personhood. The first is our experience of sharing with others in universally human capacities, activities and situations, while the second is the experience of intrinsic relatedness to other persons based on our uniqueness and mutual otherness. The natural unity provides the ontological milieu in which human persons can freely unite with each other in love, just as it provides the milieu in which Christ can in love unite them with himself.

However, this points to a new and greater unity beyond the natural and interpersonal unities embedded in the structure of humankind as God created it. Human unity is only fully actualized in the Body of Christ, the communion of saints and of all the faithful in God's Kingdom. It is the saints who are

most aware of natural human unity and unity in Christ, and they pray fervently for every person's ultimate inclusion in the eschatological unity of
God's kingdom, as Christ himself prayed for it (Jn 17). In this final unity
humankind is embraced within the mutual love and self-offering of the Father,
the Son and the Holy Spirit.

Personalism, Human Nature, and Ascetic Tradition

Two approaches to Orthodox theology and spiritual life have emerged in our
time, and they appear to some to be mutually exclusive and irreconcilable,
though in reality both have important insights. One school of thought derives
from the spiritual and intellectual renaissance of the early twentieth century
Russian diaspora, has spread to many other places in the Orthodox world
including Greece, Romania, Western Europe and North America, and has
influenced Western Christians as well as Eastern. This is the personalist
school, which values human uniqueness, creativity and spiritual freedom as
the best gifts we can offer to Christ and the Church, humankind and the natural world. Besides drawing on the Church's whole tradition including that
of the ascetic fathers, it also reflects the influence of nineteenth- and twentieth-century Russian religious philosophy and together with it yields the rich
fruit of a creative encounter between East and West. This is the tradition in
which I am rooted, though my specialty is Greek patristics. The other school
of thought draws more exclusively on the Greek fathers and the ascetic tradition summed up in the *Philokalia* and is centered in the monasteries of
Mount Athos. It emphasizes the universal human task of struggling against
passions, acquiring virtues, and receiving Christ's gift of salvation through
faith, prayer, repentance, humility and obedience. Advocates of this view
assert that sin, passions and virtues are essentially the same for everybody,
and infer further that to single oneself out as unique and called to a different
path must be a sign of dangerous pride and delusion. To be sure, there are
valuable insights here, but when they are not balanced by other insights
important in the Orthodox tradition, there is a risk of harmful distortion.

This kind of spirituality sometimes finds expression is a rigid uniformity
modeled on a particular kind of cenobitic monasticism but intended for all
the faithful. In this context personal uniqueness and spiritual freedom as such
are sometimes viewed with deep suspicion. However, this kind of spirituality
is at times expressed through the concepts of personalist theology. That is,

"personhood" is sometimes seen as opposed to "individuality," which is here defined very broadly and identified with *prelest*, self-love and self-will, and therefore suppressed. The aim of ascetic life is identified as the person's overcoming of his or her "nature," including all its individual characteristics and propensities. "Nature" in this sense is here understood as inherently fallen and opposed to authentic human identity and "freedom," Such "nature" is seen as conflicting with the "person," who must seek to combat it.

In this extreme form, the "monastic" theology (which is surely not accepted by all the monks on the Holy Mountain or elsewhere), is incompatible with the personalist view articulated in the Paris school and more recent theologians who share its ethos. Advocates of such ascetic extremism may use the language of personhood, but their position represents a distortion of personalism and empties it of substance. In this context it is important for those advocating a personalist theology to state clearly that human personhood is distinct from nature and individuality and transcends them but is not inherently opposed to them. Human nature must be understood not in negative but in positive terms, as a broader and more flexible concept than is sometimes supposed. Human nature is not a prison confining the person but a vast treasury of resources available to the person's freedom, creativity and love, resources that can be used well or badly precisely by personal freedom but are in themselves good since they are created by God. This nature is not rigid and static but capable of open-ended transformation through personal self-fashioning and interaction with other realities, and transfiguration through the reception of divine life given as grace. Through its nature, not despite its nature, the human person is open to enter into relationship with other human persons, the realities of the created world surrounding it, and, most importantly, God. A person cannot actualize and manifest its true vocation, which is self-giving love, except through the use of its nature's individual and group characteristics. These are the gifts through which one offers oneself to others. Likewise, in all their particularity, they constitute the matrix within which we are able to receive the concrete, distinctive gifts of others.

However, one must also remember that leading representatives of the personalist approach such as Bishop Kallistos of Diokleia, Archimandrite Sophrony of Tolleshunt Knights and Metropolitan Anthony of Sourozh are also deeply rooted in the ascetical tradition and embrace its key insights. Human nature as it functions in this fallen world needs to be redeemed, purified of "passionate" distortions, strengthened and further developed in virtue, and transfigured by communion with God. Hence, the anthropological concepts of the ascetic tradition can be encompassed within a broadly personalist theology, even if the insights of personalism cannot be included within certain narrowly defined versions of the "monastic" or "hesychast" anthropology.

The ascetic emphasis on human alikeness and unity is central to the Church's tradition. These insights about human identity, which are in fact affirmed by the leading personalist theologians, can and should be integrated with the concepts of personal creativity and spiritual freedom. The two positions are only irreconcilable if advocates of asceticism insist that the suppression of uniqueness, creativity and freedom is necessary to spiritual growth or to salvation. Although some people may be called to follow this path, a healthy and balanced approach to Orthodox ascetic practice will acknowledge that there are other paths as well, even within monastic life. An appreciation of such diversity-in-unity within monastic life and ascetic practice more generally can best be grounded in a theological recognition of personal uniqueness. This needs to be combined with pastoral sensitivity to particular human vocations and accurate study of the rich variety of human lives witnessing to holiness throughout the Church's history.

The ascetic tradition raises some important questions that call for further theological reflection within a broadly personalist context. Most fundamental is the ontological question, how to reaffirm the importance of alikeness and common nature in human identity without denying personal uniqueness? Along with this there is a pressing practical question, how to affirm and use uniquely personal creativity in a context of humility? The present essay will make a modest attempt to address these issues.

Unity through Otherness and Simplicity

Contemporary personalist Orthodox theologians often define human personhood as involving both creative uniqueness and intrinsic interrelatedness with others. The uniqueness of each person and the unity of humankind are seen as inextricably bound together, as mutually grounded in each other. One's unique creativity is born in a community that continually nourishes it; in turn, one's creative uniqueness is the gift one gives to others. The offering and interchange of everyone's unique gifts becomes the life of the community, which ever emerges anew as a dynamic interaction among its members. On this model human unity is the nexus of interrelatedness among persons. Since each is unique, they are united precisely by their irreducible mutual otherness, as Metropolitan John Zizioulas observes.[2] Each adds what is lacking in the others, so humankind is united as a richly variegated whole. This unity is a limitless and endlessly intricate complexity that expresses the boundless inventiveness of God's creative wisdom in synergy with the free and unique creativity of each human person, since each images the divine in a distinctive way.

Yet surely there is also an important sense in which humankind is united in simplicity. In a very basic way, people are united in sharing universal human experience. All are sinners, all are faced with death; Christ's death and resurrection can save all. At a time when some "post-modernists" envisage the fragmentation of human identity and experience and locate core identity in such group characteristics as gender, race, culture and class, the Church is called to reaffirm and bear witness to the universality of human identity.

When we are mindful that we all stand before the overwhelming majesty of God, all causes of human division appear small by comparison. The ancient fathers emphasize that all human beings share the same origin as God's creatures, the same history of sin in Adam and salvation in Christ, and the same ultimate vocation and hope in the eternal kingdom. All alike are fashioned from the dust of the earth and thus share the same intrinsic lowliness before our Creator. All have sinned and are beset by essentially the same kinds of passions, temptations, and afflictions. The ascetic fathers have analyzed these dynamics of human fallenness and discerned many universal patterns. Though not everybody has experienced all the same temptations, our passions and sins are depressingly similar. Yet all humans indeed are created in the image of God and thus are endowed with freedom, rationality, creativity and spiritual perception. When we receive God's grace and cooperate with him, since we bear his image we are all capable of practicing the virtues, keeping the divine commandments, offering ourselves in love, and thereby attaining the divine likeness and participation in the life of God. We are each free, responsible persons who decide for ourselves how to use our human faculties. So we each choose whether we accept as our own the twisted likeness of demons or the radiant likeness of Christ. We are all called to the same basic spiritual tasks of prayer, repentance, struggle against evil, practice of good, and love of God, our human neighbors, and the created world. We are all called to the same royal priesthood, to receive God's life into ourselves, each other and the created world with adoration and thanksgiving and to offer ourselves, each other and the

[2]Metropolitan John (Zizioulas), "Communion and Otherness," *Sobornost*, 16 (1994), 7–19.

whole world back to God. Ultimately, if we choose to accept it, like the thief on the cross we are all saved in the same way, by union with Christ in his death and resurrection. In the age to come we hope to share in his likeness, so that our unity in him outshines all incomplete human identities and divisive human differences as the midday sun outshines the stars.

This is why St Basil the Great speaks of human identity in terms of what everybody shares, the humility of being made from dust and the dignity of bearing God's royal image.[3] St Gregory of Nyssa's famous theological critique of slavery rests on the same foundation. For him all human beings are equal in the most important ways, and since all share in the divine image, which entails sovereignty over the whole world, how can such a person be owned or bought by another human being?[4] St John Chrysostom likens the different social locations associated with social, economic and political inequalities to the roles played by actors in the theater. Once the performance is over, those who played the king, the rich man and the slave are simply actors after all. Similarly, in the life to come the social differences that have characterized us in this life will be put aside like actor's masks.[5] The Greek fathers view such group characteristics as class, race, ethnicity and even gender, which unite parts of humankind but divide the whole, in this context. To them none of these are permanent features of human identity. In contrast, our sins and virtues, our evil and good actions, especially our love toward God and neighbor or our refusal to love, are what constitute our authentic and permanent identity; these are the things we will carry with us into eternity.

Christ offers salvation to everyone. His wisdom is expressed in simple words, in parables taken from everyday human experience. As sinners subject to disintegration and death we all need the same kind of salvation. Thus the way of humble love and self-offering that our Lord teaches is open to everyone, and this love can ultimately be taken up into participation in the eternal communion of love of the Holy Trinity. The path to salvation is a path of simplicity. We learn to forgive others because we also are sinners, they also are loved by God, we are like them and they are like us in sharing the most basic and most important aspects of human identity.

[3]Basil of Caesarea *Homily on the Words, "Give Attention to Yourself."* There is a good critical edition of this text, Stig Y. Rudberg, *L'homélie de Basile de Césarée sur le mot 'Oberve-toi toi-même': Édition critique du texte grec et étude sur la tradition manuscrite* (Stockholm: Almqvist & Wiksell, 1962).

[4]Gregory of Nyssa *Fourth Homily on Ecclesiastes* (W. Jaeger, ed. *Gregorii Nysseni Opera* [Leiden: Brill, 1960–], 5:334–38).

[5]John Chrysostom *Second Homily on Lazarus and the Rich Man* (PG 48:986).

In the ascetic saints we observe a progressive unification and simplification of self as all of their human faculties become focused on love for God, contemplation of God and love for all humankind and the created world in God. In them the extraneous aspects of human identity and activity drop away. Their prayer, too, becomes simple, often expressed in few words or in silence. Their conduct toward other people expresses a simple, direct and absolutely sincere love, free of the psychological and social complications that so often lead to impasses in interpersonal relationships. They identify with others in humility. The simple human experiences that everybody shares move increasingly into the foreground of their awareness and activity. Thus their tradition emphasizes the common features of human nature and personhood.

By long practice of prayer one comes through the Holy Spirit to a unity with Christ in one's heart. It is there, in him and within the heart, that one can become united through love with all people as St Silouan the Athonite did. Thus the Lord receives the hearts of his faithful into his heart and there makes them one. This unity in the Holy Spirit is characterized by loving simplicity. Here humankind is united in its common nature and in Christ. This is how the saints are able to love everybody, how they are also able to forgive and love their enemies. With this simple unity as a foundation, an interpersonal love and unity based on mutual recognition of uniqueness, otherness and diversity can also emerge, guided harmoniously by God's wisdom. The freedom to use human gifts of reason, talent and creativity for good in cooperation with God's creative activity is also built on this foundation.

Personal Uniqueness, Royal Priesthood and the Communion of Saints

Ascetics may be wary of affirming uniqueness, creativity and personal gifts because of a legitimate concern. It is important to honor others and to allow Christ and the shared life of the Church to be the center of one's existence and identity rather than one's own limited, isolated and self-enclosed "ego." This concern needs to be addressed, but it is also essential to affirm human uniqueness for important theological reasons. Each human being is unrepeatable and thus adds something of irreducible value to God's creation that would not otherwise exist. I remember Bob Dylan's parody of a "politically correct" over-emphasis on common humanity. On one of his early albums he sang:

I'm just average, common too,
I'm just like him, the same as you.
I'm everybody's brother and son.
I ain't different from anyone.
It ain't no use a-talking to me,
It's just the same as talking to you.[6]

On the contrary, each one of us has something unique to add to our mutual conversation. Each new person one encounters in love discloses an inexhaustible living treasure that can be found nowhere else. To use the theological language of St Maximus the Confessor, in each is present a distinctive *logos*, the divine idea and intention according to which that person was created, revealing an aspect of God's likeness that is manifest there alone. This is why the communion of saints is filled with meaning, purpose and joy. If, when reaching the perfection God intended for them, people were all merely photocopies of each other, or even merely photocopies of Jesus Christ whose likeness they indeed bear, why would God have produced so many copies? Rather, does not Christ's likeness shine forth in the saints in innumerable unique ways, each of them unrepeatable as well as entirely like him? In each generation, God adds more human persons to the eternal community of the faithful. Each one brings a new beloved presence. Each adds something fresh and unrepeatable to the joy of all the others. In this way, as their numbers increase until the end of the age, so do their love, their communion and their joy. Moreover, if St Gregory of Nyssa is correct about the unending growth of the saints in God, their joy and communion with each other must also increase without end, as they always find more in each other to love.

The human task of royal priesthood is for each a uniquely personal vocation. One must receive the life of God, the Church, other people and the created world into one's own person and from within one's own person offer it back again. In this way, the life of God is refracted through the prism of one's heart and shines forth in a distinctive spectrum of colors. When giving again to others the gifts one has received, one is also giving oneself. Thus we thank God for our human benefactors, and we also thank them. This personal human dimension is what is added when God, who needs no help from anybody, graciously allows people to participate through synergy in his activities.

[6]Bob Dylan, "I Shall Be Free Number Ten," recorded on *Another Side of Bob Dylan* (Columbia Records: 1964). Let me thank Kevin Vance of radio station KALW in San Francisco for supplying this reference.

This human contribution is always unique, whether one intends it and is aware of it or not. A great artist who seeks only to follow traditional models at the same time discloses a new beauty previously unperceived. At the heart of all cosmic and interpersonal priestly mediation is the human person's offering of self.

This is manifest in many different contexts. The artist gives concrete expression to a beauty not otherwise known and offers it to others. The scientist discovers a previously unknown facet of divine workmanship in the material world and shares it with humankind. This nurse gives this patient the particular care needed on this day. Mother and child share their unique affection for each other. All of this is profoundly creative.

Then there are the tasks directly involved in the Church's witness and worship. The iconographer, following prescribed canons, makes manifest in wood and paint the presence of Christ and his saints. Their presence is an objective, ontological truth, not a reflection of the artist's subjective imagination. Yet Fr Pavel Florensky found that each of the ancient icons he contemplated, though entirely faithful to traditional forms, was also unique.[7] This is because it manifested a unique person's authentic spiritual experience of transcendent reality. Similarly, in theological writing the author, however humble and faithful to earlier sacred texts, always contributes something personal. St Nil Sorsky, a self-effacing, reclusive monk, compiled an anthology of patristic texts about spiritual life.[8] Yet his choice of which passages to quote and in what order inevitably reveals his own teaching. This is what readers find in his book today. Similarly, because the words of Scripture contain an inexhaustible depth and breadth of meaning, when the fathers interpret the same Biblical passage they each uncover a different insight. This is true although the fathers, who share the mind of the Church, often repeat common interpretive themes and employ many of the same exegetical methods.

Humility and Creativity

Certain temptations can beset an emphasis on personal uniqueness. One is the thought that my special problems, wounds and weaknesses make me

[7]Pavel Florensky, *Iconostasis*, trans. Donald Sheehan and Olga Andrejev (Crestwood, NY: St Vladimir's Seminary Press, 1996), 83.

[8]George P. Fedotov, *The Russian Religious Mind II: The Middle Ages* (Belmont, MA: Nordland, 1975), 268.

unable to follow the path to salvation in Christ common to humankind. Yet as one makes progress one finds that God heals the wounds, supplies what is lacking and smoothes the rough edges. One discovers that Christ can save oneself as he saves others. The awareness of one's common humanity can come as a gift of hope, lightness and freedom, an occasion of deep thankfulness to God. The opposite temptation is the thought that my unique gifts make me an exception to ordinary human responsibilities. These talents can become the center of one's life instead of Christ and the shared life of the faithful in Christ. At root both of these temptations are the same. They involve arrogance, self-enclosure and isolation.

How, then, can we affirm humility while remaining mindful of our uniqueness and using our gifts? Bishop Kallistos points to the central role of the spiritual father or mother in the Church's ascetic tradition. The primary task of the wise and experienced guide is to invite the disciple into a loving and mutual interpersonal relationship. Such a guide teaches above all by example and takes great care to respect the disciple's human dignity and freedom. The bishop concludes with the following significant comment.

> Here we touch on the most important point of all, and that is the *personalism* that inspires the encounter between disciple and spiritual guide. This personal contact protects the disciple against rigid legalism, against slavish submission to the letter of the law. He learns the way, not through external conformity to written rules, but through seeing a human face and hearing a human voice. In this way the spiritual mother or father is the guardian of evangelical freedom.[9]

Often a good spiritual guide will discern, bless, encourage and enable the use of one's gifts. Obedience to the guide then allows one to escape any possible conflict between acting creatively and guarding humility.

It is also important to understand how our gifts are situated in a broader cosmic and interpersonal context. They connect us in their ontological structure and through their natural activity with God, humankind and the created world. The gifts come from God, not from ourselves, and they arise out of

---

[9]Bishop Kallistos, "The Spiritual Guide in Orthodox Christianity," *The Inner Kingdom*, Collected Works, vol. 1 (Crestwood, NY: St Vladimir's Seminary Press, 2000), 127–51, 146, emphasis in the original. Bishop Kallistos has made significant changes to the earlier article on which this chapter is based, further emphasizing the disciple's freedom and warning against possible abuse of power by the guide. The paragraph quoted here comes from the new material.

the communal context within which we always already exist. Hence they do not belong exclusively to ourselves but are given as resources to be shared with the whole community. Unique personal gifts are constituted as distinctive modes of connectedness with others. They are the tools or artistic media by which human beings enter into mutual self-giving and loving interrelatedness among persons, and by which they accomplish their priestly work of mediation so as to link together God, humankind and the created world. So the right use of one's gifts will bring a greater and greater awareness of the concurrent presence and collaborative activity of God, other people and all created beings. One becomes more and more aware of disclosing, sharing and bearing witness to realities beyond oneself, realities grounded in the transcendent mystery of God's inexhaustible wisdom and creative activity. One then recognizes that one's own contribution is small in comparison to the unfolding of these greater realities.

Some examples may help to clarify how this happens. Fr Pavel Florensky speaks of how the true artist does not express his or her own imaginative fantasies but rather uncovers the transcendent beauty that is objectively and ontologically present in the material and natural creation beneath the outward surfaces of things.[10] This is true in a special way of the iconographer, who depicts the divine radiance present in the faces and bodies of the incarnate Christ and the saints. Something similar can be said of the scientist, who, in the words attributed to Sir Isaac Newton, "thinks God's thoughts after him," and declares them to others by discerning and describing the wondrous patterns and structures inherent in the physical and biological creation. It is noteworthy that Florensky was himself a distinguished scientist as well as a religious philosopher, priest and martyr. The creative work of authentic artists and scientists is thus a labor of communication and testimony, a retrieval of realities beyond themselves so as to share them with other human persons. Such disclosure of the beauties and wonders of the created world involves the ascetic discipline of effacing oneself before the objective presence of other realities. This ultimately serves to glorify the Creator by acknowledging and honoring his works.

Post-modern literary critics have noted the inherently collaborative and interpersonal character of all written texts. Mikhail Bakhtin observes that every author's voice inserts itself into a dialogue that has already existed since the time of Adam.[11] Hence embedded in the author's text are many other

---

[10]Florensky, *Iconostasis*, 79–80.
[11]M. M. Bakhtin, *The Dialogic Imagination: Four Essays*, trans. Caryl Emerson and

voices that are quoted directly or indirectly, whether consciously or unconsciously. Yet the author is not a mere compiler but adds his or her own unique creative voice, entering into conversation with others and responding to them. Similarly, every commentator makes his or her own creative contribution when reading and interpreting texts written by others, and is thus also an author. The vast wealth of patristic commentary on Scripture is a good example of this. When reading such works we hear the voices of the fathers as well as those of the writers of Biblical texts. As the fathers observe, authors and readers alike need a similar inspiration from the Holy Spirit to arrive at genuine understanding. Likewise, all authentic scholarship is inherently dialogic and collaborative. The scholar's labor of accurately acknowledging and citing sources and submitting to peer review from colleagues is an ascetic discipline that places one's own creative work in the broader context of others' gifts and contributions. Similarly, the Orthodox theologian offers his or her work as a gift to the Church's community, mindful that at least in the long run it will be accepted if it bears witness to truth and corrected by others if it is in error.

We can conclude by recalling St Maximus' way of understanding human alikeness and distinctiveness. Human likeness to others, personal uniqueness and relatedness to others are all grounded in the divine Logos, in whose mind are the *logoi* of all human unity and diversity. Thus God's creative wisdom and activity conceptualize and fashion the structures that organize humankind, the cosmos and God into a harmonious wholeness and communion in which each entity has its particular location and dynamism.[12] Therefore, when restored to attunement with God's will, human uniqueness, alikeness and interrelatedness together come to be encompassed within the eternal unity-in-diversity and interpersonal communion of the Holy Trinity. This is sometimes adumbrated in this world but has its fulfillment only in God's Kingdom, which is to come.

Michael Holquist (Austin, TX: University of Texas Press, 1981), 279.
[12]Maximus the Confessor *Mystagogy* 1 (PG 91:664D–668C).

Embodied Word and New Creation: Some Modern Orthodox Insights Concerning the Material World

Elizabeth Theokritoff

H OW DO WE PERCEIVE the material world, and our own place within it? There is widespread awareness that the tradition of Eastern Christianity has much to offer towards an answer to this crucial question; the wisdom of early Eastern sources, found both in patristic writings and in saints' lives, is increasingly accessible in the West. But the voice of contemporary Orthodoxy is much less known. What contribution does it have to make to a renewed Christian understanding of the cosmos, ourselves included? We shall look for some answers in writings already available in English.

Even leaving aside more speculative works of religious philosophy, we find a diversity of approaches. We can, however, identify three recurrent points of reference: creation as the grounding of matter's relationship with God; the Incarnation, inaugurating the consummation of that relationship; and the Eucharist as an image of the relationship between God, man and matter.

The World as Creation

The created world is absolutely distinct from God, but has no being apart from God. This is the paradox which immediately confronts any Christian understanding of the material world, for it is inherent in the doctrine of creation out of nothing. A favorite expression of this paradox in Orthodox writers is the image coined by Metropolitan Filaret of Moscow in the nineteenth century: "All things are balanced upon the creative word of God as if on a bridge of diamond: above them is the abyss of the divine infinitude, below them that of their own nothingness."[1] This vivid image encapsulates both the fragility of creation, and the way in which that very fragility is the greatest proof of its worth: creation is "the consequence of divine choice."[2]

The doctrine of creation out of nothing entails an ontological distance separating all things from God according to their proper nature, a point stressed particularly by Metropolitan John (Zizioulas) of Pergamon. But Vladimir Lossky speaks for most of our writers when he emphasizes the grace consequently implicit in the very act of creation. Describing the notion of "pure nature" in created things as a "philosophical fiction," he points out that "such fictions tend to separate into distinct moments an indivisible reality whose appearance is simultaneous: created beings have the faculty of being assumed by God because such was the object of their creation."[3]

So "what is created is outside of God but . . . united with him," as Florovsky writes.[4] The Church Fathers, and modern theologians in their tradition, have various ways of expressing the "unitedness" of creation with the Creator without compromising the "outsideness." Crucial here is the distinction between God's essence and his divine energies. As Patriarch Bartholomew of Constantinople has pointed out, it is only the "ontological content" of God's energies that "allows us to attribute the ontological 'principle' of matter and of the world to a personal God. Not to the *essence* of God, which would lead to pantheism, but to God's hypostatic energies."[5]

There has to be what Lossky calls a "point of contact of every created thing with the Godhead;" and perhaps the most fruitful framework for conceptualizing this is that of the *logoi* ("words" or "underlying principles") in things, developed by St Maximus. As Lossky points out, this understanding is primarily grounded in the Scriptural notion of God's creative and providential word: "And God said . . ." Fr Dumitru Staniloae, who has led the way in exploring the implications of this doctrine for our use of the world, gives this account of how things relate to the creative word:

---

[1] E.g. Georges Florovsky, *Creation and Redemption*, Collected Works, Vol. 3 (Nordland, 1976), 45.

[2] Bishop Kallistos (Ware), *The Orthodox Way* (Crestwood: SVS Press, 1998), 44.

[3] Vladimir Lossky, *The Mystical Theology of the Eastern Church* (London: James Clarke and Co., 1957), 101–2.

[4] Florovsky, *Creation and Redemption*, 47.

[5] Patriarch Bartholomew of Constantinople, "The Orthodox Faith and the Environment," *Sourozh*, 62 (November, 1995), 23.

> The word "spoken" by God is a rational structure, thought by him in an active way and intended to have in reply a reality in its own image . . . All existent realities are replies to the creative word of God, replies analogous to the divine words, concrete and subsistent images of the *logoi* of God . . .[6]

This framework thus expresses divine immanence in creation; for God "conceals himself mysteriously in the *logoi* of created beings," which are in turn conceived within the eternal Word of God.[7] Paraphrasing Maximus, Bishop Kallistos of Diokleia speaks of the Creator-Logos as the "cosmic tree" to which the *logoi* of all created things come like birds to revive themselves; "the *Logos* embraces all the *logoi*, but is not himself embraced or circumscribed by them."[8]

It is clear that this vision of creation has a profound impact on how we view the material world, for it puts material creation no less than intelligible in an intimate and dynamic relationship with God. It is this same insight that Metropolitan Anthony of Sourozh expresses in poetic language when he says that

> there is not an atom in this world, from the meanest speck of dust to the greatest star, which does not hold in its core . . . the thrill . . . of its coming into being, of its possessing infinite possibilities and of entering into the divine realm, so that it knows God, rejoices in him.[9]

There is thus arguably a sense in which matter relates to God directly, apart from man, as Metropolitan Anthony contends in another powerful talk.[10] He also manages to clarify a point of some confusion: in what sense, and to what extent, is the rest of creation implicated in the Fall of man?[11]

---

[6]Dumitru Staniloae, "Christian Responsibility in the World," in *The Tradition of Life* (London: Fellowship of St Alban and St Sergius, 1971), 65; cf. 64–73.

[7]Cf. J. Chryssavgis, *Beyond the Shattered Image* (Minneapolis: Light and Life Publishing, 1999), 57, quoting Maximus *Ambigua* (PG 91:1085).

[8]Bishop Kallistos (Ware), *Through the Creation to the Creator* (London: Friends of the Centre, 1996), 11, citing Maximus *Centuries on Theology* II.10.

[9]Metropolitan Anthony (Bloom), "Body and Matter in Spiritual Life," in *Sacrament and Image* (London: Fellowship of St Alban and St Sergius, 1987), 41.

[10]Metropolitan Anthony (Bloom), "Sacred Materialism in Christianity," in *The Experience of the Incarnation: The Body as the Temple of the Holy Spirit* (Diocesan Conference 1997. Oxford: St Stephen's Press, no date), 11. Other writers draw similar conclusions, particularly with reference to animals, from the covenant with "every living creature" of Gen. 9:10; cf. Pavel Florensky, *The Pillar and Ground of the Truth*, trans. B. Jakim (Princeton University Press, 1997), 198; Tatiana Goricheva, "Les animaux dans la pensée orthodoxe" (I), *Contacts*, 145 (1989/1), 34.

[11]While some writers note that non-human creation has never ceased to do God's will, others

> ... matter [is] free to commune with God ... because it is sinless, it is
> not fallen; it has become a victim of the Fall. .... The created world,
> as we know it now ... is like a good horse ridden by a drunken rider.
> We are the drunken rider ...[12]

Accordingly, it is not in the "natural" order as we know it but in miracles that
we see "the *normal* relationship between God and his world," the order in
which "things are freed from the enslavement which we have imposed on
them."[13]

It is evident, then, that the sense of creation pervaded by the divine is richly
represented in the Christian tradition. In an important contribution to a
proper understanding of this aspect of Christianity, Fr Michael Oleksa has
explored the congruence between this and aspects of the pre-modern world-
view, exemplified in the traditional beliefs of the Alaskan tribes converted to
Orthodox Christianity in recent centuries.[14] He shows how such beliefs were
often taken up by the Orthodox missionaries: "They could affirm that the
spiritual realities those societies worshipped were indeed *logoi*, related to the
divine *Logos*, whose personal existence these societies had simply never imagined."[15] On the other hand, "there are some insights which pre-modern societies that have become Orthodox automatically understand better than we
do"—such as the cosmic significance of our worship, offered for the whole
world in recognition of "the cosmos as ... God's icon, God's self-portrait,
God's revelation to us."[16] Emphasizing the grounding of such insights in the
Christian tradition, he recalls the notion in St Maximus of the Word being
"embodied" three times: in creation, in Scripture, and finally and most perfectly as a human being. And he quotes the testimony of the twentieth-century Serbian martyr St Nikolai Velimirović to the "theophanic" character of
all creation:

stress that the whole of nature as we know it is in a fallen state—cf. Stanley Harakas, "The
Integrity of Creation: Ethical Issues," in *Justice, Peace and the Integrity of Creation: Insights
from Orthodoxy* (Geneva: WCC, 1990), 73.

[12]Metropolitan Anthony, "Sacred Materialism," 15.

[13]Metropolitan Anthony, "Body and Matter," 40; idem "Sacred Materialism," 15.

[14]See especially Michael Oleksa, "Icons and the Cosmos: The Missionary Significance,"
Sourozh, 16 (May 1984) 34–45; = *Sacred Art Journal* 5.1 (1984), 5–13; idem, *Orthodox Alaska:
A Theology of Mission* (Crestwood: SVS Press, 1992); idem, "The Confluence of Church and
Culture" in C. Tarasar (ed.), *Perspectives on Religious Education* (Syosset: Syndesmos/OCA
Department of Religious Education, 1983), 5–26.

[15]Oleksa, *Orthodox Alaska*, 61.

[16]Oleksa, "Confluence of Church and Culture," 21.

... If the whole of nature is not theology, then theology is nothing or nature is nothing. If the whole of nature does not speak about God, who will believe Isaiah or St Paul ... "Show us God," say many of our contemporaries, "and we will believe." ... We must say to them: *"Show us what is not God!"*[17]

There is a difference, certainly, between the Christian vision of God's presence in creation and that of polytheistic religions. As Bishop Kallistos points out in reference to the Burning Bush, here we see the created world as "the locus of an *interpersonal* encounter; the world acquires meaning when seen as the reflection of a reality which transcends it."[18] As Christos Yannaras puts it characteristically, the world "reveals ... the personal otherness of the creative energy of its Maker."[19] In the Christian understanding, the world can indeed be seen as a theophany; but with a view "not ... to some impersonal fusion ... but to personal communion," as the Patriarch of Antioch says.[20]

Yet the natural world itself is not lost in this communion. As Fr Alexander Schmemann emphasizes, it is precisely through the knowledge of God, expressed in thanksgiving, that we rediscover the integral *knowledge of* the world for which man was created, as opposed to merely a disintegrated *knowledge about* created things.[21] And once we "know" the cosmos in this way, we cannot go on "treating things like things," as Deacon John Chryssavgis says.[22] Fr Lev Gillet expresses this movingly when he portrays all created things as embraced by God's love, and not simply "good things" provided out of his love for *us:* "Each of us, and indeed every creature, even each microscopic grain of sand is loved by God in a divine and overwhelming manner."[23] All these things epitomize both the evolution of the world towards the "total Christ," and "love giving Itself to us." So as we "integrate our spiritual lives with the life of the universe," we learn to "recognize in every creature a spring of divine love fitting to itself alone."[24]

---

[17]Oleksa, *Orthodox Alaska*, 39.

[18]Bishop Kallistos (Ware), *Through the Creation to the Creator*, 6–8, 14. My italics.

[19]Christos Yannaras, in Sarah Hobson and Jane Lubchenco (eds.), *Revelation and the Environment: AD 95–1995* (World Scientific, 1997), 79.

[20]Ignatius IV, Patriarch of Antioch, "Three Sermons: A Theology of Creation; A Spirituality of the Creation; The Responsibility of Christians," *Sourozh*, 38 (November 1989), 7.

[21]Alexander Schmemann, *The Eucharist* (Crestwood: SVS Press, 1987), 177.

[22]Chryssavgis, *Beyond the Shattered Image*, 15.

[23]Lev Gillet, *The Burning Bush* (Springfield: Templegate, no date), 35.

[24]Ibid. 19–20.

Here we have the root of the all-embracing love and vision often summed up in St Isaac the Syrian's description of the "merciful heart" which "burns for the entire creation." As our writers frequently emphasize, this experience is no less of a reality today—as we see for example in the contemporary Elder Paisios of the Holy Mountain, who could speak of a blade of grass or a stone as an icon.[25]

The New Creation: Incarnation and Eschatology

If the Word is "embodied" in the *logoi* of created things, in St Maximus' language, then this movement awaits its fulfillment in the literal embodiment of the Word when he clothes himself in the matter of this world. The incarnation reveals to us that, in the words of Bishop Basil of Sergievo, matter is "God-friendly"; "it can only have been designed to receive him."[26] The incarnation, curiously often ignored in considering the place of material creation in Christianity, is thus absolutely central. In relation to the world of the Fall, it manifests creation made new. But it is essentially a "normative spiritual movement," as Chryssavgis writes; not a change of course, but a reaffirmation of the reality that "from the moment of creation, the world is assumed by the Word and constitutes the body of this Word."[27] Vigen Guroian insists that the incarnation "completes God's purpose at creation" because it concerns "the flourishing of all life," illustrating the point from the traditional Armenian Cross, which sprouts blossoming branches.[28] We see why some theologians can speak of creation being for the sake of the incarnation—or for the sake of the Church, within which "creation is recast within the flesh of the Lord."[29]

The material world is thus integral to the divine purpose. It is not disposable packaging for the spiritual, or a mere backdrop to the human drama.

---

[25]Alexander Belopopsky and Dimitri Oikonomou (eds.), *Orthodoxy and Ecology Resource Book* (Bialystok: Syndesmos, 1996), 55.

[26]Bishop Basil (Osborn), "Towards the Millennium: The Transfiguration of the World," *Sourozh*, 72 (May 1998), 32 (reprinted from *One in Christ* 1997/3). Cf. Metropolitan Anthony, "Body and Matter," 41.

[27]Chryssavgis, *Beyond the Shattered Image*, 54–5.

[28]Vigen Guroian, *Ethics after Christendom* (Grand Rapids: Eerdmans, 1994), 171.

[29]P. Nellas, "Redemption or Deification? Nicholas Kavasilas and Anselm's Question "Why did God become Man?" " *Sourozh*, 66 (December 1996), 27; cf. idem, *Deification in Christ* (Crestwood: SVS Press, 1987), esp. 227–237; Sergei Bulgakov, quoted in Chryssavgis, *Beyond the Shattered Image*, 154.

"The creation which we see has a goal," writes Bishop Basil, "and that goal has been revealed to us through the Incarnation of the Son of God. The goal, as we can see from the Gospel record, is transfiguration and, ultimately, resurrection."[30] We cannot realistically expect to understand the nature of transfigured matter. But since *all flesh* shall see salvation, we can affirm that earth and heaven as we know them must be "the substrate of the future transformation," as Paul Evdokimov writes in his seminal study of material creation in the Orthodox understanding.[31] Several writers emphasize the uniqueness of Christianity in this respect; notably, Metropolitan Paulos mar Gregorios contrasts the Hindu approach to matter with the Christian belief in the consummation of the entire cosmic order, organic and inorganic, in Christ.[32]

The "goal" of creation is a reality with us even now, however. By the incarnation, resurrection and ascension of Christ, a small part of this world is "pushed forward into the Kingdom," as Bishop Basil says.[33] This is the eschatological reality made manifest in the transfiguration of Christ, and also that of his saints.[34] And what happens at the transfiguration? As is often pointed out, not only Christ's face but also his clothes are transfigured; non-human creation, even human artifacts are caught up into glory. Archimandrite Aimilianos of Simonopetra speaks of Christ's clothing here as signifying "the *logoi* of created beings which have *found their fulfilment* in the divine-human person of the Word of God incarnate . . . the elements of the natural world become supple, luminous, bearers of the Spirit . . ."[35] There is a striking similarity to the way in which Metropolitan Anthony describes the impression given by Theophan the Greek's icon of the Transfiguration, depicting the moment at which "the eschatological situation is realized, and . . . God is all in all."[36]

[30]Bishop Basil, "Towards the Millennium," 36.

[31]Paul Evdokimov, "Nature," *Scottish Journal of Theology* 18 (March 1965), 22, 7.

[32]Metropolitan Paulos mar Gregorios, "New Testament Foundations for Understanding the Creation," in W. Granberg-Michaelson (ed.), *Tending the Garden* (Grand Rapids: Eerdmans, 1987), 91; cf. 89.

[33]Bishop Basil, "Towards the Millennium," 36.

[34]Bishop Kallistos, "The Transfiguration of the Body," *Sacrament and Image* (London: Fellowship of St Alban and St Sergius, 2nd edition 1987), 23; cf. L. Ouspensky, *Theology of the Icon*, Vol. 1 (Crestwood: SVS Press, 1992), 158.

[35]Archimandrite Aimilianos, "The Experience of the Transfiguration in the Life of the Athonite Monk," in Alexander Golitzin, *The Living Witness of the Holy Mountain* (South Canaan: St Tikhon's Press, 1996), 200. My italics.

[36]Metropolitan Anthony, "Body and Matter," 45; the Icon is in the Tretiakov Gallery in Moscow.

New Creation in the Church

It should be quite clear what an eschatological consciousness implies about matter: it is not a preoccupation with the "last things" but an apprehension of the *"lastness of* things," as Chryssavgis puts it.[37] This "lastness of things" is another way of expressing their "normal relationship with their Creator" as manifested in miracles—"events in advance of the surrounding world," as Bishop Basil calls them, which "allow the *eschaton* to appear locally before the end."[38] Again, things reveal their "lastness" when used in the Church and in its mysteries, those "privileged points . . . where the goal of the created order is made manifest."[39] " *'Sacramental' means no less than* 'eschatological,' " as Florovsky has said.[40]

The particular mysteries are grounded in the "great mystery of faith." "Christ walked this earth," writes Evdokimov; ". . . there is nothing in this world which has remained a stranger to his humanity and has not received the imprint of the Holy Spirit. And that is why the Church in its turn blesses and sanctifies all creation." And through the Holy Spirit, he continues, "the matter of the cosmos . . . becomes the conductor of grace, the vehicle of the divine energies."[41] Fr Alexander Schmemann frequently emphasizes that sacraments reveal the genuine nature of creation as a whole: they do not create a distinct class of "sacred objects."[42] The Eucharist is a "moment of truth" when we see the world in Christ; the blessing of waters makes the world and all creation what it was in the beginning.[43] And since this original world of God's creation has already been saved by Christ, the cosmic aspect of the sacrament is equally an eschatological aspect.[44] As Yannaras says in his development of the same theme, in the Eucharist, the world is "made word."[45]

---

[37]J. Chryssavgis, "The World as Sacrament: Insights into an Orthodox World View," *Pacifica*, 10 (February 1997), 4.

[38]Bishop Basil, "Towards the Millennium," 37; cf. Patriarch Ignatius, 4.

[39]Bishop Basil, "Towards the Millennium," 36.

[40]Georges Florovsky, "The Church: Her Nature and Task," reprinted in idem, *Bible, Church, Tradition: An Eastern Orthodox View* (Belmont, MA: Notable and Academic Books, 1987), 68. Emphases original.

[41]Evdokimov, "Nature," 16, 17.

[42]Cf. Alexander Schmemann, *Eucharist*, 61; idem, *For the Life of the World* (Crestwood: SVS Press, 1973), 132.

[43]Schememann, *For the Life of the World*, 44, 73.

[44]Cf. Schmemann, *Eucharist*, 35.

[45]C. Yannaras, *The Freedom of Morality* (Crestwood: SVS Press, 1984), 94.

All the ways in which the material world is used in the Church, both phys-
ically and in verbal imagery, can be seen as reflections of creation's renewed
relationship with its Maker: since Christ's Incarnation, everything can now
"recognize itself mysteriously in him."[46] Several writers remark how this is
expressed liturgically, notably in festal texts which speak of creation responding to its Lord.

Closely parallel to sacramental life is the witness of icons, which surround
us in the Church as "markers on our path to the new creation."[47] Interestingly, as Bishop Basil reminds us, the icon has only recently been "reborn" as
a theological concern and "seen to offer insights into the relationship of God
to man and man to the world."[48] Like the sacraments, the icon testifies by the
very fact of its existence both that our world is fundamentally "God-
friendly," and that "matter has been rendered dynamic by its sanctification in
the Incarnation."[49] The icon, too, is at once cosmic and eschatological. The
icon does not glorify matter *per se* but matter transfigured, as Mariamna Fortounatto stresses; and yet the "representatives of the created world" which
are its raw material demand of the painter a respect grounded in awareness
of creation as a divine work.[50] And the result is that materials from the ani-
mal, vegetable and mineral realms are formed into "a re-ordered microcosm
. . . re-created in such a way as to testify to the 'good news.' "[51] This "re-
ordering" is important. While it is often pointed out that most matter used
sacramentally has been worked by humans, this is most strikingly true of the
icon. It thus becomes a vitally important paradigm for human *use* of the
world, for it testifies that "man can create forms that help God to be present
in this world, forms that do not shut him out."[52]

"The life of the Church is realized eschatology," writes Fr Michael Oleksa.
"The cosmic dimension of the Orthodox faith is not the experience of a few
mystics, but the common experience of the faithful."[53] He is voicing a common conviction that liturgical life is the model and starting point for all our
relationships with the world around us. As Yannaras puts it, liturgical life
opens our eyes to see "the 'objects' of the world as *acts* of God's love, realities

[46]Metropolitan Anthony, "Sacred Materialism," 14.

[47]Ouspensky, *Theology of the Icon*, I, 193.

[48]Bishop Basil (Osborn), *The Light of Christ* (Oxford: St Stephen's Press, 1996), 49–50.

[49]Chryssavgis, *Beyond the Shattered Image*, 128–9.

[50]Mariamna Fortounatto, "The Icon: The Image of God in Matter," in *Experience of the Incarnation* (Diocesan Conference), 41.

[51]Oleksa, "Icons and the Cosmos," 41.

[52]Bishop Basil, *Light of Christ*, 52.

[53]Oleksa, *Orthodox Alaska*, 40.

of communion and relationship;" and he concludes, "one cannot participate in the life of the Church and despise material reality."[54]

Realized eschatology is never the whole story, of course; so it is also true that sacramental life exhibits the tension of "already, but not yet." Hence it both reveals and conceals the new creation. As Patriarch Ignatius expresses it, "The epiklesis involved in all sacramental acts is a prolongation of Pentecost, where the Spirit raises up the new creation in Christ . . . Christ through his incarnation, his resurrection and his ascension and his sending of the Holy Spirit, has brought about the potential transfiguration of the whole universe." But "this transfiguration remains a secret, hidden under the veil of the sacraments out of respect for our freedom."[55]

Concelebrating the Cosmic Eucharist

It is our task then, to unveil the transfiguration of the world. In the imagery chiefly favored by our writers, this means "being priests of our whole life" in the "immense cathedral which is the universe of God."[56] It requires making all our use of the world a "eucharist"—an image elaborated most extensively by Fr Alexander Schmemann. Such a relationship with the world—an attitude of thanksgiving and sacrifice, in which creation is constantly referred back to its Creator—is essentially one which undoes the Fall. In the words of Metropolitan John of Pergamon, for whom man's priesthood is a central theme: "It is precisely the reversal of Adam's attitude, who took the world as his own and referred it to himself."[57] Schmemann's classic statement of this understanding illuminates why the Church commemorates the Fall at the beginning of the Great Fast; for the Fall was an event by which man

> changed the very relationship between himself and the world. To be sure, the world was given to him by God as "food"—as means of life; yet life was meant to be communion with God . . . The unfathomable tragedy of Adam was that he ate for its own sake. More than that, he ate "apart" from God in order to be independent of him . . .[58]

[54]Yannaras, *Freedom of Morality*, 86–7.
[55]Ignatius, "Three Sermons," 6, 4–5.
[56]P. Evdokimov, *apud* Ware, *Orthodox Way*, 65.
[57]Metropolitan John (Zizioulas), "Man the Priest of Creation," in A. Walker and C. Carras (eds.), *Living Orthodoxy in the Modern World* (London: SPCK, 1996), 185.
[58]Alexander Schmemann, *Great Lent* (Crestwood: SVS Press, 1974), 94–5; cf. idem, *For the Life of the World*, 14–17, and Yannaras, *Freedom of Morality*, 91.

The eucharistic nature of the world is a given, and also a calling to us. "The whole world ought to be regarded as the visible part of a universal and continuing sacrament," writes Staniloae;[59] but it fulfils its function as a means of communion and advances towards its goal only when man returns it to God as a sacrificial gift, offering it up in thankfulness.[60] In this perception, the role of man is essential; as Metropolitan John states categorically, "the axiom promoted by most ecologists that man needs nature, but nature does not need man, does not have a place in a liturgical view of the world."[61] But at the same time, this model gives a very clear framework within which man must function in order to fulfill his indispensable role.

A crucial aspect of liturgical, eucharistic imagery is that every liturgy is in some sense a *concelebration*. The entire body of the gathered Church joins with the celebrant in the offering, albeit in differing ways;[62] and inanimate matter makes its contribution too. Thus the notion of concelebration can be applied to creation as a whole: Archimandrite Vasileios speaks of "the 'words,' the inner principles of existent things, concelebrating with the one incarnate Word, the One who offers and is offered in the Liturgy of the whole world."[63] This cosmic concelebration is the "given" which determines our use of the world. Within the framework of concelebration, there is less contradiction than at first appears between the insistence that man is the *only* link between God and creation,[64] and the emphasis on matter's own communion with God. The first way of speaking underlines our unique responsibility: there can be no liturgy without a celebrant, however much everything else is prepared. But the second, more synergistic model actually stresses the weight of our responsibility: we are in a position to realize or thwart a potential in the cosmos that cries out for fulfillment. Our task is not to redirect creation, but to *articulate* its "wordless word revealing God" rather than "exporting our fallenness" into it.[65] In the same way, the celebrant does not create the

---

[59]Dimitru Staniloae, "The World as Gift and Sacrament of God's Love," *Sobornost*, 5:9 (Summer, 1969), 667.

[60]Cf. "The Foundation of Christian Responsibility in the World," 72. Cf. Schmemann, *passim*.

[61]Metropolitan John (Zizoulas), *Revelation and the Environment*, 20.

[62]Cf. the remarks on hierarchy and liturgy in Andrew Louth, *Denys the Areopagite* (Wilton, CT: Morehouse-Barlow, 1989), 132–3.

[63]Archimandrite Vasileios, *"The Light of Christ Shines upon All" through all the Saints* (Montreal: Alexander Press, 2001), 23.

[64]Cf. esp. Metropolitan John (Zizioulas), "Preserving God's Creation," Part 2, *Sourozh*, 40 (May 1990), 40; idem, "Ecological Asceticism: A Cultural Revolution," *Sourozh*, 67 (February 1997), 23 (reprinted from *One Planet*, 7/6 [1996]).

[65]Bishop Basil, *Speaking of the Kingdom* (Oxford: St Stephen's Press 1993), 53.

Eucharist, but articulates the thanksgiving proper to the Church; and the transforming power, as Metropolitan Anthony emphasizes, is that of Christ, the true celebrant, working by the Holy Spirit.[66]

The prevailing eucharistic model means that priesthood predominates as the image of man's role. This image is grounded in the patristic understanding of man as *link* or *bridge*, in that he is at once a material and a spiritual being;[67] for the priest is "one who unites the world in his hands in order to refer it back to God."[68] The importance of this image is that it emphasizes thanksgiving and offering, and also *self-offering*; for as Bishop Kallistos underlines, in an timely corrective to the usual emphasis on love and knowledge as prerequisites for proper care of creation, "there in no genuine love without costly self-sacrifice."[69]

When other traditional images such as kingship are used, they convey something close to priesthood; they too involve sacrificial service, and, importantly, have to do with the functioning of an organic whole.[70] Whatever images are chosen for man's relationship with the rest of material creation, the way they are used underlines the significance of that relationship: as on a physical level man is absolutely dependent on his environment for survival, so on the ontological level he is absolutely dependent on the relationship with it *in order to be himself.* This ontological imperative is expressed in various ways. Schmemann speaks of man becoming himself only in thanksgiving, in eucharistic offering of creation back to God.[71] For Metropolitan John, abuse of creation is serious primarily because we are failing to fulfill our relational nature.[72] Bishop Basil reminds us that the cosmic purposes of God leave us "no real choice, if we wish to pursue our own true end, but to live in harmony with the *Logos*—and the *logoi*—of creation as well."[73]

This reveals why the drab notion of "stewardship" has almost no place here. As Mar Gregorios points out, it leaves nature as essentially "property," albeit God's, not ours—an object external to us.[74] And thus the imperative to

---

[66]Metropolitan Anthony, "Sacred Materialism," 15; cf. Metropolitan John, "Man the Priest of Creation," 184.

[67]Cf. Maximus, *Ambigua,* PG 91:1304Dff.; translated in Nellas, *Deification,* 211–16.

[68]Metropolitan John, "Man the Priest of Creation," 183.

[69]Bishop Kallistos, *Through the Creation,* 27.

[70]Cf. Yannaras, *Freedom of Morality,* 97; Goricheva, "Les animaux," 26; Archimandrite Vasileios of Iviron, *Ecology and Monasticism* (Montreal: Alexander Press, 1996), 9, 20; Guroian, *Ethics,* 160, 169.

[71]A. Schmemann, *For the Life of the World,* 60.

[72]Metropolitan John, "Ecological Asceticism," 24.

[73]Bishop Basil, "Towards the Millennium," 38.

[74]Metropolitan Paulos mar Gregorios, *The Human Presence* (New York: Amity, 1987), 87–8.

use creation in the right way is also somehow imposed from outside. In its attempt to place an external check on man's power, this image obscures the reality expressed with such compelling simplicity by Archimandrite Vasileios: "Creation seeks but one thing—for us to be fully human."[75]

If the purpose of the material world can be fulfilled only through man, it is equally true that man can fulfill his own purpose only through matter. This simply indicates that the key to the functioning—the *liturgy*—of creation is not individualism but concelebration. As Metropolitan John says, "man's relationship with God passes through other people,"[76] and also through the material world.[77] Staniloae expresses the communal nature of our calling even more positively: "Man is not called to return to God as a solitary being; he is to help his fellow man and all things to make this return."[78]

Matter and the Body

The vital role of man in material creation depends on the fact that *he partakes in its nature*. It is in man's *body*, says Yannaras, that "the sacred liturgy of uniting created and uncreated life has its origin and fulfilment."[79] With man, as with the world as a whole, it is the Incarnation that brings into sharp focus the significance of materiality; for through it, as St Gregory Palamas underlines, the *flesh* becomes a source of salvation.[80]

Fr Georges Florovsky has stressed the radical newness of the conception of the body introduced by Christianity;[81] and more recent writers have explored the significance of the body in Christian doctrine and spiritual life, and the abundant evidence from the lives of the saints for its ultimate glory.[82] A seminal study unique in its breadth and depth (if occasionally idiosyncratic) is that of Fr Pavel Florensky, who discusses at length the notion of the "holy

[75]Archimandrite Vasileios, *Ecology and Monasticism*, 19.

[76]Quoted in P. Koumarianos, "Symbolism and Realism in the Divine Liturgy," *Sourozh* 80 (May 2000), 29.

[77]Metropolitan John (Zizioulas), "Orthodoxy and Ecological Problems: A Theological Approach," *The Environment and Religious Education* (Ecumenical Patriarchate, no date), 30.

[78]D. Staniloae, "The Foundation," 68.

[79]C. Yannaras, *Freedom of Morality*, 98–9.

[80]Quoted e.g. in Bishop Kallistos, "The Value of the Material Creation," *Sobornost*, 6:3 (1971), 159.

[81]G. Florovsky, *Creation and Redemption*, especially 111–114.

[82]See especially Metropolitan Anthony, "Body and Matter in Spiritual Life," in *Sacrament and Image;* Bishop Kallistos, "The Transfiguration of the Body," in the same volume and idem, "The Value of the Material Creation."

body" which is to inherit eternal life.[83] Like others after him, he sees the
Church's affirmation of matter strikingly manifested in the veneration of
relics, which he characterizes as "the dry, lifeless seed of a holy body."[84]

A truly remarkable insight into the meaning of a "holy body" and its
cosmic significance is to be found in the writings of Iulia de Beausobre.
Meditating on approaching death, she writes of "our task—as Christians—to
use our bodies, the relics of our bodies of the resurrection, as purifiers of the
earth that we increasingly pollute."[85] Spiritual and physical pollution are
inseparable in her thinking, just as the actual, physical body is inseparable from
the process of spiritual purification and incorporation into the body of Christ
which makes our mortal remains "cleansing substances in [his] hands."[86]
Notably, a similar insight is found in Panayiotis Nellas, who writes of death as
"the means by which the human body penetrates into the interior of the earth,
reaching the inmost parts of creation . . . [which then] is dressed with a new
element which, as the human body, is receptive of incorruption."[87] This is the
way in which the eschatological transformation of the universe is realized;
"from within, organically and naturally, within the human person."[88]

These rather concrete expressions of the interaction between our bodies
and the rest of material creation suggest that human responsibility for the entire
cosmos is no arrogant metaphysical conceit, but a reasonable extrapolation
from what we know of the interrelation of all matter. "What is our body," asks
Olivier Clément rhetorically, "if . . . not the form imprinted by our 'living soul'
on the universal 'dust' which unceasingly penetrates and traverses us? There is
no discontinuity between the flesh of the world and human flesh . . ."[89]

"To Acquire a Body": The Ascetic Way

If our bodily nature gives us extraordinary potential to be a source of blessing for the whole of creation, it also means that, as corruptible beings, we are

---

[83]Pavel Florensky, *Pillar and Ground*, esp. 193–8, 211–26.

[84]Ibid. 224.

[85]C. Babington-Smith, *Iulia de Beausobre: A Russian Christian in the West* (London: Darton, Longman and Todd, 1983), 142–3. I am indebted to Dr Jurretta Heckscher for drawing my
attention to these passages.

[86]Ibid. 114.

[87]Nellas, *Deification*, 65–6.

[88]Ibid. 66; cf. Babington-Smith, *Iulia de Beausobre*, 182.

[89]Olivier Clément, "L'homme dans le monde," *Verbum Caro*, XII:45 (1958), 11–12; cited
in mar Gregorios, *Human Presence*, 81.

highly vulnerable. This tension is set out graphically by Fr John Jillions: "Cana, the body blessed; the tomb of Lazarus, the body corrupted: these two realities Jesus refuses to homogenize."[90] It is because of this potential for corruption that we need to "kill the flesh to acquire a body," in the oft-quoted words of Fr Sergei Bulgakov.[91]

Without denying that "spiritualizing" tendencies have sometimes found their way into the Christian ascetic tradition, Orthodox theologians have contributed significantly to an understanding of the essentially positive character of Christian asceticism. Florensky extols it as being "in love with creation."[92] Compellingly, he also gives us an image of such asceticism in his spiritual father, the Elder Isidore, whose loving care extended to uprooted weeds and broken branches, and who reposed in death "like a setting sun over whitened, ripe cornfields," manifesting "a flesh-bearing spiritual beauty."[93]

Fr Isidore belongs to a great lineage of ascetics, going back at least to the Fathers of the Egyptian desert, who attained "equilibrium with the whole of [their] environment," in the words of Deacon John Chryssavgis.[94] Chryssavgis' studies present these severe ascetics in their harsh landscape in an unexpected light: as witnesses to the sacredness of creation, characterized by a love for the land, a harmonious relationship of mutual care with the animals and even the elements, and joy, humility and veneration of the neighbor.[95]

Contrary to what might be assumed, asceticism has everything to do with relationship, with relatedness; it is "an ecclesial, not an individual matter," in the words of Christos Yannaras.[96] It is a natural extension, therefore, when Metropolitan John speaks of an "ecological asceticism" which "builds upon the view that we . . . are called to turn [material creation] into a vehicle of communion."[97] Others stress that we attain "communion" not only *through* material creation, but also in a certain sense *with* it: "Lent reactivates our

---

[90]John Jillions, "In the Flesh: The Body in Christ's Life and Ministry," in *Experience of the Incarnation* (Diocesan Conference), 26–8.

[91]Cf. Metropolitan Anthony, "Body and Matter," 45. Also Bishop Kallistos, "Transfiguration of the Body," 24ff., who emphasizes the essential Christian distinction between *flesh* and *body*, in contrast to the platonizing tendency to regard the body *per se* as inimical to spiritual life.

[92]Florensky, *Pillar and Ground*, 212.

[93]Pavel Florensky, *Salt of the Earth* (Platina: St Herman of Alaska Brotherhood, 1987), 71, 137.

[94]Chryssavgis, *Beyond the Shattered Image*, 95.

[95]J. Chryssavgis, "The Sacredness of Creation," *Studia Patristica* XXV (Leuven: Peeters Press, 1993), 346–51; idem, *Beyond the Shattered Image*, 90–118.

[96]Yannaras, *Freedom of Morality*, 109.

[97]Metropolitan John, "Ecological Asceticism," p. 24.

membership not only of the human community, but equally of the cosmic *koinonia*," as Bishop Kallistos writes.[98]

If our bodily nature is a bridge linking man with the rest of creation, then asceticism is the undergirding which allows the bridge to function properly; without it, the bridging structure becomes on one hand a means of "exporting our fallenness" to the rest of creation, and on the other a tie which prevents us relating to material things in freedom.[99] It is obvious how, in the words of Patriarch Ignatius, "asceticism is necessary in order to fight the instinct of possession, of blind power and a flight into hedonism."[100] But perhaps even more importantly, asceticism clears the channel of communication from the world to us: it forms in us the "eye of fire" able to perceive "the secret hiddenness of things,"[101] what Florensky calls their "original triumphant beauty."[102] The entire vision of material creation which we have presented here remains inaccessible without the cleansing of our perception.

Exercising Our Priesthood: The Jesus Prayer

Closely parallel to what is said about ascetic life, we find some compelling testimonies to the power of the Jesus Prayer in particular to transform our perceptions and our surroundings. Like asceticism, the prayer might seem at first sight self-centered and inward-looking; but Bishop Kallistos notes its "world-affirming" character and refers to one of its best-known practitioners, the anonymous Russian "pilgrim," who attained the "knowledge of the speech of all creatures" and could hear them praising God.[103] Nadiejda Gorodetzky speaks of the Prayer as a way of exercising our priestly role, "an instrument of the hidden offering of everything and everyone, setting the divine seal on the world."[104] Iulia de Beausobre provides a striking instance of this, for she records that it was her introduction to "the old prayer in its new form" by nuns in a Soviet prison camp that inspired her intuition about "de-polluting" the earth.[105] Fr Lev makes clear the intimate connection of the Name with the

---

[98]Bishop Kallistos (Ware), "Lent and the Consumer Society," in *Living Orthodoxy in the Modern World*, 82.

[99]Cf. Bishop Kallistos, "Lent and the Consumer Society," 82ff.

[100]Patriarch Ignatius, "Three Sermons," 12.

[101]Ibid. 7.

[102]Florensky, *Pillar and Ground*, 226.

[103]Bishop Kallistos (Ware), *The Power of the Name* (Oxford: SLG Press, 2nd ed. 1986), 27, 26.

[104]Nadiejda Gorodetzky, "The Prayer of Jesus," *Blackfriars* xxiii, 1942, 76; *apud* Bishop Kallistos, ibid. 27–8.

[105]Babington-Smith, *Iulia de Beausobre*, 38–9; cf. p. 234 above.

creation of the cosmos by Christ and its destiny to be transfigured into him: "all creation mysteriously utters the Name," and by pronouncing it over natural things, we "speak aloud [their] secret" and "bring them to their fulfillment."[106] Patriarch Ignatius gives an example of this in practice—a group of Orthodox physicists who used to say the Prayer while carrying out their research.[107] Here we see the key significance of the Jesus Prayer in an area of concern to several of our writers: how we are to apply our priestly ministry to modern science and technology, bridging the gap between mankind's ever-increasing functional understanding of the material world and that "science of nature" of which Philip Sherrard has written extensively, which "induces an understanding of [the] divine presence of which each sensible form is the revelation or epiphany."[108]

Images of the New Creation

For the Orthodox tradition, the new creation—the eschatological destiny of matter—is a subject less for speculation than for witness, since it is already inaugurated in the resurrection of Christ.

One such witness may be seen in monastic life. The monk "decides to tackle the fundamental causes of corruption," writes Fr Makarios, "and to restore in himself the royal but deformed image of God, in order that creation, lost in Adam, might be restored in Christ."[109] As the monk's return to God takes up the calling of every Christian, so too, in the words of a leading figure in contemporary monasticism, "every monastery remains an expression of the Church in all the fullness of her mystery"—despite the obvious fact that it is also "a human society with all the imperfections which that implies."[110] In monastic life, Fr Aimilianos shows us the true dynamic of the Church in the world, so often obscured by our sinfulness, sloth and ignorance. It is a life

---

[106]Lev Gillet, *On the Invocation of the Name of Jesus* (London: Fellowship of St Alban and St Sergius, no date), 14–16.

[107]Patriarch Ignatius, "Three Sermons," 8.

[108]Philip Sherrard, *Human Image: World Image*, 152. Most writers are less pessimistic than Sherrard about the compatibility of the two approaches. Cf. Staniloae, *Theology and the Church* (Crestwood: SVS Press, 1980), 224ff.; Bishop Kallistos, "Value of Material Creation,," 163ff.; Metropolitan John, "Preserving God's Creation" II, 39; Bishop Basil, "Beauty in the Divine and in Nature," *Sourozh* 70 (November 1997), 36.

[109]Makarios, "The Monk and Nature," in *So That God's Creation Might Live* (Ecumenical Patriarchate of Constantinople/Syndesmos, 1994), 43.

[110]Archimandite Aimilianos, "The Experience of the Transfiguration," 198.

that is "a liturgy without interruption, a daily transfiguration of the world, of matter, of space, of time, of movement, of human action and society." All work in the monastery is an image of eucharistic use of the world:

> a sacrifice pleasing to God that is illumined by prayer, and that is a col-laboration in the transfiguration of the world and the things of the world. It is a continuation of the Divine Liturgy outside the church's walls . . . both the contemplation and the use of the physical world become a light, inasmuch as that usage is . . . not like the destructive consumerism of technology, but serves to render nature a participant in the glory of the children of God, that she may join in their song.[111]

The monastic witness, then, is inseparable from the transfiguration of the world, from the new creation. A vivid expression of this is its connection with *place*: the ascetic is truly one who "acts locally." Ascesis transforms places, an effect amply attested by those who have spent time in such places as the Holy Mountain.[112] And the interaction between man and place works both ways: "I am keeping this place; and it keeps me," as Fr Vasileios says.[113]

When asceticism bears fruit in holiness, we can actually see the new cre-ation taking shape around those conformed to the image of the new Adam. This is why the use of examples taken from the experience of saints, both ancient and contemporary, has such importance. Their stories speak consis-tently of the reality set before us in the icon:

> . . . everything which surrounds a saint changes its mien. The world that surrounds man—the bearer and announcer of the divine revela-tion—here becomes an image of the world to come, transformed and renewed . . . Everything reflects the divine presence, and is drawn—and also draws us—towards God . . . This world participates in the deification of man.[114]

[111]Ibid. 205; translation adapted.
[112]Ibid. 197.
[113]Archimandrite Vasileios, *Ecology and Monasticism*, 14.
[114]Ouspensky, *Theology of the Icon*, I, 189.

PART THREE

Spiritual

Evagrius Ponticus on Monastic Pedagogy

Columba Stewart OSB

Introduction

THE GUIDANCE OF A LIVING spiritual teacher has always been regarded as indispensable to monastic initiation. The existence of monastic literature, however, shows that the process was not solely interpersonal. Monastic cultures may be embodied in their adherents, but they are propagated through their texts. Therefore the strategies devised to initiate newcomers into the forms of prayer, ascetic practice, and biblical interpretation constitutive of monastic life have typically included literary materials. The emergence of written rules in the fourth century, whether ad hoc like the Pachomian legislation, expansive like the Basilian *Askétikon*, or tightly structured like the Latin *regulae*, suggests the value of textual support for monastic stability and continuity.[1]

The most sophisticated presentation of monastic theology to survive from the literature of early Christianity is that of Evagrius Ponticus (ca. 345–399), who was a monk of the semi-eremitic settlement of Kellia in Lower Egypt for about fifteen years. For many of his contemporaries in monastic Egypt we have stories depicting their guidance of others but rather little of their actual teaching. For Evagrius it is the opposite case: we know that he was recognized as a spiritual authority but very few vignettes survive of his interaction with others. However, he left us an extraordinary collection of writings on the doctrines and developmental stages of the monastic life. They provide significant indications of how he understood the unfolding of a monastic vocation, the place of biblical interpretation in monastic development, and the role of the experienced teacher in guiding the beginner toward deepening contemplative

---

[1]Monastic and ecclesiastical authorities could also, of course, use texts to guide and control ascetic movements to ensure theological orthodoxy or observance of social and religious norms.

insight. To appreciate these precious texts fully, we must first place them in the context of Evagrius' own monastic life.

Evagrius' Life

The best source for Evagrius' life is Palladius, who was a member of his circle at Kellia in the 390s. Palladius was a Galatian some twenty years Evagrius' junior. Like his mentor, Palladius had spent time in Jerusalem with the monastic communities led by Rufinus and Melania before he went to Egypt. As a disciple of Evagrius, Palladius was hardly neutral when writing about his controversial master, but he had a unique degree of intimacy with Evagrius and, aware of the charge of favoritism, claimed that he wrote not as a partisan but as an eyewitness of the virtues he described.[2] His account of Evagrius' life in the *Lausiac History*, written about twenty years after Evagrius' death, is the most significant extant biographical record of Evagrius in the Greek tradition.[3] A more expansive Coptic version of the life seems to come from Palladius as well.[4] The fifth century historians Socrates Scholasticus and Sozomen also recounted Evagrius' life. Socrates quoted extensively from Evagrius' writings and included stories about Evagrius' monastic career not found in the Palladian accounts[5]; Sozomen re-told the story of Evagrius' premonastic life following Palladius but with a few details (or embellishments?) unique to his version.[6]

Crisis and Conversion

Evagrius had been raised in an ecclesiastical household in Pontus, where his father was a chor-bishop. Educated by theological luminaries such as Basil (who ordained him lector) and Gregory Nazianzen (who ordained him dea-

---

[2]Thus the longer version of the *Life* preserved in Coptic, ed. E. Amélineau, *De historia lausiaca* (Paris: Leroux, 1887), 105.10–13; for an English translation, see Tim Vivian, "Coptic Palladiana II: The Life of Evagrius," *Coptic Church Review*, 21 (2000), 10.

[3]*H.L.* 38 (ed. Cuthbert Butler, *The Lausiac History of Palladius*, Text and Studies 6 [Cambridge: Cambridge Univ. Press, 1904], 2:116–23). References to *H.L.* will use the section numbers in the English trans. of Robert T. Meyer (*The Lausiac History of Palladius*, Ancient Christian Writers 34 [Westminster, MD: Christian Classics, 1964]).

[4]The *Life* of Evagrius can be found in pp. 104–124 of Amélineau's *De historia lausiaca*. See Gabriel Bunge's arguments for the Palladian origin of this longer text in "Palladiana. I: Introduction aux fragments coptes de l'Histoire Lausiaque," *Studia Monastica*, 32 (1990), 106–07.

[5]*H.E.* 4.23.34–80 (ed. Günther Christian Hansen, GCS N.F. 1:252.16–257.4). Socrates also mentions Evagrius in *H.E.* 3.7.22 (Hansen, 199.16–25) and 7.17.3–4 (362.1–5).

[6]*H.E.* 6.30.6–11 (ed. Joseph Bidez, rev. Günther Christian Hansen, GCS N.F. 4:285.8–286.4).

con), Evagrius accompanied Gregory to Constantinople to help in the re-establishment of the Nicene party. When Gregory returned home in the aftermath of the Second Ecumenical Council of 381, Evagrius stayed on with the new bishop, Nectarius. Talented as he was, he also found the diversions of life in the capital to be more than he could handle. Reported to have been handsome and fond of nice clothes,[7] Evagrius fell in love with a married woman of high social standing.[8] Finding his love reciprocated, he realized that he was in an impossible situation. During prayer (Greek version of Palladius) or in a dream (Coptic and Sozomen) he received a vision promising pardon for his adultery of the heart on condition that he leave the city immediately. He packed up and took ship for Palestine. In breaking from both his beloved and his ecclesiastical career, Evagrius renounced not only lust, but also power and material comfort. Though he was a cleric he was not yet a monk, and many opportunities had lain before him.

Evagrius went directly to Jerusalem, where he settled on the Mount of Olives in the company of the brilliant and wise Melania. With her mentor Rufinus, Melania had established monastic communities likely to be hospitable to a theologically inclined deacon from Constantinople. Of his crisis, however, Evagrius said nothing. His resolve for a fresh start weakened in the cosmopolitan milieu of the Holy City, and he led what was essentially a double life.[9] He was seen frequently in the streets, so concerned about his appearance that he changed his clothes twice a day.[10] Only when his life was threatened by fever did fundamental change begin. Palladius depicts Melania as the key figure in the process, calling Evagrius to account by suggesting that his illness signified more than physical ailment. "I am not happy about your protracted illness," she says, "so tell me what is on your mind. For your illness is not without spiritual significance" (οὐκ ... ἀθεής).[11] He then revealed to Melania the full story of his affair in Constantinople. Palladius depicts her attitude as stern though compassionate. Surely she had suspected something

---

[7]Only Sozomen comments on his appearance, *H.E.* 6.30.9 (Bidez/Hansen, 285.18–19), though the point about sartorial pleasure is also in the Coptic *Life* (see below).

[8]There are variations in the accounts of this incident. Palladius writes most frankly about the intensity of their mutual attraction, and notes that Evagrius told his disciples the story himself (see *H.L.* 38.3–7 [Butler, 2:117.7–119.8]; Coptic *Life*: Amélineau, 107.6–110.6; Vivian, 12–13). Sozomen downplays the relationship itself and emphasizes the husband's jealousy (*H.E.* 6.30.9 [Bidez/Hansen, 285.19–20]). Palladius features the husband's reaction only as a guilt-induced aspect of Evagrius' decisive dream about his situation.

[9]Palladius uses the verb ἐδιψύχησε (*H.L.* 38.8 [Butler, 2:119.13]).

[10]Thus the Coptic *Life* (Amélineau, 110; Vivian, 13).

[11]*H.L.* 38.9 (Butler, 2:119.19–21).

of the sort, and had perhaps heard rumors about the liaison. Her prescription was dramatic. Evagrius was to place himself under the discipline of monastic life. Although Palladius does not say explicitly that Melania sent Evagrius to Egypt, removal to the desert made good sense given that the social atmosphere of Jerusalem had proved no healthier than that of Constantinople. Melania's own close ties to the monks of Nitria make such a recommendation likely. Rufinus (according to Evagrius himself) or Melania (according to Palladius) gave him the monastic habit, probably at Easter 383.[12] Evagrius made his way to Nitria, though as we shall see, the link with Jerusalem would last for the rest of his life and many of his key monastic writings would be directed to the monastic communities guided by Melania and Rufinus.[13]

Evagrius' Mentors

Of Evagrius' monastic life in Egypt we have, again, largely the evidence of Palladius, Socrates, Sozomen, and a few *apophthegmata*.[14] Evagrius' own writings, even his *Letters*, provide little explicitly autobiographical material. We know that Evagrius' first monastic home was Nitria, the large monastic complex built along a canal at the "Mountain of Pernouj," which Melania had visited only a few years previously.[15] From there he moved after two years to the more remote settlement of Kellia ("The Cells"), some 18 kilometers south of Nitria. There a quieter and more intense monastic life was possible than at Nitria, which had become a large and readily accessible monastic center. Evagrius lived at Kellia until his death in 399.

In his two foundational works, the *Praktikos* and *Gnostikos*, Evagrius provides a diptych of his monastic and doctrinal mentors.[16] The doctrinal panel reflective of Evagrius' premonastic life is in the *Gnostikos*, which closes

---

[12]For the attribution to Rufinus and the date, see *Letter* 22.1 (Frankenberg, 580.10–11) and Gabriel Bunge, *Briefe aus der Wüste*, Sophia 24 (Trier: Paulinus-Verlag, 1986), 184–85.

[13]Notably the trilogy of *Praktikos/Gnostikos/Kephalaia gnostika* and the two collections of *Sentences*. Rufinus was also the translator of Evagrius' works into Latin. For Evagrius' continuing links with Rufinus, Melania, and their communities, see Bunge, *Briefe aus der Wüste*, 179–88 and 193–200, and Elizabeth Clark, *The Origenist Controversy. The Cultural Construction of an Early Christian Debate* (Princeton: Princeton Univ. Press, 1992), 22 and 88–93.

[14]These are largely duplications of material found in Evagrius' works; an exception is *Apoph. Alph.* Evagrius 7 (PG 65:176A), cited below. He also appears as an interlocutor in the Coptic collection known as the *Virtues of Saint Macarius* (ed. E Amélineau, *Histoire des monastères de la Basse-Égypte*, Annales du Musée Guimet, 25 [Paris: Ernest Leroux, 1894]); see pp. 137–38, 157–58, 160–61, 195–96 (=*Prak.* 94), 200–02.

[15]On Melania's visit, see *H.L.* 9 (Butler, 2:29.10–11) and 46.2 (Butler, 2:134.11–16).

[16]*Prak.* 91–99 and *Gnost.* 44–48. Socrates Scholasticus reproduces this material in *H.E.*

with a series of five sayings attributed to theologians (*Gnost.* 44–48). Gregory Nazianzen has pride of place,[17] followed by Basil, Athanasius, Serapion of Thmuis, and Didymus.[18] None of these dicta has been located among their extant writings.[19] We do know that Gregory's formative influence continued through an exchange of letters after Evagrius' departure for Palestine and Egypt.[20] Evagrius underscores the handoff from Gregory to the Egyptian monks when he acknowledges in the *Praktikos* the prayers of "the righteous Gregory who planted me, and the holy fathers who now water me."[21] Those "holy fathers" were the monks of Nitria, Kellia, and Scetis who became the major influences on his life once he arrived in Egypt.

At the end of the *Praktikos*, Evagrius offers his monastic array of authorities in a series of nine *apophthegmata* (*Prak.* 91–99).[22] Three are attributed to famous monks: Antony the Great (92), Macarius the Egyptian (93), and Macarius of Alexandria (94). Another probably alludes to Didymus (98). Evagrius could not have known Antony, who had died in 356, but for him and everyone else in monastic Egypt, the legacy of Antony loomed large. Evagrius mentions Antony a couple of times in other writings,[23] and Gabriel Bunge has noted the influence of the *Life of Antony* on Evagrius' own teaching about demons and thoughts.[24] However, the saying that Evagrius refers to

4.23.40–71 (Hansen, 253.13–256.5), though he omits *Prak.* 96, the ban on eating with women (including one's own mother and sisters).

[17]Gregory is also named in the Epilogue to *Prak.* and in the *Letter on Faith* (=Ps-Basil, *Letter* 8.1 [Forlin Patrucco, 86.16]). He is alluded to in *Prak.* 89 and *K.G.* 6.51 as "our wise master." On Gregory's role in Evagrius' life, see A. Guillaumont in SC 170:21–24.

[18]Didymus is perhaps the monk praised in *Prak.* 89 as the "most proven of Knowers"; see the commentary by A. and C. Guillaumont in SC 171:707–08. Géhin suggests additional allusions to Didymus in *Prayer* 72 and *K.G.* 6.45; see his commentary on *Gnost.* 48 in SC 356:188–89.

[19]Géhin suggests oral transmission to Evagrius of the teaching by Gregory, Basil and Didymus, though the formulae used for Athanasius (φησί) and Serapion (ἔλεγεν), neither of whom Evagrius could have known personally, are comparable to those used for the three he had met. Given that none of the sayings has been found among the writings of these figures, there is surely some element of honorary (or strategic) attribution at work.

[20]Three of Evagrius' letters (12, 23, 46) are addressed to the "wonderful man" (*gabra tedmurtha*), most likely Gregory. See Bunge, *Briefe aus der Wüste*, 176–77; on *Letter* 46, see A. and C. Guillaumont in SC 171:715. A reference in one of Gregory's letters (*Letter* 3 [PG 37:24B]) is thought by A. Guillaumont to refer to Evagrius (see SC 170:22).

[21]*Prak.* Epil. (SC 171, p. 712.7–9); cf. a similar image, referring only to Gregory, in *Letter* 46 (Frankenberg, 596.25–26).

[22]Many of these are found in other collections of sayings, though the most "Evagrian" in tone among them are not (*Prak.* 92, attributed to Antony the Great; *Prak.* 98, anonymous but probably to be referred to Didymus).

[23]*Antirr.* 4.47 (Frankenberg, 508.19–20), *Thoughts* 35.

Antony is not found elsewhere in the Greek tradition of *apophthegmata*,[25] and its articulation of Evagrius' own doctrine on the "contemplation of created beings" (see below) makes the attribution suspect. Evagrius, like others eager to locate themselves in the monastic mainstream, sought to link his own teaching to Antony's authority and fame.[26]

The sayings Evagrius attributes to the two Macarii are quite credibly theirs. Other references to these two great monks in Evagrius' writings establish clearly that he regarded Macarius the Egyptian ("the Great," †390), who lived at Scetis, and Macarius the Alexandrian (†393), who was priest at Kellia, as his principal teachers in the monastic life.[27] The historian Socrates Scholasticus observed that Evagrius learned from them the "philosophy of deeds" to complement the "philosophy of words" he had known previously.[28] The influence of Macarius the Alexandrian would have been aided by his proximity, though Evagrius uses more reverent language when speaking of Macarius the Egyptian, "our holy and most disciplined (πρακτι-κώτατος) master" (*Prak.* 29).[29] We know from the *Apophthegmata* that the latter was a frequent visitor to Nitria, and presumably also to Kellia.[30] Eva-

---

[24]"Évagre le Pontique et les deux Macaire," *Irénikon*, 56 (1983), 332.

[25]It does appear in Rosweyde's edition of the 6th century Latin version of John (reprinted by Migne), along with *Prak.* 93 and 96 (*V.P.* 6.4.16–19 as in PL 73:1018B-D). This section of Rosweyde's edition is an assortment of material not found in the better MSS. and thought to be a later addition; the source is probably the *Praktikos* itself, so it is not an independent attestation to the saying.

[26]Cf. John Cassian's analogous use of two otherwise unknown (and decidedly Evagrian) sayings of Antony in *Conf.* 9.31 (ed. M. Petschenig, CSEL 13:277.1–13). Another example of the literary invocation of Antony can be found in the Pachomian tradition, where Antony is depicted as praising the cenobitic life over the anchoritic, to the dismay of his own disciples. The textual situation for this incident is particularly complex; see most easily Armand Veilleux's translation in *Pachomian Koinonia*, vol. 1, Cistercian Studies Series 45 (Kalamazoo: Cistercian, 1980), 179–87 (from the Coptic) and 382–83 (from the Greek).

[27]On Evagrius' mentors, see Bunge, "Évagre le Pontique et les deux Macaire," 215–27, 323–60. The spiritual paternity of the two Macarii was noted by Socrates Scholasticus (*H.E.* 4.23.34; Hansen, 252.23–24), and of Macarius the Great in the Coptic *Life of Macarius* (ed. M. Chaîne, "La double recension de l'*Histoire Lausiaque*," ROC 25 [1925–26], 240.6–8). The Coptic *Life of Evagrius* (Amélineau, 112.5–9), refers to a Macarius who is probably the Alexandrian; see Gabriel Bunge and Adalbert de Vogüé, *Quatre ermites égyptiens*, Spiritualité orientale 60 (Bégrolles-en-Mauge: Abbaye de Bellefontaine, 1994), 33 and 158 n. 28. The advice cited there is similar to that in *Prak.* 94, identified by A. and C. Guillaumont (SC 171:699–700) and Bunge ("Évagre le Pontique et les deux Macaire," 221–22) as referring to the Alexandrian even though the story was included in the Coptic *Virtues of Saint Macarius* [the Great] (Amélineau, *Histoire des monastères*, 195.14–96.4). See also A. Guillaumont, "Le problème des deux Macaire," *Irénikon*, 48 (1975), 57.

[28]*H.E.* 4.23.34 (Hansen, 252.23–24).

[29]Cf. *Prayer* Prol.: "great teacher and master (καθηγητής καὶ διδάσκαλος)," *Prak.* 93: "ves-

grius is a frequently cited source for sayings and stories about both Macarii in the Coptic tradition.[31]

Evagrius' circle of monks at Kellia included as its other leading figure Ammonius (†403), one of the "Tall Brothers," whom Evagrius praised as "the most passionless" person he had ever known.[32] Ammonius was an Egyptian with an impeccable monastic pedigree. With his three brothers he had been a disciple of Abba Pambo (†374/5), one of the first-generation monks of Nitria. But Ammonius was also theologically sophisticated, having read (and, according to Palladius, memorized) great quantities of the works of Origen, Didymus, and others.[33] This is the circle to which Palladius attached himself when he went to the desert.[34] While both Ammonius and Evagrius were deeply committed to the traditional monastic wisdom taught by venerable fathers like Pambo and the Macarii, they represented a monasticism that was receptive to theological literature and, in Evagrius' case, open to literary composition (indeed, Palladius notes that Evagrius supported himself by copying manuscripts).[35] Clearly Evagrius was trying to link the best of his past to the demands of his present circumstances.

The custom at Kellia was for the monks to spend weekdays in solitude but to come together on Saturdays and Sundays for liturgy and conversation. The Coptic version of Palladius' *Life of Evagrius*, describes gatherings at which monks would discuss their thoughts with Evagrius either in the group or pri-

---

sel of election" (also used of Gregory Nazianzen in the *Epistle on Faith* [Ps-Basil, *Ep.* 8.1; Forlin Patrucco, 86.15–16]). Macarius the Alexandrian is "holy" and "blessed" (*Prak.* 94, *Antirr.* 4.23 [Frankenberg, 506.1–3], 4.58 [p. 510.12]; perhaps 8.26 [p. 540.26]; see Bunge, "Évagre le Pontique et les deux Macaire," 222), also used for Macarius the Egyptian in *Antirr.* 4.45 (Frankenberg, 508.16).

[30] *Apoph. Alph.*, Macarius the Egyptian 2, 34, 39 (PG 65:260B, 277C, 280C).

[31] See the *Virtues of Saint Macarius*, which purports to be about Macarius the Egyptian but actually mixes traditions about both Macarii (Amélineau, *Histoire*, 137.16–138.10, 157.9–58.3, 160.11–61.10, 195.14–96.4, 200.5–202.3). As noted above, Guillaumont suggests that the material on pp. 195–96 is actually about the Alexandrian, and further notes that the material mentioning Paphnutius (pp. 191.3–94.3) should be referred to the Alexandrian as well ("Le problème des deux Macaire," 57).

[32] *H.L.* 11.5 (Butler, 2:34.11–12). See also *H.L.* 24.1 (2:77.18–78.1).

[33] *H.L.* 11.4 (Butler, 2:34.5–9): Palladius alleges some 6,000,000 lines. Bunge contrasts this bibliography (and a similar list attributed to Melania in *H.L.* 55.3 [Butler, 2:149.13–15]) with the entirely post-Nicene authorities cited by Evagrius in *Gnost.* 44–48. See "Origenismus— Gnostizismus. Zum geistesgeschichtlichen Standort des Evagrios Pontikos," *Vigiliae Christianae*, 40 (1986), 36–44.

[34] On Palladius' association with Evagrius, see *H.L.* 23.1 (Butler, 2:75.5), 35.3(2:101.4–5, 102.9–11), 47.3 (2:137.8–9).

[35] *H.L.* 38.10 (Butler, 2:120.11–12).

vately afterwards. Palladius notes that Evagrius always had visitors from abroad.[36] His fame was such that Theophilus of Alexandria offered him the bishopric of Thmuis. Evagrius briefly fled Kellia, probably sometime in the early 390s, to foil those plans.[37]

Because the monastic culture of Lower Egypt placed a great value on consultation, traveling to seek or to offer spiritual guidance was standard practice. Evagrius joined the network established among the prominent monks of late fourth century Egypt and went to meet at least some of them. Even Palladius, a devoted disciple of Evagrius, sought help from monks beyond Kellia, and made the dangerous journey to Scetis to find help for particularly embarrassing sexual temptations.[38] Evagrius probably went to Scetis to visit Macarius the Great; he also mentions John Colobos, another famous monk of Scetis (*Prayer* 107). We know that he and Ammonius went south to ask John of Lycopolis (whom Evagrius calls "the Prophet" or "Seer," †394/5) about the light seen while at prayer.[39] It is impossible to say whether Evagrius visited the Pachomian monks of Upper Egypt, though he introduces a story about Abba Theodore by saying, "And you have surely read the *Lives* of the Tabennesiote monks" (*Prayer* 108).

Evagrius' Monastic Struggles

When Evagrius became a monk he made a definitive break with his past. Cassian records a story about "a brother from Pontus" who saved and then burned all of his letters from home, unread.[40] This is usually understood to refer to Evagrius, though we know he continued to correspond with Gregory Nazianzen. Palladius records Evagrius' particular struggles with lust, blasphemy, and anxieties about accusations of heresy.[41] He is known to have

[36]On Palladius' memories see the Coptic *Life* (Amélineau, 105.7–10); on the gatherings with Evagrius, see pp. 114.8–115.6.

[37]See the Coptic *Life* as in Amélineau, 115.9–11, and Socrates, *H.E.* 4.23.75 (Hansen, 256.12–14).

[38]*H.L.* 23.1 (Butler, 2:75.1–8).

[39]All of the references to John are in the *Antirrhetikos*: 2.36 (Frankenberg, 490.4), 5.6 (p. 512.36), 6.16 (p. 524.7–14), 7.19 (p. 532.30). This suggests that *Antirr.* must have been written after the visit to John described both in *Antirr.* 6.16 and *H.L.* 35.11 (Butler, 2:104.19–105.2), which can be dated between 391 (when Palladius went to the desert) and 394/5 (when John died). The abundance of references suggests that the *Antirrhétikos* was written while the visit was still fresh in Evagrius' memory.

[40]*Inst.* 5.32.1–3 (ed. M. Petschenig, CSEL 17:105–06); cf. *Prak.* 95, an anonymous saying about earthly vs. divine fatherhood that Palladius attributes to Evagrius (*H.L.* 38.13 [Butler, 2:123.1–3]).

practiced a severe alimentary discipline that included homophagy, the avoidance of cooked food, and xerophagy, the consumption of dried foods to the exclusion of fresh vegetables and fruit.[42] His dietary practice was linked to the battle with sexual temptation, for Evagrius frequently underscored the connection between gluttony and lust.[43] The reliance on dried bread and water, supplemented occasionally by a little oil, damaged his digestive system to the point that senior monks had to intervene and insist that he take some cooked food.[44] He himself later warned against the dangers of misdirected ascetic zeal.[45] He was finally granted the peace he sought, noting near the time of his death, "This is the third year that I have not been tormented by carnal desires."[46] Of his prayer the best witness we have is his teaching, particularly in the treatise *On Prayer*.[47] The Coptic *Life* notes that he spent much of the night walking in his courtyard, "meditating and praying," "making his intellect search out contemplations of the Scriptures."[48]

Evagrius' talents were widely recognized, but his monastic career was not smooth sailing. One of the sayings about him (the last of seven included in the Alphabetical Collection), records the rebuke he received from one of the priests at Kellia after he spoke up at a monastic gathering. "We know, Abba, that if you were still in your own land you would be a bishop and leader of many; however, here you sit as a foreigner."[49] When he asked Macarius the Great for a word to live by, he was told that he must cast far from himself the glory of worldly rhetoric.[50] Evagrius' brilliance would have made him a natural target for the envious or those suspicious of intellectual monasticism. He himself recorded the pain of feeling persecuted by one's fellow monks and

[41]*H.L.* 38.11 (Butler, 2:121.2–122.1).

[42]Cf. *Prak.* 16–17, 91, 94 on recommending a dry diet; in *Antirr.* 1.32 (Frankenberg, 478.16–18), 45 (p. 480.13–21), 53–54 (p. 482.3–7) he mentions the allure of vegetables and fruit, and 1.59 (p. 482.18–20) is about the temptation of cooked food.

[43]E.g., *Thoughts* 1.6–8, 27.21–22; *Gnostikos* 31; *De octo* 1–3 (PG 79:1146A-48C).

[44]*H.L.* 38.12 quotes Evagrius himself as claiming that he had never eaten lettuce, green vegetables, fruit, grapes, or meat since coming to the desert (Butler, 2:122.8–10). The regimen described in *H.L.* 38.10 consisted of bread and a little oil (Butler, 2:120.8–9). For the last two years of his life, however, he ate vegetables and pulse or porridge. The Coptic *Life* provides a more graphic description of the illness and notes the role of the elder monks, a detail not found in the Greek (Amélineau, 112.12–113.5).

[45]*Thoughts* 35 and *Antirr.* 1.27 (Frankenberg, 478.4–6), 37 (p. 478.26–30).

[46]*H.L.* 38.13 (Butler, 2:122.15–123.1).

[47]See my article, "Imageless Prayer and the Theological Vision of Evagrius Ponticus," *Journal of Early Christian Studies*, 9 (2001), 173–204.

[48]Amélineau, 113.5–13.

[49]*Apoph. Alph.* Evagrius 7 (PG 65:176A).

[50]*Virtues of Saint Macarius* (ed. Amélineau, 157.9–58.3).

the temptation to counter-attack those who have caused distress,[51] though Sozomen commends his detachment from both praise and criticism.[52] Palladius recounts the sad tale of Heron, an over-zealous young monk who in a fit of pride told Evagrius, "Those who put faith in your teaching are deceived: for there is no need to pay attention to teachers other than Christ."[53]

Much of Evagrius' distress would have come from the ecclesiastical campaign against monastic "Origenists" that began during his lifetime.[54] Given his teaching about imageless prayer, one of the major points of contention in monastic circles in the late 390s,[55] and the similarities between the cosmology of his *Kephalaia gnostica* and Origen's *On First Principles*, the fact that his name first appears in the literature about the controversy only in 415 is puzzling.

One possibility is that Evagrius chose to lay low and was not widely known outside of monastic circles. According to Socrates, Evagrius jokingly noted to Ammonius that he himself had escaped ordination without self-inflicted bodily harm (Ammonius had cut off his ear to avoid the episcopate). Ammonius replied, "But you, Evagrius, do you not think that you are liable to judgment, you who from self-love have cut out your own tongue and not used the gift that has been given you?"[56] Though the reference is most evidently to the episcopal ministry of preaching, there may also be hints of a more general reluctance to wade into ecclesiastical affairs.

In his own allusions to the developing Origenist controversy in correspondence with Bishop John of Jerusalem (dated by Gabriel Bunge to 393–94[57]), Evagrius sounds quite detached even as the campaign seems to draw closer to him.[58] In letters addressed to other monks he speaks more frankly of criticism directed at him.[59] Evagrius' well-established connection

---

[51]*Antirr.* 5.34 and 5.56 (Frankenberg, 516.24–26 and 520.9–11) about feelings of persecution; 5.32 (Frankenberg, 516.20–21) on the urge to write vicious letters in response to criticism. It is notable that *Antirr.* 5.32 and 5.56 are the only two scenarios (of 64) in Book 5 that are described in the first person. See also the material from his *Letters* described below.

[52]*H.E.* 6.30.7 (Bidez/Hansen, 285.12–15).

[53]*H.L.* 26.1 (Butler, 2:81.4–7). Cassian relates a story about an old monk named Heron who suffers from similar, though more extreme, delusions (*Conf.* 2.5.1–5; Petschenig, 44–45); one suspects a common tradition of some kind despite the discrepancy in age. The fact that Cassian does not mention Evagrius is unsurprising since he never names his mentor.

[54]Evagrius alludes to opposition apparently related to this campaign in *Letters* 51–53 and 59 (Frankenberg, 598.13–602.3 and 608.14–27).

[55]The so-called "anthropomorphite" controversy. See Clark, *The Origenist Controversy*, 43–84.

[56]Socrates, *H.E.* 4.23.76 (Hansen, 256.16–18).

[57]*Briefe aus der Wüste*, 198.

to Melania and Rufinus, especial targets of Jerome's fanatical reaction against the work of Origen and its propagators, also makes anonymity unlikely. When Evagrius does appear in Jerome's famous *Letter to Ctesiphon* of 415, he is the target of Jerome's wrath as a close associate of Melania and Rufinus, and indeed as a theological influence upon them.[60] Gabriel Bunge has argued that Evagrius' absence from the literature of the early stages of the Origenist controversy suggests that he was not considered to be an "Origenist" of the ilk of his friends in Jerusalem. Bunge suggests further that Evagrius' writings were at least partially intended to save Melania, Rufinus, and their followers from theological error.[61] The later imputation of heterodox views to Evagrius himself was, in Bunge's mind, a reaction by concerned authorities to the misuse of Evagrius' teaching by Palestinian monastic enthusiasts.[62] Elizabeth Clark, on the other hand, sees Evagrius as lurking throughout the Origenist controversy in both Egypt and Palestine.[63] However one interprets the finer points of Evagrian theology (and especially the Christological issues that came to the fore in sixth-century Palestine), it is undeniable that Evagrius followed Origen's lead in both cosmology and biblical intepretation. It may be that Evagrius' seeming absence from the polemical literature is simply an accident of textual survival. Whatever Evagrius' own role in the developing Origenist Controversy, things became much worse after his death. Indeed, Theophilus of Alexandria, who had previously sought to make Evagrius bishop of Thmuis, mounted a military raid against suspected Origenist monks in Nitria within the year.

Evagrius' years as a monk, however difficult, were also creative and fruitful. His unique combination of excellent education, penetrating psychologi-

[58]In *Letter* 51 he has received word from John through Palladius of the troubles in Palestine (Frankenberg, 598.13–16) and is grateful to be in a very different situation himself; in *Letter* 52.4–5 (Frankenberg, 600.8–21) he includes himself among those attacked and reflects on the way that controversy destroys "pure prayer."

[59]In *Letter* 59.2, to a monk named Kekropios, he writes: "You sent a blessing upon those who dwell with me, but it is the *meek* who are *blessed* (Matt. 5:5). Those who dwell with me are anxious dogs who daily lick my blood (cf. Luke 16:21). Understand what I am saying!" (Frankenberg, 608.20–22). Actually this text is more ambiguous than either Frankenberg's retroversion (p. 609.23–25) or Bunge's German translation (p. 279), since the word *yasipha*, which they render as "shameless," has more of a sense of "anxious, careful, solicitous." In any case the metaphor is unpleasant. He is milder in *Letter* 53.2, writing to an unknown monastic correspondent: "Do not marvel if some among the brethren speak evilly of us" (Frankenberg, 602.1–2).

[60]*Ep.* 133.3.5–6 (ed. Isidorus Hilberg, CSEL 56:246).

[61]This is the thrust of Bunge's "Origenismus—Gnostizismus." See also n. 78 below.

[62]See n. 78 below.

[63]*The Origenist Controversy*, 60–84, 107, 114–17, 188–93.

cal insight, and a rich theological imagination generated a substantial corpus of writings in a variety of genres. He worked through the fundamentals of monastic asceticism and developed a cosmic vision placing monastic life within a theological "unified theory of everything." He would have been a Christian intellectual force of some renown. The anonymous author of the *History of the Monks in Egypt* described him as "wise and learned (λόγιος), with considerable discernment of thoughts, a skill acquired from experience. He would often go down to Alexandria to refute the Greek philosophers."[64]

His literary career had already begun in Constantinople, which is unsurprising given his education and patronage.[65] His most famous monastic writings, the trilogy *Praktikos / Gnostikos / Kephalaia gnostika*, and the treatise *On Prayer*, are addressed to particular individuals. The trilogy is dedicated to a monk living in Jerusalem named Anatolios, who was probably associated with the communities on the Mount of Olives founded by Melania and Rufinus.[66] The two collections of sentences were probably also destined for Melania and Rufinus,[67] and Jerome records that Rufinus translated Evagrius' works (at least the *Sentences* and the *Praktikos*) into Latin.[68] The recipient of *On Prayer* is not named, and the grammatically masculine forms do not narrow the field very much.[69] But there is no reason to consider that these dedications exclude a broader audience for the texts.[70]

As we shall see, Evagrius worked within a particular pedagogical tradition and made his own contributions to its development. We do not know why he wrote. Evagrius may have felt a need to pull together resources for the formation of his disciples and visitors, especially as his health began to

[64]H.M. 20.15 (ed. A.-J. Festugière, *Historia monachorum in Aegypto*, Subsidia hagiographica 53 [Brussels: Société des Bollandistes, 1961], 123.80–83).

[65]Evagrius' *Letter on Faith* was probably written in 381, while he was still in Constantinople; the influence of Gregory of Nazianzus' thought is manifest throughout. See Bunge, *Briefe aus der Wüste*, 190–93 and 380–90.

[66]See *Prak*. Prol. ll. 1–2 on Anatolios. For "holy mountain" as referring to Jerusalem and speculation about Anatolios' identity, see the Guillaumonts' commentary in SC 171:482–83 and Bunge, *Briefe aus der Wüste*, 33–36, and "Origenismus—Gnostizismus," 39. On the links with Rufinus and Melania see also Clark, *The Origenist Controversy*, 188–92.

[67]See Bunge, "Origenismus—Gnostizismus," 36–37, and Susanna Elm, "Evagrius Ponticus' *Sententiae ad Virginem*," *Dumbarton Oaks Papers* 45 (1991), 115–16.

[68] *Ep*. 133.3.5–6 (CSEL 56:246): *huius libros . . . interpretante discipulo eius Rufino Latinos*, referring back to the claim that Evagrius had written to virgins, to monks, to Melania, and had produced a book and sentences "about *apatheia*," surely a reference to the *Praktikos*.

[69]The prologue to *Prayer* concludes with a mention of "true brothers."

[70]See Elm's remarks about the distribution of the *Sentences to a Virgin* in "Evagrius Ponticus' *Sententiae ad Virginem*," 115–20.

fail. As he saw the climate turn against those who shared his theological interests, he may also have become concerned about the future, wanting to safeguard his legacy in case living tradition were compromised or broken. It is noteworthy—and poignant—to observe that he sent so many works to the communities in Jerusalem. Both before and after his death they were more hospitable to his ideas than were most monastic groups in Egypt. We should not exclude the possibility that he wrote in obedience to his own imperative to create, for it is obvious that he had developed a comprehensive Christian vision and worked out the place of monastic life within that larger story.

The Content of Monastic Instruction

The Three Aspects of the Monastic Life

Evagrius' model of the monastic life was based on a traditional division of philosophy into ethics, physics, and logic or contemplation.[71] Origen had adapted this program to serve as a schema for biblical interpretation. Although Evagrius did use the threefold system for exegesis, he also made it his way to describe stages of moral and intellectual development. The basic program is explicit in both the basic trilogy of *Praktikos/ Gnostikos/ Kephalaia gnostika* and in his biblical scholia, and is found in varying degrees throughout his other works. Indeed, as Gabriel Bunge has pointed out, it marks even Evagrius' first known work, the *Letter on Faith*, written before his departure from Constantinople.[72] Evagrius' adaptation of the tripartite model presents monastic life as composed of three aspects: *praktiké, theoria physiké, theologiké* (ascetic discipline, natural contemplation and theology).[73] These aspects are cumulative rather than discontinuous. Ascetic discipline (*praktiké*), for example, does not cease even if it is no longer the principal focus of an advanced monk's monastic experience, and contemplation of the natural creation (*theoria physiké*)

---

[71]For overviews, see my *Cassian the Monk* (New York: Oxford, 1998), 50–51; A. Guillaumont's introduction to the *Praktikos* in SC 170:38–49; Gabriel Bunge, "*Praktike, Physike, und Theologike* als Stufen der Erkenntnis bei Evagrios Pontikos," *Ab oriente et occidente (Mt 8,11). Kirche aus Ost und West. Gedenkschrift für Wilhelm Nyssen*, ed. Michael Schneider and Walter Berschin (St. Ottilien: Eos Verlag, 1996), 59–72. For analysis of the philosophical model itself, see Pierre Hadot, "Les divisions des parties de la philosophie dans l'Antiquité," *Museum Helveticumi*, 36 (1979), 201–23.

[72]"*Praktike, Physike* und *Theologike*," 61. The terminology is found in *Letter on Faith* 15 (=Ps-Basil, *Ep.* 8.4; Forlin Patrucco, 94.19–22).

[73]His terminology for the three stages varies slightly but these are the most typical labels.

remains a vivid aspect of the monastic quest in this life even as one approaches knowledge of God (*theologiké*).

The fundamental aspect of monastic life is the *praktiké*, the "practical life" of asceticism (πρακτικὸς βίος / πρακτική), understood in the monastic context as sustained attention to the "thoughts" that captivate the mind. These thoughts, presented under eight headings (gluttony, lust, avarice, sadness, anger, accidie, vainglory, pride), distract from the pursuit of knowledge and twist both experience and perception. The goal of the *praktiké* is freedom from preoccupying thoughts and the emotional distortions they encourage. Evagrius followed the Stoics and Clement of Alexandria by calling the resulting peace of soul *apatheia*. The blessing of *apatheia* is twofold: it makes genuine love possible and allows clarified spiritual vision for the purpose of contemplation.

The adept *praktikos* monk is then ready to learn the skills of the *gnostikos*, the "knower."[74] Spiritual knowledge begins with *theoria physiké*, "natural contemplation." Contemplation and knowledge were inseparable for Evagrius, educated as he was in an intellectual milieu imbued with Platonic epistemology. Understanding the purpose (*logos*) of God's creatures, both visible and invisible, and of God's actions in "judgment" and "providence" toward them was an essential stage of the journey toward knowledge of God as Trinity, the ultimate goal of human existence. The primary contemplative medium for *theoria physiké* was the Bible, for there most directly, though not always plainly, the *gnostikos* monk reads the traces of God's work. As we shall see below, biblical interpretation was a key element of both monastic formation and contemplative practice.

Evagrius' Program of Monastic Instruction in the Basic Trilogy of Writings

Evagrius' most systematic exposition of his program of monastic instruction is in the three works entitled *Praktikos*,[75] *Gnostikos*, and *Kephalaia gnostika*. They were composed as a trilogy, reflecting Evagrius' tripartite model of monastic development. As we shall see later, that model is used in other works and can be considered typical of Evagrius' monastic theology. Although each

---

[74]On this terminology and Evagrius' debt to Clement of Alexandria, see Antoine Guillaumont, "Le gnostique chez Clément d'Alexandrie et chez Évagre le Pontique," *Alexandrina: Mélanges offerts à Claude Mondésert SJ* (Paris: Cerf, 1987), 195–201.

[75]Evagrius also referred to this work as the *Monachos*, "The Monk," surely because it covers both the fundamentals of monastic asceticism and their goal, the attainment of *apatheia*. See the discussion of titles by the Guillaumonts in SC 170:399–408.

of the three works focuses on a particular area of concern, all three include references to the other aspects of monastic growth.

Evagrius devotes the *Praktikos* to the eight thoughts and the process of growth into *apatheia*. The work consists of 100 chapters, of which the final nine are the testimonies from and about great teachers of the ascetic life. Much of the *Praktikos* concerns the "philosophy of deeds" Evagrius learned from the two Macarii and other monastic teachers, but the framework and terminology owe more to his pre-monastic philosophical and doctrinal masters. The *Praktikos* was the most widely circulated of Evagrius' works, copied far more often than its two companion texts. Although the primary emphasis is on attention to the thoughts, the work includes a significant discussion of the qualities and stages of *apatheia*, as well as several remarks about the conditions required for attainment to knowledge of God. The work therefore keeps the beginner grounded in basic ascetic discipline while clearly outlining its goal.

The *Gnostikos*, understood by Socrates Scholasticus as addressed "to one who has been judged worthy of knowledge (πρὸς τὸν καταξιωθέντα γνώσεως),"[76] is best understood as a manual for monastic teachers. That orientation is an unmistakable signal of Evagrius' pedagogical interests. For him monastic life was essentially a quest for knowledge of God, and advancement in the life drew one into teaching as well as learning. The work is composed of 50 chapters, of which numbers 44–48 invoke Evagrius' theological masters in a way analogous to the citation of monastic authorities in the final chapters of the *Praktikos*. In exercising the role of spiritual guide, the "knower" uses skills based on insight into both human nature and the broader creation, that is, the *theoria physiké* that Evagrius establishes as the hinge between self-awareness and knowledge of God. His several cautions to the knower about the insidious persistence of anger even among those experienced in the life remind us that Evagrius does not understand the stages of monastic growth to be discrete. While teaching "spiritual knowledge," that is, ways of interpreting Scripture according to Evagrius' schema of Christian and monastic life, the knower continues to be an example and guide in the practice of physical and spiritual disciplines. Furthermore, monastic instruction requires the teacher's keen sensitivity to the readiness of the student to venture beyond the fundamentals of ascetic self-awareness: "the knower offers a word (*logos*) of salt to the impure and of light to the pure" (*Gnost.* 3).

The *Kephalaia gnostika*, the longest and most challenging of the three works, consists of six books of 90 chapters each.[77] In them Evagrius roams

[76]*H.E.* 4.23.36 (Hansen, 253.4–5).

around the vastness of his theological vision, exploring the scope of *theoria physiké* and demarcating it from the "essential knowledge" of the Holy Trinity belonging to the ultimate stage of human progress. In the *Kephalaia gnostika* the depth of Evagrius' fascination with the speculations of Origen in the treatise *On First Principles* becomes most evident. The significance of the *Kephalaia gnostika* for Evagrius' own view of monastic life as well as their relationship to Origen's thought remain controverted points.[78] These texts puzzle and even disturb those readers of Evagrius who seek to reconcile the astute desert ascetic and loyal disciple of the Cappadocians with the esoteric thinker at work in the dense, often cryptic, paragraphs of the *Kephalaia gnostika*. The *Letter to Melania*[79] is a helpful key to some of the ideas contained in the *Kephalaia gnostika*, but the text remains difficult. The theological framework explored in the *Kephalaia gnostika* is evident throughout Evagrius' works, including the *Praktikos, Gnostikos*, and the biblical scholia, suggesting that it cannot be relegated to a purely accessory role in his thought.

A Developmental Pedagogy

Evagrius was quite aware that the farther reaches of his theology could be risky footing for those without proper training. When describing his trilogy of *Praktikos/Gnostikos/Kephalaia gnostika* to its dedicatee, Anatolius, he writes: "we have concealed (ἐπικρύψαντες) some things and veiled (συσκιά-

---

[77]Guillaumont suggests that six refers to the days of creation (thus the work is a kind of *Hexaemeron*), and that 90 represents the sum of the 40 days before, and the 50 days of, Easter (*Les 'Képhalaia gnostica' d'Évagre le Pontique et l'histoire de l'Origénisme chez les grecs et chez les syriens*, Patristica Sorbonensia 5 [Paris: Éditions du Seuil, 1962], 19–22); cf. *K.G.* 2.38–41. We have no complete Greek text of the *K.G.* though about a quarter of the original can be reconstructed from fragments preserved in various MSS. The whole work exists in two Syriac versions edited by Antoine Guillaumont.

[78]The standard account emphasizing the "Origenism" of Evagrius is Antoine Guillaumont's *Les 'Képhalaia gnostica' d'Évagre le Pontique*. Gabriel Bunge has vigorously disagreed with Guillaumont, suggesting both that Evagrius' seemingly "Origenist," i.e. speculative and esoteric, statements were actually anti-gnostic formulations and that Evagrius has been read in light of later writers who used seemingly similar formulations but in a manifestly unorthodox manner. See "Origenismus—Gnostizismus," 24–54, and "Mysterium unitatis. Der Gedanke der Einheit von Schöpfer und Geschöpf in der evagrianischen Mystik," *Freiburger Zeitschrift für Philosophie und Theologie*, 36 (1989), 449–69; on a more technical level, see "Hénade ou monade? Au sujet de deux notions centrales de la terminologie évagrienne," *Le Muséon*, 102 (1989), 69–91. A good overview of the various positions is provided by Michael O'Laughlin in "New Questions Concerning the Origenism of Evagrius," *Origeniana Quinta*, ed. Robert J. Daly (Leuven: Leuven Univ. Press/ Peeters, 1992), 528–34.

[79]Bunge thinks the letter may actually have been addressed to Rufinus, and sent after the

σαντες) others, lest we give holy things to the dogs or cast pearls before swine. However, these things will be clear to those who have begun to track them down."[80] Central to Evagrius' pedagogical program is presentation of material suited to the learner's stage of development. He had support for this pedagogy from St. Paul.[81] Indeed, the whole thrust of Evagrius' spiritual theology, with its emphasis on asceticism, progressive forms of natural contemplation, and entry into theology, is developmental.

Central to the *Gnostikos* is the importance of teaching in a way that can be grasped and applied constructively to the learner's situation. Evagrius cautions that monastic teachers must not teach beyond the capacity of their students, especially of those "embattled by the passions."[82] Such people may desire the "sweet" diversion of discussing the purpose (*logoi*) of creation but are not ready for it: "they resemble sick people who discuss health." One must not speak to them of such matters, nor allow them to read books about "gnostic things" (*Gnost.* 25), presumably Origen's *On First Principles* or Evagrius' own *Kephalaia gnostika*.[83]

Instead, one must keep them focused on morals rather than doctrines (*Gnost.* 13 and 35; cf. 17), exercising particular caution when speaking of eschatology lest the hearers lose a salutary fear of final judgment. Presumably this could be a consequence of learning the doctrine of the *apokatastasis*, the ultimate restoration of all things (*Gnost.* 36). One should even feign ignorance in the face of importunate questioning, a dissimulation not entirely false since no one still joined to a body, no matter how spiritually advanced, can have true knowledge of things (*Gnost.* 23). There are also pitfalls for the teacher, who may become over-confident or careless, and be susceptible to "false knowledge," that is, heretical teaching (*Gnost.* 42–3).

latter's departure for Italy in 397, i.e., while he was translating Origen's On First Principles; see *Briefe aus der Wüste*, 193–200.

[80]*Prak.* Prol. ll. 58–62.

[81]E.g., 1 Cor 3:1–3, Heb 5:12–14; cf. Eph 4:13–14.

[82]See *Gnost.* 25 and 29. He is equally hesitant to be explicit about the stratagems of demons lest he frighten the inexperienced: see *Prak.* 46.1–4; *Thoughts* 16.1–3, 37.7–11.

[83]Cf. the *Letter to Melania* 17 (Frankenberg, 616.5–6), where he refers to the danger of writing about esoteric teaching lest it be seized upon by the presumptuous: this may be a reference to opponents (as in Bunge, *Briefe aus der Wüste*, 393 n. 29), though it may also be a caution analogous to that of *Gnost.* 25.

The Form of Monastic Instruction

Evagrius' Use of Kephalaia

Evagrius presents his teaching in brief textual units that he calls *kephalaia*. In Classical and Patristic usage, *kephalaion* signifies "main point" or "gist," "topic" or "proposition," as well as the familiar "text division."[84] The format is almost ubiquitous in Evagrius' works. In the Prologue to the *Praktikos*, Evagrius describes the trilogy of *Praktikos/ Gnostikos/ Kephalaia gnostika* as collections of 100, 50, and 600 *kephalaia*.[85] He also characterizes the treatises *On the Thoughts* and *On Prayer* as *kephalaia*.[86] Some of Evagrius' *kephalaia* are expository paragraphs, many are definitions of biblical or technical vocabulary, and others are maxims or proverbs akin to the *gnomai* common in Greek literary and philosophical tradition.[87] The biblical scholia, to be considered in more detail below, contain a mix of styles. In almost every instance, however, the *kephalaia* present Evagrius' teaching in a concise manner conducive to memorization and meditation.

Evagrius did not invent the genre of *kephalaia*, though he was the first Christian writer we know to have used it.[88] The most famous earlier philosophical examples are the *Manual* of Epictetus and the *Meditations* of Marcus Aurelius, though there were many other works composed as *kephalaia* (in

[84]For the first, see Liddell and Scott, *Greek-English Lexicon*, 944b; for the second, see Lampe, *A Patristic Greek Lexicon*, 748b.

[85]*Prak.* Prol. ll. 56–58. On the discrepancy between 600 and the actual 540 of the *K.G.*, see note 77 above.

[86]In *Thoughts* 24.4–5 he refers the reader back to an earlier *kephalaion*; in the Prologue to *On Prayer*, he twice refers to the work as a collection of *kephalaia*; cf. *Thoughts* 22.22, referring to *On Prayer* as the "Chapters on Prayer."

[87]Some works, such as the *Sentences for Monks* and *Sentences for a Virgin*, consist entirely of proverbs. On this format and on the sophisticated arrangement of the former, see Jeremy Driscoll, *The 'Ad monachos' of Evagrius Ponticus*, Studia Anselmiana 104 (Rome: Pontificio Ateneo S. Anselmo, 1991); on the latter, see Elm, "Evagrius Ponticus' *Sententiae ad virginem*." It is interesting to note the terminology used in manuscripts of the *Sentences for Monks*: *Barberini graec. 515* (13thC.) is headed: εὐαγρίου κεφάλαια διάφορα ψυχωφελή (the text of *Sentences for a Virgin* in the same manuscript has no title); in *Vat. graec. 703* (14/15th C.) they are συμβουλείαι (see Hugo Greßmann, "Nonnenspiegel und Mönchsspiegel des Euagrios Pontikos," *TU* 39.4, p. 153). The Latin version in the 9th C. Fleury MS. *Reginensis 140* (fols. 114v-118v) calls them *proverbia* (see Jean Leclercq, "L'ancienne version latine des Sentences d'Évagre pour les moines," *Scriptorium* 5 [1951], 204). On the *gnomai* see the entries in *OCD*, 640b; *Der Kleine Pauly*, 822–29.

[88]See E. von Ivánka, "ΚΕΦΑΛΑΙΑ. Eine byzantinische Literaturform und ihre antiken Wurzeln," *Byzantinische Zeitschrift*, 47 (1954), 285–91, and the Guillaumonts' introduction to *Prak.* in SC 170:113–14.

the *Praktikos* Evagrius seems to quote from one of them, Porphyry's *Aphormai*).[89] Evagrius used this succinct format for the same reason as the philosophers: to assist intellectual and moral formation by way of fairly brief, easily memorized condensations of the teacher's instruction. Such points for meditation, to have at hand when needed,[90] were key elements of philosophical training, as Pierre Hadot and others have demonstrated.[91] Evagrius' choice of format, as well as his arrangement of the *kephalaia* into "centuries" (ἑκατοντάδες), groupings based on divisions or multiples of the perfect number 100, were to prove highly influential with later Christian authors, notably Diadochus of Photiké and Maximus the Confessor.[92]

There were also biblical and monastic analogues to the philosophical models. The Book of Proverbs and other Wisdom writings are in the same broad category of formative moral instruction, and as we will see, Evagrius wrote scholia on Proverbs, Ecclesiastes, Job and the Psalms. While the *form* of some of his *kephalaia*, especially those in the *Sentences for Monks* and *Sentences for a Virgin*, closely resembles the biblical Book of Proverbs, Evagrius' *use* of *kephalaia* adheres more closely to the philosophical models. His own clear program of monastic instruction means that his writings are not general-purpose moral guidance but initiatory aids for a specific manner of life. They feature a high proportion of technical vocabulary related to the theological and spiritual system Evagrius constructed from the various components of his own education and experience.

The *Apophthegmata patrum* are another obvious parallel, and Evagrius cites several to conclude the *Praktikos*. It is important, however, to remember that there were collections of philosophical *apophthegms* in circulation long before the appearance of Egyptian monastic compilations, which themselves post-dated Evagrius' works.[93] Furthermore, in contrast to the collections of monastic *Apophthegmata*, Evagrius' *kephalaia* are virtually all his own work, arranged by their creator in specific collections with at least some ordering within them (even if it is not always readily apparent). The numerological

---

[89]*Prak.* 52; see the note in SC 171:619.

[90]Thus Epictetus' Ἐγχειρίδιον, "Manual." On this terminology, see Paul Rabbow, *Seelenführung* (Munich: Kösel, 1954), 334–36.

[91]See Hadot's "Spiritual Exercises," tr. Michael Chase, in *Philosophy as a Way of Life*, ed. Arnold I.Davidson (Oxford: Blackwell, 1995), 85–86, and "Ancient Spiritual Exercises and 'Christian Philosophy'," in *Philosophy as a Way of Life*, 133–34.

[92]See SC 170:114–16; Irénée Hausherr, "Centuries," *D.Sp.* 2:416–18.

[93]See, e.g., the entry for "Apophthegma" in *RAC*, 545–50. The *apophthegmata* at the end of the *Praktikos* are actually the earliest ones extant; see A. Guillaumont in SC 170:118–20.

significance of the gathering into "centuries" or other groupings such as the 153 *kephalaia* on prayer (interpreted both in terms of the 153 fish mentioned in John 21:11 and according to Pythagorean symbolism[94]) further demonstrates the careful construction and pedagogical orientation of the works: even the total number of *kephalaia* can make an instructive point.

Evagrius' *kephalaia* have two distinguishing characteristics: they are usually quite succinct, and they become briefer and more difficult as one moves into the more advanced stages of monastic instruction. Somewhat more than half of the 100 *kephalaia* in the *Praktikos* are six lines or less in the standard edition; a quarter are no more than three lines long. Only two exceed 15 lines. The *Gnostikos* is even more concise: half of the chapters are shorter than three lines, and almost all are briefer than seven lines. None exceeds 15 lines. The *Kephalaia gnostika* are the briefest of all: few are longer than three lines of printed text. A similar shrinking scale is evident in the works *On the Thoughts/ On Prayer/ Reflections (Skemmata)*, which although not a trilogy in the formal sense of *Praktikos/ Gnostikos/ Kephalaia gnostika*, are nonetheless related in a similarly graduated manner. The original structure of *Thoughts* and *Reflections* is unclear since the arrangement of both seems to have been disturbed in later transmission; even the exact number of *kephalaia* in each work is uncertain.[95] Even so, the trend toward greater brevity as the level of difficulty rises is evident in these works as well. Some of the *kephalaia* in *On the Thoughts* are substantial, and most are longer than 20 lines. When one turns to *On Prayer* and the *Reflections*, the *kephalaia* are comparable in length to those of the *Gnostikos* and *Kephalaia gnostika* respectively.

The teaching in the *Praktikos* and *On the Thoughts* is reasonably accessible to the general reader. The *Gnostikos* and *On Prayer* present few difficulties for someone who has been introduced to Evagrian theology (although the loss of the Greek text for certain chapters of the *Gnostikos* creates some problems of interpretation).[96] In the *Kephalaia gnostika* and the *Reflections*, however, the texts become extremely dense, and are often koan-like in requiring focused meditation in order to crack them. The interpretative challenge is matched to the presumed level of initiation and insight of the reader,

---

[94]See the decryption by Simon Tugwell in *Evagrius Ponticus: Praktikos & On Prayer* (Oxford: Faculty of Theology, 1987), 26–29.

[95]For *Thoughts*, see Paul Géhin's description of the textual situation in SC 438:34–136; for the *Skemmata*, see J. Muyldermans, "Evagriana," *Le Muséon*, 44 (1931), 37–68, and "Note additionnelle," 369–83.

[96]An exception would be *Gnost.* 50; this final chapter has the allusive quality more typical of *K.G.* and thereby functions as a hinge linking *Gnost.* to the more advanced work.

capturing the interest of those advancing in the formational program and precluding access by the uninitiated.

Most of Evagrius' writings in the *kephalaia* format open with a series of definitions that locate the collections within his theological framework.[97] As the table below indicates, the *Praktikos* and *Gnostikos* both begin with three *kephalaia* defining basic terms and a fourth *kephalaion* describing the epistemology appropriate to the developmental stage represented by the work. Evagrius opens the *Praktikos* by keying some fundamental Christian terminology to his monastic theological framework. By contrast, the opening definitions of the *Gnostikos* operate entirely within Evagrius' own system. The epistemology he identifies as important for the reader of the *Praktikos* centers on the role of the senses in arousing the passions, while in the *Gnostikos*, Evagrius distinguishes between two kinds of intellectual apprehension.

Praktikos	*Gnostikos*
1: "Christianity" = *praktiké/physiké/theologiké*	1: "*Praktikoi*" and "*Gnostikoi*" = those understanding *logoi* *praktikoi* or who see *gnostika*
2: "Kingdom of Heaven" = *apatheia* + *gnosis* of beings	2: "*Praktikos*" = *apatheia* of impassioned part of soul
3: "Kingdom of God" = *gnosis* of Trinity	3: "*Gnostikos*" = offers *logos* of salt for the impure and of light for the pure
4: sensation, desire, and pleasure	4: two ways the mind receives *logoi*

On the Thoughts and *On Prayer* exhibit analogous opening sequences that lay a foundation for what follows. When the two sequences are compared, it is clear that *On Prayer* is pitched to a more advanced reader.

Thoughts	*Prayer*
1: "three demons vs. the *praktiké*"	1: four virtues
2: depictions (*noemata*) of sensory objects	2: purification of soul and preparation of mind for prayer

[97]The same parallelism is evident in *Prak.* 74–75 and *Gnost.* 42–43, which use the same formulae "The temptation of the monk (or the 'knower') is . . ." and "The sin of the monk (or the 'knower') is . . . ."

| 3: must deal with desire and reaction | 3: "prayer"
= conversation of mind with God, proper mental state to converse with God |
| 4: memory and dreams create fantasies | 4: put away all depictions (*noemata*) to see and converse with God |

In the initial sequences of *Praktikos/Gnostikos* and (less obviously) in *On the Thoughts/ On Prayer*, Evagrius gives his readers a foretaste of what they will find throughout the *Kephalaia gnostika* and *Reflections* in a much more challenging form. Both advanced works consist almost entirely of brief definitions or maxims referring to elements of the advanced stages of Evagrian theology. The strong emphasis on spiritual knowledge in these works makes epistemology a central concern. What Antoine Guillaumont noted of the *Sentences for Monks* applies especially to these works: "These collections are not composed to be read straight through, but to be meditated sentence by sentence, and the enigmatic touch is justified by the need to hold the reader's attention and to demand reflection."[98]

Evagrius' Biblical Scholia

According to the Coptic *Life*, Palladius learned two things from Evagrius at Kellia: the spiritual interpretation of Scripture and cautions about false knowledge.[99] The same text describes Evagrius as spending much of the night "making his intellect search out contemplations of the Scriptures."[100] Evagrius' emphasis on biblical interpretation and instruction is evident even in the most cursory overview of his literary output. His biblical commentaries, presented in the form of scholia, that is, brief notes on particular texts, constitute the major part of his written works. The scholia are not commentary in any conventional sense, but rather a re-tuning of biblical texts to his theological framework. Evagrius' effort to connect each biblical *lemma* to some aspect of his spiritual theology is sustained and even relentless: with every biblical verse meditated, the monk's attention was to be directed to the bigger picture. In the scholia we see Evagrius bringing together the two facets of his

[98] Les 'Képhalaia gnostica', 33 n. 54.
[99] Amélineau, 105.4–7. For interpretation, see Bunge and Vogüé, *Quatre ermites*, 153 n.3, and Bunge, "Origenismus—Gnostizismus," 37–38.
[100] Amélineau, 113.12–13.

own life as ascetic practitioner of biblical meditation and as creative philosophical theologian.

Evagrius lays out his strategy of biblical interpretation in chapters 16–21
of the *Gnostikos*. Because most of these *kephalaia* survive only in Syriac and
Armenian, precise interpretation is difficult. Obviously Evagrius was concerned that the teacher be adept at fielding questions about specific biblical
texts. Such skill would require knowing the ways of the Bible, its *ethos* or
sunetheia, and the ability to demonstrate that knowledge with specific examples.[101] This is exactly what Evagrius does in the scholia. He remarks in one
of the *Scholia on Proverbs* that someone who has rejected evil through the
power of the virtues becomes an "*oikonomos* of the mysteries of God, giving
spiritual knowledge to each of the brothers appropriate to his condition,"
that is, to his degree of progress in the monastic life.[102]

Evagrius writes in the *Kephalaia gnostika*, "The divine Book does not
make known what the contemplation of [created] beings is, but it openly
teaches how one approaches it by practice of the commandments and by true
doctrines."[103] To go deeper, one needs a guide, the "*oikonomos* of the mysteries of God." Thus he opens his *Scholia on Ecclesiastes* by interpreting the
"Ecclesiast" to be either Christ or "one who purifies souls through ethical contemplations (τῶν ἠθικῶν θεωρημάτων) and leads them to natural contemplation (τῇ φυσικῇ θεωρίᾳ)."[104] By "contemplations" (θεωρήματα) Evagrius
means here understandings of Scripture,[105] and these are what he provides in
his scholia on Psalms, Proverbs, Ecclesiastes, and Job. Evagrius seems more
concerned to provide a firm grasp on the text in a way related to his theological framework than to encourage creative exploration of possible meanings.
In the *Gnostikos* he provides a concise summary of his own method of biblical interpretation, which is more restrictive than Origen's in that Evagrius limits each text to one literal and one spiritual signification. Each is keyed to one
of the three divisions of knowledge: practical, natural, or theological.[106]

Evagrius chose those particular books for commentary for at least two
reasons, one monastic and one traditional. The Psalms were the staple of

---

[101]*Gnost.* 19. The Greek is not extant; see Géhin's rationale for this terminology in SC
356:118–19.

[102]*Prov.* 17:2 (G 153.3–6).

[103]*K.G.* 6.1.

[104]*Eccl.* 1:1 (G 1.4–6).

[105]Cf. *Prov.* 30:9 (G 288.3–6) for a clear example of this use of θεώρημα.

[106]*Gnost.* 18 and 20. The literal and spiritual meanings can relate to different kinds of
knowledge. See Paul Géhin's remarks on Evagrian exegesis in SC 340:26–32.

monastic prayer night and day, and were obvious matter for commentary. The Book of Proverbs was especially popular in monastic circles for both its format and ethical orientation, as witnessed by Evagrius' own imitation of the genre in, for example, his *Sentences for Monks* and *Sentences for a Virgin*. Like the Psalms, the Proverbs would have been memorized for use in meditation. Evagrius also knew and was influenced by Origen's allegorical understanding of Proverbs/ Ecclesiastes/ Song of Songs as pertaining respectively to ethical, natural and contemplative knowledge.[107] As we have seen, Evagrius based his whole doctrinal system on that tripartite division. In explicitly relating his scholia on Proverbs and Ecclesiastes to it, he applied the schema more rigorously than did Origen himself. Although we have no scholia by Evagrius on Song of Songs and he rarely cites it in his extant works,[108] he did write brief pastiches based on each of the three "Solomonic" books.[109] The choice of Job may seem odd, though in the Septuagint tradition Job follows the other three books.[110] Therefore in his scholia Evagrius was working with the books at the heart of the monastic Bible.

Evagrius is the first Christian author known to have composed scholia, but as with the *kephalaia*, he did not invent the genre. Explications, typically brief, of particular points in authoritative texts are extant from at least the time of Cicero, who seems to have been the first actually to use the word.[111] However, the term and probably the genre were not in Christian use until the fourth century despite Jerome's claim that Origen had written scholia (*excerpta . . . quae graece σχόλια nuncupantur*).[112] Éric Junod has argued that Origen's so-called scholia do not fit the criterion of "brief notes on a particular difficulty of interpretation" but are a "developed, though discontinuous,

---

[107]See Origen's prologue to the *Comm. on Song of Songs* (GCS 33:76–77); Evagrius cites the schema in *Prov.* 22:20 (G 247).

[108]Never in *Prak./Gnost./K.G.*; once in *Thoughts*, never in *Prayer* or *Reflections*.

[109]See Paul Géhin, "Evagriana d'un manuscrit basilien," *Le Muséon*, 109 (1996), 71–73, 75–85. A partial Greek text of the compilation based on Proverbs can be found in J. Muyld-man's edition of codex *Barberini Gr. 515*, fols. 60v-61r (*Le Muséon*, 45 [1931], 20–21), there sentences 50–67; a more complete Syriac version is in Muyldermans' *Evagriana Syriaca*, Bibliothèque du *Muséon*, 31 (Louvain, 1952), 135–38 (Syriac) and 165–67 (French trans.). The Greek text of the compilation based on Ecclesiastes remains unpublished; Géhin signaled its rediscovery in his 1996 article, in which he publishes an Arabic version on pp. 76 (Arabic) and 78–79 (French trans.). The Greek text of the compilation based on the Song can be found on pp. 71–73 of the same article.

[110]In the Hebrew Bible, Job is situated between Psalms and Proverbs; in the Vulgate and modern western Christian Bibles, it appears before Psalms.

[111]See M.D. Reeve, "Scholia," *OCD*, 1368.

[112]In the prologue to his translation of Origen's *Homilies on Ezekiel*, SC 352:30–33.

commentary on certain passages requiring explication," perhaps preliminary to continuous commentary.[113] They may also indeed be "excerpts" from works not preserved in their original form.

Like the *kephalaia* they so often resemble, the form of Evagrius' scholia varies from that of notes to more extended reflections. On three occasions, once each in the scholia on Psalms, Proverbs, and Ecclesiastes, he cuts short his explication, noting that it would not be in accord with the scholial genre to be more expansive.[114] His scholia are in fact typically quite brief: two-thirds of those on Proverbs are four lines or less, and few exceed ten lines.[115] Many are simply terminological notes, neither explicative nor commentarial in a traditional sense. They are instead ways of keying these fundamental, popular, widely memorized biblical texts to Evagrius' understanding of monastic life.[116] When he defines or explicates a biblical word, he is matching it to a term or concept from his monastic theology. One could, therefore, devise an Evagrian exegetical lexicon based on those matches.

Many of Evagrius' scholia do advance beyond mere decoding and recoding of the biblical text, resembling the longer *kephalaia* in containing sections of instructional material. In every case, however, Evagrius works closely with the biblical text even if his interpretations seem constrained by his theological framework. All commentary is to some extent a recoding of the source text to a particular cultural or religious situation, and sometimes even the simplest gloss can show us the interpretative location of the commentator. However, Evagrius' interpretative program is much more explicit than the commentary of Philo and Origen. The reason for this tighter focus, of course, is that Evagrius was serving as spiritual guide to a group with very particular formational needs. Evagrius' understanding of those needs was highly developed and, to the extent such a term is appropriate for pre-modern texts, systematic.

[113] "Que savons-nous des ‹Scholies› (ΣΧΟΛΙΑ-ΣΗΜΕΙΩΣΕΙΣ) d'Origène?," in *Origeniana Sexta: Origène et la Bible*, ed. Gilles Dorival and Alain Le Boulluec, Bibliotheca Ephemeridum theologicarum Lovaniensium 118 (Leuven: Leuven Univ. Press/ Peeters, 1995), 147.

[114] *Prov.* 25:26 (G 317.16–17): τὸ εἶδος τῶν σχολίων πολυλογίαν μὴ ἐπιδεχόμενον; *Eccl.* 5:17–19 (G 42.5–6): μὴ συγχωροῦντος τοῦ τῶν σχολίων κανόνος. In *Psalms* he observes that he would like to give an explanation of a "deep contemplation" but is forbidden to do so by the rules of the scholia (παρελεύσεται τοὺς τῶν σχολίων κανόνας) *Sch. 5 in Ps. 88:9* [Pitra, 160]).

[115] Of a total of 386 scholia (four of the 382 contained in Géhin's edition are two-part), 264 are 1–4 lines long in the SC edition; another 99 are 5–10 lines. Those on Ecclesiastes tend to be somewhat longer since the biblical *lemmata* commented on by each scholion are longer than for the *Scholia on Proverbs*; thus 31 of 73 are 1–4 lines, another 29 are 5–10 lines. The *Scholia on Psalms* are similar in length to those on Proverbs; the surviving *Scholia on Job* are very brief but too few to draw any conclusions about the whole collection.

[116] See Géhin's overview of types of Evagrian scholia in SC 340:15–18.

Evagrius' scholia fulfill and model that vital aspect of the monastic teacher's role as described in the *Gnostikos*: "to know the ways of divine Scripture and to establish them, as far as possible, by means of examples" (*Gnost.* 19). The opening scholia for both Proverbs and Ecclesiastes follow the pattern established in the opening *kephalaia* of the *Praktikos* and *Gnostikos*, which had probably already been written when Evagrius was composing the scholia.[117] As in the *Praktikos* and *Gnostikos*, the opening sequences of the two scholial collections are pitched to different levels of spiritual progress, beginning and intermediate respectively. Once again we find a series of definitions that key fundamental terms to Evagrian theology, followed by an epistemological orienting of the work. Both sets of scholia present an overview of the entire spiritual trajectory, but the opening scholia on Proverbs posit a move from ethics to knowledge of creation as the goal, while those on Ecclesiastes focus on *theoria physiké*, with hints of the ultimate goal of knowledge of the Trinity. The difference reflects the traditional understanding of the two biblical books inherited from Origen.[118] The epistemological specification is crucial, since for Evagrius, *how* you know is as important as *what* you know, and both have a developmental progression.

Scholia on Proverbs	*Scholia on Ecclesiastes*
1: "proverb" = saying that uses sensory things to signify intellectual ones	1. "*Ekklesia*" = true knowledge of ages and worlds, judgment and providence

---

[117]In *Sch. in Ps.* 143:1 Evagrius refers to the "*Monachos*," which should be taken as a reference to the *Praktikos* and his discussion there of the parts of the soul; see the analysis of this passage (and of its misreading by editors of printed editions) by M.-J. Rondeau in "Le commentaire sur les Psaumes d'Évagre le Pontique," *OCP* 26 (1960), 312–18. Géhin suggests that the scholia were written in canonical order (Psalms, Proverbs, Ecclesiastes, [Song], Job), and after *Praktikos* (at least its first redaction), *Gnostikos*, and *Kephalaia gnostika* (SC 340:20–21). In content, the scholia on Psalms are closest to *Thoughts* and *Reflections*; those on Proverbs and Ecclesiastes place less emphasis on Evagrian mystical themes such as the "place of God" or the light seen in prayer. See Stewart, "Imageless Prayer and the Theological Vision of Evagrius Ponticus," 191–8.

[118]Another indication of the difference between the two sets of scholia is that those on Proverbs contain "antirrhetic" scholia directed at particular temptations, while those on Ecclesiastes do not (although verses from Ecclesiastes are used in the Evagrian work entitled *Antirrhetikos*); see Géhin in SC 340:18 and 356:9–10. The current state of the scholia on Psalms and Job does not allow comparison of the opening sequences; the relationship established in the opening sequences of the scholia on Proverbs and Ecclesiastes parallels both Origen's understanding of the two books and the progression Evagrius establishes from *Praktikos* to *Gnostikos*.

"Ecclesiast"= Christ OR one who
purifies souls through ethical
contemplations and leads them
to *theoria physiké*

2: "Kingdom of Israel"
= spiritual knowledge about
incorporeal and corporeal
beings, judgment and
providence; or contemplation
about *ethiké*, *physiké*, or
theologiké

2: "vanity of vanities"
= *logoi* of ages and worlds
compared to knowledge of
Trinity

3: "wisdom"
= knowledge of corporeal and
incorporeal beings, judgment
and providence
"*paideia*"
= *metriopatheia* of the passions

3: contemplation of God requires
separation from all depictions
(*noemata*) of things

4: three faculties of judgment:
sensation, reason, and intellect

5: *nous* perceives sensory things
through the senses, intellectual
things by the virtues

There is another point of convergence between Evagrius' *kephalaia* and his scholia. He was very concerned that the *kephalaia* be copied correctly lest the format, essential to the pedagogy, be obscured. There is a note at the head of some copies of the *Praktikos* in both Greek and Syriac traditions that Antoine and Claire Guillaumont attribute to Evagrius himself: "I implore the brothers who read the book and want to copy it, that they not link chapter (κεφάλαιον) to chapter, nor put on the same line the ending of the chapter being written and the beginning of the one [next] to be written, but begin each chapter with its own beginning, just as we have marked them with numbers. Thereby the arrangement in chapters (κεφαλαιώδης . . . κανών) can be preserved and what is said will be clearly seen."[119] In the surviving manuscripts of the *Praktikos*—all dating from centuries later than Evagrius—his plea was only sometimes effective.[120]

[119]Text: SC 171:498 n.1; interpretation: SC 170:384–85.
[120]Claire Guillaumont provides detailed information about each manuscript used in her edition in SC 170. Of the five MSS. containing the complete text of the Praktikos (i.e., all 100 *kepha-*

The original manuscript format of the scholia was similar to that of the *kephalaia* in presenting each scholion as a distinct textual unit written after its biblical *lemma*, creating a sequence of biblical text/scholion/biblical text/scholion, etc. This format survives in manuscripts preserving the Evagrian scholia in their integrity, that is, unmixed with scholia by other writers.[121] It preserved Evagrius' intention that the scholia, like the *kephalaia*, nourish focused meditation. In later transmission, the scholia were usually mixed with glosses by other authors to create collections of *eklogai*, "excerpts," of which the earliest were perhaps those of Procopius of Gaza (6th century). In later practice these collections, later known as "chains" (*catenae*), were often formatted as marginal commentary surrounding the biblical text.[122] Such arrangement was useful for purposes of study but was a dramatic departure from the original *Sitz im Leben* in which scholia, like *kephalaia*, were linked to Evagrius' theological vision and pedagogical program.

Conclusion

Evagrius Ponticus was not a typical desert father. His education, experience, and brilliance set him apart from his contemporaries, for better or for worse. These qualities compel our attention, for through Evagrius we have privileged entree into the ascetic and intellectual world of one strand of fourth-century monasticism in Lower Egypt. Evagrius' literary program for monastic formation, so highly structured and presuming his own understanding of monastic life, would have been difficult to apply *in toto* even for his contemporaries.

laia), two begin each *kephalaion* on a new line (*Casinensis Arch. Abbatiae 231* contains the admonition to copyists, *Chozobiotissis 10* does not, though it seems to have been copied from an exemplar containing it); one often starts each on a new line (*Paris gr. 1056*, though it does not contain the admonition); two do not start each on a new line, even though one contains the admonition (*Paris gr. 1188*) while the other does not (*Coislin 109*). Of three MSS containing the earlier, shorter, version (90 *kephalaia*), none contains the admonition or appears to begin each *kephalaion* on a new line (*Protaton 26, Lavra G 93* [*Athous 333*], *Panteleimon 635* [*Athous 6142*]).

[121]For Proverbs, codex *Patmiacus 270* (10th C.) contains all of the Evagrian scholia; for Prov. 1:1–9:10a they are written without biblical *lemmata*, though these were added in the margin; for Prov. 9:12a to the end, the *lemmata* are included in small script, followed by the scholia (see Géhin in SC 340:61). For Ecclesiastes, all 73 scholia are in *Parisinus Coislinianus gr. 193* (11th C.), where each biblical *lemma* is written in gold, the Hexaplic variants are provided where they exist, and each scholion follows its *lemma* (see Géhin, "Un nouvel inédit d'Évagre le Pontique: son commentaire de l'Ecclésiaste, *Byzantion* 49 [1979], 188–89).

[122]See Robert Devreesse, "Chaînes exégétiques grecques," *Dictionnaire de la Bible, Supplément* 1:1084–1233, esp. 1084–99; Carmelo Curti, "Catenae, biblical," *Encyclopedia of the Early Church*, 1:152–53.

The program is a resource and artifact rather than an immediately applicable system, representing the crystallization of Evagrius' monastic and pedagogical experience toward the end of his life. More transferable would have been his emphasis on both a coherent theological vision of monasticism and pedagogy suitable for initiation into it.

However, after Evagrius' death and the controversies of the late fourth to sixth centuries, his program shattered. The *Praktikos*, the treatise *On the Thoughts*, and the two collections of *Sentences* continued to be admired and widely copied for their ascetic wisdom. Many of the scholia were absorbed into the *eklogai / catenae*, preserved alongside the commentary of other writers. The treatise *On Prayer* was reassigned to Nilus and circulated under that safer cover. The more advanced works, the *Gnostikos*, *Kephalaia gnostika*, and *Skemmata*, fell more readily under the ban. The first two survive only partially in the original Greek, the third has been recovered through patient textual study. Only in the east, in Armenian and Syriac speaking regions, did the whole Evagrian textual tradition survive, though even there his program was a resource and inspiration rather than a living process of monastic initiation. The influence of Evagrius' thought—and even his choice of literary format—was enormous, directly in Greek and in the translations, indirectly through the work of those shaped by his thought, including John Cassian in the Latin west.

Apart from lessons particular to the case of Evagrius, the fate of his formational program reminds us that monasticism is *lived*, and is learned primarily from living it under the guidance of those who have grown wise in the life. Traditions, whether literary or customary, may support this living guidance but they can never substitute for it. Evagrius himself knew this well, which is why he placed his manual of monastic pedagogy, the *Gnostikos*, at the heart of his comprehensive trilogy of monastic writings. Mediating between asceticism and knowledge stands the teacher. Aiding discernment and interpreting the Bible, the monastic teacher points toward Christ and the fullness of life found ultimately in the Holy Trinity, source and goal of all Christian aspiration.

Works of Evagrius

Antirrhetikos. Syriac version ed. Wilhelm Frankenberg, *Euagrius Ponticus*, Abhandlungen der königlichen Gesellschaft der Wissenschaften zu Göttingen, Philologisch-historische Klasse, Neue Folge 13.2 (Berlin: Weidmann, 1912), 472–544.

Ecclesiastes=Scholia on Ecclesiastes. Ed. Paul Géhin, *Évagre le Pontique: Scholies à l'Ecclésiaste,* SC 397 (Paris: Cerf, 1993). Cited according to biblical verse being commented upon. G + number= Géhin's numbering of the scholia.

Eight Spirits (De octo spiritibus malitiae). PG 79:1145A-64D.

Eulogios (Ad Eulogium). PG 79:1093C-1140A.

Gnostikos. Extant Greek chapters ed. Antoine and Claire Guillaumont, *Évagre le Pontique: Le Gnostique,* SC 356 (Paris: Cerf, 1989); Syriac version (S1) in Frankenberg, *Euagrius Ponticus,* 546–52. Reference is to the Greek text where extant, otherwise to Frankenberg's edition of the Syriac (key to differences in numerotation in SC 356, p. 195).

Job=Scholia on Job. Ed. Ursula and Dieter Hagedorn, *Die älteren griechischen Katenen zum Buch Hiob,* PTS 40/48 (Berlin/New York: De Gruyter, 1994–). Reference is to the biblical verse being commented upon as well as to the chapter and section of the *Catena.*

K.G.=Kephalaia gnostika. Syriac version ed. Antoine Guillaumont, *Les Six Centuries des 'Kephalaia gnostica' d'Évagre le Pontique,* PO 28. Paris: Firmin-Didot, 1958. Citations are to version S2, printed on the odd-numbered pages of the edition; references there to Greek fragments.

Letter on Faith (Epistula fidei). Preserved as *Letter* 8 of (Ps-) Basil. Ed. Jean Gribomont in M. Forlin Patrucco, *Basilio di Cesarea. Le Lettere,* vol. 1 (Turin: Corona Patrum, 1983), 84–112 (text) and 296–97 (commentary).

Letter to Melania. Partial Syriac text in Frankenberg, *Euagrius Ponticus,* 610–19, remainder in G. Vitestam, "Seconde partie du traité qui passe sous le nom de 'La grande lettre d'Évagre le Pontique à Mélanie l'Ancienne'," *Scripta Minora Regiae Societatis humaniorum litterarum Lundensis 1963–1964,* 3 (Lund: C.W.K. Gleerup, 1964); English trans. and commentary by Martin Parmentier, "Evagrius of Pontus' Letter to Melania," *Bijdragen,* 46 (1985), 2–38; German translation (based directly on the manuscripts) and commentary by Gabriel Bunge, *Briefe aus der Wüste,* Sophia 24 (Trier: Paulinus-Verlag, 1986), 303–28 (=Letter 64). References are to Bunge's section numbers, Frankenberg's or Vitestam's editions of the Syriac, and Parmentier's translation.

Letters. Syriac version in Frankenberg, *Euagrius Ponticus,* 562–634; section divisions as in the German translation of Gabriel Bunge, *Briefe aus der Wüste.*

Praktikos. Ed. Antoine and Claire Guillaumont, *Évagre le Pontique: Traité pratique ou le moine,* SC 170–71 (Paris: Cerf, 1971).

Prayer= Chapters on Prayer (De oratione). Ed. Simon Tugwell (Oxford: Theology Faculty, 1981). Tugwell's edition is based on Paris MS. *Coislin 109* and other manuscripts superior to those used for the edition found in PG 79:165A-1200C; Tugwell's ch. 35 is the final part of ch. 34 in PG 79, and from that point until ch. 78 the chapters in PG are numbered one less than those in Tugwell's edition.

Proverbs=Scholia on Proverbs. Ed. Paul Géhin, *Évagre le Pontique: Scholies aux Proverbes,* SC 340 (Paris: Cerf, 1987). Cited according to biblical verse being commented upon. G + number= Géhin's numbering of the scholia.

Psalms=Scholia on Psalms. Pitra= Ed. Jean Baptiste Pitra, *Analecta sacra,* vol. 2 (Frascati, 1884), 444–83, for Pss. 1–25 and vol. 3 (Paris, 1883) for Pss. 26–150. Other texts in Migne, PG 12:1054–1686 and 27:60–545. Key in Marie-Josèphe Rondeau, "Le commentaire sur les Psaumes d'Évagre le Pontique," *OCP* 26 (1960), 307–48.

Reflections (Skemmata, Capita cognoscitiva, "Pseudo-supplement to Kephalaia Gnostika"). Ed. J. Muyldermans, "Evagriana," *Le Muséon*, 44 (1931), 374–80.

Sentences for a Virgin (Ad virginem). Ed. Hugo Greßmann, "Nonnenspiegel und Mönchsspiegel des Euagrios Pontikos," *TU* 39.4 (Leipzig, 1939), 146–51.

Sentences for Monks (Ad monachos). Ed. Hugo Greßmann, "Nonnenspiegel und Mönchsspiegel des Euagrios Pontikos," *TU* 39.4 (Leipzig, 1939), 153–65. Greßmann's Greek text, English translation and commentary in Jeremy Driscoll, *The 'Ad monachos' of Evagrius Ponticus. Its Structure and a Select Commentary*, Studia Anselmiana, 104 (Rome: Pontificio Ateneo S. Anselmo, 1991).

Thoughts=On the Thoughts (De malignis cogitationibus). Ed. Paul Géhin, Claire Guillaumont, Antoine Guillaumont, *Évagre le Pontique: Sur les pensées*, SC 438 (Paris: Cerf, 1998).

❁ · ❁

❈ The Vision of God and the ❈ Form of Glory: More Reflections on the Anthropomorphite Controversy of AD 399*

Alexander Golitzin

The Problem

IN LATE WINTER OF AD 399, the annual paschal epistle of Patriarch Theophilus of Alexandria took occasion to condemn at length the teaching that God has a human form. The letter itself is no longer extant, but John Cassian, together with Palladius and the Church historians, Sozomen and Socrates, all agree that it hit a nerve among the monks of Egypt.[1] Cassian tells us that the priests in three of the four churches of Scete refused to accord the patriarch's letter a public reading,[2] while Sozomen and Socrates report a mob of angry ascetics converging on the patriarchal residence bent on lynching the offending prelate.[3] Although both Church historians leave the reader with the impression that they would have quite liked to have seen Theophilus dangling from a handy lamp-post, neither evinces much sympathy for the protesting monks. The latter are portrayed as unlettered peasants whose simplicity regarding both the nuances of biblical interpretation and the twists of ecclesiastical power politics allows the patriarch to direct their anger against

---

*See also the related article: A. Golitzin, "The Demons Suggest an Illusion of God's Glory in a Form," *Studia Monastica*, 44.1 (2002), 13–43, for discussion of the same line in monastic texts related to, though mostly different from, the ones considered here.

[1]John Cassian, *Collatio* X, in *Collationes*, ed. M. Petschenig, CSEL 13:288–308; ET: *John Cassian. The Conferences*, tr. O. Chadwick (NY: 1985),125–140; Socrates, *HE* VI.7, PG 67:684A-688C; ET: NPNF 2nd Series, II:142–143; Sozomen, *HE* VIII.1–12, PG 70:1344C-1349A; ET: NPNF 2nd Series, II:406–407; Palladius, *Dialogue sur la vie de S. Jean Chrysostome*, ed. Malingrey and P. LeClerc, SC 341:138–140.

[2]Cassian, *Coll* X.2 (CSEL 287:18–24; ET: 126).

[3]Socrates 684B (ET: 142); Sozomen 1544A-C (ET: 406).

certain targets within the Egyptian Church whom he has singled out for elimination, notably the Tall Brothers and their associates.[4] According to the two historians, Theophilus redeems the situation and quite possibly his life with a single remark: "In seeing you," he tells the mob, "I behold the face of God."[5] The answering demand that he demonstrate his repentance by condemning Origen provides him with with the opportunity he has been seeking to begin his purge.

Elizabeth Clark has dealt admirably with the politics and sociology of this prelude to the first Origenist controversy, while others—such as Antoine Guillaumont, Gabriel Bunge, Jeremy Driscoll, Michael O'Laughlin, and Columba Stewart—have examined the thought of the Egyptian Desert's "Origenist-in-chief," Evagrius Ponticus, together with the latter's disciples and admirers,[6] which categories include all four of the reporters noted above. Comparatively little attention, on the other hand, has been devoted to the thinking of the monks who objected to Theophilus' letter. Most modern scholars, when they note the protesters at all, reflect the assessment of Sozomen and Socrates and dismiss the "crude forms of folk religion" which the monks must have represented. Among the very few who have troubled to look more deeply, Edouard Drioton at length in 1915–1917 and Guy Stroumsa very briefly just a couple of years ago have argued that the Egyptian protesters took their cue from the Audians, a Mesopotamian ascetic sect whom Epiphanius of Salamis had criticized a generation earlier.[7] Stroumsa adds the suggestion of interesting parallels with currents in then contemporary Jewish thought concerning the divine form.[8] Against Drioton, Georges Florovsky in the 1960's held that the anthropomorphite "heresy" of the monks was in fact a construction placed upon their thought by their enemies, precisely by those Evagrian sympathizers who constitute nearly the only sources that we have for the debate. Rather than believing in the human shape of the Godhead, the monks in Florovsky's eyes were defending the enduring reality of the Incarnate Word

[4]Thus Sozomen 1544C (406).

[5]Socrates, 684BC; Sozomen, 1545A; both: *hōs Theou prosōpon*.

[6]E. Clark, *The Origenist Controversy: The Cultural Construction of an Early Christian Debate* (Princeton: 1992), esp. 43–84.

[7]E. Drioton, "La discussion d'un moine anthropomorphite audien avec le patriarche Theophile d'Alexandrie," *Revue de l'orient chrétien*, 20 (1915–1917), 92–100 and 113–128.

[8]G. G. Stroumsa, "Jewish and Gnostic Traditions among the Audians," in *Sharing the Sacred: Religious Contacts and Conflicts in the Holy Land*, ed. A. Kofsky and G. G. Stroumsa (Jerusalem: 1998), 345–358 (my thanks to Professor Stroumsa for the offprint of this article); and, briefly, idem, "The Incorporeality of God: Context and Implications of Origen's Position," *Religion*, 13 (1983), 345–358, esp. 354.

against the solvent of Evagrian spiritualism.[9] The accusation of anthropomorphism in the controversy of 399 was therefore a kind of theological phantom conjured up by Evagrius' disciples, Cassian and company, in order to stigmatize their in fact more orthodox opposition. Thirty years later, in 1992, Graham Gould wrote in support of Florovsky, arguing on the basis of selected fourth and early fifth century monastic texts that there is no clear evidence for anthropomorphism among the Egyptian monks, and so concluding that their detractors were guilty of "serious misrepresentations of their opponents' theological outlook"[10]—Florovsky's phantom, in other words, if more cautiously phrased.

In what follows, I would like to offer the suggestion that, while each of these four men has contributed something toward explaining the controversy of 399, the heart of it lay in what Drioton felt was at issue, the matter of God having a body, together with Stroumsa's perception of a parallel in then contemporary Jewish mysticism. I admit that to look, as I propose to do, for the elucidation of a theological controversy involving turn of the fifth century Christian monks in, on the one hand, Old Testament theophanies and the apocalyptic texts of the later Second Temple and, on the other hand, the rabbinic-era mysticism of ascent to the *merkavah* or chariot throne of God, must seem odd at best. I hope to render it less outrageous by turning next to a capsule investigation of certain themes in the Old Testament and in the intertestamental era, particularly as these have been illumined by the work of scholars in both Judaica and Christian Semitic studies, and then by providing a sketch—of necessity exceedingly brief—of evidence for these ideas in pre-Nicene Christianity. Given this basis, I shall conclude with a reading of the two texts, Cassian's tenth *Conversation* and the Coptic *Life of Apa Aphou of Pemdje*, which have come down to us from opposite sides of the controversy.[11]

---

[9]G. Florovsky, "Theophilus of Antioch and Apa Aphou of Pemdje," in *The Collected Works of Father Georges Florovsky* (Belmont MA: 1975), Vol. 4:97–129, and more briefly, "The Anthropomorphites in the Egyptian Desert," Ibid. Vol. 4:89–96.

[10]G. Gould, "The Image of God and the Anthropomorphite Controversy in Fourth Century Monasticism," in *Origeniana Quinta*, ed. B. Daley (Louvain: 1992), 549–557, here 555, basing himself on Evagrius' *de oratione*, the *Apophthegmata Patrum*, the *Vita Prima* of Pachomius, and the *Letters of Anthony*.

[11]The limitation is deliberate, held to the texts dealing with 399, in order to keep the paper to a reasonable length. For a more extensive account of the other Egyptian, Syrian, and Latin Christian materials, see the earlier version of this essay in Romanian translation: "Forma lui Dumnezeu si Vederea Slavei: Reflectii asupra Controversei Anthropomorphite din annul 399 d. Hr," in A. Golitzin, *Mistagogia: Experienta lui Dumnezeu in Ortodoxie*, tr. I. Ica Jr. (Sibiu, Romania: 1998), 184–267, esp. 196–223.

Background, Part I: Glory, Image, and the Vision of God from Ezekiel to 2 Enoch

In the Old Testament, I turn primarily to one term, glory (*kavod* in Hebrew), and two texts, Ezk 1:26–28 and Gen 1:26–27. The former is Ezekiel's vision of God's chariot throne. What is significant for us is what he sees upon it:

> And above the dome over their [the cherubim's] heads there was something like a throne, in appearance like a sapphire; and seated above the likeness of a throne was something that seemed like a human form [*dmwt kmr'h adam*]. Upward from what appeared like the loins I saw something like gleaming amber . . . and downward from what looked like the loins I saw something that looked like fire, and there was splendor all round. Like the bow in a cloud on a rainy day, such was the appearance of the splendor all around. This was the appearance of the likeness of the Glory of the Lord [*hw' mr'h dmwt kbwd YHWH*], and I saw it and fell upon my face . . . [Ezk 1:26–28, NRSV]

While every detail of this vision is important for subsequent tradition, for our purposes I underline the repetition of *demut*, "likeness," and its identification at once with the human form and with the appearance of the divine glory, the *kevod YHWH*. "Glory" may admittedly have several senses in the Hebrew.[12] Its initial meaning has to do with weight, and by extension wealth, power, honor, or praise. In connection with theophany, as in for example Ex 24:16–17, and elsewhere in the Priestly source, it seems to denote the fiery stufff of divinity, or God's light, splendor, or sovereignty, as in Is 6:3: "the whole earth is full of his glory." Isaiah's vision of the king enthroned, however, directs us back to what we find highlighted in Ezekiel's vision: the frequency—not to say near (though not total[13]) ubiquity—of anthropomorphism in the Old Testament theophanies. Thus, to return to Ex 24, Moses and the chosen elders "see the God of Israel" in v.10 from, apparently, beneath the "sapphire"

---

[12]Most recently, see M. Weinfeld, "*Kabod*," *Theological Dictionary of the Old Testament*, ed. G. J. Botterwick et alii, tr. D. E. Green (Grand Rapids: 1995), Vol. VII: 22–38.

[13]Thus see in contrast Dt 4:12, "The Lord spoke to you out of the fire. You heard the sound of words, but saw no form [*tmwnh*]," and Mettinger's suggestion of a conscious theology of transcendence, strongly aniconic, to supplant the older traditions of divine manifestation specifically linked with the Temple (T. D. N. Mettinger, *Dethronement of Sabaoth: Studies in the Shem and Kabod Theologies* [Lund, 1982], 38–79), and quite distinct (Ibid. 80–115), from the *kavod* theology of Ezekiel and the Priestly source—thus see the link (denied in Dt. 4:12) between *tmwnh* and *kavod* in my remarks below.

pavement of his throne, and eat and drink with him in v.11 as sign of the new relationship inaugurated in the covenant—a scene which serves in Is 24:3 and in rabbinic *midrashim* as an image of the eschaton. The rabbis write of both the biblical and the eschatological events as a sharing with the angels who "feed on the light of the *Shekinah*."[14] Again, in the scene of Moses' encounter with God and transfiguration in Ex 33–34, the Lawgiver asks to see the Glory and is granted the vision of its "back parts." Here the human form of the Presence is presupposed—the huge divine hand sheltering Moses in the cleft of the rock, and then God standing "beside him" in Ex 34:5. We may add to these scenes the innumerable evocations, like Is 6, of God enthroned as a king elsewhere in the prophets and Psalms, or the visitations of the "angel of the Lord," normally a circumlocution for God himself, to the Patriarchs (Gen 18 and 32, esp.), to Joshua (Jos 5:13ff), or to Manoah and his wife in Jdg 13, and who is regularly introduced as "a man [*ish, adam*]."[15] In Nu 12:8 and in Ps 17:15, the divine form (*tmwnh*) is the object of Moses' vision and of the Psalmist's plea. The LXX, significantly, will assimilate the *tmwnh* of both these texts to the word which it uses to render the Hebrew *kavod*, such that Moses sees, and the Psalmist asks to see, God's *doxa*.[16]

We arrive thus back again at Ezekiel's pairing of the Glory with the human likeness, the *demut adam*, which leads us to my second text: the "image [*tslm*] and likeness [*dmwt*] of God" in Gen 1:26–27. In a perceptive article on the theophanies for *Vetus Testamentum* some years ago, James Barr wrote cautiously that "the naturalness or propriety of the human likeness for divine appearances . . . may have been one element in the thinking of those who developed the thought of the *tselem elohim* [image of God]. Certainly," he continues, "the word *tselem* should lead us towards the thought of a kind of manifestation or presentation, such as a statue."[17] The *imago* of Genesis

---

[14]Thus R. Rav in the *Babylonian Talmud*, tractate *Berakot* 17a: "In the coming aeon there is neither eating nor drinking nor procreation . . . rather the righteous sit with their crowns on their head and feed upon the splendor of the Shekinah [*mziv haShekinah*], as it is said, 'And they beheld God and ate and drank'" (Ex 24:11), cited in I. Chernus, *Mysticism in Rabbinic Judaism* (Berlin/NY: 1982), 75. Chernus' whole chapter, "Nourished by the Splendor of the Shekinah," Ibid. 74–87, is of interest for our theme. For the vision of the Glory as eschatological beatitude in the Old Testament, see also Is 40:5.

[15]J. Barr, "Theophany and Anthropomorphism in the Old Testament," *Supplements to Vetus Testamentum* VII (Leiden: 1960), 31–38, here 37.

[16]On the importance of this glory-form equivalence in the LXX and subsequent writings, see J. Fossum, "Jewish-Christian Christology and Jewish Mysticism," *Vigiliae Christianae*, 37 (1983), 260–287, esp. 263 ff.

[17]Barr, "Theophany," 38.

1:26–27 is linked thus—in all likelihood—to the theophany tradition, in particular, I would add, to the *kevod YHWH*, and carries a definite physical sense, that is, it refers to the human body and so at the least suggests that God himself also has a body.[18] The linkage between the Glory and the (human) form certainly appears to have been assumed in the LXX usage I cited above. The human shape as the *imago*, and even Barr's likening of the *tslm* to a statue, appear in an early rabbinic saying attributed to R. Hillel the Elder. Asked why he understands bathing as religious duty, the sage replies by citing Gen 9:6:

> If the statues of kings . . . are scoured and washed by the man appointed to look after them . . . [and who, as a result] is exalted in the company of the great—how much more shall I, who have been created in the image and likeness; as it is written, "For in the image of God made he man."[19]

For R. Hillel, while God is assuredly of a different "stuff" than we—recall the brilliance and fire of Ezekiel's *kavod*—as the wood or stone of an emperor's image differs from the latter's living flesh, it is nonetheless his form which is the model for ours. This view appears to have been a constant in the rabbinic tradition. As Alon Goshen-Gottstein recently pointed out, writing in opposition to Arthur Marmorstein's attempt earlier this century to find both anthropomorphites and anti-anthropomorphites among the sages: "In all of rabbinic literature there is not a single statement that categorically denies that God has a body or form."[20] The rabbis were building here on ancient foundations.

It was the great merit of Gershom Scholem to have first argued the case some sixty years ago for a clearly related continuity between rabbinic mysticism of the divine form and earlier apocalyptic literature, on the one hand, and medieval Kabbala, on the other. He found the linkage in the texts of mystical ascent to the chariot throne, the so-called *hekhalot* literature (from

[18]Thus, for example, G. Quispel, "Ezekiel 1:26 in Jewish Mysticism and Gnosis," *Vigiliae Christianae*, 34 (1980), 9: ". . . the Jewish-biblical concept . . . that God has a shape, and . . . that the image of God in man is to be found not in his soul . . . but in the outward bodily appearance."

[19]R. Hillel in *Leviticus Rabbah* 34.3, tr. J. Israelstam and J. S. Slotki (London: 1939), 428, citing Gen 9:6. I am grateful to M. Smith, "The Image of God: Notes on the Hellenization of Judaism, with Especial Reference to Goodenough's Work on Jewish Symbols," *Bulletin of the John Rylands University Library of Manchester*, 40 (1958), 473–512, here 475–476, for directing me to this passage.

[20]A. Goshen-Gottstein, "The Body as Image of God in Rabbinic Literature," *Harvard Theological Review*, 87.2 (1994), 171–195, here 172.

hekhal, the heavenly palace or temple) and, in a related tradition of the divine form, texts devoted to the *shi'ur qomah,* the "measure of the extent [of the divine body]," which married the traditions of Glory and Image to the *Song of Songs,* especially 5:10–16 on the limbs of the beloved, in order to arrive at descriptions of the presumably mystical vision of the divine body and its inconceivably vast dimensions.[21] His thesis has had a remarkably fertile effect on several related fields of inquiry: the intertestamental era, including Qumran and apocalyptic texts, Christian origins and Gnostic studies, as well as Judaica. For our purposes here, it is particularly his effect on work in apocalyptic literature and Christian origins which is significant. Concerning the former, Scholem's influence appears notably in a new prominence accorded the visionary element in these ancient documents by such scholars as, for example, John Collins and Christopher Rowland, who point especially to the motifs of the heavenly journey, the revelation of the divine throne, and disclosure of heavenly secrets which appear as early as just prior to 200 BC in *I Enoch* 1–36, the "Book of the Watchers."[22] "To speak of apocalyptic," Rowland writes, "is to concentrate on the direct revelation of heavenly mysteries." He adds the observation later on in his book, *The Open Heaven,* that these works also accord an important prominence to the visionary in the very fact that "certain individuals have been given to understand the mysteries of God, man, and the universe."[23]

I suggest that these two elements, the nature and content of the apocalyptic visions, and the recipient of those experiences, are both important for the study of early Christian monasticism. Concerning the latter point, I cannot resist the opportunity here to register my sense that the seer of the apocalyptic texts, transformed as the result of visionary experience, is a basis —arguably even *the* basis—for the eventual portrait of the ascetic holy man, the elder or "Abba," as initiate and guide into heavenly mysteries. The same figure could also serve others as a demonstration for the soteriology of

---

[21]First in G. Scholem, *Major Trends in Jewish Mysticism* (Jerusalem: 1941, rep. 1973), on the *hekalot* texts in 40–79, and then in a series of essays published in his *Jewish Gnosticism, Merkabah Mysticism, and the Talmudic Tradition* (NY: 1960, 2nd ed. 1965), esp. 36–42 on the *shi'ur qomah.* For texts and translations of the *shi'ur qomah,* see M. S. Cohen, *The Shi'ur Qomah: Texts and Recensions* (Tübingen: 1985).

[22]See *Semeia* 14 (1979), ed. by J. Collins, *Apocalypse: The Morphology of a Genre,* particularly Collins' own contributions in the latter, "Towards the Morphology of a Genre," 1–20, and "The Jewish Apocalypses," 21–59 (note esp. 48–49 on Qumran and the *Merkavah*).

[23]C. Rowland, *The Open Heaven: A Study of Apocalyptic in Judaism and Early* Christianity (NY, 1982), 14 and 76, resp.

deification, as in, for example, the hero of Athanasius' *Vita Antonii*.[24] These, together with the other points we have been considering in this section, find startlingly clear expression in the likely first century apocalypse, *II Enoch*. There is first of all a striking anticipation of the rabbinic *shi'ur qomah* tradition in *II Enoch* 39:5–6:

> You, my children, you see my right hand beckoning you . . . but I, I have seen the right hand of the Lord beckoning me, who fills heaven. You, you see the extent of my body . . . but I, I have seen the extent of the Lord, without measure and without analogy.[25]

The patriarch's vision of the divine form is perhaps the most uncompromisingly anthropomorphic of any such in the ancient literature, as again in *II Enoch* 39: "I saw the view of the face of the Lord, like iron made burning hot in a fire . . . and it emits sparks and is incandescent." Finally, there is the note of transformation. Enoch is "clothed with the clothes of glory," anointed with oil whose "shining is like the sun," and so becomes "like one of the glorious ones," that is, the angels.[26] To see the divine body is to become oneself light, "a reflection," as Goshen-Gottstein remarks, "of the body of light"[27] and, I would add, in fulfillment of our creation in the image.

Background, Part II: From Apostle to Apocryphal Acts

Sometime around the turn of the seventh century, the presbyter Timothy of Constantinople compiled a list of the heresies of certain ascetic groups. Eighth on that list is the following: "They say . . . that the body of the Lord was uncircumscribed [*aperigrapton*], like the divine nature."[28] I would like to offer the suggestion that this statement, tantalizingly brief though it be, hints at least at the continuation within Christianity of those traditions of the divine form we have been tracing in pre-Christian and later Jewish sources. What evidence, though, can I offer for the presence of this current in Christianity between first

---

[24]See the discussion of the *Vita Antonii* as theological advertisement in D. Brakke, *Athanasius and the Politics of Asceticism* (Oxford, 1995), 142–200, esp. 153–161, and 239–244.

[25]Translated by F. I. Andersen, in *Old Testament Pseudepigrapha*, ed. J. H. Charlesworth (NY: 1983), Vol. I:163.

[26]Ibid., *OT Pseudepigrapha* I:138–139.

[27]Goshen-Gottstein, "The Body as Image," 188.

[28]Greek text and English translation in C. Stewart, *"Working the Earth of the Heart": The Messalian Controversy in History, Texts, and Language to A.D. 431* (Oxford/NY: 1991), 278.

century apocalyptic and seventh century heresy hunting? I submit that there is a very great deal of evidence, indeed, though much of it lies in obscure, out of the way places, such as in the Old Testament Pseudepigrapha themselves, nearly all of which, like *I* and *II Enoch*, were to the best of our knowledge preserved exclusively by Christians (and, from the fourth century on, perhaps primarily by monks), together with New Testament apocrypha, with patristic and monastic polemic against our themes (as, for example, in Origen, or in his great admirer in the Egyptian desert, Evagrius Ponticus[29]), with the universal, pre-Nicene patristic tendency to identify the visible manifestations of God in the Old Testament with the Second Person, and with the odd remark or detail dropped here and there, such as, for example, Abba Silvanus' visionary ascent to heaven to stand before "the Glory" in the *Apophthegmata*,[30] or the mid-fourth century *Liber Graduum*'s casual equation of "our Lord (*moran*)" with the "Glory [*shubho*]" which appeared to Moses and all the prophets "as a man (*a[i]k bar nosho*).[31]

Since I have neither time nor space to expand on this list in the present essay, allow me simply to point to a few suggestive elements in the earliest Christian writer whose works we possess, St. Paul, and then conclude this background survey with one citation from a New Testament apocryphon from around the turn of the third century. Paul calls Christ "the Lord of Glory" in I Cor 2:8. In 2 Cor 3:7–4:6, he compares Moses' encounter with the Glory atop Sinai and consequent, temporary transfiguration with the greater and permanent transformation afforded the Christian in Christ, thus at least implying that Christ was himself the Glory that Moses had glimpsed.[32]

---

[29]For Origen and anthropomorphism, see D.O. Paulsen, "Early Christian Belief in a Corporeal Deity: Origen and Augustine as Reluctant Witnesses," *Harvard Theological Review*, 83.2 (1990), 105–16.

[30]Silvanus 3 (*PG* LXV:409A); and for monastic transformations in the *Apophthegmata* reminiscent of the transfigurations of apocalyptic seers, see again Silvanus 12 (412C), Sisoes 14 (396B), Pambo 12 (372A), Joseph of Panephysis 7 (229CD), and Arsenius 27 (96BC).

[31]*Liber Graduum* XXVIII.10–11, in *Patrologia Syriaca* III, ed. M. Kmosko, 802, ll. 4–24. In the latter's Latin rendering: "Item apparuit Moysi in monte velut homo [*a(i)k bar nosho*] . . . et videre gloriam Domini [*moryo ahid kul*, i.e., of the Father] omnipotens [then quoting Ex. 33:11, 25:9–10, and Nu 12:8]," and below, "Vides quomodo Dominus [*moran*, "our Lord," i.e., the Son] ostenderit velut homo [*a(i)k bar nosho*] omnibus prophetis."

[32]On Christ as the Glory of 2 Cor 3–4, see C. Stockhausen, *Moses' Veil and the Glory of the New Covenant*, Analecta Biblica 116 (Rome: 1989), esp. 176–177; A. A. Moses, *Matthew's Transfiguration Story and Jewish-Christian Controversy* (Sheffield: 1996), esp. 239–244; A. Segal, *Paul the Convert: The Apostolate and Apostasy of Saul the Pharisee* (New Haven, 1990), esp. 9–11, 58–64, and 152–157; and C. C. Newman, *Paul's Glory Christology: Tradition and Rhetoric* (Leiden/NY, 1992), 229–235.

The apostle speaks in the third person of his own rapture to "the third heaven," "Paradise," and subsequent "revelations" in 2 Cor 12:1–7.[33] By now, this is surely familiar territory: Sinai, the Glory, transfiguration, and heavenly ascent. "It may be," as Martin Hengel has remarked, "that Paul's contemporaries and opponents in Corinth had much more to say about the Glory and [Christ's] sharing of the throne [with the Father] . . . than Paul would have preferred," but, as Hengel himself goes on to assert,[34] the experience of 2 Cor 12 was indeed a throne vision, akin to what we have seen earlier in apocalyptic literature, and which appears later on in Jewish tradition, such as the story of the four sages' entry into the "Garden," *pardes*, found in the Talmud.[35] Likewise, Luke's account of the Damascus Road conversion, especially the versions in Acts 9 and 22, recall the elements of light and overwhelming force ubiquitous in the throne visions—though without the heavenly setting. There is enough in just these texts to suggest, as Alan Segal and others have argued recently, the possibility of affinities between Paul and the later rabbinic *merkavah* traditions.[36]

We arrive clearly at the tradition of the glorious form in the opening to the hymn of Phil 2:6–11: "Who though he was in the form of God [*en morphē theou hyparchon*] . . ." Gilles Quispel, who was, I think, one of the first to link this phrase with the Glory and image traditions twenty years ago, summed up his argument as follows: "The implication of the *morphē* is obviously that it is the divine body, identical with the *kavod*, Glory, and equivalent with the *eikōn*."[37] The phrase, "body of his glory" [*sōma tēs dōxes autou*], to which Christians are called to be "conformed" (*symmorphon*) in Phil. 3:21, recalls the "body of the glory" (*guf haKavod*), or "body of the Shekinah" (*guf haShekinah*), of later rabbinic and kabbalistic thought, as well as, of course, the manlike form of the Glory which appears in apocalyptic

---

[33]Here see esp. J. Tabor, *Things Unutterable: Paul's Ascent to Heaven in its Greco-Roman, Judaic and Early Christian Contexts* (Lanham, MD, 1986) 19–21 and 113–124.

[34]Hengel, "Setze dich zur meinen Rechten!," in *Le trône de Dieu*, ed. M. Philonenko (Tübingen, 1993), 108–94, here 136.

[35]*Babylonian Talmud*, tractate Hagigah 14b; *Palestinian Talmud*, Hagigah 2.1, 77b; and *Tosefta*, Hagigah 2.3–4. For discussion of the sources and the scholarship from Bousset to Scholem and Schäfer, see D. Halperin, *Faces in the Chariot: Early Jewish Responses to Ezekiel's Vision* (Tübingen, 1988), 11–37, for the sceptical side, and C.R.A. Morray-Jones, "Paradise Revisited (2 Lev 12:2–12): The Jewish Mystical Background of Paul's Apostolate," *Harvard Theological Review*, 86 (1993), 177–217 and 265–92, for argument in favor of a mystical tradition in connection with Paul.

[36]Segal, *Paul the Convert*, loc.cit.

[37]Quispel, "Ezekiel 1:26," 9.

texts, in the Pentateuch, and in the throne visions of the psalms and prophets.[38] The deutero-pauline epistles, Ephesians and Colossians, feature similar expressions. Eph 4:13 calls on its hearers to arrive at "the perfect man [*andra teleion*], to the measure [*metron*] of the stature of the fulness of Christ." The "man" and the phrase, "measure of the stature," in this verse are at the least reminiscent of what we find in the phrase, *shi'ur qomah* (indeed, the Greek and Hebrew phrases are identical in meaning), and the Rabbinic tradition.[39] The divine, that is, the preexistent and not just postresurrectional body of the Savior appears very clearly in Col 1:10–15. The Lord is "the *eikōn* of the invisible God, the first-born of all creation, for in him all things . . . were created." Here Christ, Jarl Fossum writes, is "the physical embodiment of divinity . . . the *kavod* of God which could be seen . . . the Heavenly Man,"[40] which last expression we also find nearly verbatim in St. Paul: *ho deuteros anthrōpos ex ouranou* in I Cor 15:47, and two verses later his promise that we shall carry the "image [*eikōn*] of the heavenly [man]."

In the Colossians passage, Christ's body contains the universe, and this may in turn provide a key for the interpretation of the *kenosis* of Phil. 2:7, that is, that it denotes precisely the contrast between the weak, tiny and sinful "body of our humility," which the Savior assumes for our sake, with the cosmic "body of his glory" (both bodies in Phil 3:21) in which we are called to participate through his saving condescension. Like the *shi'ur qomah* texts, the *metron* of Eph 4:13 and the emptying of Phil 2:7 deal in measurements. The *kenosis*, as Stroumsa has suggested, was "an originally mythical conception rather than being simply metaphorical . . . The Incarnation implied that Christ [gave] up the greatness of his previous cosmic dimensions."[41] Like the *shi'ur qomah*, and other *merkavah* texts as well, the glorious body is also seeable, if only under special circumstances. It can be experienced, as we saw St. Paul himself testify. Unlike the later Jewish writings, however, and of importance for subsequent Christian—especially, I would add, for ascetic Christian—tradition, the possibility of this experience has eschatological and

[38]Scholem, *Jewish Gnosticism*, 36–42, and more recently, A. Segal, *Two Powers in Heaven: Early Rabbinic Reports about Christianity and Gnositicism* (Leiden, 1977), 210–212; Fossum, "Jewish-Christian Christology"; and G. G. Stroumsa, "Form(s) of God: Some Notes on Metatron and Christ," *Harvard Theological Review*, 76.3 (1983), 269–288, esp. 282–287.

[39]On Eph 4:13, Phil 2:6–7 and 3:21, see the brief but penetrating remarks of M. Fishbane, "The Measures of God's Glory in Ancient Midrash," in *Midrash and Christos*, ed. I. Gruenwald, S. Shaked, and G. G. Stroumsa (Tübingen: 1992), 70–72.

[40]J. Fossum, "The Magharians: A Pre-Christian Jewish Sect and Its Significance for the Study of Gnosticism and Christianity," *Henoch*, IX (1987), 338–339.

[41]Stroumsa, "Form(s) of God," 283.

soteriological significance. Whether here or in the world to come, it is the very stuff of transfiguration and beatitude.[42]

We find a remarkable reprise of just these Glory and Image traditions in one last witness, the late second century, early third century *Acts of John*. Chapter 90 of that work is set at the transfiguration:

> He takes me, James and Peter to the mountain where it was his custom to pray, and we saw on him a light which it is not possible for mortal men using words to express what sort it was . . . And he takes us three up again to the mountain . . . and I, because he loved me . . . get close to him and stand looking at his backparts . . . his feet were whiter than snow, so that the ground was lit up by his feet, and . . . his head stretched up to heaven . . . and [then] he, turning around, appeared as a little man.[43]

Fossum, in an article appropriately entitled "Posteriori dei," pointed out the echo here of Moses' vision in Ex 33–34, especially in John's view of Christ's "backparts," and concludes: "The *Acts of John*, chapter 90, portray the transformed Christ as the heavenly Glory. This is further corroborated by the exceedingly great stature . . . ascribed to him"[44]—the *shi'ur qomah* parallel, in short. I would myself add that Christ's reversion to ordinary stature, becoming again "a little man" at the end of the episode, is again a recollection of the *kenosis* and the "body of our humility"/"body of his glory" contrast of Phil 2:7 and 3:21.

With this sketch of the background in place, it is time to turn to our controversy.

---

[42]The rabbinic *merkabah* tradition appears to have played down the *visio gloriae* as an eschatological anticipation. See Chernus, *Rabbinic Mysticism*, 88–107. By contrast, see the discussion of Cassian, Evagrius, and of the *Macarian Homilies* below and nn. 77–79.

[43]*Acta Ioannis* 90, in *Acta Apostolorum Apocrypha*, Bonnet ed., II.1:199–200. For similar elements in the apocryphal Thomas tradition, see the *Gospel of Thomas*, esp. *logia* 13, 50, 59 and 82–83, together with A. DeConick, *Seek to See Him: Ascent and Vision Mysticism in the Gospel of Thomas* (Leiden: 1996), esp. 43–125 on the *imago* and *kavod* traditions. Cf. also the *Acta Thomae*, esp. the clothing with the robe of light and the luminous image, increase in stature, and ascent to heaven in 112, *AAA* II.2:223–224, to worship the "radiance [*pheggos*] of the Father," i.e., Christ.

[44]J. Fossum, *The Image of the Invisible God: Essays on the Influence of Jewish Mysticism on Early Christology* (Freiburg/Göttingen, 1995), 106.

The Anthropomorphite Controversy, Part I: In the Aftermath of Nicea

The Anthropomorphite Controversy was played out against the background of the most important doctrinal development of the fourth century: the debate over the Nicene *homoousion* and the latter's emergence at century's end as the official teaching of the imperial church. I read this development as necessarily affecting the traditions of the Glory, chiefly by way of cementing the latter's transition from a term intimately associated with and occasionally identifying the Second Person, the "heavenly man," to its employment as a synonym for, to paraphrase an expression from Evagrius, the shared and blessed light of the consubstantial Trinity.[45] The "heavenly man" becomes entirely the Word *incarnate*, and does so because the Logos can no longer serve, as he certainly does for Origen, Clement, Philo, and in a different way for those people and works we have just finished considering or alluding to, as mediator by virtue of his very essence. His being is now one with the Father and Spirit. They constitute a single *ousia*, and thus share in a single, absolutely transcendent divinity—infinite, unknowable, invisible, etc., or, briefly, in all the apophatic qualifiers and terms of transcendence that had formerly been ascribed to the Father alone. This "paradigm shift" is well enough known for me not to have to belabor it here, but what I do feel obliged to underline is the seal which the imperial church in effect set on the labors of an Origen through its final approval of the *homoousion*. Obviously, I do not mean by this either Origen's subordinationism or all of his quirks—double creation, inadequate treatment of the material cosmos, christology of the *nous* of Jesus, *apokatastasis*, etc.—which were the cause of debate and adjustment for more centuries to come, and which are just as well known as the Nicene shift in trinitarian understanding, but rather his overall project of rationalization and spiritualization or, put another way, his baptism of Hellenistic philosophy. Here, too, he was scarcely the first in line to engage in this project, but he was surely its most powerful and influential advocate in the centuries prior to Nicea. In a nutshell, the *homoousion* confirmed forever the place and necessity of philosophical expression in the self-articulation of the Christian faith, whether that articulation dealt with doctrine *per se* or, as in our case, with "spirituality." To borrow a pungent phrase, Nicea and its aftermath

---

[45]For Evagrius on the "light of the Holy Trinity," see again *de orat.* 73–74, with "Chapters Supplementary to the *Kephalaia Gnostica*" 4 and 26, in W. Frankenburg, *Evagrius Pontikus* (Berlin: 1912), 427 and 450.

represented "Philo's revenge on the rabbis."[46] The full meaning of this shift was bound thus to meet opposition since, as in the case of the monastic anthropomorphites whom we shall take up next, it meant that a most ancient way of understanding and approaching the Christian mystery had become an anachronism. They were slow to become aware of it, especially since most of them doubtless considered themselves orthodox communicants and defenders of the Great Church. I would therefore like to take this opportunity to suggest that the rumblings in 399 were but the single instance of a vast realignment which stretched over the entire extent of the Christian Church and which required decades for its completion, and in some places—as Timothy of Constantinople's list seems to indicate—centuries.

The Anthropomorphite Controversy, Part II: Cassian and the Life of Apa Aphou

Cassian's tenth *Conversation* opens with the discussion and rebuttal of the Egyptian anthropomorphites. In view of what we have seen above concerning the Glory and theophany, it is surely not accidental that this is the *Conversation* which is devoted to Abba Isaac's discussion of "imageless prayer" and the *visio dei*. A certain old and devout monk, Serapion,[47] is enlisted as Abba Isaac's foil. Serapion is aghast at the Patriarch Theophilus' "new-fangled teaching [*novella persuasio*)" on the incorporeality of the image of God as taught by Genesis 1:26. Once he has registered his protest, however, he is promptly pounded into submission by the arguments of a learned deacon, Photinus, visiting from Cappadocia. The latter explains that the "divine nature is incorporeal, without composition and simple," and that God's *maiestas* is therefore "incomprehensible and invisible."[48] The *imago dei* of Gen 1:26 must therefore also be understood "spiritually [*spiritualiter*]," and the patriarch was thus correct to "deny that almighty God [*deus omnipotens*] is of a human form."[49] Serapion is silenced, but later that evening at vespers cannot contain his distress: "Woe is me!" he weeps, "They have taken my God away from me, and now I no longer know whom I may have to hold, or whom I may call upon anymore, or whom adore!"[50]

[46]Expression used by a friend, Professor R. D. Young of Catholic University.
[47]Cassian, *Collatio* X.3–4 (288–289; ET: 126–127).
[48]Ibid. X.3 (288:8 and 23; ET: 126).
[49]Ibid. (288:19), and X.2 (287: 16).
[50]Ibid. (289:12–14; ET: 126).

The old man's grief provides Cassian with his opening to move on to the real subject of the *Conversation*, prayer in its highest form, though we certainly continue to pick up traces of polemic along the way. Abba Isaac is asked how so good and pious an elder could have been so wrong—indeed, put in peril of his soul—as to subscribe to the anthropomorphite "heresy."[51] Isaac replies that Serapion's lack of instruction in the "nature and substance [*natura atque substantia*]" of the Godhead is at fault. The matter "of his abominable interpretation [*detestandae huius interpretationis*]" of Gen 1:26 betrays a residual paganism, like that condemned by Paul in Rom 1:23, "exchanging the glory [*gloriam*] of the incorruptible God for a human likeness," or by Jeremiah's similar charge against Israel (Jer 2:11).[52] True prayer, on the other hand, requires an inner eye purged of everything material and earthly, and that purification includes even the memory of any shape or form [*forma*]."[53] In order to see Jesus in the splendor of his *maiestatis*, one must be free of that "Jewish weakness" condemned by Paul in 2 Cor 5:16, since the Lord is no longer to be known "according to the flesh."[54] The Abba continues with an evocation of the Transfiguration. Only purified eyes, by which the elder means the eyes of the soul cleansed of matter and form, may "gaze [*speculantur*]" on Jesus in his divinity.[55] The monk must therefore withdraw with Christ to the "mountain of solitude" so that the Lord "may reveal," even if not so clearly as to Peter, James and John on Mt. Tabor, "the glory of his countenance and the image of his splendor [*gloriam vultus eius et claritatis revelat imaginem*]."[56] Thus, even in this life, one may enjoy a foretaste of heaven and, filled with the indwelling love of the Father and the Son (citing here Jn 17:22 and 24–26), be joined to them in order to become oneself a single prayer without end.[57]

The argument is nearly pure Origen, or at least Origen as mediated by Nicea and Evagrius, and shorne of the double creation. Its core are two of the key texts which the Alexandrian had deployed in *On Genesis* and *On Romans* against the anthropomorphites of his own day: Gen 1:26 and Rom

[51]Ibid., X.5 (291:5–6); cf. also X.2 (287:7–8).
[52]Ibid. (290:22–291:9; ET: 128).
[53]Ibid. (291:11–16).
[54]Ibid. X.6 (291:1–17). Note also the *sub illa quodammodo Iudaica infirmitate* of 291:25; and the *in maiestatis suae gloriae* of 291:22–23.
[55]Ibid.
[56]Ibid. 292:1–13 (ET: 128–129). Note the parallel drawn between the Apostles on Mt. Tabor and Moses and Elijah on Sinai and Horeb (i.e., Ex. 24 and 33–34 once again, and I Kg 19).
[57]Ibid. 293:18–294:2 (ET: 130).

1:23.[58] Cassian adds the references to Jn 17, which were not in Origen's treatise *On Prayer*, but the emphasis on Christ's indwelling is the same in both.[59]
The account of prayer is, again, largely what one may find in Origen's treatise on that subject, particularly the cleansing away of form and matter, and
the "eyes of the soul."[60] There are some important differences, however. First,
there is the background of the *homoousion*. Serapion is not merely stupid, a
vir simplicissimus, and uneducated, but is specifically uninstructed in the
"divine nature and substance," that is, in the one *ousia* of God shared by
Father and Son. The divine *substantia* is equated with the Son's *maiestas*,
while the same holds for the latter's divine *forma*, *claritas*, *gloria*, *conspectus*,
vultus, etc. This lack of instruction in the truth of God's essence, which is now
also the ecumenical teaching of the Church, makes Cassian's foil not merely
a bumpkin, but a heretic, however inadvertently, and classed—not altogether
consistently—at once with pagans and Jews. The phrase, "Jewish weakness"
also appears in Origen, and by now we should recognize it as code for a real
exegetical tradition, whose outlines Cassian may well have known, but he is
not about to give it a hearing.[61] Serapion, unlike Origen's lively anthropo-

[58]See n. 69 below and, for a more general account of Origen's program see his *Comment.
in Jo.* 32, where, defining *doxa* in Jn 12:41 (Isaiah saw "his glory"), he notes Ex 33–34 and I Kg
8, then in the NT the Transfiguration in Lk 9:28, esp. "they saw his glory" (9:32), and concludes
with 2 Cor 3:7–4:6, in order to discover two senses to the word: first and generally, a divine
epiphany; second: "the visible manifestation of God that *is contemplated by the mind which* . . .
has ascended above all material things" (SC 385, pp. 328–344; ET: *Commentary on the Gospel
according to John*, in Fathers of the Church, 89, pp.404–11. Emphasis added). The ascent
becomes at once a stripping away of matter and an inward movement. This is the basis for both
Cassian and his master, Evagrius.

[59]See his *On Prayer*, ed. Koeteschau, *Origenes Werke* II:297–403, ET: Chadwick, *Alexandrian Christianity* (Philadelphia, 1954), 238–329, esp. the following: IX.2 on partaking of the
divine glory (318–319; ET: 256); XX.2 on the vision as within the intellect (344; 278); XXII.4
on the believer's incorporation into the body of Christ's glory, citing I Cor 14:49 and Phil 3:21
(348–349; 288); XXIII on "demythologizing" the throne texts, esp. Is 66:1 (351; 284–285);
XXV.3 on every saint as "city and kingdom" of God because of the latter's indwelling, citing Jn
14:21 (357; 289); and XXV.3 on each saint as paradise in whom God and Christ are enthroned,
again citing Is 66:1 (359; 291). Chadwick, esp. 355–356, notes that Origen is addressing himself to anthropomorphite opinions here.

[60]On the expression, "eyes of the understanding," see again *On Prayer* IX.2 (Koeteschau
318–319; ET: 256); and on the "spiritual senses," *Dialogue with Heraclides*, SC 67 pp. 78–102;
and Chadwick, *Alexandrian Christianity*, 449–452.

[61]See E. Wolfson, "Images of God's Feet: Some observations on the Divine Body in Judaism,"
in *People of the Body: Jews and Judaism from am Embodied Perspective*, ed. H. Eilberg Schwarz
(Albany, 1992), 143–181, here 132, on Origen *vs.* the literal reading of Is 66:1 in *Selecta in Gen.*
(cf. nn. 54 and 59 above): "A literal reading of Is 66: 1 is, in fact, an exact parallel to what one
finds in the *shi'ur qomah* material." "Jewish weakness" is therefore "not a stock phrase against
'Jewish' literalists . . . but represents a very specific exegesis."

morphites, whom we can almost hear citing their several texts, has only Gen 1:26 to quote, and nothing very much to say thereafter. He is a cipher, a polemical straw man.[62] The second point worth signaling is Cassian's emphasis on ascent, the "mountain of solitude," here an inner event or condition, and the *visio dei claritatis* as clearly an imminent and not just post mortem possibility, partial to be sure, but real nonetheless.[63] The last is not so clear in Origen, at least so far as I could tell, though it certainly is in Cassian's teacher, Evagrius, and it is a difference from the Alexandrian master that marks an important note of agreement between both sides of the monastic debate—a point I shall come back to in my concluding remarks.

From a muddled and ignorant Serapion, we move to a confident and even sophisticated statement of the anthropmorphite position in *The Life of Apa Aphou of Pemdje*. The latter comes to us from a Coptic MS rescued from fragments and published late last century. In 1915–1917, Drioton republished it, together with a French translation and accompanying commentary, while Florovsky supplied an English translation in the course of his reply to Drioton. Both men, together with the original editor and publisher, Reveillout, and more recently Gould and Clark, agree that the *Life* is a rare, not to say unique souce from the people whom Cassian, Socrates, *et alii* were writing against.[64] Florovsky feels that the document's value as a witness is enhanced by the fact, as he sees it, that the Egyptian editor or compiler is free of polemic and writing probably at a somewhat later period after the heat of the controversy had died down.[65] I am not so sure myself about the lack of polemic. While it is true that, unlike Cassian, the author does not use such harsh expressions as "stupid heresy" (*inepta quoque haeresis*) and "simpleton" (*simplicissimus*) for the beliefs and person he is opposing, the ease with which Apa Aphou triumphs in his exchange does somewhat resemble Deacon Photinus' dispatch of poor Abba Serapion. The Patriarch Theophilus, who is Aphou's interlocutor, does have a little more to say than Serapion had had, but not much. The advantage is wholly on Aphou's side.

The scene from the *Life* that we are interested in opens with the elder trou-

---

[62]See C. Stewart, *Cassian the Monk* (Oxford, 1998), 86–90, on Serapion as possibly a literary creation.

[63]See Ibid., 95–99, esp. the citation of Cassian's *De Incarnatione* 3.6.3 on p. 96: "I see the ineffable illumination, I see the unexplainable brilliance, I see the splendor unbearable for human weakness and beyond what mortal eyes can bear, the majesty of God shining in unimaginable light."

[64]Most recently Gould, "The Image of God," 550.

[65]Florovsky, "Theophilus of Alexandria and Apa Aphou," 100–101.

bled by the Patriarch's infamous encyclical which, we are told, had sought to "exalt the Glory [*mpeooy*] of God" by denying the image in man. Encouraged by an angelic visitation, the old man goes off to Alexandria to have a heart to heart talk with the archbishop.[66] In the first section of the ensuing exchange, Aphou reproaches Theophilus with Gen 1:26, and the patriarch replies with the assertion that the *imago* was lost with the Fall. Aphou counters by citing Gen 9:6, in order to imply that the image endured. This is the same tack that Epiphanius' Audians had also taken, the logic being that, since God is telling Noah that murder is forbidden because man is "made in the image," and since Noah is a postlapsarian figure, the *imago* likewise remained after the Fall.[67] The same thinking may have been involved in R. Hillel's citation of Gen 9:6 that I quoted earlier. Theophilus, in any case, then objects that the *imago* is not consonant with human weakness and filth. Can the "true and unapproachable light" (cf. I Tim. 6:16), he asks, have anything to do with a beggar defecating in the gutter?[68]

So far, then, we find the following: the Genesis texts, their connection with the language of glory and light, and Theophilus' assumption, redolent of Origen on the same subject, that the corruptible body is inadequate to God.[69] In what follows, however, we break into new and interesting territory. Aphou appeals to the Eucharist. If, he argues, the latter is truly the body of Christ, and if Christ, who said "I am the living bread come down from heaven" (Jn 6:51), is the very same one who spoke to Noah and warned him against murder because "man has been created according to the image of God," then the patriarch, by acknowledging the sacramental reality, must perforce recognize the *imago*'s presence even in fallen humanity.[70] The elder concludes, and I translate with gratitude from Drioton's French:

---

[66]Drioton, "La discussion," 95 (see l.10 for "the Glory [*mpeooy*] of God").

[67]Ibid. 97. See Epiphanius, *Panarion*, 70.2.4–5, GCS (Berlin: 1985), 243; ET: F. Williams, *The Panarion of Epiphanius of Salamis* (Leiden: 1987), Vol. II:404. For discussion, see Golitzin, "Forma lui Dumnezeu," *Mistagogia*, 188–192.

[68]Ibid. 98. On Theophilus' appeal to I Tim 6:16, see Gould, "Image of God," 551.

[69]See, for example, Origen's account of the creation of the "two men" of Gen 1:26 (the intellect) and 2:7 (the body) in the "Prologue"to his commentary to the Song of Songs (SC 375, p. 92): "We find mention of the creation of two men, the first made according to the image and likeness of God, the second molded from muddy earth [*e limo terrae fictum*]"; and recall above, n.58, the *Commentary on John*'s "stripping of materiality" on the inner ascent to the *visio gloriae*. Florovsky, "Anthropomorphites," 91–95, is particularly sensitive to these echoes of Origen as reflected, here, in Cassian.

[70]Drioton, "La discussion," 99.

As for the glory of the greatness [*peooy de mpmegethos*] of God, which it is impossible for anyone to see because of its incomprehensible light, and as for human weakness and imperfection . . . we think that it is like a king who orders "the making of an image which everyone is to acknowledge as the image of the king." Yet everyone [also] knows perfectly well that it is only [made] of wood, together with other elements . . . [but] the king has said, "This is my image" . . . How much the more so, then, with man . . . ?[71]

Aphou's thinking is densely phrased and quite complex, qualities which have led all the distinguished scholars who have dealt with it so far into misinterpretation. Drioton got very close in his recognition that Aphou believed in a divine body, "clothed with incomprehensible light," which provided the model for our own bodies,[72] but his simple equation of this with the Audians prevented him from looking more closely. For, unlike the Audians, and here Florovsky had the right of it, the elder is not talking about the Father, or the Trinity, but the Second Person, the Son, though not the Son simply *incarnate*. There Drioton was correct: the divine body pre-exists the historical Incarnation, and in the latter point lies the value of Stroumsa's recent contribution, that is, the presence here of a Jewish—or, more accurately, Second Temple—mystical traditon of the divine form. Gould rightly picks up on the importance of the Eucharistic allusion, but his accounting also misses the mark by moving too swiftly to an invocation of mystery, after the example of Epiphanius in the latter's quarrel with the Audians on the image, and together, perhaps (though not mentioned specifically in his article), with a couple of passages in the *Apophthegmata Patrum*.[73]

I do not think that we have here a simple equivalence of the sort that would have Aphou saying in effect: "If you believe the words of institution, 'this is my body,' you are also obliged to believe the words of the same Lord to Noah, 'this is my image' "; and then adding: "But how the eucharistic body and *imago* are what they are, we cannot know since this is a mystery." If this were the case, then surely the elder would have been better served to quote one of the Synoptic narratives of the Last Supper, or else Paul in I Cor 11:24.

[71]Ibid. 99–100, the "Glory of the Greatness [*peooy de pmegethos*]" on last 2 lines of p.99.
[72]Ibid. 126–127.
[73]Gould, "The Image of God," 551–552. Note the latter's appeal, 553 (consciously paralleling Eusebius' invocation of mystery for the *imago* in *Panarion* 70.3.1–5), to Sopatros 1 (*PG* LXV:413A) in the *Apophthegmata*. He could as well have cited Daniel 7 (156D–160A).

Instead, he appeals to Jn 6:51 and the "living bread come down from heaven." I maintain that his choice is deliberate here, and that answering the "why" of it will supply us with an important key to understanding his argument. The latter will indeed provide us with mystery in plenty, but in just a little stranger form than we are used to.

Let us proceed step by step to assemble what I take to be the elements of Aphou's thinking, beginning with a rehearsal of the texts involved: Gen 1:26, Gen 9:6, I Tim 6:16, and then Jn 6:51. Second, let us recall the vocabulary in the order that it appears: the Glory of God (and later, Glory of the Greatness), the image, "unapproachable" or "incomprehensible light," the body of Christ, the "living bread come down from heaven," and the image or statue of the king. Third, there is the passage I cited earlier from R. Hillel, the parallel between the statue of the king and the *imago*. From Hillel, let us move, fourth, to James Barr's comparison between the image of God and a statue, suggested by the Hebrew word itself, *tselem*, and the connection he suggested—if very delicately—between the idea of the image and the manlike appearances of God's fiery Glory, the *kavod*, usually in the form of a king enthroned. We then bring to the bar, fifth, the continuous witness to a mysticism of the divine form, beginning with Second Temple apocalypses and extending into the rabbinic era—from *I Enoch*, as it were, to *3 Enoch*. Sixth, we recall the echoes of this tradition that we find in the New Testament, the "Heavenly Man" of I Cor 15:47 and 49, the *morphē* of Phil 2:6 and the "body of humiliy"/"body of glory" contrast of 3:21, the *eikôn* of Col 1:15, and the *metron tes hēlikias* of Eph 4:13, to which I would add the Son of Man come "down from heaven" in Jn 3:13, Christ as light (many texts, e.g., Jn 1:9 and 8:12), as "Lord of Glory" in I Cor 2:9, and as "King of kings" (e.g., Rev 17:14), to cite some of the most important loci, and the equation which all of these texts, especially when *taken together*, presume thus as obtaining between Christ, Glory, Image, Light, Body, the Heavenly Man "come down from heaven," and the King Enthroned. I am convinced that this is exactly what is going on in the *Life of Aphou*. We have the same equation: image = Christ = bread "come down from heaven" = "Glory of the Greatness" clothed with "incomprehensible light." The "come down from heaven" of the bread in Jn 6:51 matches the "come down from heaven" of the Son of Man in Jn 3:13. Both are speaking of the descent of the Heavenly Man, the Glory, and this is why, I submit, we find Aphou's otherwise puzzling invocation of the Johannine text.

I have not yet finished my assembly, however. In connection with the "heavenly bread," we have also to recall, seventh, what I mentioned some time ago, the rabbinic *midrashim* which speak, first, of the "light of the *Shek-inah*" as the food of the angels, second, of the same light as the meal enjoyed by the elders of Israel who ate and drank before the Presence in Ex 24:10–11, and, third, the latter as anticipation of the eschaton.[74] Tying it all up and together, and providing as well evidence that neither Aphou—nor I—invented all of these connections, but that many of them had been around, and moreover around in Egypt, for some time, there is, eighth, the witness of the *Excerpta ex Theodoto* where we find Clement of Alexandria calling Christ "the Power," "the light unapproachable," form, "Face of the Father," and "the heavenly bread" giving "life as nourishment and knowledge" to both angels and the saints.[75] Now, it is true that Clement does not bring up as such the notion of the *imago*, though he does mention specifically the Son's heavenly form and body.[76] He wants these ideas spiritualized, as did Philo before him, and overall treads gingerly around the matter of the human form of the Second Person. Aphou, on the other hand, is explicit and emphatic. The same traditions appear in him in purer form, which is to say that I take him to be untroubled by the difficulties that they would pose for someone shaped by Hellenistic philosophy, such as, precisely, a Clement or a Philo. The point here is that we do find the same traditions in both men, especially the identification of the Son of God with the "unapproachable light," and the linkage which both understand Jn 6:51 as supplying between the Eucharist, on the one hand, and feeding on the light of the *Shekinah*, the Man from Heaven, on the other.

Given this background, the exchange with Theophilus makes perfect sense from beginning to end. The latter's attempt to "exalt the Glory" by denying the image would appear to Aphou as a flat contradiction or, worse, as a denial of Christ in favor of some abstract divinity. So far, then, Florovsky had it mostly right, but not in what follows. Christ, the Son of God, *is* the image. To misuse a modern American idiom, he is quite literally "the Man." Aphou thus goes off to explain things to the patriarch and instruct him, patiently and kindly, in the basics he seems to have forgotten. These include the making of man after the model in heaven, who is the *kavod*, the *morphē theou*, and, when Theophilus, probably confused by all this Greek philo-

---

[74]See n. 14 above.

[75]See Clement, *Excerpta ex Theodoto* (SC 23), 4 (58–61) on Christ as the "Power" of the Father and on his light at Tabor; as himself the "unapproachable light" and "Face of the Father" in 10.5 (78–81); and, following the invocation of his face "as bright as the sun" (Mt 17:2), as the "bread from heaven" given as "nourishment and knowledge" in 12.4 (82–85).

[76]Ibid. 10.1 (76).

sophical business, together with the baneful effect of Origen's related mis-
chief, tries to bring up the discrepancy between corrupt human flesh and
divine light, the gentle reminder of the Eucharist as marking the new covenant
through the regular and direct anticipation of that day when we shall be fed
by the light of the Body of the Glory—and, indeed, where we are fed even
now by the same Body. Israel ate from it only once, in other words, but we
have it as our "daily bread." The good bishop can surely not have forgotten
that! Then we have the little illustration of the king's image to wrap it all up:
the living flesh of the emperor is to the wood of his image as the living and
"incomprehensible light" of God's Glory, Christ, is to our flesh. True, the discrepancy is vast, absolute in fact, but then he has given us that same flesh of
light to eat, has he not? And—which is also not asked openly, but surely we
can hear by now the force of a series of unspoken, mild, but still insistent
questions directed at the archbishop—eating it, do we not become it? And in
what else would his Eminence say our salvation might consist? And so, what
else in turn could Theophilus do but surrender? As indeed, according to the
Life—and according to Sozomen and Socrates as well—he did.

A Few Concluding Thoughts

Some or most of the monks who stormed the patriarchal palace and cried first
for Theophilus' blood, and then later for Origen's, may well have been ignorant simpletons, but if so, they were simpletons in defense of traditions that
were much older and more sophisticated than they. Apa Aphou is neither a
naive country bumpkin nor a fanatic. His thought is neither crude, nor obvious, nor simplistic. It is scriptural, entirely, but in no way some rough and
ready literalism. The voice we hear in the *Life* is that of a teacher who is
patient, humbly remorseless, and wise and confident in his learning. The latter is not the product of the schools of Athens or of glittering Alexandria, but
learning it remains all the same: complex, subtle, allusive and indirect, content to evoke with a minimum of words and texts whole clusters of association, and all the while—since its workings are never without discipline or
forethought—directing its listener to certain definite conclusions. I might be
tempted to call it the learning of the deep desert, but I think it is a good deal
older than the monastic movement as we know the latter from its emergence
in the fourth century. It is Christian, profoundly, but not quite the Christianity that we are used to, since its profundity draws so very deeply and confi-

dently on the wealth of its Jewish roots. Some of those roots strike us, as they struck other and equally Christian contemporaries at the time, as outlandish and quite incredible, but they are very, very old. They antedate Paul and the Gospels, though I think that they are also the stuff out of which the Gospels and Paul's theology are largely made, and they reach back into the foundations of Israel and, even before, into the ancient Near East. Aphou's learning is one which lives in myth, but never in foolishness, and it is, again, supremely confident—a word that I have now used three times in the space of this paragraph and do so without hesitation or regret because it fits.

It certainly fits the old ascetic in his poverty and rags who comes with his (to us) archaic myths and weird theology to confront the great prelate in the splendor of the latter's wealth and of his power and of his learning in the wisdom of the Greeks. What a mismatch, one thinks. And, indeed, according to the *Life*, so it was: poor Theophilus never stood a chance. Patience, after all, together with learning in the divine word, wisdom and holiness will always win out, in the end. Such was the perspective that could watch empires roll in and out, controversies over doctrine crash and roar, and not be moved. It could and did accept Nicea-Constantinople, though only, I think, because the latter affirmed that the Lord Jesus is divine, and it had always known *that*, but it cared not a whit for the fine points of the debate, nor for the unspoken but necessarily philosophical commitment of the *homoousion*. It could and did ignore Chalcedon three generations later, and continues to do so to this very day. We would do well, I think, to explore more than we have done the connections between those Jewish roots I sketched earlier—Glory and Image and the "body of light"—and the so-called "Monophysitism" of both Egypt and Syria, or, for that matter, perhaps, even of Apollinaris and Eutyches themselves. Nor, similarly, is it so very difficult to see how Apa Aphou's "body of the Glory" might begin to explain the marks of Pachomian manufacture on the Nag Hammadi codices. It was a notion that could easily devolve into the sort of "popular docetism" of the Apocryphal Acts, and the Nag Hammadi materials bear this out, representing in fact a broad spectrum which ranges from the perfectly "orthodox" and in fact ascetically inclined *Teachings of Silvanus*, through an encratite mysticism of the divine form in the *Gospel of Thomas*, and on down to the wild jungle of mythical beings and dualist speculation called Gnosticism.

By way of a final word, I should like to narrow somewhat the contrasts I have drawn, and therewith make up a little for the injustices I may have done a Cassian, an Origen, or an Evagrius in the course of making my argument.

It is true that what we have in the Anthropomorphite Controversy of 399 is a real difference of opinion, and that our controversy is but the visible tip of a much larger affair, but I would still insist that the difference lies within a common tradition. Both sides of the debate were Christian, rooted in the evangel of the risen Jesus, worshipping him as God and Lord, and committed to the faith that, in him, all things have become new, that the eschaton has already entered into time, and that that same world to come may on occasion be glimpsed, felt, or sensed, especially in the persons of living saints. The "two" are really shadings of a single Gospel of transfiguration and theosis, of participation in the life of God through Christ, and of hope for the vision of the light of glory. Evagrius and Cassian, or—far away and just a few years earlier—the Macarian homilist,[77] are seeking to phrase the ancient hope in a newer way, consonant at once with the ecumenical creed and with Greek learning. They are, in short, advocating a kind of "interiorized apocalyptic," emphasizing the relocation of the heavenly throne and the place of ascent to the hidden places of the human heart, thus Cassian's inner "mountain of solitude" and Evagrius' deliberate interiorization of the Sinai theophany of Ex 24:10–11, where the *nous* becomes the sapphire throne and waits "at the time of prayer" to feed on the "light of the Trinity."[78] The *Macarian Homilies* are engaged in exactly the same project at nearly the same time, as, for

[77]See A. Golitzin, "Temple and Throne of the Divine Glory: Pseudo-Macarius and Purity of Heart," in *Purity of Heart in Early Ascetic and Monastic Literature*, ed. H. A. Luckman and L. Kulzer (Collegeville, 1999), 107–29, here 122–9. For two particularly striking examples of the Macarian Homilist's awareness of the currents under discussion, see n. 79 below, and Homily XXXIII.2–3 and 6 in Collection I, ed. H. Berthold, *Makarios/Symeon Reden und Briefe: Die Sammlung I des Vaticanus Graecus 694 (B)*, GCS (Berlin: 1973), Vol. II:30:13–22 on the "camps of the angels" and "heaven of light," 31:15–18 on the "palaces" (recall *hekhalot*), and "glorious vesture" of the heavenly kingdom, and cf. Homily X.4.7, Vol. I:36, ll.23 ff. on the city and "palace" God builds for His dwelling within the soul.

[78]See esp. "Supplementary Chapter" 25 (Frankenberg 449): "When the intellect takes off the old man and is clothed by grace with the new, then as well it will see its constitution at the time of prayer likened to a sapphire and the form of heaven. This is what was called the 'place of God' by the elders of Israel when he appeared to them on the Mountain," and cf. chp.s 2 and 4 (425 and 427) and Ep. 39 (593). See also G. Bunge, "Nach dem Intellekt Leben? Zum sogenannten 'Intellektualismus' der evagrianischen Spiritualität," in *Simandron, der Wachkopfer: Gedankenschrift für Klaus Gamber*, ed. W. Nyssen (Köln: 1989), 195–109, esp. 101–4 for texts and discussion of the Evagrian intellect as feeding on the "bread of angels" (*In Ps.* 23:6), and as "body of God" (Ep. 64), the latter even with echoes of the Song of Songs, thus, though unstated as such in Bunge, an interiorization of the *shi'ur qomah* traditions. On Evagrius' knowledge and deployment of Targumic *haggadah*, and as providing "the first interiorization [of the Sinai theophany] of which we have written attestation," see N. Séd, "La shekinta et ses amis araméens," *Cahiers d'Orientalisme*, XX (Geneva: 1988) 233–247, esp. 240–2.

example, in their use, which Scholem himself noted, of nothing less than the *merkavah* of Ezekiel: a type, says "Macarius," of the heart which is to become the throne of Christ's glory.[79] This approach, too, had its dangers, as Hans-Veit Beyer pointed out—though not altogether justly or accurately—some years ago,[80] chiefly in a potential denigration of the visible sacraments and the Church hierarchy. That would be the work of later monks and thinkers to correct, not least of whom, I would submit, was the unknown Syrian who wrote under the name of Dionysius the Areopagite.[81] For now, though, allow me to close by suggesting that we can hear the echoes at once of our controversy and of the form its resolution took, at least in the Greek Church, in the words of a Constantinopolitan abbot at the turn of the eleventh century. That visitation of Christ which comes to the sanctified believer, Symeon the New Theologian tells us:

> . . . is not an apparition without substance . . . but appears in a light which is personal [*hypostatikon*] and substantial [*ousiōdē*]. [It is] in a shape without shape and a form without form [*morphē amorphōtos*] that he is seen invisibly, and comprehended incomprehensibly.[82]

❀ · ❀

[79]See esp. Homily I.2, in Collection II, ed. H. Doerries et. al., *Die 50 geistlichen Homilien des Makarios* (Berlin: 1964), 1–2, and Scholem, *Major Trends*, 79, on this text as a "mystical reinterpretation of the *Merkabah*."

[80]See H.-V. Beyer, "Die Lichtlehre der Mönche des vierzehnten und des vierten Jahrhunderts, erörtet am beispiel des Gregorios Sinaites, des Evagrios Pontikos, und des Ps.-Makarios/Symeon," *Jahrbuch des österreichischen Byzantinistik*, 31.1 (1981), 473–512, an insightful article especially valuable for its pinpointing of the central scriptural texts, but quite wrong in its ascription of the *Lichtleib* (p.509)—precisely the "Body of Light"!—to Neoplatonic provenance (478), and, secondly, as voiding the Eucharist of significance (485 and 509). Beyer is still laboring under a set of outdated scholarly fixations: "Hellenistic Betrayal," "Messalianism" (491 ff.), and especially the anti-Palamite polemic which frames his article (473–474 and 510–512). The Jewish roots are completely overlooked.

[81]See A. Golitzin, "Hierarchy versus Anarchy? Dionysius Areopagita, Symeon New Theologian, Nicetas Stethatos, and Their Common Roots in Ascetical Tradition," *St Vladimir's Theological Quarterly*, 38.2 (1994), 131–179.

[82]Symeon New Theologian, *The Ethical Discourses* X, Greek in SC 129, pp.322–324; ET: *Symeon the New Theologian on the Mystical Life: The Ethical Discourses*, tr. A. Golitzin (Crestwood, NY: 1995), Vol. I:169.

From Egypt to Palestine: Discerning a Thread of Spiritual Direction

John Chryssavgis

Introduction

T HIS PAPER EXAMINES the concept of spiritual direction with particular
reference to representative literature from early Egyptian (fourth-fifth
century) and Palestinian (sixth century) monasticism. The purpose is to clarify the somewhat mystified concept of the spiritual director by turning to the
early sources of this tradition. The fathers and mothers who moved away
from society into the desert of Egypt in the fourth century acquired considerable spiritual authority among their contemporaries. By totally rejecting
ordinary human structures and almost provocatively renouncing worldly
institutions, they paradoxically came to represent another kind of power.
Their advice was sought in matters of spirituality, salvation, doctrine, even
social life and political action. In the popular perception, the desert ascetics
clearly enjoyed a position of spiritual prestige; yet the desert fathers and
mothers did not accept this picture of themselves. Although Anthony and his
contemporaries constituted prototypes of spiritual direction for subsequent
generations, they deliberately avoided any promotion of themselves as *models*. Vainglory was a temptation to be avoided and a trap that went "against
the grain" of the desert.

Toward the end of the fourth and the early fifth centuries, the monks of
the Egyptian desert were characterized by a sense of *movement*. For instance,
after the death of the founding fathers of monasticism, Abba Silvanus
migrated to Palestine around the year 380. Some time later, during the 430s,
Abba Isaiah settled in Gaza. It is from here that we have a series of twenty-
nine *Ascetic Discourses* attributed to Isaiah and written in the latter part of
the fifth century. Abba Isaiah sought in various ways to enhance the spiritual

formation of the monastics that he directs. In his discourses, the constant implication is that community comprises exchange of honest communication and humble reconciliation.

In the following century, Barsanuphius and John offered spiritual guidance to numerous visitors, again defying the romanticized picture that gradually develops in Eastern Christendom of the "spiritual director." These two "old men" never claim to be experts, nor do they expect those who seek their advice to bare their souls to them. They do not provide "wisdom" on request, nor do they attempt to solve all problems brought before them. What characterizes them, like the desert dwellers of Egypt, is a flexibility that is reflective of the Spirit of God that "breathes where it wills" (Jn 3:8).[1]

The Desert Fathers Revisited

The Apophthegmata: "Text" and "Context"?

When we consider the sayings of the desert fathers and mother, we must imagine the "secret" of the spiritual relationship that is concealed, and the sacrament of spiritual mentoring that is conveyed. These *Sayings* tell the story of their spiritual journey; like any story, they are not the history of the actual relationship. They constitute a kind of map requiring unfolding and careful reading. In order best to understand the story, correctly to follow the map, one needs to be on the same journey with a guide: "One who climbs a mountain the first time needs to follow a known route, and he needs with him, as a companion and guide, someone who has been up before and is familiar with the way."[2]

The ascetic inhabitants of the fourth-century Egyptian desert were aware of the tensions and problems inherent in spiritual direction. It is unfortunate that those who subsequently edited these "sayings" failed to pass on the rich texture of the spiritual lives behind them, conveying instead only the results of their knowledge. What has come down to us through the centuries is, therefore, the distillation of wise words, without the description of the process of wise living. The revision and rearrangement of the "sayings" over generations

[1]On the *Sayings of the Desert Fathers*, see J. Chryssavgis, *In the Heart of the Desert* (Bloomington IN: World Wisdom Books, 2003). On Isaiah of Scetis, see J. Chryssavgis and R. Penkett, *Abba Isaiah of Scetis: Ascetic Discourses* (Kalamazoo MI: Cistercian Publications, 2002). On *Barsanuphius and John*, see J. Chryssavgis, *Letters of Barsanuphius and John* (Kalamazoo MI: Cistercian Publications, forthcoming).

[2]K. Ware, "The Spiritual Father in Orthodox Christianity," in *Cross Currents*, 24 (1974), 296.

inevitably reduced the focus, even distorted the original, oral tradition that would have conveyed a more comprehensive vision of the ascetic mindset and desert lifestyle.

The *Sayings of the Desert Fathers* narrate many legends of spiritual direction; they describe the leading figures, recount their memorable words, and portray their outstanding examples. Yet these tales must be understood within their context. No "abba" or "amma" was declared a spiritual authority or an oracle of wisdom.[3] Each belonged to a long tradition of spiritual authority that is associated with these titles. Elders were themselves disciples of other elders. There existed a kind of "charismatic succession" alongside of—and, to varying degrees, congruent and overlapping with—the more institutional "apostolic succession."[4] A deep awareness of the sacredness of this tradition maintained a strong sense of responsibility and accountability on the part of spiritual directors, primarily to God and toward their own elders from whom and through whom they received the gift of spiritual authority.

Idols of Power or Icons of Love ?

There is a temptation for contemporary readers to romanticize the early ascetics. Discernment—a virtue highly prized among the desert elders—needs to be exercised, so that the true meaning of spiritual authority may be discovered.[5] Eccentricities unraveled and illusions unmasked, the desert dwellers always remain fully human. The intensity of their struggle revealed the love for their neighbor as the integrity of their heart, and the love for God as the intention of their life. So it is not so much the great fast or the impressive feat that mattered in the desert but the principle of love.[6] This principle is supremely important for the evaluation of spiritual authority and the evasion of its abuses. The ascetics are not idols of supreme power, but icons of sublime love:

> They said of Abba Macarius the Great that he became, as it is written, a god upon the earth. Just as God protects the world, so Abba Macarius

[3]Cf. P Rousseau, *Ascetics, Authority, and the Church in the Age of Jerome and Cassian* (Oxford: Oxford University Pres, 1978), 25.

[4]Cf. D. Chitty, *The Desert A City* (London and Oxford: Mowbray, 1966), 67–8.

[5]Cf. Anthony 8, Agathon 5, John the Dwarf 34, and Syncletica 16. The sayings can be found in B. Ward, trans. *The Sayings of the Desert Fathers* (London and Oxford: Mowbray, 1975).

[6]Moses 2, Poemen 92, and 109. Cf. D. Burton-Christie, "The Call of the Desert: Purity of Heart and Power in Early Christian Monasticism," in *Pro Ecclesia*, VII, 2 (1998), 216–34.

could cover the faults which he saw, as though he did not see them; and those which he heard, as though he did not hear them.[7]

Fully conscious of their own limitations, the desert elders were able to show great compassion for the weaknesses of others.

Ascetic Terminology

There are certain terms in "the way of the ascetics"[8] that require unpacking in order to be properly understood. In this section, two ascetic terms will be briefly discussed: "obedience" and "dispassion."

Obedience was clearly very important for the Desert Fathers (cf. also Heb. 13:17). It was out of obedience that John the Dwarf watered a piece of dry wood for three years, and it bore fruit.[9] It is not one's free will that one is called to surrender, but one's willfulness. The ascetic went to extremes at times in cutting off altogether the fallen, individual will and in acquiescing to the will of God. Extreme measures merely reflected the extremity of human estrangement from God. The renunciation of the fallen will is undoubtedly a slow, painful process. It is likened to bearing one's cross (cf. Luke 22:42). It might also be paralleled with bearing a child. The "death of one's will" is the first step to resurrection and new life.[10]

The biblical command holds true in the desert of Egypt: "do not become servants of human masters" (I Cor 7:23). Obedience is neither submissiveness nor servility. For, obedience is *also due from the elder*, not simply to abstract rules but to another specific person. Abba Mios states: "Obedience responds to obedience"[11]—not to authority. The understanding at all times is that both elder and disciple are subject to the same conditions and commandments, both accountable before the living God. The two are traveling together, though they may not be on equal footing.[12]

The second term that needs clarification is *apatheia*, variously translated as "dispassion" or "passionlessness." In its negative sense, dispassion may be

---

[7]Macarius 32.

[8]Title of a book by Tito Colliander (new ed. London & Oxford, 1983).

[9]*Saying* 1. Cf. also Anthony 36, Agathon 28, John the disciple of Paul 1, Mark 1, Poemen 103, Pambo 3, Rufus 2, Sisoes 10, Saios 1, and Syncletica 16.

[10]Cf. John Climacus, *Ladder* Step 4, 4 (PG 88:680A); Sisoes 3, Zacharias 3, and Hyperechios 8.

[11]Mios 1. See also Poemen 65, Sisoes 45, and Psenthaisios 1.

[12]Cf. J. Aumann, *Spiritual Theology* (Westminster, MD: Christian Classics, 1987), 391–93.

linked with mortification of vices and purification of life through obedience; in its more positive aspect, it implies resurrection and restoration of the will.[13] Now, in the Christian practice, *apatheia* is neither aloofness nor insensitivity. Rather, it is freedom from misdirected passions and the suffering they cause. It involves, as Abba Abraham says, not the elimination of the passions but their "control."[14] This discipline of control is required not only of the disciple, but also of the elder who must practice "nonattachment" (*apotage*) in the exercise of spiritual authority. *Apatheia*, then, has nothing to do with apathy; on the contrary, it is the ultimate expression of empathy for others. The greatest gift on the part of the elder to the spiritual directee is the least imposition on the will of the latter. Dispassion is the ground of compassion and is closely linked with charity:

> One of the Fathers used to say: eat a little without irregularity; if charity is joined to this, it leads the monk rapidly to the threshold of dispassion.[15]

This gives dispassion an extending, impelling significance. For no longer is it seen as a self-regarding condition. Rather, it is identified with love, constituting the other side of the same coin, inseparable and "distinguished [from love] only in name."[16]

A Remarkable Model

The director is encouraged to empower, and the disciple is encouraged to exercise his/her own judgment:

> A brother asked Abba Poemen: "I am harming my soul through staying near my Abba. Should I still stay near him?" The old man said: "Stay, if you want." So he went back and stayed there. He came again and said: "I am losing my soul. Should I leave?" But the old man did not say: "Leave." He came for a third time and said: "I really cannot stay any longer. I am leaving." Abba Poemen said to him: "See, now you have been healed. Go, and stay no longer."[17]

[13]Cf. *Ladder*, Step 15, 4(881A) and 65 (873CD), as well as 29, 1–4 (1148).
[14] Abraham 1.
[15]Evagrius 6.
[16]*Ladder*, Step 30,4 (1156 B).
[17]The text is from the collection edited by J.C. Guy, *Recherches sur la tradition grecque de*

In this remarkable story, Abba Poemen seems to be struggling to exclude his own will, while expanding that of the disciple. He knows that healing is found not through *what is done by others to us*, but in the final analysis through *what is done by us in ourselves*. His aim is to assist the disciple to assume responsibility for personal healing and to honor proper limits.[18]

From Egypt to Palestine: Abba Isaiah of Scetis

An Asceticism of Sensitivity

Drawing on a rich monastic tradition that defines regulations for those living in a religious community,[19] as well as on basic evangelical precepts of charitable conduct (cf. Mat 7:12 and Lk 6:31), Abba Isaiah of Scetis delineates clearly the limits of respect in regard to personal and interpersonal relations. The *Ascetic Discourses* open with a firm clarification that "condemning" and "correcting others" are to be avoided (*AD* 1). This was, after all, the primary task of the Scetiote monks, as reported by Abba John the Dwarf:

> Such was the work of the monks of Scetis: [not to judge, but] to give heart to those who were in conflict.[20]

Abba Isaiah agrees:

> Without charity, the virtues are merely an illusion. (*AD* 21)

It is significant, however, that Abba Isaiah should observe this at the very outset of his monastic treatise because charity is also deeply connected to the virtue of renunciation, which is the first step in the ladder of ascetic spirituality: "Above all else, renunciation is the first ascetic struggle."[21]

Sensitivity in brotherly relations is part and parcel of monastic detachment, the radical surrender of all sense of individual possession. The ultimate aim of

Apophthegmata Patrum, Subsidia Hagiographica, 36 (Brussels, 1962; repr. 1984), 29–30.

[18]Poemen 174.

[19]Cf. Pachomius *Canons* 8 and 9 (PG 40: 948); John Cassian, in PL 28: 860; and Palladius, *Lausiac History* 7 (PG 34: 1019). References to the *Ascetic Discourses* of Abba Isaiah are cited in parentheses *(AD)*.

[20]John Colobos (the Dwarf) 18 (PG 65: 209–212).

[21]Cf. John Climacus, *Ladder* Step 1 (PG 88: 632–644). Step 3 (664–672), "on exile," also precedes Step 4 "on obedience," which is the longest step in the *Ladder* (677–728).

giving up is learning to give; to give freely of one's own and one's self. The desert ascetic in Egypt—so Isaiah would have recalled from his own sojourn there—was called to let go of all material, verbal, and spiritual control:

> Our fathers of old said that the flight is one from one's own body. (*AD* 26)

"Letting go of oneself before God," "letting go of other people," and "letting be of things in general" are phrases often repeated in Isaiah's writings (cf. esp. *AD* 4).

The Power of Will

Letting go of one's individual will and right, *especially* when one believes these to be according to God, is a great matter for a person. (*AD* 8)

The purpose of "surrendering the will of the passions" is "submission to the will of God" (*AD* 16). This struggle is intense because the will is hardened:

> Every person is either bound to hell or loosed therefrom through personal will. For there is nothing harder than the human will, whether it is directed toward death or else toward life. (*AD* 18)

Asceticism is not the denial of will, of life, or "of the will to live." It is the liberation of passion, the redirection of desire, the transformation of power, and the transfiguration of choice. As such, it becomes the way of dependence and trust, the way toward confidence and community. This is why submission of the will is in fact a protest against, and not a prolongation of authoritarian structures. It is a contradiction, and not simply the continuation of institutional roles of power. Obedience is subversion, not subservience. Or, as Abba Isaiah himself puts it: "The one who obeys is actually the great one." (*AD* 3)

The Notion of Obedience

The proof of "letting go" and of "surrendering" (*AD* 3) lies in the practice of obedience. The monastic is called to obey the words of the elder, even when it comes to making decisions on affairs that appear to be good:

> If some of the elders are speaking the word of God, ask your abba whether you should stay and listen, or else withdraw to your cell. And do whatever your elder tells you. (*AD* 3)

Abba Isaiah is familiar with the ascetic tradition of Egypt, where the desert fathers emphasized obedience to the "t." Abba Mark did not even complete the letter "omega" when called away by his elder, Abba Sylvanus;[22] this is a story which Isaiah may have either heard or even experienced first hand in Scetis. Abba Isaiah translates this tradition to the region of Palestine with his own pithy statements about obedience to one's elder:

> Neither add anything, nor take away anything [from whatever he tells you]. (AD 3)[23]

> If your brother calls you, do not say: 'Wait a little, until I finish what I have started,' but obey at once. (AD 5)

> We are to be obedient to our fathers in God *in everything*." (AD 25)

> . . . even in the slightest details: whether it is a matter of speaking or doing something, of receiving or eating or drinking something, of sleeping, or indeed of anything at all. In order first to test whether something is according to God, you should confess the root cause of everything, and then do what must be done before God. (AD 27)

The Role of the Spiritual Elder

Abba Isaiah recognizes that subjection to one's elder should be both confident and complete:

> Bare all your thoughts to your elder with confidence. (AD 4)

The elder is naturally someone "spiritually superior" (AD 4). A weak person can destroy one's own soul in presuming the authority of spiritual direction (AD 5). The elder is also a "wise accomplice" (AD 8), who "remains with us" (*ibid.*) throughout the intensity of the ascetic struggle.

However, Abba Isaiah appears to be flexible in regard to the number of spiritual directors consulted. He understands well that the monastic life is not a life characterized by isolation, but rather a life that is constituted by

---

[22]Mark (disciple of Abba Sylvanus) 1 (PG 65: 273–296).

[23]Cf. also Barsanuphius *Letter* 305. See footnote 29, below, for bibliographic details on these letters.

encounters. Thus, in *Discourse 9*, he refers to confiding in one's "fathers" (*sic*; note the plural), as well as "giving one's heart to the obedience of one's elders." This multiplicity of spiritual direction was practised during the next century in the nearby monastery by the founder and abbot Seridos and by Dorotheus of Gaza, who enjoyed "dual fatherhood"[24] from the "great old man" Barsanuphius and "the other old man" John the Prophet. The aim is never "to be or to act alone" (cf. also *AD* 12), but always to act in consultation: "Always consult your elders." (*AD* 16)[25]

Abba Isaiah is perhaps the first to introduce into the monastic milieu of Palestine and Gaza a life-style that acquires prominence in the next generation with the peculiar practice of the popular "old men," Barsanuphius and John. From the seclusion of his cell, Barsanuphius directed a nearby monastery (formally supervised by Seridos). Barsanuphius may well have learned this manner of spiritual direction from Isaiah and his own relationship to Peter (who may have acted as administrative superior in the nearby community). If this is so, then with the most renowned disciple of Barsanuphius and John, Dorotheus of Gaza, and before these Isaiah and his own disciple Peter, we have four generations of an ascetic "pedigree," a monastic "succession" or evolution that begins in the Egyptian desert.

The context of obedience to a spiritual elder is always one of spiritual continuity (cf. also *AD* 26), which protects the community from the inherent dangers of self-designated directors, from those who "want to have authority over others, who enjoy talking with . . . or who enjoy teaching others, without themselves actually being questioned . . ." (*AD* 17). Outside of this line of spiritual succession, the advice is to avoid teaching and counseling.

The Temptation to Counsel

Abba Isaiah warns against the temptation to counsel others:

> Again he said about teaching: "There is a fear you can fall into that which you teach. For so long as you submit to a weakness, you cannot teach others about it" . . . (*AD* 26)

[24]Cf. L. Regnault in his introduction to *Maîtres Spirituels au Désert de Gaza: Barsanuphe, Jean et Dorothée* (Solesmes: 1967).

[25]Cf. also Symeon the New Theologian, who encourages his monks to disclose their thoughts to a brother whom they trust in the monastery, even if this is not the abbot. See ed. I. Hausherr and G. Horn, *Un grand mystique byantin. La Vie de S. Syméon le Nouveau Théologien par Nicétas Stéthatos*, in Orientalia Christiana, 12 (Rome, 1928), xlix-xlxx.

We cannot teach or counsel others about a passion that continues to control us (*AD* 26):

> For it is shameful to teach others, before one has been liberated from the passion about which one is teaching. (*AD* 26)

Furthermore, Abba Isaiah is critical of any form of "self-reliance" or "self-righteousness." How can a person who is "holding onto one's own will . . . either find rest or else see what is lacking" (*AD* 8)? There is fundamental humility in the recognition that each of us must "repent for our own sins" (*ibid.*). Indeed, the desert elders preferred to be taught, rather than to teach.[26]

Conversely, if a disciple does not follow the advice of an elder, then the solution does not consist either in imposing or insisting upon one's own way, but rather in desisting or detaching oneself:

> So detach yourself, otherwise your own soul is in danger of dying. (*ibid.*)[27]

This advice is again understood within the context of community and in light of Abba Isaiah's firm conviction that "all of us are in need of medical attention: someone feels pain in the eye, another in the hand; some require vaccinations, or other medical treatment" (*ibid.*).

The Way of "Humi-Limit-ation"

Abba Isaiah understands well the significance of self-discipline and of setting boundaries in this regard. One of his favorite phrases is "set boundaries for yourself" (*typoson seauton*: *AD* 4). Limitation of oneself is connected with respect of the other; one is called neither to "betray oneself" (*ibid.*) nor to wound another, but to be "generous to one's body" (*ibid.*) and gentle toward others. Ascetic struggle ultimately implies an attitude of charity. This is precisely why Abba Isaiah treats of diet and vigil as a prelude to his discussion about friendship. Abstinence is a way of "agape;" restraint is the other side of the same coin known as respect.

If individual limits or measures are to be curtailed, it is in order that they

---

[26]See *Vitae Patrum* V, 81 PL 73: 967. Also Sisoes 16 (PG 65: 397), and Macarius 2 (PG 65: 260).

[27]Cf. Theodore of Pherme 20 (PG 65: 192).

may be tailored to a fullness according to the measure of Christ (cf. Eph. 4: 13). Paradoxically, for Abba Isaiah, this does not entail the maturity of adulthood, but the integrity of infancy. In the final analysis, one is called not to increase in spiritual complication, but—paradoxically—to decrease in simplicity. The aim of *ascesis* is "to come to the measure of a child," "to reach the measures of sacred infancy" (*AD* 25). This child-mindedness, or holy innocence, provides for Abba Isaiah the key to the heavenly kingdom (Matt. 18: 3) and holds the secret to his understanding of spiritual direction. The efficacy of spiritual direction depends more on the disciple's innocent trust than on the elder's spiritual maturity.

Ultimately, in the monastic community, discipline and discipling are interconnected; if we are to limit ourselves, it is in order to "liberate our conscience" (*AD* 4). Such is the meaning of obedience in spiritual direction, the privilege of submission to a spiritual elder. It is humbly to dwell on the margins of surrender, and there to discover the limitless space of freedom. It is *a gift to be obedient*: the openness of the heart is a gift; the insight of an elder is a gift; the possibility of community is a gift. It is *a gift also to be free*. The mystery lies in the reality that the first gift generates the last. We grow in the spiritual way when we give in acts of sharing; we begin to live even as we are—"behold"—prepared to die (cf. II Cor. 6: 9); and we attain genuine freedom only through total obedience and surrender (cf. *AD* 4).[28]

The Palestinian Tradition

The "two old men": Barsanuphius and John

The great age of Palestinian monasticism constitutes a link between the earlier Egyptian movements of the third and fourth centuries and the later Byzantine developments of the seventh and eighth centuries. Monastic life flourished in Palestine during the fifth and sixth centuries, coming to an end in 638 when Jerusalem fell to muslim Arabs and the centers of monasticism shifted to the West and to Asia Minor.

The two main regions of Palestinian monastic life were Judaea and Gaza. It was in the latter region that, near the turn of the sixth century, a monk from Egypt named Barsanuphius settled to live a life of seclusion near a cenobium founded by a monk named Seridos. From his cell outside this monastery,

---

[28]Cf. also *AD* 27 and 17, where a connection is also made with "dispassion."

Barsanuphius directed the community's life through Abbot Seridos, the single person to whom he would open his door. Around the year 524–5, another hermit, named John assumed a similar life in a nearby cell. Barsanuphius, John, and Seridos all died around the middle of the sixth century (c. 542–543).

Neither Barsanuphius nor John would see anyone in person; they preferred to advise people through letters dictated to their secretary, Seridos. These letters were answers to questions addressed to them in writing. In this way they guided not only the nearby monastery but also numerous visitors from the surrounding area. Barsanuphius, known as "the great old man," is more spiritual in his responses; John, known simply as "the other old man," tends to offer more practical advice. Yet, they support each other's ministry, sometimes advising people to: "go and ask the other old man."

Often contemporary scholars, indeed the primary sources themselves, tend to emphasize the more extraordinary qualities of the early desert dwellers. However, Barsanuphius and John are less spectacular: they are not eccentric miracle-workers[29], but practical advisers; they are not extreme ascetics[30] or charismatic visionaries, offering instead simple teaching, encouragement, and hope to people in their struggle.[31]

Some 850 examples of this remarkable correspondence survive, a living testimony about diverse aspects of the spiritual and daily life. The questions addressed to the elders come from monks, ordained leaders, and laypeople. They range in content from personal temptations to interpersonal relations, from spiritual issues of depression to practical matters of employment, from social questions concerning pagans to superstitious themes about magic, from theological and liturgical directions to questions dealing with talking in church or at bath.

Barsanuphius and John have behind them two centuries of ascetic experience in the tradition of the Desert Fathers. Their spirituality is in the succes-

[29]For miracles, see Letters 1, 43, 47, 124, 171, 227, 510, 581, and 781. The letters are in Greek, though Barsanuphius himself was certainly a Copt. For the letters of Barsanuphius and John, see the Greek text cited by S. Schoinas, *Biblos Barsanuphiou* (Volos, 1960), originally edited by St Nikodemus of the Holy Mountain (Venice, 1816); the incomplete English translation by D. J. Chitty, *Barsanuphius and John : Questions and Answers*, in *Patrologia Orientalis* 31 (Paris, 1966); and the French translation and introduction by L. Regnault, *Barsanuphe et Jean de Gaza : Correspondance* (Abbaye de Solesmes: 1972). References in this paper are to the Schoinas/Volos edition.

[30]For their ascetic discipline, see Letters 72, 73, 78, and 97.

[31]For clairvoyance, see Letters 1, 27, 31, 54, 163, 777, and 800. For an example of mystic experience, cf. Letter 110.

sion of the earlier inhabitants of Nitria, Scetis, and Kellia. Indeed, "what the *Sayings of the Desert Fathers* let us glimpse only in the form of transitory flashes, is here played out before our very eyes like a film."[32]

A course by correspondence

In their *Letters*, the two elders are very clear about the need for spiritual direction. We all need an adviser; no one can travel the journey alone. This legacy they bequeathed to their own disciple, Dorotheus of Gaza, who writes:

> Do you know someone who has fallen? Well, you can be certain that this person has trusted himself.[33]

Barsanuphius and John repeatedly stress the idea of nonattachment or renunciation, which occurs through the surrendering of one's will. To this end, we are advised to do very little without the counsel of a wise elder.[34]

The two "old men," however, take pains to underline the effort required on the part of the spiritual directors.[35] The vocation of spiritual direction presupposes a life of continual prayer,[36] a temperament that is slow—indeed "foreign"—to anger,[37] as well as a nature that is both "gentle" and "generous":

> Not wounding one's neighbor, that is the way of Christ.[38]

One should not hasten to consider[39]—let alone to appoint—oneself an "abba." Barsanuphius writes almost lamentingly:

> I do not wish to become either an elder or a teacher to anyone. For I have the Apostle who rebukes me: you, then, who teach others, will you not teach yourself? (Rom 2:21)[40]

---

[32]Cf. Lucien Regnault in P. Brown, *The Body and Society: Men, Women and Sexual Renunciation in Early Christianity* (Faber and Faber: 1990), 233.

[33]*Teaching* 5, 6 (PG 88: 1680B).

[34]Cf. *Letters* 162, 344, 356, 551, 558, 583, 694, 703.

[35]Cf. *Letters* 109, and 206.

[36]*Letters* 17, 80, 109, 129, 208, 216, 235, 255, 353, 365, 645.

[37]*Letter* 23.

[38]*Letter* 26.

[39]*Letter* 570.

[40]*Letter* 162.

It is dangerous for the spiritual guide to overlook his or her own salvation by becoming distracted by the role of spiritual direction. Transferring concentration on one's personal struggle to apparent concern for others' weaknesses in the end proves self-destructive:

> God knows, that if I ignore my own salvation, how will I find the strength to care for you?[41]

These two Palestinian epistolographers emphasize the solidarity and mutuality involved in the relationship between elder and disciple. This solidarity is expressed in the respect[42] of the elder for the disciple, as well as in the elder's readiness to receive from the disciple:

> The Lord has bound your soul to mine, saying, do not leave him. So it is not for me to teach you but to learn from you.[43]

The "oneness of soul" between teacher and pupil extends beyond this life to the next.[44] For the spiritual elder, there is a greater degree of *identity with* the disciple than there is *authority over* the disciple. Therefore, the emphasis is always on "consulting," not on "compelling."[45] This insistence on not defining regulations for the spiritual life is a constant theme throughout the correspondence. A spiritual disciple should not be stuck on fixed rules; and a spiritual director must not be stuck on fixed roles. Barsanuphius continually appeals to the Gospel emphasis on free will (cf. Matt.16: 24; Mark8: 34; Luke 9:23):

> Never force a person's will, but simply sow in hope. For our Lord too did not compel but only evangelized; and whoever wanted to, heard.[46]

There is a profound respect for the free will, which can never be constrained.[47] The elder stands beside the disciple as a soul-companion and merely accompanies the will:

[41]*Letter* 77.
[42]*Letter* 208. Cf. also *Letters*, 1, 119, 121.
[43]*Letter* 164.
[44]*Letter* 5, and 305.
[45]*Letter* 187.
[46]*Letter* 35.
[47]*Letter* 51.

> Do not conceive in your heart that I have given you a rule; it is not a rule but a friendly opinion.[48]

This opinion, however, is not mere external advice. The spiritual elder teaches primarily by personal example.[49] This is what accounts for the authority of one's words.

Barsanuphius believes that this form of obedience—as openness to divine grace and not simply conforming to human laws[50]—is the way of the saints whose accountability before God confirms their *authority from God*:

> The saints do not speak of themselves, but it is God who speaks in them as God wills—sometimes in a hidden, and at other times in an open manner.[51]

With a heart open for communion with God in prayer and for communication with the disciple in care, the spiritual elder does nothing less than accept full responsibility for the souls of others:

> Although you ask something beyond my strength, I shall show you the limits of love, that it is forced to move even beyond its limits. I admire you, and I assume responsibility for you, on this one condition, that you in turn bear the keeping of my words and commandments.[52]

Sometimes the elder will assume total responsibility,[53] while at other times the responsibility is partial.[54] On occasion, the elder covers the disciple's sins from childhood and even from birth.[55] And the loving concern reaches far beyond death:

> I will never abandon you, even in the age to come.[56]

[48]*Letter* 160.
[49]*Letter* 344.
[50]Cf. *Letter* 344.
[51]*Letter* 778.
[52]*Letter* 270.
[53]Cf. *Letters* 48, 169, 231, 239, and 614.
[54]Cf. *Letter* 168.
[55]Cf. *Letters* 202, and 210.
[56]*Letter* 239. See also *Letter* 647.

There is a sense in which the compassion involved in the spiritual relationship conquers not only the guilt of sin but the very power of death. This is why the elder refuses even to enter heaven unless the disciple too is saved. The words of Barsanuphius are striking:

> Master, either take me into your Kingdom with my children, or else wipe me also off your book.[57]

This attitude of vicarious transference is legitimate inasmuch as it reveals an extraordinary ascendancy over individual human existence. For the opening up that occurs between elder and disciple is the allowing of the divine Other into the whole of one's life. Reintegration presupposes reconciliation, and repentance requires relationship. It is this spiritual relationship—and not obedience to outward rules or codes—that is unconditional and enduring. This is why the elder will in fact care for the disciple more than the disciple cares for himself or herself—quite simply, because God does![58]

Conclusion

If matters of general spiritual guidance form the central structure of these remarkable early documents, then one of their most critical and recurring themes is that of spiritual fatherhood. The tradition of the spiritual father/mother is particularly important in Eastern monasticism that is less institutional and more personal. In the East, Christians have always visited monasteries to encounter persons of profound prayer and spiritual experience, rather than to consult scholars and learned persons. Such is the chief social role of monasticism in the East.

Yet more than often, it is the privileges of spiritual direction and not its problems that are underlined among Eastern Christian authors. Throughout the centuries, people have chosen to single out the advantages of such a spiritual relationship and to cover up the disadvantages. As a result, the idea of spiritual fatherhood has been somewhat idealized and spiritual authority romanticized. We tend to ignore the fact that, according to the relentless truth of social relations in the ascetic tradition, "from our neighbor comes [not

---

[57]Letter 110. Cf. also Letters 212, 217, 573, 645, and 790.
[58]Cf. Letter 39.

only] life, but also death."[59] This is a passionate conviction of the desert experience and expectation.

Obedience and submission are qualities that may be *soul-purifying for the disciple*, but these very virtues of the disciple may become *soul-sullying for the spiritual director*. The elder must at all times be aware of limitations before God (whose divine will must be reflected), as well as of boundaries in relation to the disciple (whose free will must at all times be respected). This is why the Palestinian elders distinguish clearly between "command" and "opinion." The "other old man," John, writes:

Simple advice according to God is one thing, and a command is another. A command has an inviolable bond; but advice is *counsel without compulsion*, showing a person the straight way in life.[60]

Authority and obedience are perceived by the Desert Fathers and Mothers in the light of *continuity* in the tradition of spiritual direction, and in the context of *communion* between director and directee. Barsanuphius sums up this profound tradition as follows:

I have not bound you, brother; nor have I given you a command. I have simply offered you an opinion. Go then and do *as you will*.[61]

In this respect, the Palestinian tradition is neither an innovation in desert spiritual literature nor a deviation from the way of the Desert Fathers and Mothers. The sixth century teaching on this matter is very much a continuation of the fourth and fifth century desert practices.

---

[59]Anthony 9.
[60]*Letter* 368. Emphasis mine.
[61]*Letter* 56. Emphasis mine.

❦ "The Heir of Resurrection": ❦ Creation, Cross and Resurrection in Early Welsh Poetry

A. M. (Donald) Allchin

I

BISHOP KALLISTOS AND I have known each other for more than fifty years. Our friendship goes back to the days after World War II when we were both at Westminster School; our common interest in the Orthodox Church was one of the things which first brought us together. I think of the occasion when Nicholas Zernov came to speak to a school society in 1947; it was, I believe, for Bishop Kallistos, as for myself, a first direct encounter with an Orthodox theologian. We were both to become active members of the Fellowship of St Alban and St Sergius, and in that context we were to meet representative Orthodox figures, many from the Russian diaspora, and notable among them Vladimir Lossky.

I recall these facts not only out of sense of gratitude for a long and unbroken friendship, but also because for me, as a Western Christian who has remained part of the Western Christian world in which I grew up, the influence of Orthodox theology, an influence felt already before I came up to the University and in my first years there, has been profound and lasting. Looking back now I see how much I owe to the Orthodox teachers whom I first got to know all those years ago. My early impression of the interpenetration of Eastern and Western Christianity, my sense that the meeting with Orthodoxy was enabling me, as an Anglican, to discover things at the heart of my own tradition, which were too often ignored and undervalued, has remained with me ever since and has grown stronger with time. This article itself is a small example of one of the later developments of those early convictions and impressions. My growing involvement with the Celtic tradition of Christianity, particularly in its Welsh form, has been experienced by me, not as an abandonment of that early concern for the relationship between Orthodoxy and the West, but as a constantly unexpected reaffirmation of it.

The Heir of Resurrection, Gwrthrych Dadwyrain, the phrase which stands at the head of this article, comes from a poem of the 1130s, written by a notable poet of the early twelfth century in North Wales, Meilyr Brydydd. It is a poem which refers to the Holy Island of Bardsey, Ynys Enlli, a place of pilgrimage, famous in medieval Wales, as the place where pilgrims went at the end of their life, to die and to be buried and to find resurrection, there in "the island of the twenty thousand saints."[1] The phrase from Meilyr Brydydd's poem implies that the island itself, is in expectation, is the Heir Apparent of the gift of resurrection. As St Paul tells us in the Epistle to the Romans, all creation awaits the manifestation of the children of God and its renewal in his purposes.

Throughout the long history of Welsh poetry, Meilyr Brydydd has been regarded as the founder of a new and remarkable school of poets, who flourished for one hundred and fifty years. They are known in Welsh as the *Gogynfeirdd, The Rather Early Poets,* a name which points us back to the *Cynfeirdd, The Early Poets,* a group of writers some six centuries earlier, who had celebrated the warriors of post-Roman Britain, in their long and ultimately unsuccessful struggle to defend the island from the Anglo-Saxon invaders. Now in the twelfth and thirteenth century, another school of poets arose, who celebrated and affirmed the last independent princes of Wales, in their own bitter struggle against the Anglo-Norman invaders of their time. It was a struggle which ended in 1282 with the death of Llywelyn ap Gruffudd (Llywelyn our Last Leader, as he is always called in Welsh). Not unnaturally this same group of poets are often known as the Poets of the Princes.

These poets however were not only singers of the courage and strength of the warriors of these last small independent Welsh kingdoms. They were poets whose work of praising the princes and warriors of their people, was rooted in a powerful understanding of the nature of poetry itself as praise, and above all as praise of God. When, according to the rules of the Poetic Grammars, the chief poet sang before the prince and the court at one of the great feasts of the year, Christmas or Easter for instance, he had always to begin by singing a poem in praise of God. Only afterwards did other forms of praise follow. So

---

[1] A translation of the poem and a brief commentary on it will be found in Oliver Davies' book *Celtic Christianity in Early Medieval Wales: The Origins of the Welsh Spiritual Tradition* (Cardiff, 1996), 109–10. This is a remarkable pioneering study of its subject, indispensable for those who want to go further. A different translation and a rather fuller commentary is to be found in my own book, *Resurrection's Children: Exploring the Way Towards God* (Norwich, 1998), 90–107.

there exists in the poetry of the writers of this school, a number of Odes to God, and of other poems of a distinctly religious and theological nature, notably "death-bed" poems, *marwysgafn,* poems of repentance and entreaty written as the poet approaches the end of his life. Meilyr Brydydd's poem is not only the first of these, it is one which is commonly recognized as "the most intensely felt and tenderest of the few extant poems of this kind."[2] It is a poem which is full of sorrow for sin, and a certain anxiety at the prospect of death, but it is also full of a quiet confidence in God, "Lord of all places how good it is to praise you," as the poet exclaims in the middle of his work.

It needs also to be said that although the poem is a very personal expression of faith and entreaty it is also in some way a work representative of its age and society. The poet was a man who had played a large part in the history of his time. For a whole generation he had stood beside Gruffudd ap Cynan, the ruler of Gwynedd, supporting him in his long and difficult struggle to unify and control his small unruly kingdom, until in the end, as a very old man, Gruffudd seems to have achieved a period of stability and peace which was to become legendary in Welsh history. We have here a poem which tells us not only about a single individual, but about a whole society, a small but distinct world, in its longing to find final peace and covenant with God. I cite here the last third of the *Marwysgafn* of Meilyr Brydydd.

> I am Meilyr the Poet, pilgrim to Peter,
> Gatekeeper who measures right virtue.
> When the time of our resurrection comes
> All who are in the grave, make me ready.
> As I await the call, may my home be
> The monastery where the tide rises,
> A wilderness of enduring glory.
> Around its cemetery the breast of the sea,
> Island of fair Mary, sacred island of the saints,
> Heir of resurrection, to be in it is lovely.
> Christ of the prophesied cross, who knows me
>   shall guide me
> Past hell, the isolated abode of agony.
> The Creator who made me shall receive me
> Among the pure parish, the people of Enlli.

---

[2]*The New Companion to the Literature of Wales*, Ed. Meic Stephens (Cardiff, 1998), 490.

By a curious chance—but is it altogether chance?—one of the few people in England in the 1950s who would have known and cared about the poem, was himself a very active and influential participant in the life of the Fellowship of St Alban and St Sergius, Father Derwas Chitty. Growing up in a Shropshire rectory in the Anglo-Welsh borderland, Derwas Chitty was unusually sensitive to the distinct religious and cultural history of Wales. Since his childhood he had heard of the famous place of medieval pilgrimage, Bardsey Island, out at the end of the Llyn Peninsula, the north west tip of Wales, and already as a young priest, before the war, he had been taking parties of young people to camp on the island during the summer. Now, after the war, restored to his parish in Berkshire, he and his wife Mary were beginning a new series of visits to the holy island, taking with them some their parishioners to taste the particular quality of the place, "the island of the hermits, the island of solitude, where we are least alone," as Derwas Chitty would describe it.

How it was that Derwas Chitty had discovered Orthodoxy is another story and not one that can be told here. It is enough to say that in the 1920s he had been studying in Jerusalem with the Dominicans at the *Ecole Biblique*. He had found himself more and more drawn to the study of the origins of Christian monasticism in Palestine and Egypt, and more and more drawn in to the life and faith of Orthodoxy as he was meeting it, not only in its Russian and Greek but also in its Arab form. It was not perhaps surprising that a learned man of a deeply intuitive mind, should have seen at once the parallel between the monastic sites which he was exploring in Palestine and the ancient monastic site which lay out to the west of Britain, which he had known as a boy. Deeply influenced and moved by Jerusalem itself, and in particular by the Church of the Resurrection—the proper name of the Church of the Holy Sepulchre, as he loved to insist—he was also deeply moved by the island of Bardsey, also a place of monastic life from the beginning of the sixth century, also a place of death and resurrection. In a way which it is difficult to explain he came to feel that there was a very close relationship between the two places, the central holy place of Christendom, the windswept island off the north west coast of Wales. It was this which made him determined, when he retired from his parish, to find a place near the end of the peninsula so that he might live near the "Island of the Twenty Thousand Saints," and this he did.[3]

---

[3]Derwas Chitty retired to Llangwnnadl in the Llyn in 1967 and died in 1971. His history of early Christian monasticism, *The Desert a City*, has become well known since the time of his death. Mary Chitty still lives at Llangwnnadl, aged 96. Her two small books *The Monks on Ynys Enlli, Part I, C500–1252* (1992) and *The Monks on Ynys Enlli, Part II, C1252–1537* (2000)

II

We have been beginning to look at a twelfth century poem, itself part of the start of a new period in the long history of Welsh literature. As we have seen it is a poem of considerable skill and assured technique, a poem which looks forward through and beyond death to a resurrection which includes all of creation as well as humankind. What is it that lies behind this poem? Surely it is the product of some older tradition than itself?

To answer this question is not altogether easy. For one thing the religious element in the development of early Welsh poetry has not hitherto been very much studied. But more than that, the material available for the study is not at all abundant. If we are right in thinking that by the beginning of the twelfth century the Welsh court poet already had at least some elements of a tradition of writing sacred poetry to begin from, an idea which we shall be exploring in these pages, we inevitably must ask ourselves where and how that understanding of the poet's task as a sacred task, a task envisaged and carried out in explicitly Christian terms, came to be formulated?

The answer to that question again is not immediately clear. We can only point to certain pieces of evidence, some in Welsh, some in Latin, from the centuries which preceded the end of the first millennium, which suggest to us something of the fusion of Christian with pre-Christian theory and practice, which had in fact taken place.

We could begin with a remarkable set of verses, nine three line verses, to be found in the margin of a Latin manuscript in the University Library in Cambridge. The writing of these verses is commonly dated to the early ninth century, the poem itself may well of course be older than that. They constitute a poem which, in the judgment of an outstanding scholar on the poetry of the eighth and ninth centuries, Dr Jenny Rowland, is of the highest quality as a work of literary art and craftsmanship. The more I have looked at the theological content of this poem the more I have come to find it a work of similarly remarkable theological penetration and maturity. The nine three line verses contain a hymn to God as Trinity, to God as at once Creator and Redeemer of the whole human race, of the whole created order. It is an act of Trinitarian praise which begins and ends with a celebration of the incarnation, with the praise of Christ as Son of God and son of Mary. The way in

are an invaluable source for the history of monasticism on the island. The pilgrimage to Bardsey has grown constantly in recent years and for fifteen years towards the end of the twentieth century, the hermit life was lived there again.

which the themes of creation and redemption are woven together, the way in which the Trinitarian nature of God's action towards the world is expressed, all make this a work of remarkable consistency and remarkable depth. There lies behind it some remarkable fusion of a vernacular tradition of poetic writing with a Latin tradition of theological reflection and understanding.[4]

Looking towards the Latin side of the picture, there are fragments which surprise us by their quality and their insight. There is the late seventh century inscription for instance, to be found in the little church of Llanlleonfel, in north Breconshire, an inscription which commemorates two local chieftains buried together, in what circumstances we do not know.

> *In sindone muti Ioruert, Ruallaunque sepultus,*
> *Iudicii adventun spectant in pace tremendum.*

> Silent in the shroud, Ioruert and Ruallan lie buried here,
> Awaiting in peace the coming of the dread judgment.[5]

The two local chieftains lie together in their tomb, awaiting the day of judgment with a mingling of awe and confidence, of anxiety and peace, not altogether dissimilar from the mood we discovered in the poem of Meilyr Brydydd. But who would have expected in mid-Powys at the end of the seventh century, in a place so far as we know of no particular distinction, such powerful lines of verse, such penetrating statements of Christian faith? All this is found in a somewhat clumsy-looking inscription centered upon a cross.

Perhaps our expectations of this period are too low, in part because we have so little evidence of the inner quality of its life, in part because we have had so little regard for what evidence there is. If we look again at the Latin speaking world of Wales at this time and at a text which dates from much the same period as the Llanlleonfel inscription, in this case early in the eighth century, we shall find a window into the monastic world opened for us, by a writer at once learned and passionate, biblical and poetic. He shows considerable familiarity with the text of the Bible, in the Old Testament for instance with Genesis, the Psalms and the Song of Songs, and in the New Testament

---

[4]For this poem see Oliver Davies, op. cit. 50–52, see also my article, "There is no resurrection where there is no earth: Creation and Resurrection as seen in Early Welsh Poetry," in *Celts and Christians: New Approaches to the Religious Tradition of Britain and Ireland,* Ed. by Mark Atherton (Cardiff, 2002), 104–9.

[5]V. E. Nash-Williams, *The Early Christian Monuments of Wales* (Cardiff, 1950), 84. See also A. M. Allchin, *God's Presence Makes The World* (London, 1997), 2–4.

with the four Gospels above all. His method of interpretation, seeing Christ present throughout the pages of scripture, was the common property of first millennium Christianity east and west, but he employs the method with skill and with a real imaginative vitality. For him again it goes without saying that creation and resurrection are intimately linked and that the destiny of the individual is finally inseparable from the destiny of the universe. We see this in the lines with which he begins the first of his series of meditations on our dying and rising with Christ, on the way of repentance and forgiveness.

> I pray to God the Father, God the Son,
> And to God the Holy Spirit,
> Whose infinite greatness
> Enfolds the whole world,
> In persons three and one
> In essence simple and triune,
> Suspending the earth above the waters,
> Hanging the upper air with stars,
> That he may be merciful to me a sinner.

More striking are his two meditations on the parable of the prodigal son. Here he begins from the personal mode, describing the Father in the parable who, as we shall see, he identifies with the second Person of the Trinity,

> He from whom I hope for the robe of
>   immortality
> And the ring of dignity,
> Who for my arrival slays
> The fattened calf from the herd,
> Whose blood restored
> The structure of the whole world.[6]

We see again theological affirmations which bring together indissolubly creation and redemption, personal and universal, in a single text of prayer and meditation.

When we turn back from the world of learned Latinity to the vernacular poetry of mid-Wales in a slightly later period, we find in a very different form

---

[6]"The Prayers of Moucan," in *Celtic Spirituality*, Ed. Oliver Davies (Mahwah, NY: Paulist, 1999), 301–7.

similar basic affirmations. Here on the contested border between Powys and Mercia we find an insistent meditation on the power of death over the affairs of humanity. I am here again dependent on the work of Dr Jenny Rowland on the saga poetry, and in particular on her valuable discussion of the theme of the inexorable quality of fate/death, *tynghet*, as we find it above all in the proverbial elements of the poetry of this period. From that discussion I take just four quotations as examples of the capacity for a brief but compact state- ment of profound theological truth which we can already observe in this poetry.

First a line which can easily be related to the thought which lies behind the Llanlleonfel inscription.

> He, the Lord of Heaven, gives us a peaceful fate/death

> *Ac ef arglwydd nef tanghef tynged an dug.*[7]

Death in the context of these poems is normally death in battle and often death in defeat. But even such a death is something which can be received in peace because it comes from God who is the disposer of fate and the Lord of death who can make even death to be peaceful.

> No man alive rules according to his intentions;
> It is God who rules because of his victory.

> *Dyn yn fyw ni fedd oi arfaeth*
> *Duw a fedd oi fuddugoliaeth*

Clearly the issues of life and death are not at man's disposal; they rest in God's hands. In the context of this first millennium Christianity there can be only one possible interpretation of the reference to the victory of God. It is the moment of the resurrection, in which, by a supreme paradox, the triumphant Christ, the *Christus Victor* annihilates the power of death in the very moment of dying.

Thus on the cross the power of God is revealed to the utmost, in the utmost human weakness, as the poet affirms in the following line

---

[7]Jenny Rowland, *Early Welsh Saga Poetry: A Study and Edition of The Englynion* (Cam- bridge, 1990), 28–9.

> When it is most restricted for man, it is most expansive—
> open—for God

> *Pan vo ygaf gan dyn ehangaf vyd gan duw.*

In such small concentrated statements there appears a capacity for the poetic articulation of theological truth which is to characterize Welsh writing throughout the centuries until today.

This little group of lines may be summed up in one serene and simple statement

> In God there is no fate/death

> *En Nuw nid oes dynghedfen.*

As St Paul declares "Death is swallowed up in victory." (1 Cor: 15:51) R. S. Thomas says of such early poetry "This is the springtime of the imagination. It offers hope."[8]

III

We have been looking back in the previous section to evidence coming to us both in Latin and in Welsh from the later centuries of the first millennium, from circa 650–circa 950. We come now again to poetry not easy to date, but very possibly contemporary with the work of Meilyr Brydydd with which we began this study, that is to say poetry dating from the first half of the twelfth century or from the century following. There are two poems in particular which demand attention. The first is a short but weighty statement, a poem which both in its form and its content shows skillful and long pondered crafts-manship. Each line in the original contains internal rhyme and alliterative devices; as we shall see its theological affirmations give proof of similar pro-longed meditation on the mysteries of Christ. Second there is a longer and more expansive poem, a poem notable for the all-inclusive quality of its praise. All things in creation, in all their diversity, great and small, natural and

---

[8]R. S. Thomas from a lecture on David Jones. See *David Jones, Diversity in Unity: Studies in his Literary and Visual Art*, edited by Belinda Humfrey and Anne Price-Owen (Cardiff, 2000), 159.

human, social and personal, come together in the praise of God. In the case
of the first poem we have a concentrated statement about the nature of God's
work as creator and redeemer, in the second the stress is on the radiance of
creation itself when it is seen in the light of Christ's death and resurrection.
To come to the first poem:

> In the name of the Lord, mine to praise, of great praise,
> I shall praise God, great the triumph of his love.
> God who defended us, God who made us, God who saved
>   us,
> God our hope, perfect and honorable, beautiful his blessing.
> We are in God's power, God above, Trinity's King.
> God proved himself our liberation by his suffering,
> God came to be imprisoned in humility.
> Wise Lord, who will free us by Judgment Day,
> Who will lead us to the feast through his mercy and sanctity
> In paradise, in pure release from the burden of sin,
> Who will bring us salvation through penance and the five
>   wounds.
> Terrible grief, God defended us when he took on flesh.
> Man would be lost if the perfect rite had not redeemed him.
> Through the Cross, blood-stained, came salvation to the
>   world.
> Christ, strong shepherd, his honor shall not fail.[9]

Much of the language of this poem is close to that used in praise of a prince
or a warrior, but it is evident from line two that this is a very particular kind
of ruler. It is the triumph of his love which is being celebrated. The word triumph here could also be translated abundance, blessing, benefit. We are the
beneficiaries, the recipients of this love. The God who made us is the God who
saved us, whose creative and redeeming power is an overflowing and ever
increasing power. The first eight lines of the poem are highly theocentric, concentrated on who God is and what God does. The sixth and seventh lines
bring this first part of the poem to its climax in the two great affirmations,
"God proved himself our liberation by his suffering." and "God came to be
imprisoned in humility."

---

[9]Oliver Davies, *Celtic Christianity in Wales*, 52–6.

Here we have the work of an accomplished vernacular poet, who is also a master in the articulation of the mysteries of Christian faith. Here surely we have a man who is learned in the Scriptures, in other words a master in Latin, as well as a master in Welsh. Familiar with the Pauline understanding of the redemptive incarnation of Our Lord as we see it in the Epistle to the Philippians, in the self-emptying of the Son who comes into the depths of our human desolation in order to raise up human-kind and all creation to the Father.

The poem is at first glance centered on the suffering of the Cross, the suffering involved in the way of the Cross. "Terrible grief, God defended us when he took on flesh." In the original as well as in the translation the first two words stand out abruptly, alone, at the beginning of the line. But as we look back at the three lines which precede this exclamation we see in them already the clear affirmation of the conclusion to which this grief will come. On the day of judgment God will free his people, his whole creation, bringing us to the fulfillment and joy of his eternal kingdom. The perspective is at once that of resurrection and ascension.

In his commentary on this poem Oliver Davies dwells on the fact that it begins, in a way which could be paralleled in other works of this kind, with a phrase which is at once Welsh and Latin, *Yn Enw Dom'ni, In the Name of the Lord.* This opening at once suggests a liturgical text and the poem surely contains references both to the sacrament of baptism made through its speaking of penance and the sharing of Christ's wounds, and the sacrament of the Eucharist, "the perfect rite" which has redeemed us. Here surely we have a poem written from inside the celebration of the Eucharist, by a writer who is both priest and poet and very possibly a monk.

At this point there is an interesting contrast with the second and longer poem which we shall examine. This is a more expansive work which sees the beauty of God shining out through all creation, and it seems to be written from the point of view of the Christian layman. Amongst all the beautiful things which it celebrates from the world of nature, the specific gifts of grace are not ignored, but they are seen as it were through the eyes of one who looks towards the altar. We hear of "The beauty of a faithful priest in his church," or "The beauty of desire for penance from a priest," or again "The beauty of a strong parish, led by God," and perhaps most significant of all, at least in allowing us to place the poem in space and time, there is a line which speaks of "The beauty of bearing the elements to the altar." The poem dates from a period when the active participation of the laity in the offertory of the Eucharist was still an evident part of the rite.

But these distinctly sacramental references which come near the center of the poem are only one element in a work which, though it begins and ends with the thought of the beauty of repentance now and the ultimate beauty of repentance and covenant with God on the Day of Judgment, is for the most part an astonishingly free and seemingly spontaneous celebration of the beautiful things of creation in all their variety and difference.

> The beauty of berries at harvest time,
> Beautiful too grain on the stalk . . .
> The beauty of an eagle on the shore when the tide is full
> Beautiful too the sea gulls playing . . .
> The beauty of the moon shining on the earth,
> Beautiful too when your luck is good.
> The beauty of summer, its days long and slow,
> Beautiful too visiting the ones we love.[10]

But the feature of the poem which is likely to surprise and disconcert us at first, is that these fifty lines of affirmation are placed between a beginning and an ending in which the poet speaks above all of the beauty of doing penance for sin. Surely the twenty-first century reader will protest, here is a note of life-denial and renunciation which sits uneasily with the great affirmation of the goodness and beauty of things which comes in between. Here again we need to remember that the practice of penance was in Celtic Christianity rooted in the practice of baptism and in the constant renewal of the risen life of Christ within each Christian and within the Christian community as a whole, brought about through confession and forgiveness. What we have in this poem is a celebration of the world as seen in the light of the resurrection, seen through eyes which are themselves full of the life of the resurrection. It is a testimony to the life of the resurrection lived as a present reality here and now, in space and time, a life which cast its radiance onto the whole world of our human experience, inner and outer.

IV

We have noticed in the last poem the reference to bringing gifts to the altar, and the sense that it gives that the author is living in a church in which the

[10]Ibid. 84–5.

active participation of the laity in the Eucharistic celebration seems to be taken for granted. This sense of the active participation of the laity in the liturgy of the Church is to be observed also in the poetry of others among the *Gogynfeirdd*, and in particular in the work of the family of Meilyr Brydydd, the author of the death-bed poem from which we began. Meilyr was not only acknowledged as the founder of a whole school of poets, he was also the father of a distinguished family which for three generations produced a series of poets who played their part in the life of the Kingdom of Gwynedd in North Wales. Most famous among them was his son Gwalchmai ap Meilyr, but his three grandchildren, Einion ap Gwalchmai, Meilyr ap Gwalchmai and Elidir Sais were also distinguished poets. It is one of the poems of the latter writer which we shall look at now in this final section of our essay. It is a poem which starting on Shrove Tuesday takes us swiftly through Lent into Holy Week and then on into the heart of the mystery of Christ, in the events of Good Friday to Easter Day. There is much in this poem which merits attention, not least its Trinitarian quality, but I shall restrict myself to the six lines at its center which speak of Christ rising on the morning of Easter and the four lines which follow which speak of the Harrowing of hell.

> The next day he performed a second deed,
> He, the true Son of God, showing himself alive.
> Sunday (deepest of memories this) when the sun arose
> He rose up from his grave.
> This great message awakens us and will awaken us,
> Christ's, the Lord's awakening, the awakening of our poetic
>   art.[11]

We may begin by asking why the resurrection is spoken of as a second deed. What was the first? A possible clue is given in the lines immediately preceding which speak of the death on the Cross on Good Friday. The poet having spoken of "the Cross of Our Father," then speaks of "our total oppression," and then at once goes on the speak of Christ as the one who gave life to all things at the beginning. Here is the full paradox and mystery of the death on Good Friday, it is the author of life who is put to death. The great

---

[11]See N. G. Costigan, *Defining The Divinity: Medieval Perceptions in Welsh Court Poetry* (Aberystwyth, 2002), 37–8, for an English translation of the poem and 91–2 for a commentary. This recent book gives the English reader a quite new access to the religious poetry of the *Gogynfeirdd*.

deed of Easter Morning is the second deed seen not only in relation to Good Friday itself but also, and perhaps more profoundly, in relation to the first work of creation in the beginning. Here in the resurrection the purpose of God from the beginning of all things is brought to its conclusion.

The movement of the poem carries us at once to Easter Morning, and to the striking parenthesis, "deepest of memories." The Welsh word here for deep is *dwys*, a word which comes from the Latin densus: weighty, profound, intense would all be possible readings. The word for memory is *cof*, one of the most necessary of all words in Welsh, a word which means both memory and mind, the word which is used to speak of the three "Lores in which the poets were instructed in the bardic schools, namely the history, language and genealogy of Wales." Dr John Davies of Mallwyd, perhaps the greatest of Welsh Renaissance scholars, in his English-Welsh-Latin dictionary of 1632 suddenly moves beyond Latin into Greek at this point, giving us *commemoratio, hypomnema, memoriale, mnemosynon, reminiscentia;* all are invoked at once.[12]

Surely what the poet is telling us is that the resurrection of the dead is the bringing to light of the deepest memory buried in the human mind and heart. The memory of the beginning, the creation which in the beginning God saw and declared to be very good, was made in order that it might find its fullness of life in God himself. This it did at the moment of Christ's rising from the dead.

At once the poet goes on to tell us more of the meaning and purpose of this great deed, and in a striking way he brings us back to the Gospel narratives of the empty tomb, and their insistence that the women who have come, are to go out and proclaim the message, the good news of this deed which is for all people and for all creation, "This great message awakens us and will awaken us." The message of the resurrection is for now, in this life, in which already we share in Christ's risen life, but the message of the resurrection is also for the future, for the last day, for the eternal world, when not only we but all creation will share in this awakening.

There follows a line which suddenly brings us from the universal to the particular, from eternity to the present, and we observe a new example of one of the most characteristic features of early Welsh poems in praise of God, the way in which the poet will suddenly switch from saying that all things praise God, to saying "and here am I praising you O Lord." Suddenly we see that the act of prayer and praise as it is understood in this tradition is at once

[12]*Geiriadur Prifysgol Cymru*, Volume I (1967), 536.

all-inclusive and yet profoundly personal and intimate, realized in the voice of the one who is making this act of praise, making it his or her own and making it on behalf of all. The Welsh bards were fully convinced that their poetic art was at once a gift and a task, a gift which came from God, a task whose fulfillment would bring them to God.

At times they were clearly overawed by the greatness of this calling as they understood it, a calling which goes so far beyond human capacity. At times they seem overwhelmed by their awareness of the darkness and cruelty and tragedy of the world they are living in, poets whose principle earthly task is the praise of warriors who are necessarily called to overcome their enemies by killing them. Here indeed, in the resurrection of the dead, is the answer to their fears and griefs, their sense of total unworthiness, here in the death in which by dying, life triumphs forever over death, in which that life gives itself wholly in the moment of dying, to us and the whole world. Here the poets discover the meaning and the motivation of their art.

This celebration of the gift of life on Easter Day at once goes forward to a celebration of the harrowing of hell, the liberation of the souls of the departed from prison.

> The Son of God led souls out from fire and terror,
> From the cold marsh of hell, redemption from its quagmire,
> From earth's disturbance, from its quaking,
> From the cold comfortless prison.

It is sometimes said that these early poets loved to dwell on the pains of hell, and it is true that there are in their work one or two notable examples of a detailed description of the torments of hell which may well trouble and pain us. Here the poet is not so specific. What surely is significant is that he deliberately uses clashing, contradictory images to describe this marginal condition of utter loss, as if to show that his language is the language of image and not of literal truth. It is hot, it is cold, it is a marsh which clings to us, a prison which confines us, an earthquake which scatters us. The poet concludes this part of the poem with two lines which for him sum up the whole mystery of Good Friday and Easter.

> On this account, the multitude of the children of men fall
>   down
> In worship around the Creator and his blood-stained Cross.

Here in the work of one of the lesser-known of the *Gogynfeirdd*, a poem which has so far escaped the attention of commentators both in Welsh and in English, we see something of the quality of theological insight and affirmation which this early Welsh poetry contains.

In the conclusion to his remarkable and pioneering study *Celtic Christianity in Early Medieval Wales: The Origins of the Welsh Spiritual Tradition*, Oliver Davies, having spoken of the Trinitarian, Incarnational and cosmic dimensions of this poetry adds, "In addition it is a form of Christianity which affords a special value to the creativity of the poet as one who both instructs the people and speaks before God on their behalf, and yet who also, in himself, embodies the inspirational power of art which is the sublime gift of God. It is above all here, in the implicit notion of a poetic priesthood in which the poet—touched by a particular grace—speaks in and for the spiritual community, that we find the most distinctive aspect of the Welsh tradition."[13]

V

I spoke at the beginning of this article of a sense of the hidden, as yet unrealized affinity with Orthodoxy which is to be found in the Welsh tradition. This is something to be found not only in its early centuries, but something which seems to occur again and again. Perhaps it is most strikingly and unexpectedly realized in the work of the four great Welsh language poets of the mid-twentieth century, John Saunders Lewis, David Gwenallt Jones, Waldo Williams and Euros Bowen who together, but in startlingly different ways, made a great affirmation of the Christian faith in the middle of an age when such an affirmation was hardly to be expected. In this essay we have been looking at a much earlier stage in the development of that tradition, a stage in the early middle ages when a school of intensely traditional poets made a remarkable statement about the nature and content of that tradition as they understood it, a statement which had both sacred and secular implications.

It will not have escaped the notice of the Orthodox reader that many of the poems we have quoted date from after 1054 and one or two from after 1204. But the vision of Christian faith which they express is, I would maintain, the vision of first-millennium Christianity, the vision of a Christian world in which communion between East and West has not been broken, in

[13]Oliver Davies, *Celtic Christianity*, 144.

which the Christians of this Western part of Britain look not only to Rome but also to Jerusalem, and to the monasteries of the Egyptian desert. In their assurance that Creation, Cross and Resurrection belong together, there is a wholeness of Christian faith and understanding which has continued to inform the development of the Welsh poetic tradition down until today. Despite all the dislocations and disasters which have affected that tradition in the course of history, despite times of outward failure and defeat, something of that inner assurance of the reality of resurrection, of new life gained and given through the death on the Cross, has remained at its heart. We hear it for instance in the victorious affirmations of Pantycelyn or Ann Griffiths in the eighteenth century. We find it, as has already been suggested, in the middle of the last century in the work of Saunders Lewis and Gwenallt, of Waldo Williams and Euros Bowen. The poetic gift and the poetic task of making *anamnesis* has never been altogether lost. Rather the deepest of memories has been preserved and renewed, the memory that the earth itself and all creation waits in eager expectation for the coming of the day of final resurrection.[14]

---

[14]For a first introduction to these four writers see A. M. Allchin *God's Presence Makes the World*, Chapters 5–7, 88–151.

❀ "What Kind of Fool Am I?" ❀
Further Gleanings from Holy Folly

Peter C. Bouteneff

Bishop Kallistos (Ware) has written more than once on the phenomenon of holy foolishness in the Christian East. "The Fool in Christ as Prophet and Apostle"[1] is a historically incisive and spiritually profound essay on the meaning of holy folly in the Christian East, drawing largely on the example of the sixth-century saint Symeon of Emesa. A few years later he wrote about a fourteenth-century athonite fool, Maximos of Kapsokalyvia.[2] This latter study introduced a wider public to a little-known saint, and through him to the explicit connection between holy foolishness and athonite hesychasm. The former article is so full of scholarly and spiritual insight in its twenty-three pages that, especially when taken together with G. P. Fedotov's masterful essay focusing on the Russian fools (*iurodivye*),[3] and Lennart Rydén's (much shorter) piece focusing on the Byzantine ones,[4] it is difficult to think of what more could be said in something less than a book.

Yet, while honoring and drawing upon the aforementioned essays, further observations can be made about the holy fool. The primary aim of this contribution is to show that while there are factors which unite the various Christian holy fools under one category, there are also significant features which make a clear subcategorization inevitable. We will explore, in turn, what it is that divides the fool into three kinds, and what it is about the fool that has justifiably compelled Christians to revere and canonize them as a particular

---

[1] *Sobornost*, 6:2 (1984), 6–28; repr. with revisions in Bishop Kallistos Ware, *The Inner Kingdom*, vol. 1 of the Collected Works (Crestwood, NY: SVS Press, 2000), 153–180.

[2] "St Maximos of Kapsokalyvia and Fourteenth Century Athonite Hesychasm," in ΚΑΘΗΓΗΤΡΙΑ, Festschr. Joan Hussey (Porphyrogenitus, 1988), 409–430.

[3] "The Holy Fools," in *The Russian Religious Mind* (Cambridge, Mass.: Harvard University Press, 1946), vol. II, 316–343.

[4] "The Holy Fool," in *The Byzantine Saint*, special issue of *Sobornost* (1981); repr. (Crestwood, NY: SVS Press 2001), 106–113.

type of saint. In both cases, examples will be taken both from the Christian and the non-Christian world, drawing attention to both the universality and the Christian uniqueness of the fool-for-Christ's-sake.[5]

The Phenomenon of Holy Foolishness

The Orthodox Church has recognized the holy fool (in Greek *salos;* in Russian *iurodivy*) as a particular type of saint, and endowed the fools for Christ with their own liturgical hymnography:

Troparion Tone 1

Having heard the voice of your apostle Paul: "We are fools for
    Christ's sake,"
Your servant _____, Christ God, lived the life of a fool here on
    earth for your sake.
Therefore, as we venerate his memory, we entreat You, O Lord, to
    save our souls.

Kontakion Tone 8

Desiring heavenly beauty, you left the low delights of the flesh.
You passed away, blessed _____, after leading a life like the
    angels,
empty of any desire for the things of this vain world.
Together with them, intercede without ceasing for us all!

The secondary literature also treats holy fools together as one type of saint. There are good reasons for doing so. While the fools for Christ (as we know them from their *vitae*) are a diverse group of people, with sometimes widely differing dispositions and different ways of reflecting Christ, there are also several defining features which they hold in common together and in distinction from other types of saints. These substantiate the overarching category of "holy fool" in the face of the variety of fools. They also remind us of the unique significance of this brand of sanctity. A brief review follows:

---

[5]In the present essay I focus on the Byzantine and Russian traditions. Holy Folly in the Christian West is a related phenomenon, also with some marked differences. The most useful single study of the western fools remains John Saward's *Perfect Fools: Folly for Christ's Sake in Catholic and Orthodox Spirituality* (Oxford, 1980).

A quality of the fool which stands out in a particular way in Bishop Kallistos' assessment is his *freedom*. He (or she) secures this freedom by at least two means. The fool, regardless of what kind, bursts into the society, sometimes seemingly out of nowhere. The fool is a *stranger*, either actually originating from a foreign place or simply seeming to be from an alien land, a foreign psychological terrain. It is virtually impossible to be prophetic in one's own country, among one's own kin, as Our Lord recognized clearly:[6] there are too many ties and associations, people will place you and categorize you. The fool, who is a kind of prophet, comes from somewhere else, irrupting into the society with no such ties.

Similarly, the fool owns nothing, wears almost nothing, and wants nothing material. In this way he is *free from attachment*. He has absolutely nothing to lose, except his health and his comfort (he is always exposed to the elements, and often beaten for his activities). But he does not care about these either. The fool is a peculiar gift to the world, which comes with no strings attached. In these ways is the fool a free being, although this freedom is hard-earned.

Stemming from this freedom is the fool's *truth-telling*, his ability to speak the unspeakable, to overturn societal and religious hypocrisies. It is not for nothing that the fools' *vitae* often dwell on the spirit world—they are full of accounts of angels and demons—for the fool is an exorcist. The demons with which he wrestles are not only of the hypostatic variety: he is a discerner of good and evil, of genuineness and falsity, wherever he goes, in the marketplace as well as in the church. The fool reveals facades, dismantles empty societal constructs, overturns values which have been taken for granted. The world seeks riches, authority, and intelligence; the fool exults in destitution and the renunciation of intelligence and cleverness.

The fool has a kinship with the lowly of society, the outcasts, the "dregs," insofar as they are like him, but also perhaps because they tend to remain unaffected by the crippling mores of respectability. Like Christ, the fool enjoys their company more than anyone else's.

Proceeding from and underscoring the fool's freedom are his strange and often scandalous public activities. The fool is a *non-conformist*, to the highest degree. Hence the pranks, the absence of regard for bodily functions, the societal and even religious outrages, such as public fast-breaking and disruption of the liturgy. His pranks have the double function of exposing and

---

[6]Mark 6:4, with parallels in all of the gospels.

awakening a self-satisfied public, while at the same time removing from them any suspicion that the fool might indeed be a holy one. For nothing is more dangerous to the fool's freedom than the praise and veneration of others. For him to be caught in the net of respectability would end it all.

In his nonconformity as with everything else, the fool is a *maximalist*. In the Book of Revelation, when God speaks to the church of Laodicea, he says: "I know your works: you are neither cold nor hot. Would that you were cold or hot! So, because you are lukewarm, and neither cold nor hot, I will spew you out of my mouth" (Rev 3:15–16). The fool is anything but lukewarm. By the radical nature of his life, he takes the tepid lives of the people and brings them either to freeze or to boil. This is another of his distinctive gifts to mankind.

The fool's maximalism is certainly applied to his asceticism, and perhaps more than anything else the fool is an *extreme ascetic*. Most fools, of whatever ilk, are noticed first for being ill-clad—they let the elements work to mortify their flesh. The rest of the fool's asceticism is often practiced away from the public eye. Whatever the public outrages, mutterings, and digestive indiscretions, in private he abases himself, prays and fasts more than anyone else. The "blessed idiot" likewise lives in humble self-denial. The extreme asceticism of the fool is that which grounds everything else that he does. In self-abasement he finds—again—freedom, and the humility to withstand the scorn and beatings that are a part of his daily existence. In his intense passion-fighting, prayer and fasting, the fool grounds his profound sense of discernment.

And *discernment* is crucial for the fool. For it is only to the extent that the fool is a true discerner of spirits, a truly pastoral and mysteriously insightful person, that his pranks and outrages, or his mental condition, do not merely scandalize people or drive them away from the Church, but somehow strangely bring them nearer to God, to the Church, to the genuine, to the eternal. For the role of the prophet is not only to rebuke but to build up, to console and to encourage (cf. I Cor 14:3).

Three Types of Fool

The features set out above apply to virtually anyone given the title of "holy fool." Yet this does not do justice to the significant differences between types of holy fool, their function and their effect on the society. Reading the *vitae* it is possible to discern at least three kinds of Christian holy fool. The categories

I am suggesting are of course flexible, and the saints themselves do not always fall neatly in to any one of them. Nonetheless, the examples provided from the vitae together with their resonances from broader sociological and religious types across the cultures, point towards the following categorization.

The Scandalous Prankster

The most fully-developed portrait we have of the "scandalous prankster" is St Symeon of Emesa, of whom we know thanks to a glorious seventh-century *vita* by Leontius of Neapolis.[7] This *vita,* which becomes a type for those of many later fools, describes a man who, after 29 years in the desert as an ascetic, heeds the calling to return to the city under the guise of a madman, in order to "mock the world."

By now many scenes in Symeon's life are well known. His antics were designed to unmask and unsettle social and religious hypocrisy, as well as to remove the impression from people's minds that he was actually a holy man. In church, he extinguished the oil lamps and hurled nuts at the faithful. He ate sausage on the cathedral steps on Great and Holy Friday. In the public baths, he took off what little clothing he was wearing, wrapped it around his head like a turban, and promptly entered the women's section. He burned incense in the palms of his hands. He would enter the homes of the wealthy and pretend to fondle the female servants. He would go around limping, dancing, dragging himself along on his buttocks. He enjoyed sticking his foot in front of running people in order to trip them.

Symeon's scandal-mongering ways of foolishness found reflection in several subsequent saints. Isaac the Syrian could write of some monks who, "lest they should be praised on account of wonderful deeds performed in secret, assumed the habits of lunatics, though they were in full possession of their wits and their serenity."[8] A later Isaak, the eleventh-century recluse of the Kievan Caves, began to be bothersome after he "miraculously" caught a pesky raven in the kitchen with his bare hands. As soon as the brothers began to consider him a wonderworker he began "to make trouble, now for the

---

[7] *Vie de Syméon le Fou et Vie de Jean de Chypre,* trans. and commentary by A.-J. Festugière, Greek text ed. by Lennart Rydén (Paris: Geuthner, 1974). See also Derek Krueger, *Symeon the Holy Fool: Leontius's Life and the Late Antique City* (University of California Press, 1996), featuring a full English translation of the *vita.*

[8] *The Ascetical Homilies of Saint Isaac the Syrian* (Brookline, MA: Holy Transfiguration Monastery, 1984), 55.

abbot and now for the brethren."[9] The fourteenth-century Nicholas and Theodore, both fools in Novgorod, parodied the political factionalism of that city by holding mock battles, throwing stones or cabbage at each other across the Volkhov river. (The *vitae* note that at some points in their mock cabbage-hurling battles, the saints would return to their respective riverbanks walking over the water as if it were dry land.)[10]

The antics of Isaak were about shunning praise; those of Nicholas and Theodore exposed absurd societal pretense. Both motivations are typical for the holy fool, and the means, in the case of these particular fools, is prankishness. Symeon and the fools like him are both playful and serious, clowning and somber, scandalous and ascetical. Mysteriously, amazingly, they point to the age to come by means of their pranks. These are often quite outrageous, including frequent public defecation and wind-breaking: in this kind of holy fool, eschatology meets scatology.

The scandalous conduct of the *salos* has been compared to the nonconformist and anti-intellectual ways of the Cynics, in particular to their celebrated Diogenes of Sinope (4th c. BC), whose biographical details are often strikingly similar to those of Symeon.[11] More generally, the "scandalous prankster" type can to some extent be interpreted along the lines of the classic trickster figure, a commonplace in folklore in all places and times. At their best, tricksters are in the business of exposing falsehoods. Like clowns (a related category) they often make use of masks, although the trickster's mask is figurative: it is his eccentricity, or sometimes a feigned madness. But their use of the mask is conscious and deliberate.

One of the better-known tricksters of (non-Christian) history is Nasreddin Hodja, of thirteenth-century Anatolia. Anecdotes and sayings about this highly popular figure multiply with each century. Some of these anecdotes themselves fall into types, such as the at least three instances where he is seen to be riding his donkey backwards.[12] Lao-tzu, sixth-century BC author of the

---

[9]See Fedotov, *Russian Religious Mind* vol. 2, 324f. See also Kovalevsky, *Khrista Radi Iurodivye Vostochnoi i Russkoi Tserkvi* (Moscow, 1895; third edn. Moscow, 1902, repr. Ontario, 1984), 163–67. There is a suggestion that Isaak's "feigned" foolishness had its roots in an actual mental instability expressed earlier in his life.

[10]See Kovalevsky, ibid. 191–205.

[11]See Derek Krueger, *Symeon the Holy Fool: Leontius's Life and the Late Antique City.*

[12]Here is one of the three dialogues that is told: One day Nasreddin Hodja was riding his donkey, facing towards the back. "Hodja" the people said, "you are sitting on your donkey backwards!"—"No," he replied. "It's not that I am sitting on the donkey backwards, I'm just more interested in where I have been coming from than where I am going."

Tao Te Ching, is sometimes also depicted as the "sacred fool," riding his ox backwards, as is the sixteenth-century Zen master Seiogyu.[13] As it happens, the Blessed Staretz Feofil (19th c.) of the Kiev-Caves Lavra, was known for riding his ox backwards too. (Sometimes he would ride facing forwards, not on an ox, but on an exceptionally small horse. He would guide either beast not by holding any reigns, but with a kind of telepathy.)[14] The prankster, across times and cultures, is particularly adept at communicating his message through inversion (or shall we say, reversal), on which more will be said below.

The Terrifying Ascetic

The Life of Symeon of Emesa finds a kind of counterpart in another archetypal *vita,* that of St Andrew *Salos* of Constantinople.[15] Dating probably from somewhere in the tenth century,[16] this *vita* presents a dramatic and pious portrait of a figure who was supposed to have lived in the fifth century.[17] Andrew, like Symeon, feigns his madness, and mostly pretends to be either mad or drunk, sometimes dancing about, or muttering. Like Symeon, he on occasion relieves himself in public. He drinks from puddles and lives off of the scant alms of only certain givers deemed by him to be acceptable.

He is revealed as an intense ascetic, and one who is very much in communication with the spirit world. He levitates during prayer, and at one point, when confronted by the devil and his demons, he calls upon St John the Theologian and his band of fighters to come and give them a "supernatural beating" as Andrew stands by and laughs.[18] At another point, the apostles Peter and Paul come to his rescue, hovering in midair. He ascends into paradise and is given a tour of the heavens. His companion Epiphanios forgets to mind his

[13]See *Parabola,* 26, iii (Aug., 2001), special issue on The Fool, cover illustration.

[14]See Vladimir Znosko, ed., *Hieroschemamonk Feofil, Fool for Christ's Sake* (Jordanville, NY, 1987).

[15]*The Life of St Andrew the Fool* (2 vols.), commentary, critical text and translation by Lennart Rydén, *Studia Byzantina Upsaliensia,* 4:1 (Uppsala, 1995). See also J. Grosdidier de Matons, "Les thèmes de l'edification dans la vie d'André Salos," in *Travaux et Mémoires,* 4 (1970), 277–328.

[16]The date of this *vita* has been disputed by Rydén and Cyril Mango in a series of articles from 1978–1983. Rydén's final appraisal, accounting for Mango's views, are to be found in vol. 1 of his *Life of St Andrew the Fool,* 41–56.

[17]Abundant anachronisms in the vita show him to be either transplanted in time or entirely fictitious. Yet it would be unlikely in the tenth century to invent, out of nothing, behavior such as is attributed to Andrew in order to make a pious, edifying story. It would seem probable that his character has basis in the behavior of one or more actual people.

[18]*Life,* vol. 2, p. 22.

kitchen fire when he goes off to church, but returns to find an angel cooking his bean soup, testing it for readiness.[19]

Andrew is constantly in conversation with angels and in battles with demons, the latter always in the guise of Ethiopians. He describes his visions to the hagiographer, apparently so that the latter could record it for the edification of his readers. But it is edification of a peculiar kind: many of his dealings with the spirit world are scare tactics, designed to frighten the wits out of the sinners whom he encounters. This is a portrait of a saint who is acutely attuned to good and evil, spiritual and material. But it sometimes appears that Andrew's chief aim, which he effects almost exclusively via the spirit world, is to terrify or effectively to bully his hearers into repentance. Certainly this is the attitude the hagiographer wishes to inculcate in his readers. As one commentator on Andrew's life puts it, ". . . the author, a penitent's penitent, aims to keep his sheep on the narrow path by instilling in them an obsessive fear, whose desired effect is to limit their freedom of choice between good and evil."[20]

In one episode Andrew warns a grave-robber, on his way to a theft, that he will not see the sun again if he carries through with his deed. The thief ignores him. But when he steals the clothing off a dead woman, her corpse comes alive, as it were, and strikes him so hard on the face that he goes blind. She then stands and lectures him. He spends the rest of his life a blind beggar, remembering Andrew's warning, and praising God.[21] Other sinners, likewise, after their encounters with Andrew (during which he slaps and beats them), end up as beggars, have demons unleashed at them (by Andrew), or are given guided tours of hell in order to give them a taste of what is in store for them.

In some ways not unlike Andrew is St Procopius of Ustiug, of the thirteenth century. His sixteenth-century *vita*, which in places borrows directly from that of Andrew, is characterized again not by pranks but by severe asceticism. His chief "foolish" eccentricity lay in the pokers he carried in his hand at all times, which the people of the city began to rely on with something of a superstitious certainty that they would portend a good or bad harvest, depending on which way they were facing. Generally, Procopius resembles Andrew primarily in his stark, somber asceticism, and his Jonah-like prophecy to the people. As Fedotov sums up Procopius' vita, "Not foolishness

[19]Ibid. 75–9.
[20]Grosdidier de Matons, "Les thèmes," 328.
[21]*Life*, 137–41.

but inhuman ascetic sufferings and humiliations are offered to the pious meditation of the reader."[22]

Andrew's harsh tactics are recalled in several events in the life of St Basil the Blessed (†1552), a beloved saint especially in his native Moscow. In one episode, three girls who laugh at the saint are made to go blind, until they repent before his feet in tears. He blows into their eyes, and their sight is restored. More chillingly, when a youth tries to extort a fine cloak from the saint by pretending to be dead, Basil changes the ruse into reality—and the man actually dies—"for the wicked shall be destroyed" (cf. Ps 37:38).

As it happens, the majority of the Russian *iurodivye* resemble Andrew more than they do Symeon. The characteristics of the classic holy fool in Russia have less to do with prankishness than with the severest forms of asceticism; they are sooner somber than playful. As a telling example we take the life of the sixteenth-century St John the Hairy. Little is known about this saint; we are even left guessing about the reason for his nickname (although an icon manual specifies that the hair on his head must be "great"). His life is described as "in the manner of a *iurodivy*, suffering scorn and needfulness, without home or place to lay his head . . . spending his time in humility, patience, and unceasing prayer."[23] For this Russian hagiographer, "the manner of a *iurodivy*" consists essentially in lowliness and the suffering of scorn, rather than in any "foolishness" as such.

This type of holy fool is not always as "terrifying" as that of the prototypic Andrew of Constantinople. And while there can be something of the trickster figure in him as well, he is defined primarily by a radical and somber urban asceticism, rather than by high jinks. The extreme ascetic is a primordial religious type, and one need not look far outside Christianity to find examples of severe self-denial, exposure to the elements, and the wearing of heavy chains, much like the ascetical *iurodivyi*. E. M. Thompson shows a direct linkage between the asceticism of the Russian holy fool and the Ruthenian shaman.[24] But to limit the spiritual provenance of the *iurodivyi* to one people is unnecessarily narrow.

---

[22]*Russian Religious Mind*, vol. II, 329.
[23]Kovalevsky, ibid. 260f.
[24]*Understanding Russia: The Holy Fool in Russian Culture* (University Press of America, 1987).

The Blessed Idiot

The question of the feigned nature of the fools' "madness" is difficult to discern. We are effectively at the mercy of the hagiographer, whose piety leads him to assert in nearly every case that the mask of madness was donned as a deliberate camouflage, a chosen disguise for someone who was entirely in possession of his wits. But there are cases where the reader may suspect a genuine mental disorder, disturbance, or deficiency, of which God makes use for salvific ends. The Russian word "blazhenny," which is most commonly translated as "blessed," can also mean "innocent," denoting the kind of purity of heart and love that one can often behold with a particular clarity and beauty in the mentally handicapped. The "foolishness" of this kind of saint, whether feigned or with roots in a genuine mental condition, is manifest not in prankishness, nor in demon stories, but usually in an intellectual and physical simplicity and lowliness.

There are at least three stories from the fifth and sixth centuries which describe strikingly similar occurrences and persons, probably "blessed" ones. The first and most celebrated is found in Palladius' *Lausiac History*,[25] and recounted again in Bishop Kallistos' essay,[26] where Abba Pitiroum is told in a vision of a woman who is "more excellent" than he, and is instructed to go and find her in the monastery at Tabenna. Arriving there, the Abba has all the nuns brought before him—all but one, for she is "mad" and "of no account." Insisting that she be brought out, Pitiroum recognizes her instantly as the one described in his vision. As soon as he praises her publicly she flees and is never heard of again.

Of the two virtually identical stories, one concerns a nameless "idiot" monk.[27] When three monks (who were in fact angels in disguise) visit a certain monastery, they are shown all but one brother, who was thought to be an embarrassment. He ends up greatly impressing the visiting Abbot, in his wisdom and asceticism. The sixth-century *Life of the Abbot Daniel of Scetis*[28] describes another visit, this time again to a woman's monastery, where all are shown to the visitor but one woman, also nameless, who is constantly seeming drunk, passing the night by the latrines. The visitor, Daniel himself, singles her out, sensing that it was obviously in order to see her that he came to

[25]For this account, cf. Budge, W., ed., The Paradise of the Fathers (by Palladius), Vol I, Chatto & Windus, 1907, 147–9.

[26]In *Sobornost*, p. 10, in the SVS version, 157.

[27]Patrologia Orientalis 8, 178ff., ed. F. Nau.

[28]Ed. L. Clugnet (Paris, 1901), 22–25.

this place.[29] As the nuns and the abbess begin to revere her she flees, making off with Daniel's cap and staff.

A later such figure may be the fourteenth-century St Savas the Younger.[30] Savas was associated with Mount Athos (like his contemporary, Maximos the Kapsokalyvite), but also journeyed for nearly twenty years throughout the Near East and Asia Minor. Other than his nakedness or near-nakedness, his foolishness was expressed neither through pranks nor through aggressive acts, but passively: he was simply silent. People took him not for a madman, but for a dimwit.

The greatly venerated St Xenia of Petersburg, also called "blazhennaya," is another example of someone whose strange behavior was not a put-on. After her husband's death, she donned his clothing and ceased to acknowledge her own name, answering only to his. She lived as an ascetic, and had the gift of clairvoyance that is common to most of the holy fools. No matter what was her mental state before the death of her husband, she clearly suffered a certain breakdown which, again, was sublimated into a special kind of sanctity, of a very great and enduring kind.

Like the trickster, the blessed idiot figures into history and fiction across time and space. Nineteenth-century Russian novels feature several characters who fall into the mold of the "blessed," such as Marie in Dostoevsky's *The Idiot*,[31] and "Smerdiashchaya [Stinking] Elizaveta" in his *The Brothers Karamazov*. Both were "idiot girls" who would spend nights outside, ill-clad and ill-shod, the scorn of the town, until they came to be venerated as "blazhennye." Real-life examples from the same period are seen in Sarov, in the persons of Pelagia Ivanovna and Paraskeva (Pasha) Ivanovna.[32] No claim is made that their madness is pretended; their hagiographers, or at any rate their

---

[29]Elements of these three stories are reflected in the Cinderella folktale, of which there are hundreds of known version in all continents and which dates, in its written form, at least as far back as the ninth century.

[30]Cf. A.-J. Festugière, *Vie de Syméon le Fou*, 223–249. Also see Rydén, "The Holy Fool," 112.

[31]Contrary to the superficial reckonings of some observers, the protagonist of this novel, Prince Myshkin, is not himself a *yurodivy* but Dostoevsky's notion of "a wholly beautiful individual" or "the perfect man," as the author's correspondence indicates. His Christ-like simplicity, along with his epilepsy (and the book's title) have led many to associate him with the holy fools, although he shares virtually none of their actual characteristics. On this issue, cf. Ludmilla Buketoff Turkevich, "Religious Aspect [sic] of Dostoevsky's 'Idiot'," *SVTQ* 33 (1989), 377–391.

[32]See *Seraphim's Seraphim* (Boston: Holy Transfiguration Monastery, 1979); Kovalevsky, ibid. 289–370.

redactors, freely admit a certain mental handicap, which "even aided [Blessed Pelagia] in her foolishness for Christ's sake."[33]

Looking now outside Russia and Christendom, the Zen poet-lunatic Ryokwan (d. 1831), was one who "lacked what is known as common sense, of which we people of the world have too much," but "had a most sensitive heart for all things human and natural."[34] Once, in his grass hut, a bamboo shoot sprouted of which he grew very fond. When it began to outgrow his hut, he attempted to burn a hole in the roof for it, and managed to burn down his entire hut. Does not the mind move instantly to St Maximos the Kapsokalyvite, who, though for somewhat different reasons, regularly burnt his hut down to the ground?[35]

†

The categories explored above interpenetrate each other, and some fools can be seen to embody elements of more than one of them. In places it is only a fine line that separates Symeon and Andrew: Andrew too dances about, and Symeon has his own exchanges with demons, conversations with angels, and at one point he blinds a woman until she renounces "the acephalic heresy" and becomes Orthodox. It is a question of overall focus, where the difference in character between the saints is significant.

There is surely a place in Christian spiritual life for each type of fool, for each type of hagiography. Different temperaments are suited to these different styles, and each person will be taught in a different way. In each case, the story of the fool is no doubt challenging: to learn from the pranks of Symeon is not necessarily easy, and some indeed are left scandalized rather than edified. Neither is it natural, to some, to be edified by the likes of Andrew, although the type of episode described in his *vita*—focusing on the spirit world more than the human, on gloom rather than joy, on fear more than love—are typical of the stories recounted in many settings to this day. And for many, the idiot is just an idiot; the homeless, ill-clad one on the street is a subject of pity, or even annoyance, not of reverence. But when it works

[33] *Seraphim's Seraphim*, xiv-xv.

[34] D. T. Suzuki, *Zen and Japanese Culture* (Princeton, 1970; orig. 1959), 364f.

[35] See Kallistos Ware, "St Maximos of Kapsokalyvia and Fourteenth Century Athonite Hesychasm" (cf. n. 2). Also cf. R. M. Dawkins, *The Monks of Mount Athos* (London, 1936), 79, where we learn that Maximos was known not only for his cottage-burning, but for his ability to fly.

properly, the foolishness of any true *iurodivy* can open the eyes of the spiritually blind.

In setting out the categories of holy fool, our forays outside of the Christian world have helped to illustrate the distinctions between them. Looking again at the broader phenomenon of foolishness, we can also see something of the unifying principle of "the holy fool," for the defining features of the *iurodivy* are reflections of wider archetypes.

The fool is an example of the phenomenon of *inversion,* where the straight is manifest through the crooked, the forward is seen in the backward. It is a strange but universal phenomenon that humans are often most profoundly enlightened through reversal. This is why, in some of the accounts of Abbadisciple relationships, the spiritual father tells the monk to plant the cabbage upside down, or to water a dead stick for years. He is not only teaching obedience, but illumining his disciple to the truth through inversion, which is liable to operate on a deeper, intuitive level.

This reverse logic is familiar from the Taoist and Zen koans and fables, whose goal is to enlighten through first confounding and then bypassing our logic, our conscious deliberations—or, as the Orthodox pray, to "release us from slavery to our own reasonings." The koans work by placing illogical scenarios before us, such as the contemplation of "the sound of one hand [clapping]." In a particularly extreme example of Zen "inversion," the ninth-century master Chu-chih (a.k.a. Gutei), brought on the enlightenment of his disciple when, having perceived just the precise moment, he cut off the disciple's finger.

As the Spanish Jesuit Balthasar Gracian observed, "The things of this world can be truly perceived only by looking at them backwards."[36] Or, to paraphrase Kierkegaard, while we live life forwards, we often understand it backwards.[37] This is the logic of inversion.

The Christian Particularity of the Holy Fool

While it is almost superfluous to set out the Christian particularity of the fool-for-Christ's-sake, it is worth revisiting. For one, the fools-for-Christ represent just the kind of foolish wisdom that Paul wrote about (1 Cor 1:20; 1:27;

[36]Cited in Barbara A. Babcock (ed.), *The Reversible World: Symbolic Inversion in Art and Society* (Ithaca: Cornell U. Press, 1978), 13.

[37]Cf. Patrick L. Gardiner, *Kierkegaard* (Oxford, 1988), 90.

3:18). But the ultimate Christian example of inversion is the life-giving death of the Savior. The cross, as we know, is seen as "foolishness" and "scandal" (cf. 1 Cor 1:23). Not all could accept that "Lo, through the cross, joy has come into the world."[38] And while he was neither prankster, nor super-ascetic, nor blessed idiot, Christ—the *crucified* Christ—represents the ultimate prototype for the inversion that is holy foolishness. In and through Christ, joy comes out of suffering, strength is manifest through weakness (2 Cor 12:9). The Orthodox take a special pleasure in oxymorons, speaking and singing of bright sadness, sober inebriation, dazzling darkness. And we are in perpetual awe of the irony of Christ: the One who hung the earth upon the waters is hung upon the tree.

The fools-for-Christ's-sake represented a Christianization, a baptism of the types of folly found elsewhere. Much like the Zen stories or the Zen poet lunatics, like Hodja the trickster, like the extreme renunciants everywhere, the fools-for-Christ seek to cultivate freedom, genuineness and detachment in themselves and in others. For some people, this detachment is an end in itself. But for the Christian holy fool, the sought-for freedom, spontaneity and wakefulness is a space that is ready to be filled by the presence of Christ, a silence into which can be breathed the living Word. The *iurodivyi* are renunciants, but they are not Messalians—they do not renounce the Church and her sacramental life. The *vitae* concur in showing them to be publicly strange or scandalous, sometimes even at the liturgy, but privately, or to the eyes of a precious few, they were extremely pious and explicitly Christ-loving. Their lives are oriented towards Christ.

The Unique Lesson of the Fool

The fool for Christ, in more ways than one, is an exceptional phenomenon, distinct from other types of sanctity. One indicator of this uniqueness is that the fool (together with that similarly extreme nonconformist, the stylite) is alone in being a kind of saint whose life we are *not* called to imitate. The Church tells us: be a prophet, be a martyr, be a healer, a preacher, a pastor, a missionary. But don't be a fool, for Christ's sake. That is because so few people have the calling for this inherently rare and different path; so few have the necessary discernment to make the inversion into something life-giving.

All of the various types of sanctity are interpenetrating: martyrdom, apostleship, prophecy, asceticism, healing—they go hand in hand. And the fool,

---

[38]Sung at Matins after the Gospel reading.

as Bishop Kallistos showed in his eponymous essay, is part prophet, part apostle. But he is also ultimately an ascetic, and he often ends his life by being martyred, effectively for telling too much truth. The prophetic and apostolic qualities of the fool's life stand as examples for us, but the *means* of his prophecy, which largely revolve around scandal and shock, are like a fire which is too dangerous for the rest of us to touch. Again, it takes an exceedingly refined and rare perspicacity to make an otherwise merely scandalous act into prophecy, building up the people and calling them to repentance.

The saying of St John Climacus applies particularly to the holy fool, be he prankster, scare-monger, or "blessed" simpleton: "To admire the labors of the saints is good; to emulate them wins salvation; but to wish suddenly to imitate their life in every point is unreasonable and impossible."[39] And yet, the ways in which the fool is prophet, apostle, martyr, ascetic, and the ways in which he is like a child—innocent and simple—these stand as a kind of cumulative example for Christians. Don't be a *iurodivy*, the Church says, but *like* him be a prophet. Be intellectually pure and humble. Be a person of prayer. Check your conformity, shun ideologies, and tell the truth.

---

[39] *Ladder of Divine Ascent*, Step 4:42.

❦ The Theology of the *Philokalia* ❦

Andrew Louth

I N THE YEAR 1782, there was published in Venice the first edition of a
work called Φιλοκαλία τῶν Ἱερῶν Νηπτικῶν, "Anthology of the Sacred
Ascetics," compiled by St Makarios, Bishop of Corinth, and St Nikodimos, a
monk of the Holy Mountain of Athos. This marked a turning point in Orthodox theology, for it can be argued that all that has been most vital in Orthodox theology over the last couple of centuries has been inspired, or at least
touched, by this work. For the *Philokalia* was part of a movement of renewal
within Orthodoxy at the end of the eighteenth century, a movement of
renewal that was to be tested in the nineteenth century in the Balkans, as
Greece, Bulgaria, Serbia and Romania threw off the Ottoman yoke, and that
in more propitious conditions inspired literary, philosophical and theological
movements in nineteenth-century Russia. This movement of renewal ran parallel with similar movements in Western Europe that may loosely be classified
in the term "Romanticism"; how much the Philokalic movement shared with
these contemporary movements is a subject that is still largely to be explored.
In the twentieth century the inspiration of the *Philokalia* is perhaps even more
striking: the so-called "Paris school" was both directly, in so far as it embraced
Palamism, and indirectly, through its roots in nineteenth-century Slavo-
philism and Symbolism (Khomiakov, Dostoevsky, Solov'ev), indebted to the
Philokalia; and particular theologians, most notably Fr Dumitru Stăniloae,
but also Christos Yannaras, Olivier Clément, Paul Evdokimov, and certainly
Bishop Kallistos himself, display a similar indebtedness. But the influence of
the *Philokalia* has been felt beyond such intellectual circles, and indeed
beyond Orthodoxy itself: it has been remarked that the practice of the Jesus
Prayer, surely the spiritual heart of the *Philokalia*, became in the course of the
twentieth century more widespread than at any earlier time; and the monastic spirituality of the *Philokalia* also found a distinctive voice in that century
through such as St Silouan and his disciple, Fr Sophrony, the Romanian
monk, Fr Cleopa, and various abbots of the Holy Mountain, such as Fr

Aimilianos of Simonpetra, though perhaps the most poignant manifestation of the spirituality of the *Philokalia* was in the notorious prison camps of Soviet Russia and other countries that fell under the Communist yoke in the twentieth century.

Among the many lasting achievements of Bishop Kallistos, one that will perhaps have the widest influence is his part in producing the first complete English translation of the *Philokalia*.[1] It is, therefore, especially appropriate that at least one contribution to a volume in his honour should seek to explore something of the theological vision that the *Philokalia* both has expressed and continues to inspire.

To mention the date 1782 in connexion with the *Philokalia* is somewhat deceptive. The year before, 1781, was the date of the publication of the first edition of Immanuel Kant's *Critique of Pure Reason*. The significance of that date is clear: in that year Kant declared to the world the principles of his critical philosophy, which was to transform the history of philosophy in the Western world. 1781 is the beginning, faltering at first, to be sure, of that influence. Certainly Kant's critical philosophy can be related to movements in philosophy earlier in the eighteenth century, but its origins prior to 1781 lie essentially in the intellectual biography of the sage of Königsberg. The significance of 1782 in relation to the *Philokalia* is rather different. The *Philokalia* is an anthology of theological and ascetical texts, collected and arranged by Makarios and Nikodimos (it seems likely that Makarios had most to do with the collection, and Nikodimos most to do with arrangement). Such a collection of texts belongs to a monastic tradition: a monastic tradition, on the one hand, of very great antiquity, and, on the other, of more immediate provenance. For the collecting of such texts by individual monks is something that most likely goes back to the very origins of Christian monasticism: collections of biblical texts, psalm verses, sayings of notable ascetics, striking passages from books read. The *Philokalia* itself contains examples of such collections (most notably, the huge collection ascribed to the otherwise unknown Peter of Damascus, that comprises nearly an eighth of the whole work). To begin with, perhaps, such collections were made by individual monks as an aid to their life of prayer and contemplation: they were texts to meditate upon. Some

---

[1] *The Philokalia. The Complete Text*, compiled by St Nikodimos of the Holy Mountain and St Makarios of Corinth, translated from the Greek and edited by G.E.H. Palmer, Philip Sherrard and Kallistos Ware, 4 vols. (out of 5) so far, London: Faber and Faber, 1979–95. Bishop Kallistos also wrote the article on the Philokalia in the *Dictionnaire di Spiritualité*: vol. 12, part 1, Paris: Beauchesne, 1984, cols. 1336–52, *s.v.* "Philocalie".

of these collections may have circulated more widely, among the disciples of a notable master, for example. Such collections paralleled the practice, much in evidence from the fifth century onwards, of compiling collections (*florilegia*) of passages from the fathers on theological matters, particularly the most contested theological issue in the East at that time, the doctrine of Christ. One of the most famous of these collections, which attempted to cover the whole range of Christian doctrine, was St John Damascene's *Exact Exposition of the Orthodox Faith*. That collection, like many such collections, took the form of a century, that is, a collection of 100 chapters or paragraphs. The first, apparently, to compile such centuries was Evagrios, the disciple of the Cappadocians and the great exponent of the spirituality of the fathers of the Egyptian desert, where he spent the last dozen or so years of his life. The "century" was a monastic literary genre; with its relatively short chapters, such a century would constitute a convenient booklet that a monk could copy for himself and keep by him. But such centuries, or the materials from which the chapters were drawn, could be gathered together, sometimes to produce quite a substantial work, such as the "Collection" (*Synagoge*) made by Paul of the Constantinopolitan monastery of the Mother of God Evergetis in the eleventh century. So, on the one hand, the *Philokalia*, as a collection, belongs to an ancient monastic literary genre. But, on the other hand, it belongs to a more defined monastic tradition: that associated with the revival on the Holy Mountain of Athos that began in twelfth century, called "hesychasm." This spiritual movement attracted criticism in the fourteenth century, was defended by Gregory Palamas, and upheld by synods in Constantinople in the 1340s and 1350s. As one goes through the collection of writings in the *Philokalia* (they are arranged in what is intended to be chronological order), one finds that they converge on works by St Gregory Palamas and his disciples, precursors and supporters: the *Philokalia* is a hesychast anthology. At the heart of hesychasm as a mediæval movement (the word "hesychasm" can be used much more widely to denote the form of the monastic ideal that values contemplative quiet or ἡσυχία) lay the use of the Jesus prayer as a way of achieving prayer of the heart: it is for this reason that I earlier described the Jesus prayer as the spiritual heart of the *Philokalia*.

The very collection constituted by the *Philokalia*, then, belongs to a tradition, defined both simply as monastic, and more specifically as hesychast. The date 1782 is therefore much less significant that the date 1781 in relation to Kant's *Critique of Pure Reason*. It is not even the case that 1782 has much significance so far as the precise collection of works comprised by the

Philokalia is concerned, as the date 1861 has in relation to Palgrave's *Golden Treasury*, for instance. This is evident from the fact that the Slavonic *Dobrotoliubye*, published eleven years later in Moscow, was probably already in the process of translation, when the saints Makarios and Nikodimos published their collection in 1782. They were drawing on an already fairly fixed canon of hesychast works, just as St Païssy Velichkovsky was in his collection. Simply reflecting on the fact of the publication of the *Philokalia* has forced on our attention the place of tradition in the formation of the work.

Tradition, then, is perhaps where we should start in our consideration of the theological vision of the *Philokalia*. The publication of such an extensive collection of texts is to make certain claims about the tradition that these writings represent. This can be put in two ways: first, the selection of texts has the effect of defining the shape of the tradition, and secondly, the nature of the texts themselves serves to define what is essential about this tradition. In general terms, of course, the tradition claimed by the *Philokalia* is that of the fathers. But the notion of patristic authority, the authority of the fathers, is one that requires some definition: which fathers? And why? Are certain fathers more important than others? Is there a hierarchy, as it were, among the fathers claimed as authoritative? The selection presented by the *Philokalia* suggests certain answers to these questions. At first sight these answers seem strange: where are the great fathers of Orthodoxy, St Athanasios and St Cyril, and particularly the "three great hierarchs and universal teachers," St Basil the Great, St Gregory the Theologian, and St John Chrysostom? Could it be that the *Philokalia* is setting aside doctrinal orthodoxy in favour of ascetic authenticity, for all the fathers chosen are, as the title of the work indicates, "neptic" Fathers, that is ascetics, those trained in watchfulness or vigilance? That suggestion can be set aside for two reasons. It would not be true to suggest that the saints who compiled the *Philokalia*, Makarios and Nikodimos, sat light to doctrinal orthodoxy; Nikodimos himself shows his concern for correct doctrine both in his collection of and commentary on the Sacred Canons, the *Pedalion*, or the "Rudder," and, more engagingly, in his commentary on the liturgical canons for the Great Feasts, the *Heortodromion*. Furthermore, the two fathers to whom individually most space is devoted in the *Philokalia*, St Maximos the Confessor and St Gregory Palamas, are two saints who set such great store by doctrinal orthodoxy as to face persecution, and in the case of Maximos, martyrdom, for its sake. Doctrinal orthodoxy is hardly set aside, then, rather the selection of fathers in the *Philokalia* has another motive: to take one directly to engagement with God, leading to deification, that it is the whole point of doctrinal orthodoxy to safeguard. The fathers mentioned above are omitted, not because what they have to say is unimportant, but because the *Philokalia* starts from a different starting-point, namely, what is required of us in our search for the truth that Orthodoxy enshrines. The *Philokalia* has a particular purpose, but it presupposes the whole context of Orthodox monasticism, or better, of faithful Orthodox living, especially the Divine Liturgy, in which the mysteries of the faith are proclaimed and celebrated and the faithful offered participation in the divine life through communion in the Precious Body and Pure Blood of Christ. If the texts selected in the *Philokalia* are not directly concerned with doctrinal orthodoxy, equally they are little concerned with the sacraments and the sacramental life, and yet both St Makarios and St Nikodimos were fervent advocates of a return to frequent communion on the part of the faithful in the Body and Blood of Christ.

Nevertheless, the fathers selected in the *Philokalia* represent a particular complexion; if we approach the fathers through the *Philokalia*, we enter the world of the fathers from a particular direction, so to speak. We do not, at first, encounter the great preachers, or the great thinkers, as such (that qualification is necessary, since both Maximos and Gregory Palamas were great thinkers, and Palamas a great preacher); we may later advance to them, but they are not the first we meet on the way of the *Philokalia*. We meet first those who have lived the Christian life with an uncompromising directness, we meet those who devoted their lives to prayer and communion with God. Ivan Kireevsky, the Russian intellectual who supported the monks of Optina Pustyn' in their enterprise of making known in Russian the works of the fathers, primarily the fathers of the Philokalic tradition, said of the fathers that they were "eyewitnesses concerning a country they have been to."[2] They are not simply right or eloquent and moving, they speak of what they know, they speak from experience of a country where they have been. It is as such that the *Philokalia* introduces us to the fathers.

The particular approach of the *Philokalia* is made clear in one of the shortest (and also one of the latest) pieces included: the "Fourteen chapters on prayer"[3] by Kallistos the Patriarch.[4] Kallistos begins his treatise with the

---

[2]I.V. Kireevsky, *Otryvki*: in *Polnoe Sobranie Sochineniy*, vol. 2 (Moscow, 1861, reprinted Ann Arbor, 1983), 334, cf. 340; English translation in *On Spiritual Unity, A Slavophile Reader*, translated and edited by Boris Jakim and Robert Bird (Hudson NY: Lindisfarne Books, 1998), 283, cf. 288.

[3]Not reached yet in the English translation referred to above. It can be found in the first edition (Venice, 1782) on pp. 1100–2.

[4]Either Kallistos I, patriarch 1350–3, 1355–63, a former Athonite monk who presided over

words, "If you want to learn the truth, take as your example the lyre-player."
Note that it is the *truth* Kallistos is concerned with, even though it is the skill
and discipline of the lyre-player that he evokes. He begins to develop his
theme thus: "For even here below he inclines his head and gives what is heard
the additional force of a song, holding the plectrum in his hand. And as the
strings skilfully sound together with one another, the lyre gives out music, and
there wells up within the lyre-player the sweetness of honey." Kallistos picks
up this image of something "welling up" (ἁλλόμενος) within the lyre-player,
and links it with the living water Jesus promised to the Samaritan woman at
Jacob's Well. One who wishes to know the truth is like the lyre-player in that
this truth comes from within, from the heart, that we must discover: "for she,
seeking this water perceived by the senses, found the water of life in herself,
welling up within. For as the earth has water naturally and it straightway
flows forth, so also the earth of the heart has this water naturally, welling up
and pouring forth, that is the fatherly light, which that Adam destroyed
through disobedience." Kalllistos' example of such water flowing from within
is St Ignatios, the bearer of God, the first-century martyr-bishop of Antioch:[5]
"For just as water flows from an ever-flowing fountain, so the living water,
that wells up, flows from the soul. As was also the case in the soul of the God-
bearing man, Ignatios, which prepared him to say: There is in me no fire that
loves matter, but it is water, active and speaking."[6] The discovery of this living water, radiating light, within is a matter of our removing obstacles within
ourselves: it is a matter of discipline, which Kallistos summarizes in terms of
ascetic struggle, purifying the intellect so that the divine rays of truth are
reflected in it, and bringing calm to the heart, thus making possible prayer in
which we are "transformed by the ray of the divine light and given shape by
the burning fire of the divine spirit." This purified and transformed state is,
however, fragile: "the intellect, purified through watchfulness, is easily dark-
ened, if it does not continuously devote itself to the memory of Jesus": there
are still constant distractions, but "the soul, wounded with divine love for
Christ, follows him as his beloved." In fourteen short paragraphs, Kallistos
weaves together all the themes of the *Philokalia*, taking his example the

the synod that upheld the hesychasts in 1351, or Kallistos II Xanthopoulos, patriarch in 1397:
Bishop Kallistos himself tentatively suggests the latter (op. cit., col. 1342).

[5] Does this suggest that Kallistos was Kallistos II Xanthopoulos, whose brother was called
Ignatios?

[6] The quotation from St Ignatios is one of the most famous: "My love is crucified, and there
is not in me any fire that loves matter. It is water, living and speaking in me, saying to me from
within: Come to the Father!" *Romans* 7. 2.

musician playing his lyre, so that the pray-er is one who turns his life into a song, a love-song to Christ.

The *Philokalia*, then, points to a particular understanding of tradition: patristic, certainly, but in the sense that these fathers can become our fathers, and take us along paths of the Spirit that they know by experience. The purpose of this is, as stated on the title-page of the *Philokalia*, that "through ethical philosophy, in accordance with *praxis* and contemplation, the intellect is purified, illuminated and perfected." In those few words there is packed a wealth of meaning. The *Philokalia* invites those who use it on a quest, a quest for truth (philosophy). But this quest, as we have seen Patriarch Kallistos makes clear, is not simply a matter of intellectual investigation: it is a quest that involves the whole human person, the whole way in which we conduct our lives (*ethical* philosophy). What this means is spelt out by talking of "*praxis* and contemplation," terms that go back to Aristotle, but are here used in the sense they had acquired in monastic use since the fourth century, *praxis* meaning what we do, mainly in trying to live out our Christian lives and struggle against temptations to compromise, "contemplation" meaning the undistracted, non-possessive knowledge of reality, preeminently the transcendent reality of God. *Praxis*, ascetic struggle, prepares the way for contemplation by purification, and contemplation itself finds its fulfilment in illumination and ultimately in perfection or union with God or *theosis*, deification.

Such a work would be classed in the West as one of practical piety (albeit monastic), rather than a work of theology: to be placed alongside Jeremy Taylor's *Holy Living and Holy Dying*, for example, rather than Karl Barth's *Church Dogmatics*. Nikodimos' own interest in works of practical piety such as Scupoli's *Unseen Warfare* and the Jesuit Pinamonti's *Spiritual Exercises*, both of which he translated into Greek, might encourage such a classification. That would be a mistake, and a serious one, for much of the historical importance of the *Philokalia* lies in the way it has revealed the essential unity of what have come to be called in the West "theology" and "spirituality," a unity that Orthodoxy, at its best, has preserved.

The first point we might note about the programme of the *Philokalia*, as stated on the title-page, is that it concerns the *nous*, the intellect. That ought, from the perspective of Western theology, to occasion pause for thought, for we have argued that the *Philokalia* characterizes the patristic tradition as fundamentally experiential. In the West, an emphasis on experience normally entails opposition to the intellect: to quote the *Cloud of Unknowing*, "by love may he [God] be getyn & holden; bot bi thought neither."[7] In the East, on the contrary, it is the *nous*, the intellect, that comes to know God. This is not a simple contrast, for the Greek word *nous* embraces a richer concept than the English word "intellect" (which is why the word "intellect" sounds odd in this context in English, and is thus often avoided). Whereas "intellect" can refer simply to the human ability to argue and calculate (as in the notion of an IQ), *nous* is the means by which the soul "aspires to a knowledge that is a direct contact, a 'feeling' (*sentiment*), a touching, something seen. It aspires to a union where there is total fusion, the interpenetration of two living beings," as Festugière once put it.[8] The ætiolated sense of the English word "intellect" reflects our normal experience of intellectual activity: normal, that is, in a fallen world, where the intellect devotes its energies to negotiating the world of the senses, calculating and planning. The Greek word *nous* still trails clouds of the glory that it is meant to be: that in virtue of which we human beings are created in the image of God, and therefore capable of entering into communion with God and, in some sense, knowing him and his creation. This kind of knowledge is contemplation: simple regarding, beholding, without the necessity of seeking to control or manipulate. And such contemplation entails transformation of the one who contemplates: what the *Philokalia* calls perfection, union or deification.

This is an intensely practical matter. Here again we find ourselves tripping over our words: for us, "practical" is opposed to "theoretical," whereas in the world of the *Philokalia* what is "practical," that is, a matter of ascetic struggle, prepares the way for *theoria*, contemplation. To say that this is a practical matter is to say that the way to contemplation is a way to be pursued, not just something to think about. The *Philokalia* is a manual of practical advice, presented in a host of differing, though related, forms, because the way to contemplation is an intensely personal matter, taking different forms in accordance with the different unique persons that we human beings are. It is intensely personal because contemplation is another way of talking about the fulfilment of the unique personal relationship existing between each of us and our God, and this fulfilment involves the discovery of ourselves, the discovery of our *heart*. It is because of this personal dimension that the *Philokalia* does not, and was never meant to, stand alone. Throughout the

[7] *The Cloud of Unknowing*, chapter 6, ed. Phyllis Hodgson, Early English Text Society, Original Series, no. 218 (London-New York-Toronto: Oxford University Press, 1944), 26.
[8] A.-J. Festugière, *La Révélation d'Hermès Trismégiste*, vol. 1 (Paris: J. Gabalda et Cie, 2nd ed., 1950), 65.

Philokalia, the importance of finding a spiritual father is emphasized, for it is only under such guidance that one has much hope of finding one's own way through ascetic struggle to contemplation. Wherever the influence of the *Philokalia* has been felt, it has been accompanied by a renewal of the idea of spiritual fatherhood; that is strikingly true of nineteenth-century Russia, where the novelty of the renewed institution of *starchestvo* is palpable in Dostoevsky's *Brothers Karamazov*. This is another aspect of patristic tradition to which the *Philokalia* provides access: not so much a tradition of the fathers, as a fatherly tradition, in which fathers help their children to enter into the fruits of their experience.

The heart—the prayer of the heart: these are closely associated with the *Philokalia*. But such terms are easily misunderstood, especially in the West. It is not the heart in opposition to the intellect; nor is prayer of the heart an emotional prayer involving the feelings (even though one of the signs of true prayer of the heart is, we are told, the gift of tears). It is the heart, as we find it in the Scriptures, particularly the Old Testament, and especially the Psalms: the heart that meditates, desires, pants, is vexed, that has secrets, and is deep, that can be fixed, smitten and withered like grass, or like wax, that cries out to God, that can be broken and contrite, and made clean. It is the centre of the human person, the source of everything that we are. It is not opposed to the intellect, or rather opposition between the heart and the intellect is a sign—the sign, the cause, even—of the fragmented state that we ordinarily experience. In that fragmented state, we no longer live from the centre of ourselves, we have become genuinely "eccentric" beings, lost within ourselves, easily taken unawares by aspects of ourselves of which we are scarcely conscious, or which we have suppressed. Our task in prayer is to unite the intellect and the heart, to find the place of the heart and draw the intellect down into it: there, when the heart has been found and the intellect is devoted to guarding it, true prayer, the prayer of the heart, becomes possible. Our holy fathers, says the unknown author of *The Three Methods of Prayer*,

> concentrated wholly on this one task of guarding the heart, convinced that through this practice they would also possess every other virtue, whereas without it no virtue could be firmly established. Some of the fathers have called this practice stillness of heart, other attentiveness, others the guarding of the heart, others watchfulness and rebuttal, and others again the investigation of thoughts and the guarding of the

intellect. But all of them alike worked the earth of their own heart, and in this way they were fed on the divine manna.[9]

The theology of the *Philokalia* is, then, a true theology in that it envisages a genuine understanding of God. But such understanding of God is not, and could never be, an understanding of God in which God becomes a province of human understanding: *si enim comprehendis, non est Deus*.[10] It is rather a knowledge of God through genuine participation in God, in which the human person is made whole and reunited, in which the intellect finds the place of the heart, and is able once more to contemplate God. The *Philokalia* is less concerned with what we know in such contemplation, than with the way back to such contemplative experience. The way of return is arduous, because human beings have become so thoroughly lost in the thicket that creation becomes if it is perceived in detachment from the Creator to whom it owes its being. There would be no return at all, if God had not, in his Son, shared human experience of a fallen world to the point of dying, thereby making death the gateway of life. But not even the mystery of the Incarnation enables human beings to find their way to God unless they themselves learn to "cleanse the doors of perception," in William Blake's phrase.[11] Perhaps the most eloquent evocation of the nature of the Philokalic experience is to be found in the introduction to the English translation:

> "Philokalia" itself means love of the beautiful, the exalted, the excellent, understood as the transcendent source of life and the revelation of Truth. It is through such love that, as the subtitle of the original edition puts it, "the intellect is purified, illumined and made perfect." The texts were collected with a view to this purification, illumination and perfection. They show the way to awaken and develop attention and consciousness, to attain that state of watchfulness which is the hallmark of sanctity. The describe the conditions most effective for learning what their authors call the art of arts and the science of sciences, a learning which is not a matter of information or agility of mind but of a radical change of will and heart leading man towards the highest

---

[9]*The Philokalia. The Complete Text*, vol. 4, p. 71.

[10]Augustine *Sermo* 117 (PL 38. 663).

[11]Cf. William Blake, *The Marriage of Heaven and Hell*, "If the doors of perception were cleansed everything would appear to man as it is, infinite" : in *The Poetry and Prose of William Blake*, ed. Geoffrey Keynes (London: The Nonesuch Press, 1946), 187.

possibilities open to him, shaping and nourishing the unseen part of his being, and helping him to spiritual fulfilment and union with God. The *Philokalia* is an itinerary through the labyrinth of time, a silent way of love and gnosis through the deserts and emptinesses of life, especially of modern life, a vivifying and fadeless presence. It is an active force revealing a spiritual path and inducing man to follow it. It is a summons to him to overcome his ignorance, to uncover the knowledge that lies within, to rid himself of illusion, and to be receptive to the grace of the Holy Spirit who teaches all things and brings all things to remembrance.[12]

---

[12]*The Philokalia*, vol. 1, pp.13–14.

List of Writings by Kallistos (Timothy) Ware, Bishop of Diokleia

Items marked with an asterisk are included in *The Inner Kingdom* (2001).

" 'Economy' according to Orthodox Theology: Its Application to Non-Orthodox Sacraments," *Chrysostom*, 5 (1961), 6–8.

" 'Guarding the Walls': The Greek Orthodox Monk and his Service to the World," *Chrysostom*, 9 (1962), 5–7.

"Between Heaven and Earth: Some Notes on Contemporary Greek Monasticism," *Sobornost*, 4.7 (1962), 398–408.

The Orthodox Church (Pelican Original: Harmondsworth: Penguin Books, 1963), 352pp. [New edition, fully revised (Harmondsworth: Penguin Books, 1993). Translated into various languages.]

"The Transfiguration of the Body," *Sobornost*, 4.8 (1963), 420–434. Reprinted (with revisions) in A. M. Allchin (ed.), *Sacrament and Image* (London: Fellowship of St Alban & St Sergius, 1967), 17–32.

"Saints and Beasts: The Undistorted Image," *The Franciscan*, 5.4 (1963), 144–52.

"The Communion of Saints," in A. J. Philippou (ed.), *The Orthodox Ethos*, Studies in Orthodoxy, 1 (Oxford: Holywell Press, 1964), 140–9.

"The Orthodox Church in England," in Zoe Brotherhood (ed.), *A Sign of God: Orthodoxy 1964* (Athens: Zoe, 1964), 47–62.

Eustratios Argenti: A Study of the Greek Church under Turkish Rule (Oxford: Clarendon Press, 1964), xii + 196pp. [Photographic reprint (California: Eastern Orthodox Books, 1974).]

Edited, with an introduction: Igumen Chariton, *The Art of Prayer: an Orthodox Anthology*, translated by E. Kadloubovsky and E. M. Palmer (London: Faber & Faber, 1966), 287pp. [Introduction: pp. 9–38.]

"Intercommunion: The Decisions of Vatican II and the Orthodox Standpoint," *Sobornost*, 5.4 (1967), 258–72.

"Patmos and its Monastery," *Eastern Churches Review*, 1.3 (1967), 231–7.

"Orthodoxy in Alaska: The Centenary of the Sale to America," *Eastern Churches Review*, 1.4 (1967–8), 395–8.

"The Doctrine of the Church in Reunion Discussions," *Eastern Churches News Letter*, 48 (1968), 4–13.

"Metropolitan Philaret of Moscow," *Eastern Churches Review*, 2.1 (1968), 24–28.

"Orthodoxy in America: Some Statistics," *Eastern Churches Review*, 2.1 (1968), 70–3.

"A Conference on the Problems of the Orthodox Diaspora," *Eastern Churches Review*, 2.2 (1968), 185–9.

"Inter-Orthodox Committee at Geneva, 1968," *Eastern Churches Review*, 2.2 (1968), 189–90.

Translated and edited with Mother Mary (of Bussy-en-Othe), *The Festal Menaion* (London: Faber & Faber, 1969), 564pp. [The introduction and appendices are by KW; the translation was made jointly.]

* " 'Pray without Ceasing': The Ideal of Continual Prayer in Eastern Monasticism," *Eastern Churches Review*, 2.3 (1969), 253–261.

"Orthodoxy and the Ecumenical Movement: Recent Developments in America," *Eastern Churches Review*, 2.4 (1969), 422–4.

"The Mother of God in Orthodox Theology and Devotion," in the series "Mother of Jesus," No. 6 (Ecumenical Society of the Blessed Virgin Mary), 1970, 14pp. [Reprinted in A. Stacpoole (ed.), *Mary's Place in Christian Dialogue* (Slough: St Paul's Publications, 1982), 169–81.]

* "The Theology of Worship," *Sobornost*, 5.10 (1970), 729–37.

Introduction to Bishop Ignatius Brianchaninov, *The Arena: An Offering to Contemporary Monasticism*, trans. by Archimandrite Lazarus Moore (Madras, 1970), iii–xvi.

"The Sacrament of Baptism and the Ascetic Life in the Teaching of Mark the Monk," *Studia Patristica*, X, Texte und Untersuchungen, 107 (Berlin, 1970), 441–52.

"Primacy, Collegiality, and the People of God," *Eastern Churches Review*, 3.1 (1970), 18–29. [Reprinted in A. J. Philippou (ed.), *Orthodoxy: Life and Freedom. Essays in honour of Archbishop Iakovos* (Oxford: Studion Publications, 1973), 116–29].

"Orthodox Patriarchate of Antioch" (recent events), *Eastern Churches Review*, 3.l (1970), 78–81.

"Tradition and Personal Experience in Later Byzantine Theology," *Eastern Churches Review*, 3.2 (1970), 131–41.

Introduction to Leo Allatius, *De Ecclesiae Occidentalis atque Orientalis Perpetua Consensione*, reprint (Farnham: Gregg International Publishers, 1970), 5pp. [Not numbered.]

"The Value of the Material Creation," *Sobornost*, 6.3 (1971), 154–65.

"The Mystery of God and Man in St Symeon the New Theologian," *Sobornost*, 6.4 (1971), 227–36.

"Autocephaly Crisis: Deadlock between Constantinople and Moscow," *Eastern Churches Review*, 3.3 (1971), 311–15.

"Members of Christ: Extracts from the Hymns of St Symeon the New Theologian (949–1022)," *Eastern Churches Review*, 3.4 (1971), 415–18.

"Chalcedonians and Non-Chalcedonians: The Latest Developments," *Eastern Churches Review*, 3.4 (1971), 428–32.

"Orthodox and Catholics in the Seventeenth Century: Schism or Intercommunion?" in Derek Baker (ed.), *Schism, Heresy and Religious Protest*, Studies in Church

History, 9 (Cambridge: Cambridge University Press, 1972), 259–76.

"The Jesus Prayer in St Gregory of Sinai," *Eastern Churches Review*, 4.1 (1972), 3–22.

"The Jesus Prayer and the Mother of God," *Eastern Churches Review*, 4.2 (1973), 149–50.

"The Ecumenical Patriarch Athenagoras I" (obituary), *Eastern Churches Review*, 4.2 (1972), 156–62.

"Towards the Great Council?" *Eastern Churches Review*, 4.2 (1972), 162–8.

"Scholasticism and Orthodoxy: Theological Method as a Factor in the Schism," *Eastern Churches Review*, 5.1 (1973), 16–27.

"Thessalonika and Crestwood: Two International Conferences of Orthodox Theologians," *Eastern Churches Review*, 5.1 (1973), 60–2.

"Orthodoxy and the Charismatic Movement," *Eastern Churches Review*, 5.2 (1973), 182–6.

The Power of the Name: The Jesus Prayer in Orthodox Spirituality, Fairacres Publications no. 43 (Oxford, 1974), 25pp. [New edition: Oxford: Fairacres Publications, 1986.] [Reprinted in Elisabeth Behr-Sigel, *The Place of the Heart: An Introduction to Orthodox Spirituality* (Torrance, CA: Oakwood Publications, 1992), 135–73.]

"The Ecumenical Councils and the Conscience of the Church," in *Kanon*, II, Jahrbuch der Gesellschaft für das Recht der Ostkirchen (Vienna, 1974), 217–33.

"Derwas James Chitty 1901–1971" (obituary), *Eastern Churches Review*, 6.1 (1974), 1–6,

"Solzhenitsyn and the Moscow Patriarchate," *Eastern Churches Review*, 6.1 (1974), 94–7.

"Cyprus" (recent events), *Eastern Churches Review*, 6.1 (1974), 100–2.

"Greece" (recent events), *Eastern Churches Review*, 6.1 (1974), 103–7.

"Athos" (recent events), *Eastern Churches Review*, 6.1 (1974), 108–11.

"The Monk and the Married Christian: Some Comparisons in Early Monastic Sources," *Eastern Churches Review*, 6.1 (1974), 72–83.

"The Problem of Mixed Marriages: A Recent Correspondence," *Eastern Churches Review*, 6.2 (1974), 194–8.

*"The Spiritual Father in Orthodox Christianity," *Cross Currents*, 24.2–3 (1974), 296–313. [Reprinted (with revisions) in *Spiritual Direction: Contemporary Readings*, ed. K. G. Culligan (Locust Valley: Living Flame Press, 1983), 20–40.]

*"Silence in Prayer: The Meaning of Hesychia," in A. M. Allchin (ed.), *Theology and Prayer*, Studies Supplementary to *Sobornost*, no. 3 (1975), 8–28. [Also in M. Basil Pennington (ed.), *One Yet Two: Monastic Tradition East and West*, Cistercian Studies 29 (Kalamazoo, MI: Cistercian, 1976), 22–47.]

"God Hidden and Revealed: The Apophatic Way and the Essence-Energies Distinction," *Eastern Churches Review*, 7.2 (1975), 125–36.

"Death and Life," *Christian*, 2.4 (175), 363–9.

"The Fifth Earl of Guilford (1766–1827) and His Secret Conversion to the Orthodox Church," in D. Baker (ed.), *The Orthodox Churches and the West*, Studies in Church History, 13 (Oxford: Basil Blackwell, for the Ecclesiastical History Society, 1976), 247–56.

"Mount Athos Today," *Christian*, 3.4 (1976), 322–33.

"The Theology of the Icon: A Short Anthology," *Eastern Churches Review*, 8.1 (1976), 3–10.

"Religious Persecution and the Nairobi Assembly," *Eastern Churches Review*, 8.1 (1976), 74–8.

"A Common Easter: How Soon?" *Eastern Churches Review*, 8.1 (1976), 79–81.

" 'Separated from All and United to All': The Hermit Life in the Christian East," in A. M. Allchin (ed.), *Solitude and Communion*, Fairacres Publications, 66 (Oxford: Fairacres Publications, 1977), 30–47.

"The Moscow Conference, 1976," in Kallistos Ware and Colin Davey, *Anglican-Orthodox Dialogue*, (London: SPCK, 1977), 39–81. [French trans. *Istina*, 24 (Jan–Mar 1979), 7–43.]

"The Debate about Palamism," *Eastern Churches Review*, 9.1–2 (1977), 45–63.

"Conversation with Kallistos Ware," in E. Robinson (ed.), *This Time-Bound Ladder: Ten Dialogues on Religious Experience* (Oxford: The Religious Experience Research Unit, Manchester College, 1977), 107–23.

"Man, Woman, and the Priesthood of Christ," in Peter Moore (ed.), *Man, Woman, and Priesthood* (London: SPCK, 1978), 68–90, 177–80. [Reprinted in Thomas Hopko (ed.), *Women and the Priesthood* (Crestwood: St Vladimir's Seminary Press, 1983), 9–37.]

"The ARCIC Agreed Statement on Authority: An Orthodox Comment," *One in Christ*, 14.3 (1978), 198–206.

Translated and edited with Mother Mary (of Bussy-en-Othe), *The Lenten Triodion* (London: Faber & Faber, 1978), 699pp. [The introduction is by KW, the translation was made jointly.]

"Catholicity and Nationalism: A Recent Debate at Athens," *Eastern Churches Review*, 10.1–2 (1978), 10–16.

"Archbishop Makarios of Cyprus" (obituary), *Eastern Churches Review*, 10.1–2 (1978), 151–2.

"Archbishop Evgenios of Cyprus" (obituary), *Eastern Churches Review*, 10.1–2 (1978), 152–3.

"Church and Eucharist, Communion and Intercommunion," *Sobornost*, 7.7 (1978), 550–67. [Issued also as a pamphlet: *Communion and Intercommunion* (Minneapolis Mn: Light and Life Publishing Company, 1980), 39pp.]

Contributions to H. Cunliffe-Jones & B. Drewery (edd.), *A History of Christian Doctrine* (Edinburgh: T & T Clark, 1978 [in fact 1979]): "Christian Theology in the East 600–1453," pp. 181–225; "A Note on Theology in the Christian East: The Fifteenth to Seventeenth Centuries," pp. 307–9; "A Note on Theology in the Christian East: The Eighteenth to Twentieth Centuries," pp. 455–7.

"Orthodoxy and the World Council of Churches," *Sobornost* (incorporating *Eastern Churches Review*), new series 1.1 (1979), 74–82.

Translated and edited with G. E. H. Palmer and P. Sherrard, *The Philokalia. The Complete Text compiled by St Nikodimos of the Holy Mountain and St Makarios of Corinth* (London: Faber & Faber, vol. I, 1979, 378pp.; vol. II, 1981, 414pp.; vol. III, 1984, 379pp.; vol. IV, 1995, 458pp.).

The Orthodox Way (London & Oxford: Mowbrays/Crestwood, NY: St Vladimir's Seminary Press, 1979), 195pp. [Translated into various languages.]

Translated with Mother Mary (of Bussy-en-Othe), *The Lenten Triodion. Supplementary Texts*, duplicated publication by the Orthodox Monastery of the Veil of the Mother of God, Bussy-en-Othe, 1979 [in fact 1980], 305pp.

*"The Orthodox Experience of Repentance," *Sobornost* (incorporating *Eastern Churches Review*), new series 2.1 (1980), 18–28.

"Archbishop Athenagoras of Thyateira (1909–79)" (obituary), *Sobornost* (incorporating *Eastern Churches Review*), new series 2.1 (1980), 58–68.

"The Holy Spirit in the Personal Life of the Christian," in *Unity in the Spirit—Diversity in the Churches*, The Report of the Conference of European Churches, Assembly VIII, 18th-25th October 1979, Crete (Geneva: WCC, 1980), 139–69.

"Kirkon Salaisuus" ["The Mystery of the Church"], *Ortodoksia*, 29 (1980), 7–75. [In Finnish: the English original remains unpublished.]

"The Mystery of the Human Person," *Sobornost* (incorporating *Eastern Churches Review*), new series 3.1 (1981), 62–9. [Translated into Greek, 1991].

"Nicolas Zernov (1898–1980)" (obituary), *Sobornost* (incorporating *Eastern Churches Review*), new series 3.1 (1981), 11–32.

"Patriarch Benedict of Jerusalem" (obituary), *Sobornost* (incorporating *Eastern Churches Review*), new series 3.1 (1981), 102.

"Mother Mary" (obituary), *Sobornost* (incorporating *Eastern Churches Review*), new series 3.1 (1981), 103.

"The Monastic Life as a Sacrament of Love," Ἐκκλησία καὶ Θεολογία, 2 (1981), 690–700.

" 'One Body in Christ': Death and the Communion of the Saints," *Sobornost* (incorporating *Eastern Churches Review*), new series 3.2 (1981), 179–91.

"Diadochus von Photice," *Theologische Realenzyklopädie*, 8 (1981), 617–20.

"Patterns of Episcopacy in the Early Church and Today: An Orthodox View," in Peter Moore (ed.), *Bishops: But What Kind?* (London: SPCK, 1982), 1–24.

"The Library of the House of St Gregory and St Macrina, Oxford: The D. J. Chitty Papers," with S. Brock, *Sobornost* (incorporating *Eastern Churches Review*), 4.1 (1982), 56–8.

"The Exercise of Authority in the Orthodox Church," Ἐκκλησία καὶ Θεολογία, 3 (1982), 941–69. [French trans. *Irenikon*, 54.4 (1981), 451–71; 55.1 (1982), 25–34.]

"The Holy Name of Jesus in East and West: The Hesychasts and Richard Rolle," *Sobornost* (incorporating *Eastern Churches Review*), new series 4.2 (1982), 163–84.

"Anglican-Orthodox Dialogue, 1982: A Second Spring," *Sobornost* (incorporating *Eastern Churches Review*), new series 4.2 (1982), 219–22.

Introduction to John Climacus, *The Ladder of Divine Ascent*, The Classics of Western Spirituality (New York NY: Paulist Press, 1982), 1–70.

*"What is a Martyr?" *Sobornost* (incorporating *Eastern Churches Review*), new series 5.1 (1983), 7–18.

"Joice Loch" (obituary), *Sobornost* (incorporating *Eastern Churches Review*), new series 5.1 (1983), 71–2.

"Wolves and Monks: Life on the Holy Mountain Today," *Sobornost* (incorporating *Eastern Churches Review*), new series 5.2 (1983), 56–68.

"L'unité dans la diversité: La vocation orthodoxe en Europe occidentale," *Contacts*, 35.2, no. 122 (1983), 179–90.

"The Church: A Time of Transition," in R. Clogg (ed.), *Greece in the 1980s* (London: Macmillan, 1983), 208–30.

"Salvation and Theosis in Orthodox Theology," in *Luther et la Réforme allemande dans une perspective œcuménique* (Chambésy: Éditions du Centre Orthodoxe du Patriarcat Œcuménique, 1983), 167–84.

"Unity and Mission," in *Unity and Mission*, The Report of the Eleventh General Assembly of Syndesmos, (Kuopio: Syndesmos, 1984), 5–15.

"In Memoriam Demetrios Koutroubis" (obituary), *Sobornost* (incorporating *Eastern Churches Review*), new series 6.1 (1984), 67–71.

"The House of St Gregory and St Macrina: The First Quarter Century," with Ralph Townsend, *Sobornost* (incorporating *Eastern Churches Review*), new series 6.2 (1984), 55–63

"Philocalie," in *Dictionnaire de Spiritualité*, 12 (1984), cols. 1336–52.

Edited with George Every and Richard Harries, *Seasons of the Spirit: Readings through the Christian Year* (London: SPCK, 1984), x + 259pp. [Published in the USA by St Vladimir's Seminary Press, Crestwood NY with the title *The Time of the Spirit*].

"The Sanctity and Glory of the Mother of God: Orthodox Approaches," *The Way*, Supplement 51, Papers of the 1984 International Congress of the Ecumenical Society of the Blessed Virgin Mary (1984), 79–96.

*"The Fool in Christ as Prophet and Apostle," *Sobornost* (incorporating *Eastern Churches Review*), new series 6.2 (1984), 6–28.

«Ἡ δόξα τῆς Μεταμόρφωσης. Θέματα ἀπ' τα λειτουργικὰ κείμενα,» in *Μεταμόρφωση* (Athens: Akritas, 1984), 13–33.

"The Humanity of Christ," The Fourth Constantinople Lecture, 29/30 November 1984 (London: The Anglican & Eastern Churches Association, 1984), 12pp.

"Bishop Kallistos of Oxford Looks at Ecumenism" (Interview with A. Kelleher), *Diakonia*, 19.1–3 (1984–85), 132–6.

"Image and Likeness: An Interview with Bishop Kallistos Ware" (by J. Moran), *Parabola*, 10.1 (1985), 62–71.

"Why I am an Orthodox," *The Tablet* (16 February 1985), 159–60.

Introduction to *Marc le Moine*, translated by Soeur Claire-Agnes Zirnheld, Spiritualité Orientale, 41 (Abbaye de Bellefontaine, 1985), ix-li.

"The Jesus Prayer in St Diadochus of Photice," *Aksum Thyateira: A Festschrift for Archbishop Methodios* (London, 1985), 557–68.

"Nous and Noesis in Plato, Aristotle and Evagrius of Pontus," *Diotima* 13, Proceedings of the Second International Week on the Philosophy of Greek Culture, Kalamata 1982, Part II (1985), 158–63.

"Ways of Prayer and Contemplation. I. Eastern," in B. McGinn & J. Meyendorff (edd.), *Christian Spirituality: Origins to the Twelfth Century*, World Spirituality: An Encyclopedic History of the Religious Quest, vol. 16 (New York: Crossroad, 1985), 395–414.

"Gottesdienst. Orthodoxe Kirche," *Theologische Realenzyklopädie*, 14.1–2 (1985), 46–51.

"Archbishop Basil of Brussels" (obituary), *Sobornost* (incorporating *Eastern Churches Review*), new series 8.1 (1986), 51–4.

Contributions to Cheslyn Jones, Geoffrey Wainright & Edward Yarnold (edd.), *The Study of Spirituality* (London: SPCK, 1986): "The Eastern Fathers, Introduction," pp. 159–60; "The Origins of the Jesus Prayer: Diadochus, Gaza, Sinai," pp. 175–84; "The Spirituality of the Icon," pp. 195–8; "Symeon the New Theologian," pp. 235–42; "The Hesychasts: Gregory of Sinai, Gregory Palamas, Nicolas Cabasilas," pp. 242–55; "The Hesychast Renaissance," pp. 255–8.

"The Human Person as an Icon of the Trinity," *Sobornost* (incorporating *Eastern Churches Review*), new series 8.2 (1986), 6–23.

Praying Home: The Contemplative Journey, with Mary Clare and Robert Llewelyn (Cambridge, MA: Cowley Publications, 1987).

Contributions to Mircea Eliade (ed.), *The Encyclopedia of Religion* (New York: Macmillan, 1987): "Cyril I (Loukaris)," 4.189–91; "Eastern Christianity," 4.558–76; "Petr Moghila," 11.260–1.

"The Theology and Spirituality of the Icon," *From Byzantium to El Greco*, Royal Academy of Arts, (London, 1987), 37–9.

"Spirit, Church, Eucharist," *The Franciscan*, 29.2 (1987), 77–84.

"The Unity of the Human Person according to the Greek Fathers," in Arthur Peacocke and Grant Gillett (edd.), *Persons and Personality. A Contemporary Inquiry*, Ian Ramsey Centre Publication no. 1 (Oxford: Basil Blackwell, 1987), 197–206, 215–17.

Edited: A Monk of the Eastern Church (Lev Gillet), *The Jesus Prayer* (Crestwood NY: St Vladimir's Seminary Press, 1987), 120pp. [Foreword on pp. 5–20.]

How to Read your Bible (Mt Hermon, Ca: Conciliar Press, 1988), 16pp.

"Orthodoxy in Britain: Its Origins and Future," in *Directory of Parishes and Clergy in the British Isles 1988/89* (Stylite Publishing and Orthodox Fellowship of St John the Baptist, 1988), 3–6.

"St Maximos of Kapsokalyvia and Fourteenth-Century Athonite Hesychasm," in Julian Chrysostomides (ed.), *ΚΑΘΗΓΗΤΡΙΑ: Essays presented to Joan Hussey for her 80th birthday* (London: Porphyrogenitus, 1989), 409–30.

"Mary Theotokos in the Orthodox Tradition," *Epiphany*, 9.2 (1989), 48–59. [Reprinted in *Marianum 52*, 1–2 (1990), 210–27.]

"The Feast of Mary's Silence: The Entry into the Temple (21 November)," *The Month*, August/September (1989), 337–41. [Also printed in Alberic Stacpoole (ed.), *Mary in Doctrine and Devotion*: Papers of the Liverpool Congress of the Ecumenical Society of the Blessed Virgin Mary (Dublin: The Columba Press, 1990), 34–41].

*"Time: Prison or Path to Freedom?" *Fairacres Chronicle*, 22.3 (1989), 5–15.

"The Monastic Ideal according to St Christodoulos of Patmos," in Διεθνὲς Συμπόσιο. Πρακτικά. Ἰ. Μονὴ Ἁγ. Ἰωάννου τοῦ Θεολόγου. 900 Χρόνια Ἱστορικῆς Μαρτυρίας (1088–1988), Πάτμος, 22–24 Σεπτεμβρίου 1988, Ἑταιρεία Βυζαντινῶν καὶ Μεταβυζαντινῶν Μελετῶν. Διπτύχων Παράφυλλα 2, (Athens, 1989), 23–35.

"The Meaning of 'Pathos' in Abba Isaias and Theodoret of Cyrus," *Studia Patristica*, XX (Leuven: Peeters, 1989), 315–22.

"Orthodoxy in Britain: Its Origins and Future," *Sourozh*, 42 (1990), 23–8.

"The Spiritual Father in St John Climacus and St Symeon the New Theologian," *Studia Patristica*, XVIII.2 (Kalamazoo: Cistercian Publications/Leuven: Peeters, 1989), 299–316. [Reprinted in Irenée Hausherr, *Spiritual Direction in the Early Christian East*, Cistercian Studies Series, 116 (Kalamazoo: Cistercian Publications, 1990), vii-xxxiii.]

"Eastern Christendom," in John McManners (ed.), *The Oxford Illustrated History of Christianity* (Oxford: Oxford University Press, 1990), 122–61.

"David Balfour" (obituary), *Sobornost* (incorporating *Eastern Churches Review*), new series 12.1 (1990), 52–61.

"The Meaning of the Divine Liturgy for the Byzantine Worshipper," in Rosemary Morris (ed.), *Church and People in Byzantium*, Twentieth Spring Symposium of Byzantine Studies, Manchester, 1986 (Birmingham: Centre for Byzantine, Ottoman and Modern Greek Studies, University of Birmingham, 1990), 7–28.

* "A Sense of Wonder," in Dan Cohn-Sherbok (ed.), *Tradition and Unity: Sermons Published in Honour of Robert Runcie* (London: Bellew Publishing, 1991), 79–83.

"Tradition, the Bible and the Holy Spirit," *Epiphany*, 11.2 (1991), 7–16.

"Saints in the Image of the Trinity," in *The Reckless Saints: Sermons from All Saints Margaret Street*, Festival 1990 (London, 1991), 1–5.

"The Sacrament of Love: The Orthodox Understanding of Marriage and its Breakdown," *The Downside Review*, 109, no. 375 (April 1991), 79–93

«'Ενορία καὶ Εὐχαριστία. Ἡ ὀρθόδοξη ἐμπειρία στὸν Δυτικὸ Κόσμο,» in 'Ενορία. Πρὸς μία νέα ἀνακάλυψή της (Athens: Akritas, 1991), 125–34.

Contributions to Nicholas Lossky et al. (edd.), *Dictionary of the Ecumenical Movement* (Geneva: WCC Publications/Grand Rapids: W.B. Eerdmans, 1991): "Ethnicity," p. 373; "Tradition and traditions," pp. 1013–18.

"The Spirituality of the Philokalia," *Sobornost* (incorporating *Eastern Churches Review*), new series 13.1 (1991), 6–24.

"Possiamo parlare di spiritualità della Filocalia?" in Olivier Racquez (ed.), *Amore del Bello: Studi sulla Filocalia*, Atti del "Simposio Internazionale sulla Filocalia," Pontificio Collegio Greco, Roma, novembre 1989 (Magnano: Edizioni Qiqajon, Comunità di Bose, 1991), 27–52.

Preface to George Maloney, *Pseudo-Macarius: The Fifty Spiritual Homilies and the Great Letter*, The Classics of Western Spirituality (Mahwah, New Jersey: Paulist Press, 1992), pp. xi-xviii.

"Praying with the Body: The Hesychast Method and Non-Christian Parallels," *Sobornost* (incorporating *Eastern Churches Review*), new series 14.2 (1992), 6–35.

"Praying with Icons," in Paul McPartlan (ed.), *One in 2000? Towards Catholic-Orthodox Unity* (Slough: St Paul's, 1993), 141–168.

"Athos after Ten Years: the Good News and the Bad," *Friends of Mount Athos, Annual Report 1992* (published 1993), 8–17.

"Address on Orthodox/Catholic Dialogue," *Sobornost* (incorporating *Eastern Churches Review*), new series 15.1 (1993), 44–5.

Le royaume interieur (Pully, Switzerland: Le Sel de la Terre, 1993; 2nd edn. 1994), 112pp. [Introduction by Maxime Egger, pp. 6–17. French trans. by Lucie & Maxime Egger of: "Go Joyfully: The Mystery of Death and Resurrection" (1995); "The Mystery of the Human Person" (1981); "The Orthodox Experience of Repentance" (1980); "The Spiritual Father in Orthodox Christianity" (1974); "Silence in Prayer: The Meaning of Hesychia" (1975).] (1) Greek trans. Ἡ ἐντὸς ἡμῶν βασιλεία, trans. Joseph Roilidis (Athens: Akritas, 1994), 151pp.; (2) Italian trans. *Riconoscete Cristo in Voi?*, trans. Riccardo Larini (Magnano: Edizioni Qiqajon, Communità di Böse, 1994), 128pp.

"How to Read the Bible," in Peter E. Gillquist (ed.), *The Orthodox Study Bible: New Testament and Psalms* (Nashville, Tennessee: Thomas Nelson, 1993), 726–70 (revised version of 1988 Conciliar Press pamphlet).

"The Church of God: Our Shared Vision," *Logos*, 34.1–2 (1993), 10–29.

"Response to the Presentation by His Grace Bishop Basil (Losten): 'The Roman Primacy and the Church of Kiev,' " *Logos*, 34.1–2 (1993), 107–16.

"Father Lev Gillet and the Fellowship of St Alban and St Sergius," *Sobornost* (incorporating *Eastern Churches Review*), new series 15.2 (1993), 7–15. [French trans. *Contacts*, 36 (1994), 36–44.]

" 'The Monk of the Eastern Church' and the Jesus Prayer," *Sobornost* (incorporating *Eastern Churches Review*), new series 15.2 (1993), 17–27. [French trans. *Contacts*, 36 (1994), 60–70.]

Foreword to *Journals of the Priest Ioann Veniaminov in Alaska, 1823–1836*, trans. by Jerome Kisslinger, ed. by S. A. Mousalimas, The Rasmuson Library Historical Translation Series, Vol. VII (Fairbanks: University of Alaska Press, 1993), ix–xi.

"Prayer and the Sacraments in the *Synagogue*," in Margaret Mullett and Anthony Kirby (edd.), *The Theotokos Evergetis and Eleventh-Century Monasticism*, Belfast Byzantine Texts and Translations 6.1 (Belfast, 1994), 325–47.

"The Tension Between the 'Already' and 'Not Yet,' " in Colin Davey (ed.), *Returning Pilgrims. Insights from British and Irish participants in the Fifth World Faith and Order Conference Santiago de Compostela 3–14 August 1993* (London: Council of Churches for Britain and Ireland, 1994), 29–33.

«Πορεύεσθε μετὰ χαρᾶς» Τὸ μυστήριο τοῦ θανάτου καὶ τῆς ἀναστάσεως, in Σύναξη, 49 (Jan.-March, 1994), 19–33.

"Father Dumitru Stăniloae" (obituary), *Forerunner* (The Orthodox Fellowship of St John the Baptist), no. 23 (Summer, 1994), 14–17.

Foreword to Dumitru Stăniloae, *The Experience of God*, trans. Ioan Ioniță and Robert Barringer (Brookline, MA: Holy Cross Orthodox Press, 1994), ix–xxvii.

"The Understanding of Salvation in the Orthodox Tradition," in Rienk Lannoy (ed.),

For Us and For Our Salvation, IIMO Research Publication 40 (Utrecht-Leiden, 1994), 107–31. [Reprinted separately with the title *How are we Saved? The Understanding of Salvation in the Orthodox Tradition* (Minneapolis Mn: Light and Life, 1996), 19 pp.]

"Response to Fr Andriy Chirovsky: 'Towards an Ecclesial Self-Identity for the Ukrainian Greco-Catholic Church,' " *Logos*, 35.1–4 (1994), 125–31.

Foreword to David and Mary Ford, *Marriage as a Path to Holiness: Lives of Married Saints* (South Canaan, PA: St Tikhon's Seminary Press, 1994), ix-xii.

* " 'Go Joyfully': The Mystery of Death and Resurrection," in Dan Cohn-Sherbok and Christopher Lewis (edd.), *Beyond Death: Theological Reflections on Life after Death* (Basingstoke and London: Macmillan, 1995), 27–41.

"Gerald Palmer, the *Philokalia* and the Holy Mountain," in *Friends of Mount Athos, Annual Report 1994* (published 1995), 23–28.

"Philip Sherrard" (obituary), *Sobornost* (incorporating *Eastern Churches Review*), new series 17.2 (1995), 45–52. [Reprinted with corrections in *Friends of Mount Athos, Annual Report 1995* (published 1996), 26–34.]

"C. S. Lewis: An 'Anonymous Orthodox'?" *Sobornost* (incorporating *Eastern Churches Review*), new series 17.2 (1995), 9–27.

"The Way of the Ascetics: Negative or Affirmative?" in Vincent L. Wimbush and Richard Valantasis (edd.), *Asceticism* (New York & Oxford: Oxford University Press, 1995), 3–15.

"A Fourteenth-Century Manual of Hesychast Prayer: The *Century* of St Kallistos and St Ignatios Xanthopoulos" (Toronto: Canadian Institute of Balkan Studies, 1995), 32pp.

" 'Act out of Stillness': The Influence of Fourteenth-Century Hesychasm on Byzantine and Slav Civilization," The "Byzantine Heritage" Annual Lecture, 28 May 1995, ed. Daniel J. Sahas (Toronto: The Hellenic Canadian Association of Constantinople and the Thessalonikean Society of Metro Toronto, 1995), 25pp.

" 'In the Image and Likeness': The Uniqueness of the Human Person," in John T. Chirban (ed.), *Personhood: Orthodox Christianity and the Connection Between Body, Mind, and Soul* (Westport, CN: Bergin & Garvey, 1996), 1–13.

Spirituality: Eastern and Western Perspectives, talks given by Bishop Kallistos Ware and Philip Sheldrake, Great St. Mary's Papers, Two (Cambridge, 1996), 41pp.

*"Strange Yet Familiar," in Thomas Doulis (ed.), *Towards the Authentic Church. Orthodox Christians Discuss Their Conversion: A Collection of Essays* (Minneapolis: Light and Life, 1996), 145–68.

Foreword to Mother Thekla, *The Dark Glass: Meditations in Orthodox Spirituality* (London: Harper/Collins (Fount), 1996), v-vii.

"Has God Rejected His People? Saint Paul on the Vocation of Israel," *Saint John of Kronstadt Bulletin* (September 1996); also *In Communion*, Journal of the Orthodox Peace Fellowship (October 1996), 1–4.

"Lent and the Consumer Society," in Andrew Walker and Costa Carras (edd.), *Living Orthodoxy in the Modern World* (London: SPCK, 1996), 64–84.

Introduction to Nikolai Velimirović, Bishop of Ochrid, *Homilies*, 1, translated by Mother Maria (Rule) (Birmingham: Lazarica Press, 1996), v-vii.

"The Estonian Crisis: A Salutary Warning?" *Sobornost* (incorporating *Eastern Churches Review*), new series 18.2 (1996), 59–68.

«'Αθήνα καὶ 'Ιερουσαλήμ: ἡ Κλασσικὴ Παράδοσι καὶ οἱ "Ελληνες Πατέρες,» in *'Ορθοδοξία 'Ελληνισμός: Πορεία στὴν Τρίτη Χιλιετία*, 2, 'Ιερὰ Μονὴ Κουτλουμουσίου, "Αγιον "Ορος, (1996), 43–9.

"St Athanasius the Athonite: Traditionalist or Innovator?" in Anthony Bryer and Mary Cunningham (edd.), *Mount Athos and Byzantine Monasticism.* Papers from the Twenty-Eighth Spring Symposium of Byzantine Studies, Birmingham, March 1994, Society for the Promotion of Byzantine Studies Publications, 4 (Aldershot: Variorum/Ashgate Publishing Ltd., 1996), 3–16.

"An Icon of Human Freedom," in Mircea Păcurariu and Aurel Jivi (edd.), *Teologie, Slujire, Ecumenism: Inalt Prea Sfinţului Dr Antonie Plămădeala, Mitropolitul Ardealului, la împlinirea vărstei de 70 de ani* (Facultatea de Teologie "Andrei Şaguna"), extract from *Revista Teologică*, 3–4 (Sibiu, 1996), 103–9.

Through the Creation to the Creator (London: Friends of the Centre, 1997), 30pp.

Foreword to Donald Nicholl, *Triumphs of the Spirit in Russia* (London: Darton, Longman and Todd, 1997), ix–x.

" 'My Helper and My Enemy': The Body in Greek Christianity," in Sarah Coakley (ed.), *Religion and the Body* (Cambridge: Cambridge University Press, 1997), 90–110.

" 'We Must Pray for All': Salvation according to St Silouan," *Sobornost* (incorporating *Eastern Churches Review*), new series 19.1 (1997), 34–51.

"The Trinity, Heart of Our Life," in James S. Cutsinger (ed.), *Reclaiming the Great Tradition* (Downers Grove, Illinois: InterVarsity Press, 1997), 125–46.

"Prophet, Liturgist, Hesychast: *Orientale Lumen* on the Monastic Vocation," pp. 37–58; "Closing Remarks," pp. 173–4; in *Orientale Lumen Conference Proceedings 1997* (Eastern Churches Journal: Washington D.C.).

"Confession" *Saint John of Kronstadt Bulletin* (December 1997).

Mary Theotokos in the Orthodox Tradition (Wallington, Surrey: The Ecumenical Society of the Blessed Virgin Mary, 1997), 20pp.

"The Place of Mary: 1. No New Dogmas, Please," *The Tablet* (17 January 1998), 93. [Reprinted in Edward Yarnold (ed.), *The Place of Mary in the Church: Mariologists on Mary—Co-Redeemer* (Wallington, Surrey: Ecumenical Society of the Blessed Virgin Mary (1998), 3–5.]

Foreword to Barbara Pappas, *The Christian Life in the Early Church and Today according to St Paul's Second Epistle to the Corinthians* (Westchester, Illinois: Amnos Publications, 1998), ix–xi.

Introduction to Philip Sherrard, *Christianity: Lineaments of a Sacred Tradition* (Brookline, MA: Holy Cross Orthodox Press, 1998), ix–xiv.

"L'éducation théologique selon l'Écriture et les Pères," in *Planète St-Serge: Les feuillets de Saint Serge*, 4 (Nov. 1998), 3–11. [Romanian trans. in *Renaştearea* (Archdiocese of Cluj), nos. 10–11 (1994).]

*"Dare We Hope for the Salvation of All?" *Theology Digest*, 45.4 (1998), 303–17.

"God of the Fathers: C. S. Lewis and Eastern Christianity," in David Mills (ed.), *The

Pilgrim's Tale: C. S. Lewis and the Art of Witness (Grand Rapids, MI: Eerdmans, 1998), 53–69.

"Man, Woman and the Priesthood of Christ" [revised version of 1978], in Thomas Hopko (ed.), *Women and the Priesthood* (Crestwood, NY: St Vladimir's Seminary Press, 1999), 5–53. [Reprinted in Elisabeth Behr-Sigel and Kallistos Ware, *The Ordination of Women in the Orthodox Church* (Geneva: Risk Book Series, WCC Publications, 2000), 49–96. French trans. "Homme, femme et prêtrise du Christ," in Elisabeth Behr-Sigel (ed.), *L'ordination des femmes dans l'Église orthodoxe* (Paris: Cerf, 1998), 51–96].

"The Soul in Greek Christianity," in M. James C. Crabbe (ed.), *From Soul to Self* (London & New York: Routledge, 1999), 49–69.

Foreword to Columba Graham Flegg, *An Introduction to Reading the Apocalypse* (Crestwood, NY: St Vladimir's Seminary Press, 1999), vii-viii.

Foreword to Elisabeth Behr-Sigel, *Lev Gillet* (Oxford: Fellowship of St Alban and St Sergius, 1999), 9–13.

Preface to Alphonse and Rachel Goettmann, *Prière de Jésus: Prière du Cœur* (Paris: Albin Michel, 1999), 11–21.

«Ἀληθῶς Θεὸς καὶ Ἀληθῶς Ἄνθρωπος,» in Athenagoras Dikaikos et al. (edd.), *2000 Χρόνια μετά. Τίνα με λέγουσιν οἱ ἄνθρωποι εἶναι;* (Athens: Akritas, 1999), 86–9.

"Prayer in Evagrius of Pontus and the Macarian Homilies," in Ralph Waller and Benedicta Ward (edd.), *An Introduction to Christian Spirituality* (London: SPCK, 1999), 14–30.

"Kenosis and Christ-like Humility according to Saint Silouan," *Sobornost* (incorporating *Eastern Churches Review*), new series 21.2 (1999), 21–31. [French trans. in *Buisson Ardent: Cahiers Saint Silouane l'Athonite* 6, (2000), 30–8; Italian trans. in Adalberto Mainardi (ed.), *Silvano dell' Athos* (Magnano: Edizione Qiqajon, Communità di Bose, 1999), 63–77].

"The Passions: Enemy or Friend?" *In Communion*, 17, Journal of the Orthodox Peace Fellowship (Fall 1999), 1–8. [Also translated into Dutch and Finnish.]

"Open to a New Situation: A Fresh Approach to Old Problems?" in *Orientale Lumen II: Conference Proceedings–1998* (Washington DC: Eastern Churches Journal, 1999), 101–20.

"Not Peace, But a Sword," in *Orientale Lumen III: Conference Proceedings–1999* (Washington DC: Eastern Churches Journal, 1999), 187–91.

Foreword to *The Blackwell Dictionary of Eastern Christianity* (Oxford: Blackwell Publishers, 1999), viii-ix.

Foreword to Emil Bartos, *Deification in Eastern Orthodox Theology. An Evaluation and Critique of the Theology of Dumitru Stăniloae* (Carlisle: Paternoster Press, 1999), ix-x.

"With All Our Heart, In Thanksgiving Let Us Offer The World Back To God," in *The Orthodox Church*, 35.10–11 (October–November 1999), 3, 9, 16.

"The Establishment of a Theological and Ecclesiastical Seminary," *The Orthodox Herald*, 128–9 (May–June 1999), 23–6.

"Personal Experience of the Holy Spirit according to the Greek Fathers," *Stranitsi* 4.1

(Moscow: St Andrew's Biblical College, 1999), 10–23. [Russian trans.; English text still unpublished.]

"What is a Saint?" Sermon at the St Birinus Pilgrimage Service, Dorchester, 11 July 1999 (issued separately).

"Body, Intellect, Heart: Prayer of the Total Self," *The St Nina Quarterly*, 3.1 (Winter 1999), 1, 9–11, 15.

"The Use of the Jesus Prayer in Daily Life," *Saint Mark Annual Review 1999* (Bethesda, Maryland: Saint Mark Orthodox Church, 2000), 1–13.

"Gefangnis oder Weg zur Freiheit?" *Oikumenische Rundschau*, 49.2 (2000), 191–200. [Translation of a University Sermon given in St Mary the Virgin, Oxford, 11 June 1989.]

"The Witness of the Orthodox Church in the Twentieth Century," Address at the Tenth Orthodox Congress in Western Europe, Paray-le-Monial, 30 October–1 November 1999, *Sourozh*, 80 (May 2000), 1–14. [Reprinted in *The Ecumenical Review*, 52.1 (2000), 46–56; also in translation in French, Italian, Flemish and Greek.]

"Saint Gregory Palamas," *The Tablet* (18 March 2000), 400

"The Nearness yet Otherness of the Eternal in Meister Eckhardt and St Gregory Palamas," *Eckhardt Review*, 9 (Spring 2000), 41–53.

"Go Forth in Peace," *In Communion* (May 2000), 1–7. [Also trans. into Dutch.]

"A Peaceful Ending to our Life," Lecture given at Vézelay, April 1999; in Finnish trans., *Aamun Koitto*, 2 (2000), 4–8.

Foreword to Hilarion Alfeyev, *The Spiritual World of Isaac the Syrian*, Cistercian Studies Series 175 (Kalamazoo, Michigan: Cistercian Publications, 2000), 9–13.

"What is Eastern Christianity? The Christian East: Unity and Diversity," in William Joseph Buckley (ed.), *Kosovo: Contending Voices on Balkan Interventions* (Grand Rapids, MI: Eerdmans, 2000), 116–19.

"Constance Babington Smith" (obituary), *Forerunner*, 36 (Winter 2000–1), 34–5.

Foreword to John Chryssavgis, *Soul Mending. The Art of Spiritual Direction* (Brookline: Holy Cross Orthodox Press, 2000), ix-xi.

"Orient et Occident: Sources et espérances de l'Église indivise," in Philipp Baud and Maxime Egger (edd.), *Les richesses de l'Orient chrétien* (Pully, Switzerland: Le Sel de la Terre, 2000), 171–92.

The Inner Kingdom, The Collected Works, vol. 1 (Crestwood, NY: St Vladimir's Seminary Press, 2000).

"Eastern Orthodox Theology," in Adrian Hastings et al. (edd.), *The Oxford Companion to Christian Thought* (Oxford: OUP, 2000), 184–7.

" 'The Light that Lightens Everyone': The Knowledge of God Among Non-Christians according to the Greek Fathers and St Innocent," *Greek Orthodox Theological Review*, 44, "1999" (in fact, 2001), 557–64.

" 'It Is Time For The Lord To Act': The Divine Liturgy as Heaven on Earth," *Sobornost* (incorporating *Eastern Churches Review*), new series 23.1 (2001), 7–22.

"The Orthodox Understanding of Pilgrimage," *Forerunner*, 38 (Winter 2001–2), 1–10.

"Glorify God with your Body," *In Communion* (Spring 2001), 7–13.

"Eastern Christianity," in Richard Harries and Henry Mayr-Harting (edd.), *Christianity: Two Thousand Years* (Oxford: OUP, 2001), 65–95.

" 'The Earthly Heaven': The Mother of God in the Teaching of St John of Damascus," in William M. McLoughlin and Jill Pinnock (edd.), *Mary for Earth and Heaven* (Leominster: Gracewing, 2002), 355–68.

"How do we enter the heart?" in James S. Cutsinger (ed.), *Paths to the Heart: Sufism and the Christian East* (Bloomington, Ind.: World Wisdom/Fons Vitae, 2002), 2–23.

❀ · ❀